ADAPTING THE PAST TO REIMAGINE POSSIBLE FUTURES: CELEBRATING AND CRITIQUING WAC AT 50

PERSPECTIVES ON WRITING
Series Editors: Rich Rice, Heather MacNeill Falconer, and J. Michael Rifenburg
Consulting Editor: Susan H. McLeod | Associate Editor: Olivia Johnson

The Perspectives on Writing series addresses writing studies in a broad sense. Consistent with the wide ranging approaches characteristic of teaching and scholarship in writing across the curriculum, the series presents works that take divergent perspectives on working as a writer, teaching writing, administering writing programs, and studying writing in its various forms.

The WAC Clearinghouse, Colorado State University Open Press, and University Press of Colorado are collaborating so that these books will be widely available through free digital distribution and low-cost print editions. The publishers and the Series editors are committed to the principle that knowledge should freely circulate. We see the opportunities that new technologies have for further democratizing knowledge. And we see that to share the power of writing is to share the means for all to articulate their needs, interest, and learning into the great experiment of literacy.

Recent Books in the Series

William J. Macauley, Jr. et al. (Eds.), *Threshold Conscripts: Rhetoric and Composition Teaching Assistantships* (2023)

Jennifer Grouling, *Adapting VALUEs: Tracing the Life of a Rubric through Institutional Ethnography* (2022)

Chris M. Anson and Pamela Flash (Eds.), *Writing-Enriched Curricula: Models of Faculty-Driven and Departmental Transformation* (2021)

Asao B. Inoue, *Above the Well: An Antiracist Argument From a Boy of Color* (2021)

Alexandria L. Lockett, Iris D. Ruiz, James Chase Sanchez, and Christopher Carter (Eds.), *Race, Rhetoric, and Research Methods* (2021)

Kristopher M. Lotier, *Postprocess Postmortem* (2021)

Ryan J. Dippre and Talinn Phillips (Eds.), *Approaches to Lifespan Writing Research: Generating an Actionable Coherence* (2020)

Lesley Erin Bartlett, Sandra L. Tarabochia, Andrea R. Olinger, and Margaret J. Marshall (Eds.), *Diverse Approaches to Teaching, Learning, and Writing Across the Curriculum: IWAC at 25* (2020)

Hannah J. Rule, *Situating Writing Processes* (2019)

Asao B. Inoue, *Labor-Based Grading Contracts: Building Equity and Inclusion in the Compassionate Writing Classroom* (2019)

Mark Sutton and Sally Chandler (Eds.), *The Writing Studio Sampler: Stories About Change* (2018)

ADAPTING THE PAST TO REIMAGINE POSSIBLE FUTURES: CELEBRATING AND CRITIQUING WAC AT 50

Edited by Megan J. Kelly, Heather M. Falconer,
Caleb L. González, and Jill Dahlman

The WAC Clearinghouse
wac.colostate.edu
Fort Collins, Colorado

University Press of Colorado
upcolorado.com
Denver, Colorado

The WAC Clearinghouse, Fort Collins, Colorado 80523

University Press of Colorado, Denver, Colorado 80203

© 2023 by Megan J. Kelly, Heather M. Falconer, Caleb L. González, and Jill Dahlman. This work is licensed under a Creative Commons Attribution-NonCommercial-NoDerivatives 4.0 International.

ISBN 978-1-64215-194-7 (PDF) | 978-1-64215-195-4 (ePub) | 978-1-64642-502-0 (pbk.)

DOI 10.37514/PER-B.2023.1947

Library of Congress Cataloging-in-Publication Data

Names: International Writing Across the Curriculum Conference (15th : 2021 : Online) | Kelly, Megan J., 1976– editor. | Falconer, Heather M., 1974– editor. | González, Caleb L., 1991– editor. | Dahlman, Jill, editor.
Title: Adapting the past to reimagine possible futures : celebrating and critiquing wac at 50 / edited by Megan J. Kelly, Heather M. Falconer, Caleb L. González, and Jill Dahlman.
Description: Fort Collins, Colorado : The WAC Clearinghouse ; Denver, Colorado : University Press of Colorado, 2023. | Series: Perspectives on writing
Identifiers: LCCN 2023025975 (print) | LCCN 2023025976 (ebook) | ISBN 9781646425020 (paperback) | ISBN 9781642151947 (adobe pdf) | ISBN 9781642151954 (epub)
Subjects: LCSH: English language–Rhetoric–Study and teaching (Higher)–Congresses. | Interdisciplinary approach in education–Congresses. | LCGFT: Conference papers and proceedings
Classification: LCC PE1404 .I5285 2021 (print) | LCC PE1404 (ebook) | DDC 808/.0420711—dc23/eng/20230802
LC record available at https://lccn.loc.gov/2023025975
LC ebook record available at https://lccn.loc.gov/2023025976

Copyeditor: Annie Halseth
Designer: Mike Palmquist
Cover Photo: The Oval in May, by Mike Palmquist. Used with permission.
Series Editors: Rich Rice, Heather MacNeill Falconer, and J. Michael Rifenburg
Consulting Editor: Susan H. McLeod
Associate Editor: Olivia Johnson

The WAC Clearinghouse supports teachers of writing across the disciplines. Hosted by Colorado State University, it brings together scholarly journals and book series as well as resources for teachers who use writing in their courses. This book is available in digital formats for free download at wac.colostate.edu.

Founded in 1965, the University Press of Colorado is a nonprofit cooperative publishing enterprise supported, in part, by Adams State University, Colorado State University, Fort Lewis College, Metropolitan State University of Denver, University of Alaska Fairbanks, University of Colorado, University of Denver, University of Northern Colorado, University of Wyoming, Utah State University, and Western Colorado University. For more information, visit upcolorado.com.

Land Acknowledgment. The Colorado State University Land Acknowledgment can be found at landacknowledgment.colostate.edu.

CONTENTS

Introduction. Complicating WAC in a Time of Transition 3
    *Megan J. Kelly, Heather M. Falconer, Caleb L. González,
    and Jill Dahlman*

SECTION 1. FACULTY DEVELOPMENT 13

Chapter 1. The Work Beyond the Workshop: Assessing and Reinvigorating
Our WAC Outreach Model 17
    *Olivia R. Tracy, Juli Parrish, Heather N. Martin,
    and Brad Benz*

Chapter 2. The University of Denver Ethnography Lab: Fostering a WAC
Community of Practice 33
    Kamila Kinyon, Alejandro Cerón, and Dinko Hanaan Dinko

Chapter 3. Assessing Faculty Members' Threshold Concepts for the Teaching
of Writing: The Challenges of Survey Validity and the Promise of Narrative
Methods. 45
    Christopher Basgier and Leslie Cordie

Chapter 4. Strengthening the Core: Designing and Implementing a New,
Sustainable WAC/WID Program 59
    *Kimberly K. Gunter, Lindy E. Briggette, Mary Laughlin,
    Tiffany Wilgar, and Nadia Francine Zamin*

Chapter 5. Growing a WAC Program alongside a New College 73
    *Elizabeth Baxmeyer, Rikki Corniola, William Davis,
    Gloria Poveda, and Christopher Wostenberg*

Chapter 6. Furthering WAC Influence Through Strategic Partnerships. 87
    Ming Fang, Kimberly Harrison, and Christine Martorana

SECTION 2. PEDAGOGICAL CONSIDERATIONS 101

Chapter 7. Accessing Critical Reflection to Promote Inclusivity in
Writing Intensive Courses 103
    Julie Birt and Christy Goldsmith

Chapter 8. Using Creative Nonfiction to Influence Student
Dispositions Toward Writing Transfer and Development: Pedagogical
Opportunities for WAC..115
   James P. Austin

Chapter 9. WAC and Writing Centers: Finding Space to Work
on Institutional Diversity, Equity, and Inclusion....................127
   *William J. Macauley, Jr., Pamela B. Childers,
and Brandall C. Jones*

Chapter 10. When Learning Outcomes Mask Learning, Part 1:
The Promises and Pitfalls of Learning Analytics.....................143
   Kathleen Daly Weisse

Chapter 11. When Learning Outcomes Mask Learning, Part 2:
Probing Assumptions about Assessment via Disciplinary Genres........155
   Angela J. Zito

Section 3. Institutional Considerations 169

Chapter 12. Built to Last: Two Decades of Sustaining WAC Programs
at CUNY 173
   Andrea Fabrizio, Linda Hirsch, Dennis Paoli, and Trudy Smoke

Chapter 13. Blurred Boundaries: Sussing Out Thresholds between
WAC and WPA in Administrative Professionalization 189
   *Mandy Olejnik, Amy Cicchino, Christina M. LaVecchia,
and Al Harahap*

Chapter 14. A WAC/WID Experience in Argentina: Working for
a High Degree of Institutionalization..............................205
   Estela Ines Moyano

Chapter 15. English as a Lingua Academica in Scholarly Publishing:
The Clash of Anglo-American and Slovak Writing Style Conventions 219
   Alena Kačmárová, Magdaléna Bilá, and Ingrida Vaňková

Chapter 16. WAC Compared to Other "Across the Curriculums".........239
   David R. Russell

Chapter 17. Imagining WAC's Future: Coloniality, Diversity, and
Sustainability..253
   Al Harahap, Federico Navarro, and Alisa Russell

Contributors 273

ADAPTING THE PAST TO REIMAGINE POSSIBLE FUTURES: CELEBRATING AND CRITIQUING WAC AT 50

INTRODUCTION.
COMPLICATING WAC IN A TIME OF TRANSITION

Megan J. Kelly
University of Denver

Heather M. Falconer
University of Maine

Caleb L. González
The Ohio State University

Jill Dahlman
California Northstate University College of Health Sciences

The Fifteenth International Writing Across the Curriculum Conference, which was postponed until August 2021 due to the COVID-19 pandemic, provided an opportunity to celebrate 50 years of WAC. As noted in this collection's call for submissions, "The Fifteenth International Writing Across the Curriculum Conference offers a space for us to come together as a community to consider the complex and complicated histories of WAC and the potential evolutions of the field." The conference was a time to collectively reflect on the past so that we could envision WAC's future. It did bring us together, on Whova rather than in Fort Collins, Colorado, but what visions of the future did this conference imagine? How much change—as people, an organization, a discipline, a world community—have we enacted or innovated since Barbara Walvoord hosted the first WAC seminar at Central College during the 1969–1970 academic year? This is a crucial question especially as WAC seeks to sustain itself in meaningful ways that impact not only our college campuses but our communities, and higher education at large.

    As we (the editors) attended conference sessions—gathering in a virtual community, but never once meeting in person—and as we read through subsequent submissions to this edited collection, we began to recognize that the impact of the last few years has brought these lofty goals of the conference into question. At least, the pandemic has demonstrated how truly complex and complicated WAC work is. Al Harahap noted as much during the final plenary on envisioning the future of WAC, during which he offered this disclaimer: "What we are charged

DOI: https://doi.org/10.37514/PER-B.2023.1947.1.03

to talk about, the future of WAC, is a huge cross to bear" (Harahap, Navarro & Russell, 2021). His words deserve our thoughtful attention as higher education continues to experience challenges related to student enrollment, institutional closures, budget cuts sparked by a global pandemic, and major shifts to the ways in which writing is taught across the curriculum globally. These realities create an increased exigency to amplify the field by forwarding tropes toward a better future for WAC and leading a movement that exemplifies greater access, equity, inclusion, and justice.

COVID-19 initiated a massive and consequential pause *and* shift that reverberated around the world—not just in our individual homes and daily practices, but in our collective organizations and academic institutions. We also note that due to the pandemic's global impact, the international WAC community experienced a pause and shift in many different ways and in various educational situations. Anecdotally, WAC coordinators were called on to help think through the sudden gymnastics faculty were asked to perform: What did we know about using discussion boards to assess disciplinary content? How do we manage the writing in our classes now that we're fully virtual, or HyFlex, or hybrid? How do we accommodate or account for students without access to the internet or who don't have a space to work at home or who are attending class via their mobile phone in their car or at their workplace? How do we support students who are caring for sick loved ones or who are sick themselves? How do we support faculty in online writing instruction in often uncertain educational situations?

As experts in writing across different contexts, many WAC coordinators (and writing instructors more broadly) found themselves positioned as the go-to person—the "access point"—for writing across modalities in *addition to* the curriculum. These challenges highlighted just how much labor often falls on WAC practitioners within institutions, without clear lines of support or successors. During IWAC's final plenary (see a revised version of this talk in Chapter 17), Alisa Russell challenged us to think about this labor and access by asking:

> Where are the access points for upcoming WAC scholars like graduate students? Where are the access points for scholars in different disciplines like those in adjacent or even non-adjacent fields who are doing this work right outside of writing studies, for faculty at our own institutions, for students at our institutions? Where are the thresholds, the crossover points, the paths in? Are they visible? Are they intentional? Are they equitable? (Harahap, Navarro & Russell, 2021)

Woven into the complexity of 2020 was the simultaneous social unrest in response to the deaths of Elijah McClain, Ahmaud Arbery, Breonna Taylor,

Daniel Prude, George Floyd, Andre Hill, and too many others to name here. Indeed, Floyd was murdered and the protests ignited just a week before the IWAC conference was originally scheduled to begin. Rather than traveling to Fort Collins, some of us were quarantining in our homes as others of us marched in the streets. As we moved through 2020, we also witnessed a contested U.S. presidential election, as well as an insurrection at the nation's capital that threatened the very foundations of our democracy. Amid this political unrest, we experienced the consequences of the ever-growing global environmental breakdown: Wildfires and hurricanes displaced many, while drought and extreme heat called the notion of "sustainability" and how best to tackle climate change into question. Business as usual simply seemed like a bad business model, ushering in a period of contemplation of not where we *would like* to go as WAC practitioners, but where we *needed* to go. How well *did* our approaches work in a virtual space? Whose languages and ways of creating knowledge are *still* not being represented, despite all that research has shown? Are we transforming as a field fast enough?

We share the preceding circumstances to situate the Fifteenth International Writing Across the Curriculum Conference within the broader social and environmental contexts in which we were operating and *continue* to operate. The unprecedented conditions of rupture and change that we find ourselves in—climate, social, pandemic—are clearly calling for innovation. But to what degree is WAC capable of, invested in, or committed to the mobilization of innovation? Christopher Thaiss spoke to this, to some extent, in his opening plenary when he observed: "There is no sustainability without adaptability" (Rutz & Thaiss, 2021). The conditions are such that we can't *not* adapt and innovate in the face of all this change. Yet, while change may be inevitable, encountering so much change at once can be paralyzing, and the process of enacting sustainable, effective change can be slow.

Despite these challenges and demands on our cognitive energy, we were at last able to gather online in August 2021 to talk and think through ideas related to "Celebrating Successes, Recognizing Challenges, and Inviting Critique and Innovation." The conference theme emerged as a call to bring together within the same space an acknowledgement of the successes over 50 years and the need to address the challenges that lie ahead. With a global pandemic on the near horizon, the IWAC advisory board had no idea the challenges that would shape the programmatic and classroom conditions related to how speakers and attendees would engage conversations of successes, challenges, critique, and innovation. The advisory board also had no idea how much innovation and challenge would be reflected in the logistical and material aspects of this conference. In many ways, this brave new world we found ourselves in was more accessible because of the pandemic. People could attend the conference without worry of location, safety, or cost of traveling, or the myriad issues that must be juggled to attend in-person conferences. The conference organizers even reduced registration fees to reflect the virtual nature of the conference. Moreover, the Fifteenth International Writing Across the Curriculum Conference emerged as the most diverse IWAC in terms of attendance. Institutionally, for example, we saw around 26 percent of attendees representing both 2- and 4-year Minority-Serving Institutions (MSIs), most of which were Hispanic-Serving Institutions (HSIs) and emerging Hispanic-Serving Institutions (eHSIs). We note that Colorado State University—the conference host—became an eHSI in 2019.

Out of 475 attendees, 128 came from an MSI context within the United States, including HSIs, eHSIs, Asian American Native American Pacific Islander-Serving Institutions (AANAPISIs), Historically Black Colleges and Universities (HBCUs), and Tribal Colleges or Universities (TCUs). Drawing on the work of writing studies scholars at HBCUs, we recognize the need for more representation of MSIs—including resources to support WAC professionals from MSIs at conferences, summer institutes, and other events (Jackson, Jackson& Tafari, 2019, p. 207). We apply this to WAC especially as we continue to examine how we support students and faculty through equitable and inclusive approaches. This need for increased representation comes at a time when higher education scholars note that "Minority-Serving Institutions have become an increasingly important part of American higher education, especially as a gateway to higher education for many traditionally underrepresented students across our country" (Conrad & Gasman, 2017, p. 1). Additionally, approximately 48 attendees joined the conference from a wide range of colleges and universities across the globe. Because many attendees were speakers, these numbers were reflected in the presentations and plenary sessions that helped shape critical conversations about the past, present, and future of WAC related to access, equity, inclusion, and justice.

We highlight MSIs as context for what we observed, particularly in the second plenary session hosted by Pamela Flash and Teresa Redd (2021): the call to better support the needs of diverse student populations who engage various modes of writing across the curriculum. While supporting the needs of diverse student populations is not exclusive to WAC practitioners at MSIs, institutional diversity at IWAC is a reminder of what Sue H. McLeod (2000) found in her 1987 national survey of WAC programs: There is a strong investment in WAC among these colleges and universities. We point to McLeod's survey to show that WAC's presence in MSIs is not new. In fact, it is linked to our history in ways that reveal that we must continue to advocate for access, equity, inclusion, and justice within our policies and practices. As Flash and Redd (2021) found through their survey of conference attendees, supporting the success of a diversity of students across the disciplines is crucial to WAC's future.

We further noticed this interest at the global level given how public universities in some countries have expanded free or reduced tuition, which has increased access to education for students beyond a select few. For example, in the final plenary session, Federico Navarro mentioned that the once "nontraditional" students at his university in Chile are now, in fact, the largest group of students enrolled in Chilean universities (Harahap, Navarro& Russell, 2021). Navarro added that, very often, their universities, their faculty, and their pedagogies of writing seem at odds with current realities in higher education. As the field of WAC continues to ask questions of what it means to support access, equity, inclusion, and justice, especially in the changing conditions of higher education, we recall just how relevant Al Harahap's heuristic, also discussed in Chapter 17, is to WAC scholars at all institutions (Figure 1).

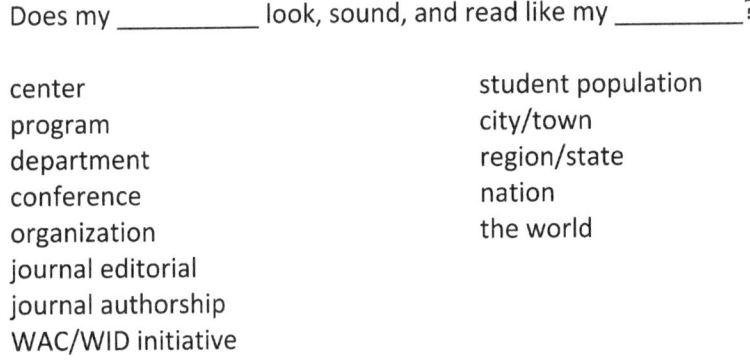

Figure 1. *Heuristic in Deciding Readiness to Do Linguistic Equity Work with Colleagues (Harahap, Navarro& Russell, 2021).*

Another highlight of the conference was the ability to recognize, in real time, the contributions to WAC from individuals across the globe. For the first time in IWAC's history, an awards ceremony was hosted in collaboration with the Association for Writing Across the Curriculum (AWAC), honoring scholarship in the field and scholars who have made critical contributions to WAC as a movement, pedagogy, and curriculum. Twenty-eight scholars were recognized, celebrating the successes of the last 50 years. Furthermore, this was the first IWAC with two multilingual sessions led by WAC scholars, including one session on installing a writing culture across the curriculum with insights from scholars in Brazil, Peru, and Colombia (Navarro et al., 2021a). The second multilingual session focused on writing engagement, self-regulation, and family support in educational communities with scholars from Chile, Colombia, and Argentina (Navarro et al., 2021b). These sessions, sponsored by the Asociación Latinoamericana de Estudios de la Escritura en Educación Superior (ALES), are just two examples of WAC functioning as a connector in building conversations between international WAC scholars and those who draw insight from these sessions given where their programs are located and their campus demographics (Harahap, Navarro & Russell, 2021). As students, teachers, and colleges and universities are more globally connected, we know that international WAC scholarship is even more crucial to the progress of the discipline. By engaging with WAC scholars around the world, we can rethink how our practices might better engage students and teachers through the various writing cultures that we build on our college campuses.

~~~

This proceedings documents some of the many conversations that were shared at the conference in August 2021. While contributors were asked to revise their initial presentations to account for the shift in genre (e.g., from a presentation to a chapter), we (the editors) were conscious that this collection is meant to be a *proceedings*, a record of some of the conversations that actually took place. As we read through the submissions to our call, we noted an array of voices and perspectives on WAC that originally took the form of panels, workshops, and roundtables, and three distinct themes began to emerge in these conversations: faculty development, pedagogical considerations, and institutional concerns. These three themes help us think about WAC in practice during times of rapid change—the challenges and innovations of working with faculty across disciplinary spaces, the practical applications of writing instruction within the classroom, and the larger systemic considerations that must be navigated in successfully building, maintaining, and adapting programs into the future.

In the first section focused on faculty development, we see six chapters that explore finding common ground through methodological, epistemological, and conceptual approaches to WAC. The authors of these chapters address such questions as: What can be accomplished with and without a stand-alone WAC program? How might integrating WAC into the vertical curriculum open other opportunities for engaging with faculty? What are the benefits and challenges to having multiple stakeholders involved in program design and implementation? The chapters in this section provide us with innovative models for creating WAC programs, as well as for assessing the impact of WAC programs on faculty development.

The second section in this collection extends these considerations to our immediate instructional spaces, be they classrooms or writing centers. What does WAC pedagogy look like when we incorporate heavy reflective and creative writing into our classrooms, for example? The approaches discussed in some of the chapters in this section come at the same time that other WAC researchers, such as Justin Nicholes (2022), analyze writing and the experiences of students describing unexpected yet meaningful creative writing approaches within their science and other research-focused coursework. Through Nicholes's work, we have seen Creative Writing Across the Curriculum (CWAC) emerge as a meaningful literacy framework to engage writers across disciplines, languages, and identities. Other chapters in this section discuss pedagogical implications beyond the traditional, face-to-face classroom, shifting our attention to writing centers and online spaces, where topics of diversity, equity, inclusion, and justice (DEIJ) require different ways of thinking about and assessing student writing and engagement.

The six chapters in the third section invite us to turn our attention outward to larger global and institutional considerations. The section opens with historical discussions of program building and professionalization, then shifts to WAC as it is enacted in two different international contexts. These chapters remind us that there is much to learn both about how this work can be performed, as well as our assumptions while *doing* this work. This final section concludes with reflections on where WAC has been and where it could be (and needs to be) if we are to be strategic in shaping cultures of writing on our college campuses.

Although not all chapters in this proceedings are directly related to DEIJ, we believe that scholarship on antiracism and access is crucial as WAC practitioners address these issues in our classrooms, our programs, and our institutions, as well as more generally as a field. Such scholarship is critical as we identify what to address in our programs (e.g., workshop topics for faculty development), in addition to how we do it (e.g., being intentional about whose expertise we invite to workshops, including the support we provide them and the partnerships we build and/or strengthen on our college campuses). In the second plenary session focused on where WAC is now at 50, Flash and Redd (2021) reported that "78 percent of [Fifteenth International Writing Across the Curriculum Conference] attendees felt that the most urgent question or work of WAC's scholar practitioners is how can we best implement antiracist policies and practices." Harahap later referenced this statistic in the closing plenary session on diversifying, professionalizing, and renovating WAC, adding that knowing how to advocate for students' right to their own language (CCCC, 1974) specifically calls for WAC to be aware of linguistic difference (Cox, 2014; Matsuda, 2001; Zawacki, 2010), antiracist writing assessment (Inoue & Poe, 2012), and linguistic justice (Baker-Bell, 2020). These are critical administrative and pedagogical concerns that shape our work today and into the future.

In some chapters within this proceedings, authors examine issues of equity and social justice by drawing on work focused on antiracism both within and beyond the field of rhetoric and composition. As we continue to integrate antiracist scholarship in our research and in future IWAC proceedings, we know that we all can do more. For example, we hope for an increase in antiracist scholarship that not only supports WAC research but that consistently (re)frames and guides the work we do in examining how language shapes worldviews both locally and globally. We believe that this approach to developing antiracist policies and practices through WAC programs and initiatives is paramount as we look to the future of the field. This, of course, requires that we revisit, as Staci Perryman-Clark states in her 2022 CCCC CFP, what our discipline historically and presently means by equity and inclusion. That is, how do we really know our pedagogical and disciplinary practices are equitable? What is our responsibility in advocating for policies and practices that expand who we want to address and reach? We know that foundational questions such as these—questions that motivate WAC in recognizing the challenges we face and the role for critique and innovation in moving the field forward—will be active at IWAC 2023 in Clemson, South Carolina.

REFERENCES

Baker-Bell, A. (2020). *Linguistic justice: Black language, literacy, identity, and pedagogy.* Routledge.

CCCC. (1974). Students' right to their own language. *College Composition and Communication, XXV*(3). https://prod-ncte-cdn.azureedge.net/nctefiles/groups/cccc/newsrtol.pdf.

Conrad, C. & Gasman, M. (2017). *Educating a diverse nation: Lessons from minority-serving institutions.* Harvard University Press.

Cox, M. (2014). In response to today's "felt need": WAC, faculty development, and second language writers. In T. M. Zawacki & M. Cox (Eds.), *WAC and second language writers research towards linguistically and culturally inclusive programs and practices* (pp. 299–326). The WAC Clearinghouse; Parlor Press. https://doi.org/10.37514/PER-B.2014.0551.2.12.

Flash, P. & Redd, T. (2021, August 2–6). *Second plenary: WAC @ 50: Where are we now?* [Conference presentation]. Fifteenth International Writing Across the Curriculum Conference, Fort Collins, CO, United States. https://youtu.be/iFOifO6KeGI.

Harahap, A., Navarro, F. & Russell, A. (2021, August 2–6). *Closing plenary: Writing across more-than-the-curriculum: A conversation toward diversifying, professionalizing, and renovating WAC* [Conference presentation]. Fifteenth International Writing Across the Curriculum Conference, Fort Collins, CO, United States. https://youtu.be/MDBbGNd-Law.

Inoue, A. B. & Poe, M. (Eds). (2012). *Race and writing assessment.* Peter Lang.

Jackson, K. K., Jackson, H. & Tafari, D. N. H. (2019). We belong in the discussion: Including HBCUs in conversations about race and writing. *College Composition and Communication, 71*(2), 184–214. https://www.jstor.org/stable/26877929.

Matsuda, P. K. (2001). On the origin of contrastive rhetoric. *International Journal of Applied Linguistics, 11*(2), 257–260. https://doi.org/10.1111/1473-4192.00017.

McLeod, S. H. (Ed.) (2000). *Strengthening programs for writing across the curriculum.* The WAC Clearinghouse. https://wac.colostate.edu/books/landmarks/mcleod_programs/ (Originally published in 1988 by Jossey-Bass).

Navarro, F., del Calle-Mora, S., Chumacero Ancajima, S. V., Lousada, E. & Thaiss, C. (2021a, August 2–6). *Installing a writing culture across the curriculum: Insights from Brazil, Colombia and Peru* [Conference presentation]. Fifteenth International Writing Across the Curriculum Conference, Fort Collins, CO, United States. https://youtu.be/zF4ur7rzw2M.

Navarro, F., Rincón Camacho, L. J., Olmos, A., Buonfiglio, Y., Velásquez, T. B. & Anson, C. (2021b, August 2–6). *Writing engagement, self-regulation, and family support in educational communities* [Conference presentation]. Fifteenth International Writing Across the Curriculum Conference, Fort Collins, CO, United States. https://youtu.be/q2frz1FmsqE.

Nicholes, J. (2022). *Creative writing across the curriculum: Meaningful literacy for college writers across disciplines, languages, and identities.* John Benjamins Publishing Company.

Rutz, C. & Thaiss, C. (2021, August 2–6). *Opening plenary: WAC fearlessness, sustainability, and adaptability over five decades* [Conference presentation]. Fifteenth International Writing Across the Curriculum Conference, Fort Collins, CO, United States. https://youtu.be/UJ9p8q-xZNo.

Perryman-Clark, S. (2022, March 9–12). *The promises and perils of higher education: Our discipline's commitment to diversity, equity, and linguistic justice* [Call for proposals]. CCCC 2022 Conference, Chicago, IL, United States.

Zawacki, T. M. (2010, May 20–22). *Researching the local/writing the international: Developing culturally inclusive WAC programs and practices* [Keynote presentation]. IWAC 2010 Conference, Bloomington, IN, United States.

SECTION 1.
FACULTY DEVELOPMENT

The first section in this collection explores the impact of WAC programs on faculty development. Regardless of other changes or evolutions throughout its history, a core component of any WAC initiative has been, and always will be, supporting faculty with writing instruction. The six chapters in this section highlight different models of engaging faculty in the teaching of writing—from offering classroom workshops to partnering with faculty teaching writing-intensive courses. In these chapters, we learn about a diverse range of programs that are reshaping how writing is taught on their campuses and, by extension, making education more accessible to students from a variety of backgrounds and experiences. We hear from WAC coordinators about programs that they have built from the ground up as well as about programs that have evolved—or are considering their need to evolve—based on assessments of their faculty development work. Ultimately, the chapters in this section are concerned with how faculty across the disciplines understand writing pedagogy and how they think about and enact aspects of writing instruction in their classes, including assignment design and expectations as well as the connection between writing and learning.

Olivia R. Tracy, Juli Parrish, Heather N. Martin, and **Brad Benz** open this section by providing insights into what faculty learn as a result of sustained WAC work, specifically the impact of classroom workshops on supporting disciplinary faculty in teaching writing. With workshops, for example, some faculty take away new and innovative ways of thinking about the composing process and how to engage students with genres and discourses; others leave with an appreciation of the work while still expecting instruction to be carried out by writing centers and WAC programs directly (i.e., conducting the same workshop term after term in a class). In this chapter, Tracy et al. report on research into the current classroom workshop model at the University of Denver and on their development of a spectrum of orientations to represent faculty engagement with this model: *a services seeker, a status quo seeker,* and a *knowledge seeker.* This spectrum provides a framework for understanding faculty motivations for partnering with a WAC program and illuminates potential limitations of a workshop model for faculty development. Tracy et al. examine some of the reasons that workshops don't accomplish the goals of faculty development, including the tendency for workshops to address the immediate needs and context of a particular class.

Section 1

Kamila Kinyon, Alejandro Cerón, and **Dinko Hanaan Dinko** then introduce readers to another way that WAC is enacted on the University of Denver campus: the University of Denver's Ethnography Lab (DUEL), an innovative space that fosters interdisciplinary collaboration around ethnographic research practices. Composed of "ethnographers from multiple disciplines and at various stages in their academic or public careers" (p. 33), DUEL offers an exciting model for how to dismantle disciplinary silos and build connection and trust across multiple stakeholders. The result is a rich, generative, sustainable initiative where faculty and student ethnographers can work toward solving pressing social problems. This chapter shares the perspectives and experiences of three stakeholders involved in DUEL: a writing professor, an anthropology professor, and a geography graduate student. Their discussions of various DUEL projects illustrate how faculty development can be a collaborative and inclusive endeavor that draws on the backgrounds, skills, and experiences of all involved.

Continuing with the theme of finding common ground, **Christopher Basgier** and **Leslie Cordie's** chapter applies a threshold concept framework to the assessment of faculty members' knowledge about writing and writing pedagogy at Auburn University. Based on the results of a quantitative inventory for assessing specific threshold concepts in WAC, Basgier and Cordie offer preliminary insights into one way to conceptualize and actively measure how faculty think about writing skills and how such skills are learned. Their findings emphasize the contextual nature of WAC threshold concepts as well as how interconnected and hard to disaggregate they are in the minds of faculty, including WAC experts. Basgier and Cordie exemplify the need to continue to innovate in our work with faculty across disciplinary and academic spaces, including in our methodological approaches, in recognizing that narrative and reflective practice are important tools for faculty development. This work becomes a critical behind-the-scenes aspect of faculty development because of the dynamic nature of evaluating program effectiveness in rapidly-changing academic environments. "Through narrative methods," they argue, "we can see how faculty encounter difficult WAC concepts, wrestle with them, test them, and (ideally) eventually internalize them as principled ways of thinking about disciplinary writing pedagogy" (p. 55). In an era of austerity, where WAC coordinators are often positioned to defend and justify their work and programs, Basgier and Cordie's inventory proves interesting and useful for considering new assessment approaches and strategies that demonstrate impact.

The next two chapters take a different approach to the theme of faculty development by illustrating how WAC can be integrated into the curriculum vertically. Helping readers conceptualize what program-building might look like "on the ground" with key institutional partners, **Kimberly K. Gunter, Lindy E.**

Briggette, **Mary Laughlin, Tiffany Wilgar**, and **Nadia Francine Zamin** explicate the development of Fairfield University's first-ever WAC program, intentionally designed to support and strengthen a new core curriculum. In their chapter, Gunter et al. showcase the transformation of their university's first-year writing requirement as well as the integration of writing intensive courses across the curriculum, all of which required a robust faculty development initiative. Like Basgier and Cordie, Gunter et al. use threshold concepts to structure curriculum design—with both faculty development and student learning in mind—and the systematic reflection demonstrated in this chapter models an important practice for ensuring program sustainability, particularly when entering into or emerging from times of transition. Gunter et al. argue that threshold concepts lead to better writing instruction because "faculty across campus can see that the writing teaching/learning they are doing with their students is connected to the writing teaching/learning happening across campus" (p. 64). This chapter is instructive for other WAC programs striving to align with best practices in WAC and writing studies while in the process of adapting to new institutional circumstances.

Similarly, **Elizabeth Baxmeyer, Rikki Corniola, William Davis, Gloria Poveda**, and **Christopher Wostenberg** discuss the development of a novel WAC program at the College of Health Sciences within California Northstate University, where faculty train students for the complex writing situations in which healthcare practitioners engage. Taking an interdisciplinary and collaborative approach in developing a writing curriculum that aligns across all disciplines at the university, Baxmeyer et al. explain how their program achieves cohesion and consistency in the student experience of writing, from lab reports to community-engaged projects: "Students find consistent language across courses and disciplines in terms of assessments, expectations, and outcomes, and faculty see direct connections between their work and that of their colleagues" (p. 75).

In addition to emphasizing the value of shared language to organize faculty development initiatives and strengthen a vertical curriculum, both accounts of these new programs demonstrate the challenging demands on WAC administrators who have to juggle being writing experts across multiple fields, while also balancing curricular and support needs for students at various levels of their academic careers.

Concluding this section, **Ming Fang, Kimberly Harrison**, and **Christine Martorana's** chapter describes the program they built at Florida International University, which is currently the largest Hispanic-Serving Institution (HSI) in the United States. Their chapter offers an important framework for thinking through the various ways partnerships might be made—from those born out of shared interest, to those imposed from administrative bodies—and strategies for capitalizing on the benefits such partnerships offer. Fang et al. highlight that a multi-pronged approach to strategic partnerships keeps their WAC program institutionally relevant and can aid them in working toward institutional transformation. Through their chapter, we learn the ways in which such relationships are beneficial in "supporting faculty as they shift from the assumption that monolingual student writers are the norm," which is crucial for mobilizing inclusive writing pedagogies that are shaped by the assets of "a multilingual, multicultural student body" (p. 90).

CHAPTER 1.

THE WORK BEYOND THE WORKSHOP: ASSESSING AND REINVIGORATING OUR WAC OUTREACH MODEL

Olivia R. Tracy, Juli Parrish, Heather N. Martin, and Brad Benz
University of Denver

In an interview with Carol Rutz (2004), Chris Anson stated that one of his goals at North Carolina State was to "saturate" the curriculum with writing. Many U.S. WAC/WID programs share this goal. Such outreach efforts are often channeled through the writing center, as faculty across campus collaborate with writing faculty to incorporate writing pedagogy into their courses (Harris, 1992; Palmquist et al., 2020; Thaiss & Porter, 2010). When WAC/WID outreach is successful, faculty in the disciplines bring a host of perspectives and levels of engagement to teaching writing in their courses (Donahue, 2002; Hughes & Miller, 2018; Miraglia & McLeod, 1997; Salem & Jones, 2010). Indeed, as Anson notes (Rutz, 2004), the most successful WAC/WID outreach results in "intellectual partnerships" across campus as faculty in the disciplines interrogate and recognize the role of writing and rhetoric in their disciplines, ultimately sharing this knowledge with students and colleagues (Carter, 2004; Russell, 1991). However, critics of WAC/WID often contend that it is accommodationist, assimilationist, and colonialist—effectively privileging academic, disciplinary discourse over other discourses (Guerra, 2008, 2016; Kells, 2001; LeCourt, 1995; Harahap et al., 2021; Poe, 2016; Villanueva, 2001). Increasingly, WPAs, as well as writing center and WAC directors, have acknowledged that their efforts are not successful if they do not also interrogate and seek change around racist and exclusionary language and teaching practices (Hopkins, 2016; Lerner, 1997, 2003, 2018; Martini & Webster, 2021).

At the University of Denver—a predominantly white, private, midsized, R1 institution—we share similar programmatic goals for WAC/WID as we partner and collaborate with faculty from across campus, quite often through the writing center. One way we try to accomplish this "intellectual partnership" is by offering and teaching writing workshops in non-writing program classes,

DOI: https://doi.org/10.37514/PER-B.2023.1947.2.01

what Rebecca M. Howard (1999) called "*in situ*" workshops (p. 40). Essentially, DU writing faculty and writing center peer consultants collaborate with faculty partners to lead hour-long workshops in their classes. This chapter examines our WAC workshop model, including the theory that informs it and the logistics of the workshops. Using findings from recent survey and interview data, we examine what faculty learn from the workshops; identify a spectrum of faculty orientations engendered by our WAC workshop model; explore three patterns emerging from the data that identified shortcomings in our model; and offer a framework from which to work moving forward as we revise our WAC efforts.

We have experienced a common challenge that David R. Russell (1991) identifies for writing faculty who collaborate with faculty from other disciplines on WAC work. Among non-writing faculty, he writes: "Because the rhetoric of the discipline appears not to be taught, efforts to teach it may require those in the discipline first to become conscious of rhetoric's role in the activities and, second, to make a conscious effort to teach it" (p. 18). Michael Carter (2007) picked up on this argument, distinguishing between what we know as writing in the disciplines with what he calls "writing outside the disciplines" (p. 385). For Carter, writing outside the disciplines can be summarized as follows: Many faculty learn to write in their discipline by writing in their discipline, without explicit instruction or sustained attention to the rhetorical practices therein. As a result, many faculty view writing as an independent skill, isolated from disciplinary practices (p. 385). Drawing on genre theory, Carter argues that successful WAC/WID collaborations occur when faculty explicitly teach their students these discipline-based ways of knowing and doing, and then connect them to writing. In the process, faculty (and students) recognize that "writing is critical to the ways of knowing valued in the disciplines" (p. 404).

OUR WORKSHOP HISTORY AND MODEL

In alignment with the goals outlined by Russell and Carter, DU has been offering WAC workshops through the writing center since 2007. The growing frequency of workshops over time suggests successful WAC/WID outreach. In our first year, we led 19 classroom workshops, a number that quadrupled over five years (see Figure 1.1).[1]

Through our classroom workshops, we connect with over 800 undergraduate and graduate students a year, on average (see Table 1.1). While these numbers demonstrate growth and increased contact with faculty and students across

---

[1] In addition to classroom workshops, we collaborate with programs and units to support student writing. In recent years, we have offered as many or more program workshops as classroom workshops. For purposes of this project, we are focused on classroom workshops only.

campus, we've grown curious about the success of our workshop model beyond these raw data.

Our model emphasizes collaboration at every step in the process as we aim for Anson's intellectual-partnership ideal (Rutz, 2004, p. 14). Workshops are coordinated by the writing center and facilitated by writing program faculty or writing center consultants. When a faculty partner contacts the writing center to request a workshop, a faculty or graduate facilitator is assigned to the workshop. The facilitator works with the faculty partner to negotiate a date for the event, inquiring about the assignment and the stage in the writing process where students will be at the time of the workshop (e.g., brainstorming, composing, revising). For example, faculty partners commonly request classroom workshops before students have begun the writing process. Conversations with faculty partners often involve negotiating a later visit, so students might more immediately apply workshop concepts to their drafts.

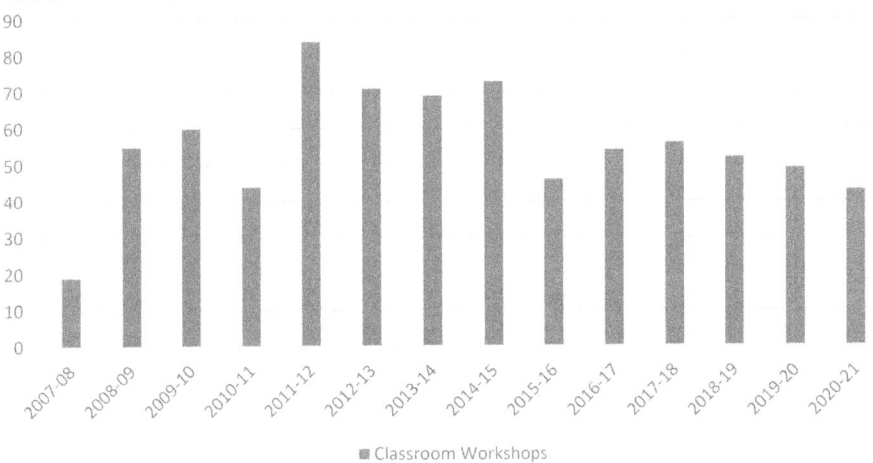

Figure 1.1. Total Classroom Workshops Facilitated by Year, 2007–2021.

Table 1.1. Total and Average Faculty and Students Involved in Classroom Workshops, 2011–2021.

Variable	Total Classroom Workshops	Unique Faculty Partners	Student Participants (Undergraduate and Graduate)
Total	574	253	~8856
Average/Year	57	25	~805

Next, the facilitator meets with the faculty partner to learn about the course and develop ideas for the workshop. The facilitator asks a lot of questions, such as: *How does this workshop complement or align with how you are teaching your students to write? Where in the assignment sequence is it located? What writing will students have completed in your course? What can/will they bring to the workshop? How do you talk about writing with your students?* These conversations surface important assumptions and expectations about writing—both ours and theirs. As part of this two-way learning process, we learn about the faculty partner's approach to writing, the conversations they have (or don't) with students about writing, and the assumptions and expectations they have for student writing. We see this work as doing some "consciousness raising" (Russell, 1991): We support the faculty partner in developing a stronger awareness of rhetoric's role in their discipline as well as their own role in teaching writing, thus making the work of writing visible in their classroom.

Finally, we facilitate the workshop. Synthesizing the information provided by the faculty partner and the facilitator's expertise in writing instruction, the facilitator develops a course-specific, interactive, hands-on workshop. Core to our model is an emphasis on students applying concepts to papers they are *currently writing*. We ask the faculty partner to remain present, both to signal to students that the work is part of the course and to involve the faculty member as a partner in learning. For example, students often raise questions about the assignment during the workshop. We view this as an opportunity for the faculty partner both to clarify expectations and better understand what might be missing or implied in their written assignments.

Via this model, we collaborate with faculty partners in the short term to develop a workshop to help students succeed with their writing assignments. In the long term, the most successful—and sustainable—partnerships occur when the faculty partner embraces Russell's second step: to "make a conscious effort to teach writing." Or, as Carter (2004) states:

> [I]nstead of perceiving of WID as asking them to become "writing teachers," they can see that their responsibility for teaching the ways of knowing and doing in their disciplines also extends to writing, which is not separate from but essential to their disciplines. The WID professional becomes an agent for helping faculty achieve their expectations for what students should be able to do. (p. 408)

By simple measures, our collaborations have been extraordinarily successful. In a 2014 assessment, for example, 96 percent of faculty reported being satisfied or very satisfied with our workshops. The increase in the number of workshops each year further reflects this success (see Figure 1.1). Indeed, workshop requests have been so robust as to stretch the writing center's resources—namely the time and energy of writing faculty and peer consultants—to the point that we no longer feel we can meet faculty demand. As we contemplated our capacity to continue this model, we likewise engaged larger questions around our efficacy in faculty development and cultivating intellectual partnerships. For example, while growth in workshop requests suggests that faculty partners see value in them, what does that growth say about faculty agency and ability to support student writing in their discipline? Or when faculty request the same workshop year after year, what does this tell us about our goal of intellectual partnership?

With these and other questions in mind, we sought to interrogate the success of our workshop model, seeking specifically to learn how and to what extent DU faculty partners and students use classroom writing workshops to develop, as writers and instructors of writing, and to learn more about the rhetoric of their disciplines. To achieve this goal, we won a modest faculty research grant to identify more clearly what faculty and students value in our workshops.

METHOD AND PARTICIPANTS

Past internal assessments over the course of our extensive workshop history focused on faculty satisfaction trends with our workshops. In this study, we wanted instead to delve deeply into three case studies, providing texture and fresh insights. The case studies consist of survey and interview data collected from faculty and student participants in three workshops; in this chapter, we focus primarily on our interviews with faculty partners. We introduce our research questions, methods, and the questions asked in surveys and interviews. Finally, we explore three through-lines that emerged in data analysis.

When we designed this project, we sought answers to the following research questions:

1. What is the value of our classroom writing workshops as defined by the faculty partners and students who attend them?
2. What writing strategies, rhetorical concepts, and vocabularies do faculty partners and students transfer to future writing situations?
3. What elements of our workshops are most important to preserve?

To explore these questions, we collected survey and interview data from students and faculty partners participating in three (out of a total of 28) workshops we offered across campus in one academic term. For each participating faculty partner, we obtained consent to observe the workshop, introduced the survey and consent process at the end of the workshop, and conducted follow-up interviews and/or focus groups with interested participants about two weeks later.

Faculty and student surveys were completed in the classroom immediately following the workshop. They consisted of three questions with Likert-scale responses and two narrative-response questions. Some questions were asked of both faculty and students, while others targeted one population and not the other. Participants were asked to indicate the extent to which they agreed with the following statements:

1. "Today's workshop was helpful." (Faculty and Students)
2. "I learned something new in today's workshop." (Faculty and Students)
3. "Today's workshop will help my students in future writing situations." (Faculty)
4. "Today's workshop will help me in future writing situations." (Students)

We then asked faculty and students to narratively respond to the following questions:

1. "What is one thing you are taking away from today's workshop? Please be specific, including examples where possible." (Faculty and Students)
2. "Why did you arrange for this workshop?" (Faculty)
3. "Why do you think your professor arranged for this workshop?" (Students)

The faculty partner interviews were conducted over Zoom. After obtaining consent to record and collecting digitally signed consent forms, we asked two sets of questions outlined in our IRB application.

The first set of questions focused on understanding what faculty and students learned in the workshops by asking faculty partners to respond to the following:

1. In addition to the evaluation you filled out after class, do you have any feedback for us about the pre-workshop meeting? The workshop itself?
2. What do you think your students learned during this workshop?
3. What do you think you, as a professor, learned from this workshop?
4. In subsequent class sessions, did you or your students refer back to the workshop?

The second set of questions created a conversation around faculty transfer by asking faculty partners to respond to the following:

1. What in this workshop might you use in or apply to . . .
   a. The same assignment in a future iteration of the class?
   b. Different assignments in the same class?
   c. Different assignments in different classes?
2. In your other classes, do you use any of the strategies discussed in this workshop?

3. How do you teach writing in your classes when you do not have a workshop?
4. What other kinds of support do you seek/use when teaching writing in your classes?

Through our conversations, we discovered that our case studies offered insight into a spectrum of faculty-partner orientations enabled by our current workshop model, including intellectual partnership through 1) a services orientation, 2) a maintenance orientation, and 3) a development orientation.

THE CASE STUDIES

As described, our *in situ* workshops provide for a spectrum of faculty-partner engagement. Even as workshop facilitators make efforts toward consciousness raising through early communications and the planning meeting, faculty-partner orientation toward this WAC work varied. We see this diversity reflected clearly in our case study findings.

One case landed firmly on the service-oriented side of the spectrum—reflected by a faculty partner who centered expectations for support and gently resisted questions about their growth as a practitioner. We conceive of this as a "services-seeking" orientation. Another case landed more in the middle—reflected by a faculty partner who was eager to engage in improving on the workshop, but less interested in pedagogical questions around writing instruction. Like many faculty partners, this individual had requested the same workshop multiple times over several years. We view this as a maintenance or "status quo" orientation. Finally, our third case reflected a strong intellectual partnership, characterized by a faculty partner who demonstrated deep engagement with pedagogical practice and development. We conceive of this as a "knowledge-seeking" or development orientation.

The Services Seeker

The faculty partner we identified as the services seeker is deeply committed to student writing, regularly meeting with students individually to talk about their writing, taking a process-driven approach to composing, and qualifies as a heavy user of writing center and WAC resources at DU. This faculty partner has requested workshops for every class taught since joining the university, indicating, when asked, "I never *not* have workshops."

In consultation with this faculty partner, the facilitator developed a workshop containing a peer-review activity and worksheet. Even as the faculty partner was pleased with the workshop and the worksheet (especially), the interview revealed only limited value to the collaboration. For example, when asked what they learned from the workshop, the faculty partner referred to the worksheet: "Those guided questions were the main thing . . . that's pretty much it." From the faculty member's perspective, both parties served as distinct content experts, noting, "I wasn't trained to be a writing teacher. So, having that pedagogical expertise is very helpful because the [peer-review] questions tend to be better when they come from the writing center." Nor did the faculty partner perceive the workshop as an opportunity to learn; rather, it was an opportunity for someone with more expertise to lend a hand. When asked about what they might transfer from the workshop to other teaching situations, the faculty partner replied, "The worksheet, obviously," noting further, "What I would like as a resource . . . are more directed peer-review questions, so [students are] looking for specific things in their assignments. I would love if someone developed that for each of my assignments." If the faculty partner sees that "the ways of knowing and doing in their disciplines also extend to writing" (Carter, 2004, p. 408), it's not clear from our interview.

Many faculty partners initially present with a services-seeking orientation. Perhaps as a consequence of our marketing strategy or broader preconceptions about writing center work, faculty often arrive with little awareness of WAC or writing center scholarship and professionalization. With this knowledge, we are intentional with our consciousness-raising efforts during workshop planning and communication. Even so, many faculty partners maintain a service orientation through various WAC engagements, some over many years.

The Status Quo Seeker

Our second faculty interview reveals another common approach to our workshops: faculty partners who regularly ask for the same workshop in the same class. These individuals are seeking the status quo. For the faculty partner in our second case study, we have facilitated the same workshop, with little variation, in eight different iterations of their course. Our workshop model has served this faculty partner and their students well, while also meeting some of our WAC/WID goals. In their interview, the faculty partner recapped the workshop meeting and workshop as follows: "I thought the pre-workshop meeting was pretty thorough. I think there was more than I could have even thought to have included in that, and then I thought the workshop went really well." They articulated awareness of the complexities of writing pedagogy, acknowledging that the workshop meeting resulted in a more enriched and intricate workshop plan than the faculty had originally envisioned. Moreover, the interview data reveal that the workshop helped students develop a more nuanced understanding of source use and the assignment, even asking "questions that were due to the workshop."

On the surface, it appears the workshop was effective, with students feeling better prepared to complete the assignment, and the faculty partner expressing interest in refining their writing pedagogy. However, on closer inspection, we see further shortcomings to our workshop model. In response to the question about modifying the workshop and assignment for a different class, the faculty partner stated: "I would probably want to do the exact same workshop again, just to have that repetition." When asked about how the faculty partner might employ writing pedagogy in their course for graduate students, they reiterated: "I'd imagine doing the exact same workshop in that class as well . . . and maybe expect a little bit more out of them in terms of the sources." The workshop itself is fine, delivering immediate results for both students and faculty partners. Yet our workshop model has enabled this faculty member to be content with the status quo, requesting the same workshop again and again. There's some movement toward Russell's consciousness-raising, some transfer of WAC/WID pedagogy, but in a limited way. This case study reflects an important limitation to our workshop model. It meets short-term goals, improves student writing on that assignment, and sparks some faculty insight into writing pedagogy. But absent a more sustained and ongoing collaboration, faculty development is stunted by continued availability of the status-quo workshop. Without further collaboration, we provide the same workshop again and again. Wash, rinse, and repeat.

The Knowledge Seeker

Our third type of faculty partner, the knowledge seeker, qualifies as an occasional user of writing center resources, having requested only two classroom workshops in five academic years, but regularly addresses writing with students, including structured peer-review activities and talking explicitly about writing in class. When asked about how they teach writing in their courses, this faculty partner mentioned offering genre samples, process guidelines, rubrics, peer reviews, and feedback, emphasizing their role in helping students understand and practice common moves in a specific genre and the importance of seeking out and using available resources.

The workshop we created with this faculty partner focused on writing literature reviews. They talked about our workshop through the lens of their own goals for teaching writing and experience in learning to write the genre, noting that the facilitator offered

> much more structure and much more context for what a literature review is trying to do than the way I can do it . . . When it comes to the literature review . . . I've only learned

it because I've done it. And I don't know how to explain why this works.

This instructor felt that the facilitator "seemed to understand" this challenge and was able to offer a "meta-perspective" to students, thus adding a necessary dimension to the course. Distinct from the other faculty partnerships we've described here, this partnership might be considered a success in both Russell's and Carter's terms: The faculty partner articulated both what they have learned in working with the facilitator and a sense of the value of writing as a way of "knowing and doing" (Carter, 2004, p. 408).

What also set this faculty partner apart was a stated desire for reciprocity with the facilitator. In their post-workshop interview, the faculty partner talked about wanting to show the facilitator that they saw the workshop as a meaningful contribution to the class—not just "a filler." Perhaps more importantly, they were particularly interested in their own role in making the workshop *count*, in avoiding a situation in which a workshop happens and is never mentioned again. In fact, this faculty member even asked about best practices, inquiring about "what workshops are and are not meant to do." In essence, this faculty member identified a gap in our model that resonated with us:

> [R]ight now, my understanding [is that] you can reach out and talk to people about how [a workshop] might fit into your class. But I was curious to know if there might be some way of going forward, people who are interested in using workshops, some fundamentals that they need to know about applying [the workshop].

In other words, the faculty partner wanted *more* than was offered. They were not content with a faculty facilitator coming to their class to teach literature reviews; rather, they wanted to understand the pedagogical principles at play, to have help understanding the role of the workshop in their course, and to better support their teaching of writing in that course.

Our current model has enabled this spectrum of faculty orientations, and we don't fault anyone for accepting what we've offered. While we might wish that our knowledge-seeker orientation was more accessible to faculty, we see how we've made the other orientations available. For example, we have chosen to do multiple workshops for faculty and likewise agreed to do the same workshop year after year; these decisions are on us.

Takeaways

During our presentation to other WAC practitioners at the IWAC Conference, our case studies resonated, suggesting faculty orientations across this spectrum present similarly in other WAC programs. It should be noted, however, that we do not offer this spectrum of faculty orientations to critique faculty partners who adopt them; rather, we seek to capture common ways that WAC programs and writing centers work with individual faculty partners.

The comments offered by these faculty partners helped us not only to recognize the spectrum of faculty orientations made possible by our current workshop model, but also to identify three patterns that emerged from that model: differences in stakeholder motivations and goals; prioritization of immediate projects over transferable skills; and recognition that our current workshop model will not be able to meet our needs and goals.

Motivations and Goals. The surveys and interviews revealed the complexity of our WAC workshop model, and the many disparate functions we hope workshops serve. Not only are our goals myriad, but often, what we want and what faculty want, what we get and what faculty get, become disconnected due to this complexity. Furthermore, when faculty partner goals do not align with facilitator goals—such as with the services seeker—our current model does little to address it.

Immediacy vs. Transfer. In both surveys and interviews, the immediate assignment often became the focus over the potential of transferable learning. In offering hands-on workshops designed to provide immediately applicable and contextual strategies, both students and faculty failed to see potential applications in other contexts, as with the status quo seeker who could not extrapolate transferable insights, but rather wanted the same workshop replicated in a higher-level course.

New or Revised Model. Finally, based on these results and previous assessments, we have concluded that it's time to do something different. Although some workshops may be achieving the goals and purposes set for them, while also supporting faculty partners' pedagogical development, we need a different workshop or WAC structure to achieve our central goals. In the next section, we explore how these patterns offer exigence for transforming our workshop and outreach goals.

ASSESSING AND REVISING OUR WORKSHOP GOALS

When we coded and analyzed the qualitative data collected from the interviews and surveys, we determined three takeaways, emerging from our through-lines:

- Our motivations and goals when offering workshops are complex and often disconnected from the motivations and goals of faculty partners requesting workshops.
- Specific assignments and faculty partners' immediate needs often take precedent over the potential of transferable learning.
- Faculty partners may be seeking services, the status quo, or knowledge,

but our current structure—which ends rather than begins with a writing workshop in a classroom—does not promote the kind of sustained engagement that successful WAC work often involves.

We set out to learn how and to what extent DU faculty and students use classroom writing workshops to develop as writers and instructors of writing and to learn more about the rhetoric of their disciplines. These takeaways showed us that our workshops *are not* meeting our current goals. In fact, our workshops as they currently exist probably *cannot* help us meet current goals. Individual faculty partnerships and workshops may be meaningful for some faculty partners, and perhaps also for their students, but we find ourselves wanting to move toward a model that achieves our goals in more intentional and sustained ways, even if it means discontinuing and rebuilding an offering we've had in place for 15 years.

In his plenary address at the IWAC Conference, Christopher Thaiss said, "There is no sustainability without adaptability" (Rutz & Thaiss, 2021). Throughout our research, we have considered how we might adapt. Could we keep our workshops but give up the WAC-iest of our goals and accept that a classroom workshop can't do what we originally wanted it to do? Could we replace our faculty and consultant-facilitated workshops? Could we offer faculty consultations, where we support faculty partners to develop and facilitate their own workshops?

In and through the process of imagining these and other futures, and considering what needs to be preserved in our workshop model, we've discovered that we need to detangle our WAC goals from our workshop model—that is, we need goals that can be applied in a variety of forms and contexts, not just through workshops. Our original workshop goals read as follows:

1. *Workshops* involve the faculty member as a collaborator.
2. *Workshops* are assignment or situation-specific, although often transferable to other writing assignments or situations.
3. *Workshops* are interactive and involve hands-on learning for students.
4. We see faculty learning from our *workshops* just as students do and want them to be able to transfer their learning (à la Russell and Carter).

We note that our original goals did not include work around antiracist practices, world Englishes, or inclusive-writing pedagogies; similarly, our assessments failed to take up questions about the ways writing conventions, practices, and genres discussed in our workshops might be shaped by racialized and culturalized expectations for student writing. We see that our case study approach did not make room for considerations of antiracist WAC either, even though we might be able to map such considerations onto our three faculty case studies.

The choice to center "work" over "workshop," we think, might help us create opportunities to put more emphasis on the work we ask faculty to do around antiracist practices and world Englishes; interrogate the intertwined linguistic and racial expectations and assumptions faculty and students bring to classroom contexts (Poe, 2016); and emphasize how "writing is not only a way of learning but also a way of fostering critical consciousness, more than a means of problem solving but also a means of problem posing" (Villanueva, 2001, p. 172). We want to think about our future WAC efforts in a similar way. As we have noted, one unintentional outcome of our workshop model was the continued perception of our workshops as stand-alone events, as one-offs that helped faculty achieve a particular goal with a particular assignment in a particular class. As we move forward, we want to stop offering workshops that solve problems *for* faculty and instead do work that poses problems *to* faculty. As Rebecca H. Martini and Travis Webster (2021) suggest, we must "reimagine how our everyday work in faculty development might change to become more antiracist through an integrated—rather than one-off or statement-centered—approach" (p. 101). This means involving faculty in our own efforts to intervene in and disrupt language, genre, and disciplinary conventions that center a narrow set of standards and in our shared discovery and implementation of instructional practices that do antiracist work. We have tried to reflect this approach in our revised WAC goals:

1. *Work* involves faculty partners as collaborators.
2. *Work* involves or leads to writing instruction that might be assignment- or situation-specific but facilitates transfer of learning.
3. *Work* involves or leads to interactive and hands-on learning for students.
4. *Work* promotes faculty learning and transfer of learning.
5. *Work* engages faculty as collaborators in antiracist instructional practices.

Even as we see problems with our workshop approach, we continue to see its value to faculty and students across campus. Thus, our intent is to keep what is meaningful by developing more intentional goals and to grow more capacious in our thinking about the mechanisms for reaching those goals. In our final section, we explore future directions for revising our workshop model to better support our re/vision of WAC work at DU.

FUTURE DIRECTIONS

Through this research, we sought to learn how DU students use classroom writing workshops to develop as writers, and how faculty partners use classroom writing workshops to develop as instructors of writing, given the rhetoric of their disciplines. In the findings discussed in this chapter, we've come to better understand not only how faculty partners engage with our workshops but also the spectrum of possible engagements our current model enables (or doesn't).

While locating the spectrum of faculty engagement has helped us understand the limitations of our current workshop model, we continue to consider how to reshape our process to emphasize the "work" rather than the "workshop." Two things we know: Our current workshop process and goals need to be disarticulated, and our revised WAC goals can help us emphasize the work beyond the workshop. As we begin to imagine these alternative approaches, we're asking the following:

- How can we continue the conversations we have with faculty, and do so in a more intentional way, to better cultivate these "intellectual partnerships" (Rutz, 2004)?
- How might we reevaluate our process through our current spectrum of faculty engagement and facilitate transfer of learning along that spectrum?
- How can different interactive, hands-on projects help us serve student and faculty needs, including through models like consultant-facilitated peer reviews or guided conversations where faculty partners develop workshops?
- How might we better support faculty learning and transfer if we could designate a writing program WAC coordinator to focus on building these relationships?
- How can we use the exigence of reinventing our WAC efforts to build in meaningful antiracist efforts and begin "cultivating more discussions and curricular changes around white language supremacy in the academy" (Inoue as quoted in Lerner, 2018, p. 116).

We understand that our workshop model needs a more comprehensive system to help us and our faculty partners achieve their writing-instruction goals. Guided by these questions, we now think beyond our workshops toward other practices. Like Steve Parks and Eli Goldblatt (2000), we believe that

> we should imagine our project as one that combines discipline-based instruction with a range of other literacy experiences that will help students and faculty see writing and reading in a wider social and intellectual context than the college curriculum. (pp. 585–586)

These continuing questions and our revised WAC goals will guide us, and perhaps inspire other writing programs, to imagine "a range of other literacy experiences" beyond the classroom workshop and develop outreach that better serves us, faculty partners, and students.

ACKNOWLEDGMENTS

Authors are listed in reverse alphabetical order. The authors thank Douglas Hesse, former DU Writing Program Executive Director; Eliana Schonberg, former Writing Center Director; and Sarah Hart Micke, former Writing Center Assistant Director, who participated in earlier assessments of our workshops that contributed to our thinking. We also offer our thanks to Corinne Lengsfeld, Senior Vice Provost of Research and Graduate Education, and Kate Willink, former Vice Provost of Faculty Affairs at the University of Denver, for providing a Faculty Research Fund grant in support of our research. The authors offer thanks as well to the editors of this volume for helpful feedback on this chapter.

REFERENCES

Carter, M. (2007). Ways of knowing, doing, and writing in the disciplines. *College Composition and Communication, 58*(3), 385–418. https://www.jstor.org/stable/20456952.

Childers, P., Johanek, C., Leydens, J., Mullin, J., Pemberton, M., Rickly, R. & Palmquist, M. (2002). Forum: Writing centers and WAC. *Academic Writing, 3.* https://doi.org/10.37514/AWR-J.2002.3.1.03.

Donahue, P. (2002). Strange resistances. *The WAC Journal, 13*, 31–41. https//doi:10.37514/WAC-J.2002.13.1.04.

Guerra, J. C. (2008). Writing for transcultural citizenship: A cultural ecology model. *Language Arts, 85*(4), 296–304.

Guerra, J. C. (2016). *Language, culture, identity, and citizenship in college classrooms and communities.* Routledge.

Harahap, A., Navarro, F. & Russell, A. (2021, August 2–6). *Writing across more-than-the-curriculum: A conversation toward diversifying, professionalizing, and renovating WAC* [Closing plenary conference presentation]. Fifteenth International Writing Across the Curriculum Conference, Fort Collins, CO, United States. https://youtu.be/MDBbGNd-Law.

Harris, M. (1992). The writing center and tutoring in WAC programs. In S. H. McLeod & M. Soven (Eds.), *Writing across the curriculum: A guide to developing programs* (pp. 154–174). Sage.

Hopkins, J. B. (2016). Are our workshops working?: Assessing assessment as research. *Praxis: A Writing Center Journal, 13*(2). http://www.praxisuwc.com/hopkins-132?rq=workshop.

Howard, R. M. (1988). *In situ* workshops and the peer relationships of composition. *WPA: Writing Program Administration, 12*(12), 39–46.

Hughes, B. & Miller, E. L. (2018). WAC seminar participants as surrogate WAC consultants: Disciplinary faculty developing and deploying WAC expertise. *The WAC Journal (29)*, 7–41. https://doi.org/10.37514/WAC-J.2018.29.1.01.

Kells, M. H. (2007). Writing across communities: Deliberation and the discursive possibilities of WAC. *Reflections, 17*(1), 87–108. https://reflectionsjournal.net/wp-content/uploads/2020/09/V6.N1.Kells_.pdf.

LeCourt, D. (1996). WAC as critical pedagogy: The third stage? *JAC, 16*(3), 389–405.

Lerner, N. (1997). Counting beans and making beans count. *The Writing Lab Newsletter, 22*(1), 1–4. https://wlnjournal.org/archives/v22/22-1.pdf.

Lerner, N. (2003). Writing center assessment: Searching for the "proof" of our effectiveness. In M. A. Pemberton & J. Kincaid (Eds.), *The center will hold: Critical perspectives on writing center scholarship* (pp. 58–73). Utah State University Press.

Lerner, N. (2018). *WAC Journal* interview of Asao B. Inoue. *The WAC Journal, 29*, 112–118. https://doi.org/10.37514/WAC-J.2018.29.1.05.

Martini, R. H. & Webster, T. (2021). Anti-racism across the curriculum: Practicing an integrated approach to WAC and writing center faculty development. *WPA: Writing Program Administration, 44*(3), 100–105. https://link.gale.com/apps/doc/A678980697/AONE?u=maine_oweb&sid=googleScholar&xid=ddce67a7.

Miraglia, E. & McLeod, S. H. (1997). Whither WAC? Interpreting the stories/histories of enduring WAC programs. *WPA: Writing Program Administration, 20*, 46–65. http://associationdatabase.co/archives/20n3/20n3miraglia.pdf.

Palmquist, M., Childers, P., Maimon, E., Mullin, J., Rice, R., Russell, A. & Russell, D. R. (2020). Fifty years of WAC: Where have we been? Where are we going? *Across the Disciplines, 17*(3/4), 5–45. https://doi.org/10.37514/ATD-J.2020.17.3.01.

Parks, S. & Goldblatt, E. (2000). Writing beyond the curriculum: Fostering new collaborations in literacy. *College English, 62*(5), 584–606. https://doi.org/10.2307/378963.

Poe, M. (2016). Reframing race in teaching writing across the curriculum. In F. Condon & V. A. Young (Eds.), *Performing antiracist pedagogy in rhetoric, writing, and communication* (pp. 87–105). The WAC Clearinghouse; University Press of Colorado. https://doi.org/10.37514/ATD-B.2016.0933.2.04.

Russell, D. R. (1991). *Writing in the academic disciplines, 1870–1990: A curricular history.* Southern Illinois University Press.

Rutz, C. (2004). WAC and beyond: An interview with Chris Anson. *The WAC Journal, 15*, 7–17. https://doi.org/10.37514/WAC-J.2004.15.1.01.

Rutz, C. & Thaiss, C. (2021, July 29). WAC fearlessness, sustainability, and adaptability over five decades. [Opening plenary conference presentation]. Fifteenth International Writing Across the Curriculum Conference, Fort Collins, CO, United States. https://youtu.be/UJ9p8q-xZNo.

Salem, L. & Jones, P. (2010). Undaunted, self-critical, and resentful: Investigating faculty attitudes toward teaching writing in a large university writing-intensive course program. *WPA: Writing Program Administration, 34*(1), 60–38. http://162.241.207.49/archives/34n1/34n1salem-jones.pdf.

Thaiss, C. & Porter, T. (2010). The state of WAC/WID in 2010: Methods and results of the U.S. survey of the international WAC/WID mapping project. *College Composition and Communication, 61*(3), 534–570. https://www.jstor.org/stable/40593339.

Villanueva, V. (2001). The politics of literacy across the curriculum. In S. H. McLeod, E. Miraglia, M. Soven & C. Thaiss (Eds.), *WAC for the new millennium: Strategies for continuing WAC programs* (pp. 165–178). The WAC Clearinghouse. https://wac.colostate.edu/books/landmarks/millennium/ (Originally published in 2001 by NCTE).

CHAPTER 2.

THE UNIVERSITY OF DENVER ETHNOGRAPHY LAB: FOSTERING A WAC COMMUNITY OF PRACTICE

Kamila Kinyon, Alejandro Cerón, and Dinko Hanaan Dinko
University of Denver

The 50th anniversary of writing across the curriculum (WAC) in 2020 motivated an exploration of the movement's historical foundations along with reflections on future directions. To best understand WAC's role in writing studies, it is important to consider how WAC comes into play in first-year writing instruction, how it promotes inclusiveness and access, and how it stimulates global collaboration (Palmquist et al., 2020, p. 5). One of WAC's important goals is to open the possibility for new types of interdisciplinary collaborative spaces (Palmquist et al., 2020, p. 6). A case in point of such a space is the University of Denver Ethnography Lab (DUEL), founded in 2019. As a collaborative ethnographic institute, DUEL is a rich site for WAC, especially given ethnography's interdisciplinary nature, commitment to social justice, and increasing value to writing studies as a scholarly method and pedagogical tool.

Initiated by anthropology professor Alejandro Cerón, DUEL seeks to serve as a catalyst for change, bringing together ethnographers from multiple disciplines and at various stages in their academic or public careers. As discussed in more detail below, DUEL members include faculty, graduate students, and undergraduates as well as community partners and interested faculty at other institutions. DUEL supports ethnographic research and writing through a range of outreach activities as well as through a center where writers can get feedback on various stages of their ethnographic work.

As a community of practice that employs ethnography in action, DUEL aligns both with WAC's commitment to social justice and public good and with the University of Denver's mission to serve these goals. Jean J. Schensul and Margaret D. LeCompte (2016) define ethnography in action through the emphasis on sustainable community-based interventions that contribute to positive change as defined by the communities themselves. Ethnography in action embodies a central mission of WAC, which is committed to serving as a force for

DOI: https://doi.org/10.37514/PER-B.2023.1947.2.02

social change, "a force that involves both the recognition of past shortcomings and the promise of taking meaningful action" (Palmquist et al., 2020, p. 37). DUEL can support scholars who are working towards community-based interventions, including, for example, those who are conducting institutional ethnography, identified by Michelle La France (2019) as a productive method for programmatic, departmental, and university focused research. Overall, DUEL's community of practice serves as a WAC resource to faculty in different disciplines who are pursuing issues of social justice in their fields.

Ethnography has become increasingly important to WAC practitioners as both a research method and a pedagogical tool, as can be seen in its growing role over the past decades. While Stephen M. North's (1987) "Making of Knowledge in Composition" deemphasized the role of ethnography, the following decade saw a rapid growth in ethnography's application to writing studies, as illustrated in the anthology *Voices and Visions: Refiguring Ethnography in Composition* (Kirklighter, 1997). In her seminal article "Ethnography in a Composition Course: From the Perspective of a Teacher Researcher" (1992), Beverly J. Moss explains how she used ethnographic methods to study her composition classroom while simultaneously assigning ethnographies to her students. This assignment fostered diversity by empowering students to incorporate their personal voice in a study of local communities. In "Putting Ethnographic Writing in Context," Seth Kahn (2011) further elaborates on the benefits of ethnography for first-year composition, since it teaches students different forms of writing as they go through the process of collecting fieldnotes, transcribing interviews, and presenting their findings to a variety of scholarly and public audiences. In addition, Durba Chattaraj (2020) draws on transfer study research (Yancey et al., 2014) to argue that ethnography should be taught in composition courses because its broad-based understanding of evidence facilitates transfer of learning skills beyond the classroom. Incorporating multiple texts within itself—academic discourse, journalistic prose, the speech of interviewees, and the native discourses of the ethnographer's own culture—ethnography helps promote inclusiveness, making this a fruitful method for countering racism. As emphasized by Charles Bazerman and colleagues (2005), it is particularly important to address "issues of race, class, and gender as they relate to the writing process and to the discourse communities which house writing" (p. 101).

Within this larger framework, our discussion below demonstrates the growing importance of ethnographic research and writing for WAC as well as the role that interdisciplinary labs such as DUEL can play in supporting a community of practice for ethnographic work. First, we'll explain the foundation of DUEL under Cerón's initiative, its mission and goals, and the way in which DUEL serves as a catalyst for change on the DU campus and beyond. Next, we'll offer an example of dissertation work about water rights in Ghana conducted by Dinko Hanaan Dinko through the Department of Geography and the Environment. Dinko's fieldwork in Ghana embodies ethnographic work for the public good conducted through a range of departments at DU. Finally, we'll illustrate the role of ethnography in research writing courses taught by Kamila Kinyon, who extends her teaching beyond the classroom through collaborations with DUEL. These examples highlight a few ways that DUEL supports WAC efforts and constitutes a new direction for interdisciplinary collaborations.

AN INTERDISCIPLINARY ETHNOGRAPHY LAB AS A CATALYST FOR STUDENT, FACULTY, AND COMMUNITY COLLABORATIONS

The prehistory of DUEL can be traced back to 2014 when Cerón started incorporating short ethnographic projects in several of his anthropology courses with the aim of combining experiential learning and community engagement. Following this approach, Cerón and his students created ethnographically informed documents for community partners on a number of different subjects. This made Cerón recognize the growing interest in ethnography from undergraduate and graduate students majoring in different disciplines. Conversations with those students offered the early motivation that led to DUEL. Subsequently, in 2015, Kinyon invited Cerón to share his research and writing about epidemiology in Guatemala in Conversations in the Disciplines (CID), an interdisciplinary annual roundtable event organized by the University Writing Program. At this event, several professors from different disciplines present their research and writing approaches to an audience of students enrolled in WRIT 1133, a research writing course that completes the program's two-quarter sequence. In participating in CID, Cerón learned about the advantages of integrating ethnographic projects into a first-year composition curriculum.

The initial concept of an ethnography lab was conceived in 2017 and refined in 2018 through informal conversations with a group of anthropology graduate students who helped flip the switch from inspiration to action. Cerón and two graduate students did a planning exercise that materialized into the initial draft of DUEL's vision, mission, and goals. They also identified websites of similar projects at other universities and reviewed relevant literature on teaching and applied anthropology (Copeland & Dengah, 2016; Schensul & LeCompte, 2016).

Although learning from other university-based ethnography labs was important, DUEL needed to be compatible with the teacher-scholar model characteristic of DU. Important to the DU College of Arts, Humanities, and Social Sciences, for example, is the goal for expanding experiential learning opportunities. Similarly, the anthropology department's vision encourages publicly-engaged anthropology through its undergraduate and graduate programs. Moreover, DU promotes the teacher-scholar as espoused by Boyer et al.'s (2016) model aimed at weaving in the teaching and research facets of scholarly work (p. 83). Conceiving DUEL within these institutional realities meant that, through integration into curriculum, the lab would not need to depend on external grants for its basic functioning.

When DUEL was founded in 2019, the lab included 14 faculty members from across DU who used ethnography for their teaching or research. They were distributed in nine academic units including geography, journalism, sociology, music, education, languages, writing, international studies, and anthropology. Each of them would potentially have students attracted to ethnographic work. The materialization of DUEL was nurtured through dialogue among those 14 DU faculty members focusing on DUEL's purpose and nature.

DUEL aspires to be a catalyst for the multidisciplinary scholarship and learning of ethnography through the promotion of collaborations among faculty, students, and the broader community. DUEL works towards four goals: (1) facilitate interactions and collaborations among faculty who use ethnography in research or teaching; (2) offer a space where students interested in ethnography can develop their ideas and skills; (3) offer faculty and students an institutional home that helps nurture sustainable community collaborations; and (4) offer faculty and students the resources needed for carrying on ethnographic projects. Consequently, collaborations among faculty and students are a vehicle for cultivating ideas and skills, developing community collaborations, and sharing resources for ethnographic projects. Hence, DUEL is conceived as a network of practitioners of ethnography, and its activities are not bounded by specific courses or projects (McCormack et al., 2021).

DUEL's organization is reflected in key projects conducted during the 2020–2021 academic year. DUEL worked with five community partners, involving seven DU faculty from four departments, five students as research assistants, and 55 students through four courses. DU faculty participated, without extra funding, as part of their normal research-teaching load, while student research assistants were compensated through small internal grants or work-study awards. Community partners participated without extra funding, but small grants supported some project-related expenses. Cerón held regular weekly meetings with research assistants, while faculty and community partners met as needed or on a monthly schedule. As a result, DUEL has started to work on a few projects. Three of the projects are described below with the hope of showing how DUEL's four goals co-construct each other, how multiple modes of experiential learning are generated for students, and how this creates opportunities for students' engagement with different aspects of writing.

For example, three anthropology faculty collaborated with a group of epidemiologists in the Colorado Department of Public Health and the Environment (CDPHE) to find ways to address the misrepresentation and invisibilization of minoritized social groups in public health data. They met every three weeks and co-developed projects for visual anthropology and museum exhibit design courses. Students who took those classes critically analyzed public health data displayed in the CDPHE website, did short ethnographic observations in a Denver neighborhood, and made suggestions for how to represent different social groups in written reports and websites.

In a different example, faculty from Spanish, journalism, and anthropology are collaborating with a historian at History Colorado Center, the State's history museum, to document stories from minoritized social groups in Colorado. With a grant supporting a research assistant and paid internships, this project involves students taking classes by each of the three faculty and provides training in oral history interviewing, processing text and audio from interviews, and producing podcasts that synthesize those stories for presentation to broader audiences.

Finally, DUEL has been collaborating with Project Protect Food System Workers (PPFSW), a coalition organized in early 2020 to promote farmworkers' rights (Project Protect Food System Workers, 2021). DUEL is supporting PPFSW in collecting data about and stories of farmworkers that illuminate their contributions to society, the ways in which their work is undervalued, and the needs that arise as a result. This has led to DUEL's involvement processing and analyzing qualitative data collected by PPFSW's network. With the vision and expertise of Esteban Gómez, a DU professor who specializes in digital and visual anthropology, DUEL is now designing a project for organizing farmworkers' personal narratives and a virtual exhibit that will be part of PPFSW's website. Students taking Gómez's visual anthropology class designed a prototype for the exhibit, and research assistants are working on implementing the design. Students taking an ethnographic methods class are processing and analyzing narrative information to help create an online community archive. Two students have written their anthropology capstone theses as ethnographically-informed reports for PPFSW, one of which is published on the organization's website (Hyde & Neiss, 2021).

Through connecting individuals of unique skills, experience, and needs, DUEL is able to catalyze mutually beneficial collaborative relationships that otherwise may not have come into being or may have done so less smoothly. At the present moment, despite the challenges of COVID-19, DUEL continues to look towards the future and its potentialities as it learns from its experience thus far, as discussed in an article co-authored by a community partner, students, and faculty involved in DUEL's work (McCormack et al., 2021).

THE BENEFITS OF INTERDISCIPLINARY METHODS IN WATER SECURITY RESEARCH

As a case in point of DUEL's capacity to stimulate productive collaboration, Dinko's involvement in the lab and interaction with Cerón influenced his approach to his dissertation work under the direction of Hanson Frimpong. In this section, Dinko discusses the utility of interdisciplinary methods in researching the spatial intersections of water insecurity and identity politics. In so doing, this section primarily focuses on methodology, not the findings of the overall dissertation, but rather the implications of certain findings for WAC.

Dinko's dissertation study aims at understanding the dynamics and lived experience of climate-induced water insecurity at the local level in Ghana's Sudan Savannah. The Sudan Savannah is the driest climate in Ghana with a distinctly short rainfall season followed by a prolonged period of drought (Dinko, Yaro & Kusimi, 2019; Wossen & Berger, 2015). With livelihoods almost entirely dependent on agriculture and the natural environment, Ghanaians need access to irrigation water in order to survive the nine-month dry season. Indeed, the centrality of water to livelihood outcomes shaped postcolonial government policy. For instance, Ministry of Finance and Economic Planning (2017) notes that between 1960 and 2015, over 240 small gravity-driven dams had been constructed by the Ghanaian state to address agricultural water insecurity and enhance the incomes of smallholder farmers.

While dams are often financed and constructed by the state, the land is controlled by customary law. That is, while dam water is effectively a state property and comes directly under statutory laws with universal usufruct access rights, irrigated lands are owned and controlled by customary norms and practices. Effectively, those who desire to access water through the land must navigate a complex system of statutory and customary laws that co-govern land and water resources allocation (Kansanga, Arku & Luginaah, 2019; Yaro, 2010). Hence, the process and struggle for gaining and maintaining access to irrigated water is spatially nested in differentiated power alignments, customary-statutory practices, and politically entangled in shifting alliances. Yet, water resources are often treated as a biophysical element devoid of historical, emotional, and political contest.

Given these inherent complexities, this dissertation project sought to investigate the spatial pattern of water access and how ingrained power structures and practices shape access rights outcomes for different social groups. Specifically, the project sought to answer the following key questions: (1) How do sociodemographic characteristics of people define the spatial organization of access to irrigation water in space and time? (2) What strategies do different social groups adopt in negotiating access to water? (3) Why do some people succeed and others fail to gain access?

To answer these questions requires combining methodological, analytical, and writing strategies that span across different disciplinary barriers. Specifically, Dinko combines participatory drone mapping, drone-based photo-elicitation interviews, ethnography, and geospatial analysis to research water rights in semiarid Ghana. Collectively, these interdisciplinary methods are called "geo-ethnographic." An interdisciplinary approach provides a breadth of opportunities to examine in detail the flux, entanglements, and messiness of struggles and politics over critical water resources and how different social groups (men, women, migrants) negotiate, contest, and renegotiate water access in semi-arid Ghana. Through these methods, Dinko draws connections between climate change, water resource contestation, and water access outcomes given the vagueness inherent in the pluralistic governance system in context. By analyzing space-making through drone images of irrigated fields, this project explored the intersections of social identities and space-making and how these are politically and spatially entangled in historical structures of inequality. In adopting an interdisciplinary approach embedded in a political ecology theoretical framework, the goal is to write a dissertation that gives both the researcher and the researched an active voice by giving them more authority to challenge the status quo, and thus addressing concerns about power, control, and social justice for the public good.

Using combined ethnographic methods with novel drone participatory mapping empowered irrigators to be co-creators of space-making and its interpretation. Drone images of irrigation fields opened up a new opportunity for farmers to visualize how irrigation water insecurity and social identities permeate water outcomes. For the first time, farmers could draw a direct link between closeness to irrigation canals and access to water through observing the greenness of vegetation. Through drone-based photo-elicitation interviews, farmers reflected on the identities of irrigators and their proximity to dams and canals. By reflecting on the intersections of identity and location of their irrigation lands, farmers were leading the discussion on how water laws and ideational systems converge to shape differentiated water outcomes. The exclusive use of ethnography alone may not have elicited such discussions. Similarly, using drone images alone for spatial analysis would have likely missed the intersection of identity politics and water access on the ground.

Relatedly, combining ethnography with participatory drone mapping stirred up discussions about distributional water justice and inclusive water governance. Seeing spaces of water insecurity on the drone images jolted the minds of farmers to how salient identities disadvantage some while privileging others (Figure 2.1).

Figure 2.1. Results of community validation of drone map. The pins closest to the dam are primarily men with ties to either Chief Tindana, or their ancestors were part of the formation of the community. Pins in the middle: primarily women. Pins at the tail end: "Outsiders"; migrants but also people in the community with weak links to powerful people.

This image resulted in a more open discussion about how these taken-for-granted identities are reflected in the quality of life. For instance, during ethnographic interviews with chiefs and water association executives, gender did not seem to matter in water access. However, the participatory drone mapping indicated otherwise. Community-validated drone maps indicated women tended to have land farthest away from the dams and were less likely to get water in time to be home for household and familial duties. With drone maps revealing the gender dynamic in water access, chiefs and the male-dominated water users association executives were compelled to discuss water insecurity more honestly. Thus, there is a huge emancipatory potential in combining ethnography with spatial science analytical methods (for example, drone mapping).

Involvement with DUEL influenced Dinko's use of interdisciplinary methods in his research while also helping create opportunities to share his research and writing with a broader network of audiences (from scholars in the field to undergraduates). The engagement with audiences from different disciplinary traditions helped refine and expand the initial methods and theorization toolbox for his project. Reciprocally, people at different levels in their own ethnographic work were able to inform their own approaches through Dinko's work, including the first-year composition students who attended his presentation in the spring 2020 Conversations in the Disciplines event (discussed in the following section). In facilitating interdisciplinary interactions like these among people working on ethnography, DUEL aligns with WAC's goal to open the possibility for new collaborative spaces.

THE ROLE OF ETHNOGRAPHY IN FIRST-YEAR RESEARCH WRITING COURSES

Since joining the DU Ethnography Lab in 2019, Kinyon has worked with DUEL members, including Cerón and Dinko, to support the work of students in the first-year writing sequence. Since the founding of the University Writing Program in 2006, ethnography has played an important role in the pedagogy of many faculty members, especially in the context of first-year research writing courses, which introduce students to qualitative, text based/interpretive, and quantitative research. From the early years of the program, many instructors gravitated towards ethnography as an engaging and productive method for teaching qualitative research and writing. This comes as no surprise, since the founding of the program came at a time when ethnography was gaining increasing attention in writing studies both as a form of research and as a pedagogical tool.

Kinyon has incorporated ethnography and autoethnography into her own classes since 2007. Initially working from Bonnie Sunstein and Elizabeth Chiseri-Strater's *Fieldworking*, she has taught her students methods for taking fieldnotes, conducting interviews, writing literature reviews relevant for ethnographies, and presenting research to different popular and scholarly audiences. Her teaching has been informed by approaches to ethnography discussed by Kahn (2011) and, more recently, by Chattaraj's (2020) ideas about connections between ethnography and writing transfer. Through collaborations with DUEL, Kinyon has been able to support student work through a range of resources and events, as discussed below.

In a Conversations in the Disciplines (CID) event during spring 2020, three DUEL members—Dinko, Kelly Fayard, and Alison Krögel—presented their ethnographic research and writing to an audience of first-year students. Representing ethnographic practice in geography, anthropology, and language departments respectively, they discussed the challenges of working with fieldnotes, interviews, quantitative data, and/or close readings to present their research to different disciplinary audiences. Students learned that there is not a single formula for ethnographic writing and that the forms that this writing takes differ in significant ways from one field to another. Students also became aware that issues of social justice, public good, and cultural understanding are important topics for ethnographic projects. Due to the COVID-19 pandemic, the event took place on Zoom and was recorded and archived on DUEL's website for future classroom use, becoming a valuable resource for future writing courses.

In addition, Kinyon used an internal grant to work with DUEL members on creating a set of ethnographic resources (archived on the DUEL Instructional Videos website) for students and faculty. This involved compiling bibliographies about ethnography and autoethnography as well as the creation of instructional and experiential videos for classroom or faculty use. For example, in "Doing Ethnography in Pandemic Times," Kinyon interviews three professors about ways that their ethnographic research was altered in 2020–21. In another video, students are introduced to ethnographic positionality, including outsider, participant observer, and autoethnographic perspectives. Other videos by professors and students participating in DUEL include an explanation of IRB protocols as well as personal accounts of ethnographic work: the study of animal healthcare practices in Guatemala, tattoo parlors, music festivals, and food and meaning. DUEL is in the process of further expanding resources such as these for faculty and students.

Especially in recent years, Kinyon's students have gravitated towards projects that reflect DU's commitment to diversity and that align with WAC's focus on community-engaged research and writing. Through ethnographic or autoethnographic methods, her students have examined topics such as the first-generation student experience, hybrid racial identities, and a range of physical and mental health issues. As DU has increasingly provided opportunities for students of diverse backgrounds—recruiting, for example, first-generation students and/or students of Latinx, Native American, African American, and other underrepresented racial backgrounds—many of her students have explored issues of social justice in their ethnographies. This emphasis aligns with larger shifts within WAC towards an activist stance aimed at the potential for change. Students leave her first-year research classes both with a solid knowledge of the writing skills that ethnographic work can provide and with an impetus to further explore how their own identities intersect with those of others. The collaboration between DUEL and the writing program has been instrumental in teaching undergraduates to effectively use ethnographic methodologies and to complete meaningful writing projects that foster social awareness. Given its success in supporting the work of faculty and students, especially as this relates to issues of community engagement, DUEL can potentially serve as a model for the establishment of WAC ethnography labs at other campuses.

CONCLUSION

Ethnographic methodologies are important for WAC, especially since WAC's goals to foster community engagement and to serve social justice parallel current directions in applied anthropology. Serving as a catalyst for change, DUEL provides support to a range of faculty members and students who are conducting ethnographic work for the public good. In multiple forms, ethnography can provide the studied subjects with access to needed resources. Cerón's study of epidemiology in Guatemala aims to provide access to medicine and healthcare; Dinko's dissertation work in Ghana aims to give people better access to clean water; and Kinyon's students' socially-engaged projects emphasize the importance of providing access to education and a better life for immigrants and first-generation students. While DUEL is centered at the University of Denver, the work of its members is having a broad impact. DUEL's experience may serve as an inspiration for other similar communities of practice, especially given the way that its approach offers multiple points of contact for individuals at different stages of their careers to get involved in ethnographic research that benefits the subjects of study.

REFERENCES

Bazerman, C., Little, J., Bethel, L., Chavkin, T., Fouquette, D. & Garufis, J. (2005). *Reference guide to writing across the curriculum*. Parlor Press; The WAC Clearinghouse. https://wac.colostate.edu/books/referenceguides/bazerman-wac/.

Boyer, E. L., Moser, D., Ream, T. C. & Braxton, J. M. (2016). *Scholarship reconsidered: Priorities of the professoriate* (2nd ed.). John Wiley & Sons.

Copeland, T. J. & Dengah, H. J. F. (2016). 'Involve me and I learn': Teaching and applying anthropology. *Annals of Anthropological Practice, 40*(2), 120–133. https://doi.org/10.1111/napa.12096.

Chattaraj, D. (2020). Anthropology and writing pedagogy: Why anthropologists should teach writing seminars. *Teaching Anthropology, 9*(10), 35–43. https://www.teachinganthropology.org/ojs/index.php/teach_anth/article/view/475/590.

Delpit, L. D. (1993). *Freedom's plow*. Routledge.

Dinko, D. H., Yaro, J. & Kusimi, J. (2019). Political ecology and contours of vulnerability to water insecurity in semiarid North-eastern Ghana. *Journal of Asian and African Studies, 54*(2), 82–299. https://doi.org/10.1177/0021909618811838.

DUEL instructional videos - University of Denver. MediaSpace. (n.d.). Retrieved March 18, 2023, from https://mediaspace.du.edu/playlist/details/1_qyfa1wc1.

Hyde, G. & Neiss, K. (2021). *Hearts of service, people like us*. Denver, CO. Project Connect Food Systems Workers. https://www.projectprotectfoodsystems.org/post/hearts-of-service---people-like-us.

Kahn, S. (2011). Putting ethnographic writing in context. *Writing Spaces: Readings on Writing, 2*, 175–195. https://wac.colostate.edu/books/writingspaces2/kahn--putting-ethnographic-writing.pdf.

Kansanga, M. M., Arku, G. & Luginaah, I. (2019). Powers of exclusion and counter-exclusion: The political ecology of ethno-territorial customary land boundary conflicts in Ghana. *Land Use Policy, 86*(April), 12–22. https://doi.org/10.1016/j.landusepol.2019.04.031.

Kirklighter, C. (Ed.). (1997). *Voices and visions: Refiguring ethnography in composition.* Boynton/Cook.

LaFrance, M. (2019). *Institutional ethnography: A theory of practice for writing studies researchers.* Utah State University Press.

McCormack P., Neiss, K., Johns, Z., Kinyon, K. & Cerón, A. (2021). Building community through ethnography in action to catalyze student, faculty, and community collaborations. *Annals of Anthropological Practice, 45*(2), 193–206.

Ministry of Finance and Economic Planning. (2017). *The budget statement and economic policy of the Government of Ghana for the 2017 Financial Year.* https://mofep.gov.gh/sites/default/files/budget-statements/2017-Budget-Statement.pdf.

Moss, B. J. (1992). Ethnography in a composition course: From the perspective of a teacher-researcher. In R. Connors & C. Glenn (Eds.), *The St. Martin's guide to teaching writing.* (2nd ed., pp. 471–482). St. Martin's Press.

North, S. M. (1987). *The making of knowledge in composition: Portrait of an emerging field.* Boynton/Cook.

Palmquist, M., Childers, P., Maimon, E., Mullin, J., Rice, R., Russell, A. & Russell, D. R. (2020). Fifty years of WAC: Where have we been? Where are we going? *Across the Disciplines, 17*(3/4) 5–45. https://doi.org/10.37514/ATD-J.2020.17.3.01.

Project Protect Food System Workers. (2021). *Our group: Protect food systems workers.* https://www.projectprotectfoodsystems.org/our-group.

Schensul, J. J. & LeCompte, M. D. (2016). *Ethnography in action: A mixed methods approach.* AltaMira Press.

Sunstein, B. S. & Chiseri-Strater, E. (2011). *Fieldworking: Reading and writing research* (4th ed.). Bedford/St. Martin's.

Wossen, T. & Berger, T. (2015). Climate variability, food security and poverty: Agent-based assessment of policy options for farm households in Northern Ghana. *Environmental Science and Policy, 47*, 95–107. https://doi.org/10.1016/j.envsci.2014.11.009.

Yancey, K. B., Robertson, L. & Taczak, K. (2014). *Writing across contexts: Transfer, composition, and sites of writing.* Utah State University Press.

Yaro, J. A. (2010). Customary tenure systems under siege: Contemporary access to land in Northern Ghana. *GeoJournal, 75*(2), 199–214. https://doi.org/10.1007/s10708-009-9301-x.

CHAPTER 3.

ASSESSING FACULTY MEMBERS' THRESHOLD CONCEPTS FOR THE TEACHING OF WRITING: THE CHALLENGES OF SURVEY VALIDITY AND THE PROMISE OF NARRATIVE METHODS

Christopher Basgier and Leslie Cordie
Auburn University

FACULTY WRITING CONCEPTIONS

Writing across the curriculum (WAC) programs support writing and writing instruction in a broad range of communicative contexts in higher education with faculty from a variety of disciplines forming the core constituency participating in WAC efforts. Therefore, it is no surprise that WAC research often examines faculty perceptions on writing and how faculty teach writing in the disciplines. These studies have taken many forms, including investigations of faculty's differing expectations for school-based and professional assignments (Herrington, 1985), their expectations for good writing (Walvoord & McCarthy, 1990), their ideas about the qualities of academic writing (Thaiss & Zawacki, 2006), the kinds of assignments they require students to complete (Melzer, 2014), and aspects of those assignments they believe impact students' learning (Eodice et al., 2016).

Recently, WAC scholars have also begun examining faculty's conceptions of writing pedagogy (e.g., Flash, 2016; Moon et al., 2018). WAC pedagogies are often counterintuitive for faculty in the disciplines, yet they can be transformative when understood and applied in a systematic, integrated fashion. For example, the notion that writing instruction ought to be a shared enterprise across disciplines might seem unreasonable to faculty who believe students should learn everything they need to know about writing in first-year composition (or in high school). However, when they come to see that even expert writers can improve with practice and feedback, they might be more apt to change the ways they think about, and thus teach, writing in the disciplines. One innovative

DOI: https://doi.org/10.37514/PER-B.2023.1947.2.03

way of researching the counterintuitive and transformational potential of WAC pedagogy is through *threshold concepts* (Meyer & Land, 2005; Timmermans & Meyer, 2017), which are complex ideas that enable learners to enter and work within communities of practice to develop interdisciplinary skills in higher education (Brew, 2012).

THRESHOLD CONCEPTS FRAMEWORK

Threshold concepts hold particular promise as a framework for investigating conceptual dimensions of writing pedagogy across disciplinary contexts. The framework holds that certain difficult concepts—often referred to as "troublesome knowledge" (Adler-Kassner et al., 2012, Meyer et al., 2008)—can act as irreversible gateways to an academic discipline's ways of knowing, doing, and communicating (Baillie et al., 2013). Much of the recent work in writing studies related to the framework focuses on how threshold concepts may help students transfer knowledge about writing to new, unfamiliar communicative contexts across the curriculum (e.g., Adler-Kassner, et al., 2016; Melzer, 2014). However, students are not the only ones who wrestle with threshold concepts.

According to Chris Anson (2015), faculty also encounter threshold concepts germane to WAC, which encourages them "to think in principled ways about incorporating writing in their courses, regardless of discipline" (p. 213). Indeed, faculty frequently turn to WAC programs after they assign writing in their courses, and the results do not go as planned, particularly when assignments do more to confuse students than improve their learning (Melzer, 2014; Walvoord & McCarthy, 1990). Through formal and informal WAC channels, including consultations, workshops, learning communities, and lunch discussions, faculty encounter principled thinking about topics such as effective assignment design, writing-to-learn, scaffolding assignments in a course, and integrating writing across a department or program curriculum. Because of the diversity of backgrounds in those seeking assistance in teaching disciplinary writing, WAC professionals who deliver such programs often find themselves wondering how to best gauge faculty participants' threshold crossings (Basgier & Simpson, 2019; Basgier & Simpson, 2020).

In previous studies, Christopher Basgier and Amber Simpson (2019; 2020) showed how faculty narratives could reveal different stages of understanding about threshold concepts for the teaching of writing in the disciplines. Basgier and Simpson (2019) created a "travel" metaphor as a heuristic for analyzing faculty members' narratives, including *roadblocks* (when they could not see a way through a teaching difficulty), *detours* (when they tried an isolated change with limited success), and *journeys* (when they told detailed stories of multifaceted solutions that manifested conceptual changes). Using this heuristic, the researchers (2020) then identified three threshold concepts for the teaching of writing in the disciplines: (a) effective writing pedagogy involves iterative, multifaceted changes; (b) students' development as writers can be supported through scaffolded interventions; and (c) genres can be taught as actions, not (just) as forms. Given these findings, Basgier wondered whether the threshold concepts suggested by WAC research could be converted into a survey instrument that would assess any changes in faculty thinking after they participated in WAC programs. Thus, the two of us, Basgier and Cordie, began a collaborative effort to develop such an inventory and research its efficacy.

Overview of Study

In this chapter, we report on our efforts to develop a quantitative inventory of approaches to teaching with writing that measured six threshold concepts: 1) writing-to-learn, 2) writing in the disciplines, 3) writing as rhetorical, 4) writing as developmental, 5) writing as a process, and 6) writing as a general skill. We begin by describing our process for creating the survey based on research in WAC and on qualitative interviews with faculty members about their pedagogical techniques and commitments. We then explain the need for survey validation and describe our use of an index of item-objective congruence (IIOC) for validation. Based on the results, we show how the survey items we developed were not strongly associated with any single concept, which suggests that in practice, the six concepts proposed are especially interconnected and difficult to isolate. We conclude by reflecting on the implications of our study for the identification and assessment of threshold concepts research more broadly. Finally, we suggest that narrative methods show future promise for WAC's work in threshold concepts.

RESEARCH METHODOLOGY

We designed the Inventory of Approaches to Teaching Writing (IATW) to measure disciplinary faculty's underlying conceptions for the teaching of writing in the disciplines in terms of our WAC program's broad definition of writing, which includes any forms of composed communication, such as text, image, and sound. We began by defining six concepts for teaching writing in the disciplines derived from the scholarly literature in WAC (e.g., Anson, 2015; Bazerman, 1988; Berkenkotter & Huckin, 1995; Carroll, 2002; Emig, 1977; Herrington, 1981; McCarthy, 1987; Russell, 2002; Russell & Yañez, 2003; Thaiss & Zawacki, 2006) as well as Basgier and Simpson's (2019, 2020) previous research on threshold concepts. The first concept—writing as a general skill—is not a threshold concept, but one many WAC specialists might consider "pre-threshold" with its focus on "writing [as] an autonomous skill, generalizable to all activity systems" (Russell, 1995, p. 57). The other five concepts are ones we believed faculty were most likely to encounter in our local WAC program or that were implied in Basgier and Simpson's (2019, 2020) research. Like Anson (2015), we recognized that other threshold concepts for WAC likely exist, yet felt the foundation for the survey was ready for testing with the six main concepts discussed next.

Concepts Measurement

The six concepts we used for the IATW included the following terms and definitions:

Writing as a General Skill (WGS). Teaching writing from a general skill perspective emphasizes rules and common expectations for writing. Faculty who hold this perspective typically focus on grammar and other surface issues when they comment on student writing— although some faculty may not feel any obligation to comment on student writing at all. Often, they believe that students ought to have learned how to write before enrolling in a specific course. They may be more interested in the content of the writing (and whether such content is correct) than in the effectiveness of the writing (e.g., for different audiences or purposes). Others may feel that students are inherently good or bad writers, which means writing instruction is not their responsibility. Broadly, this perspective treats writing as a foundational skill that transfers easily to new situations.

Writing Development (WDEV). Teaching writing from a developmental perspective involves supporting students' growth as writers. Faculty with a commitment to WDEV generally wish to help students improve as writers by teaching them the features of effective writing or the expectations for writing in a particular course. Often, faculty see themselves preparing students to write effectively in future communicative situations and may wish to help students develop identities as writers.

Writing in the Disciplines (WID). Teaching writing from a disciplinary perspective involves preparing students to write in an academic discipline, profession, or field. Faculty with a commitment to WID often ask students to use writing as a means of practicing the ways of thinking that characterize a discipline, profession, or field. To that end, they may use writing to help students answer questions, explore hypotheses, analyze data or texts, or intervene in debates with disciplinary relevance. Others with a commitment to writing in the discipline may emphasize the correct and appropriate use of technical vocabulary ("jargon"), as well as the genres or forms common in a particular field. Finally, some faculty members may use writing to help students connect their personal lives to the work of a discipline, profession, or field.

Writing-to-Learn (WTL). Teaching writing from a writing-to-learn perspective involves using writing to help students understand, and engage with, the content of a course. Faculty with a commitment to WTL may assign low-stakes writing tasks that help students engage with readings, practice applying course concepts in hypothetical situations, or wrestle with complexity. Some may be especially committed to the potential for writing to promote students' thinking.

Writing as a Process (WAP). Teaching writing as a process involves helping students manage the range of activities involved in the writing process, particularly for complex projects. Faculty with a commitment to WAP may help students learn to work with sources and/or data iteratively. They might also scaffold assignments into manageable tasks with increasing complexity. Often, these faculty build in opportunities for peer and instructor feedback, and they may guide students to use that feedback to revise effectively.

Writing as Rhetorical (WAR). Teaching writing from a rhetorical perspective involves explicit attention to audience, purpose, genre, and context. Often, faculty who teach WAR develop assignments with realistic rhetorical contexts in mind, and may even engage students in authentic writing situations for real-world audiences. Others who are committed to WAR pedagogy may ask students to analyze rhetorical situations and develop plans for creating effective pieces of communication for those situations.

Survey Development

After defining and revising these concepts for teaching writing in the disciplines, we created survey items that would potentially measure faculty members' relative commitment to each one. To do so, we adapted a framework from Daniel D. Pratt (1998), who designed the Teaching Perspectives Inventory (TPI). TPI items measured five broad concepts for teaching in general, and were grouped according to actions, intentions, and beliefs. According to Pratt (1998), actions are "the routines and techniques we use to engage people in content" (p. 17); intentions are "an expression of what a person is trying to accomplish and, usually, an indication of role and responsibility in pursuit of that" (p. 18); and beliefs "represent underlying values" that drive actions and intentions (p. 21). Using this framework, we created items representing actions, beliefs, and intentions that were associated with each of the six concepts defined above. Like the TPI, we created survey items by adapting specific statements about classes and assignments discussed in earlier research (Basgier & Simpson, 2019; Basgier & Simpson, 2020) into more general statements that we believed applied across contexts and disciplines.

The aim of the IATW was to score faculty members' responses using a five-point Likert scale on each item, with the survey designed to provide a numerical representation of faculty members' relative commitment to each conception for the teaching of writing in the disciplines. We planned to include sub-scores for actions, intentions, and beliefs, which could be particularly useful if any one of those elements was misaligned with the others. For example, we anticipated some faculty members expressing a belief that students should learn to communicate with multiple audiences for multiple purposes (a feature of writing as rhetorical), but spend more time correcting surface features of students' writing (a feature of writing as a general skill). Ideally, if such discrepancies were assessed through the survey before a WAC faculty development experience, faculty members' conceptions would be better aligned afterward through discussion or a learning activity. Additionally, if faculty expressed no commitment to, say, writing-to-learn beforehand, they might intend to do so afterward, particularly after an interval (a semester or a year) post workshop.

SURVEY VALIDITY

J. David Creswell and John W. Creswell (2017) noted that validating a new research instrument, even one derived from the literature and synthesis of other instruments, raises concerns about the instrument's utility. Arlene Fink (2003) defined validity as whether the instrument actually measures the proposed constructs. In the area of assessment research, there are several types of measurement validity recognized, with the most relevant including *face, content, criterion-related,* and *construct* validity approaches. Creswell and Creswell (2017) further noted that *content* validity is the most commonly addressed validation approach in the research literature and refers to actual content measurement in the instrument. Thus, we selected *content* validity for confirmation of the six threshold concepts and development of the IATW to establish the survey measurement.

Content Validity

Jake London et al. (2017) have noted that content validity is essential for developing accurate and consistent psychometric measures to progress theory. The concept of content validity, though, is complex and as noted by Stephen Sireci (1998) involves evaluating content representation in a survey instrument. A critical component of survey development is providing evidence that the actual items created do effectively measure the content or construct that they are defined to measure—in our case, the six concepts for the teaching of writing defined above.

Index of Item Congruence

After developing the IATW, we used the Index of Item-Objective Congruence (IIOC) to establish content validity. Ronna Turner and Laurie Carlson (2003) have emphasized that IIOC uses a panel of experts (a group of people who are familiar with the subject the instrument purports to measure) that judge the adequacy of the information and appropriateness of the items in measuring one or more constructs. Richard Rovinelli and Ronald Hambleton (1976) first developed the IIOC's procedures and test statistics for assessing the degree to which an item measures the objective or construct that it intends to measure. Turner and Carlson (2003) further developed the index to measure multi-dimensional items, including types of interaction in distance learning courses (Keeler, 2006; Lambie et al., 2017; Murphy et al., 2013). We decided to use the IIOC to validate the IATW and the threshold concepts, hoping to ensure recognition by other WAC scholars, along with transferability to WAC contexts beyond our own teaching and learning environments.

DATA COLLECTION AND ANALYSIS

After IRB approval, we emailed the IIOC survey on threshold concepts with a link to the Qualtrics® survey to 43 individuals from a range of institution types across the United States. We had identified these individuals as content experts in writing studies with backgrounds in WAC/WID administration and research. The survey included demographic data collection, such as institution and number of years working in WAC, a list of definitions for the six concepts included above, and instructions on how to complete the IIOC for this study. As recommended by Turner and Carlson (2003), experts were not told what constructs the individual items were intended to measure, so they could remain independent evaluators. Each expert was asked to evaluate each item by giving the rating of 1 (for clearly measuring the content), -1 (clearly not measuring), or 0 (measure of the content area is not clear). For each item, the goal was a 70 percent agreement rate for the target construct. As there is no statistical test for assessing significance of the measure using IIOC, Rovinelli and Hambleton (1976) recommended a procedure for setting the criterion levels. Following Turner and Carlson's (2003) recommendation, a level of 0.70 for the index was chosen as the minimum requirement because it indicates that a majority of experts agreed that the item clearly measured the content.

Eighteen (18) experts responded to the IIOC survey, or nearly a 42 percent response rate, an acceptable rate for online surveys (Fulton, 2018). The demographic data on the experts represented a diverse range of faculty ranks: two assistant professors, four associate professors, six professors, two clinical professors, one visiting professor, and three "others" responded. The respondents had worked in WAC/WID on average 19 years, with a minimum of five years and a maximum of 41 years. The broad range of ranks and years of experience implied a quality sample for the survey testing, as suggested by Fink (2003).

After reading the definitions of the six concepts, 15 respondents agreed or strongly agreed that they could distinguish among the definitions of the threshold concepts. One (1) respondent neither agreed nor disagreed, and two (2) disagreed. These differences of opinion did not appear to differ according to rank or years of experience in the field. Our analysis of respondents' evaluations indicated that only one of the 36 items met the minimum level of acceptance (0.70). Most items were below the significance level, had more than one item above the significance level, or had negative values. We then conducted a second analysis using Turner and Carlson's (2003) IIOC multi-dimensional method on the ten survey items that had more than one average value above 0.70 for multiple constructs, including WDEV, WTL, WAR, and WAP. The analysis produced similar results, with only one WGS item attaining above a 0.70 value.

DISCUSSION

Although it is possible that the survey items could be again revised and rewritten to measure each concept more independently, we believe the results of both validation attempts pointed to a generalizable result: We may be able to develop reasonably distinct definitions of different threshold concepts for the teaching of writing in the disciplines, but faculty's actual actions, intentions, and beliefs are markedly interconnected and aligned on the concepts. Overall, the experts were unable to isolate separate threshold constructs using the IIOC.

Narrative Comments

Participants' qualitative comments from the survey extended our interpretation of these data. First, several respondents noted the interconnected nature of these constructs. As one of the WAC experts wrote at the end of the IIOC:

> These 6 conceptions / labels for writing instruction are not discrete / separate, at least for me and for the faculty I work with, teachers I prepare, etc. WID is rhetorical and includes attention to process and has elements of WTL; and in all writing instruction, I see / want to see attention to the development of writer.

Similarly, another WAC expert wrote:

> These categories seem to me to be aspects that are present in nearly any writing classroom. I have difficulty separating them in many cases. A good writing teacher would make use of toolkits from any of these categories. I guess one might find some instructors who tend more in one direction. But the longer one teaches the more one draws from all of these approaches.

SCOPE OF THRESHOLD CONCEPTS

Expert respondents also suggested that these six constructs might not be fully representative of the full range of conceptions for the teaching of writing in the disciplines. When asked whether they could think of other concepts, for example, individual WAC experts noted "writing for critical consciousness" and "'civic' writing" as other possibilities. Several responses pointed to the link between writing and what might be viewed as personal growth or well-being. For instance, one respondent mentioned "writing as an aid in maintaining and improving psychological health" as a potential concept. Taken together, these suggestions indicate that WAC experts who took the IIOC did not believe the survey items represented the full range of beliefs, intentions, and actions that might characterize faculty members' conceptions for teaching writing in the disciplines. If these conceptions and related items were added to the IATW, they may still be difficult to distinguish from other conceptions. For example, civic writing would require significant attention to rhetoric and writing pedagogies that involve psychological well-being, or the development of identity could intersect with a developmental understanding of writing acquisition in the discipline.

CONCLUSION AND IMPLICATIONS

As WAC continues to evolve, the field will need to develop innovative methods for researching and assessing the efforts of our faculty development endeavors. Our study illustrates the challenges and opportunities that arise when innovating methodologies, especially those that translate across qualitative and quantitative inquiries. Based on the results from this research, the main implications from our analyses were 1) the lack of statistical indications or qualitative suggestions, and 2) that the survey items were not associated with a single threshold concept. Because the six conceptions we used in the IATW appear to have overlapping beliefs, intentions, and actions, they cannot be easily separated using this kind of quantitative instrument. Additionally, even if we were to build a more comprehensive inventory with additional conceptions, such as multimodal writing or writing for introspection, the same lack of distinction between items would likely persist. Linda Adler-Kassner and Elizabeth Wardle (2019) maintain that threshold concepts "are contingent, contextual, and threshold-for-now," so they cannot be used as a "checklist" or "reduce[d] . . . to easily accessible, ready-to-digest ideas" (p. 9). The results of our validation study provide empirical backing for their claim.

The results also suggest a potential refinement of the theory undergirding the threshold concepts framework as an explanation for transformative learning experiences in communities of practice (Cordie & Adelino, 2020). One of the many suggested features of threshold concepts is their "integrative" nature. According to Ray Land et al. (2016):

> [Threshold] concepts seem to have an integrating function in the sense of bringing what formerly appeared to be disparate elements into a coherent relationship, much as the addition of a particular jigsaw piece may bring other pieces together to provide a new and meaningful perspective. (p. xii)

Unlike a puzzle, however, a given element of writing pedagogy can figure differently from different threshold perspectives. For example, our results indicate that scaffolded writing experiences could fit into multiple perspectives on the teaching of writing in the disciplines. Similarly, interdisciplinary scholarship often makes use of diverse theories that might constitute threshold concepts in particular disciplines. Both of these scenarios suggest that certain pieces (usually called "elements" or "phenomena" in the threshold concepts framework) can fit multiple puzzles (disciplinary or interdisciplinary fields).

Finally, our results have methodological implications. Although there is no methodological consensus about the best ways of identifying and studying threshold concepts, qualitative methods appear to be the most constructive going forward. Sarah Barradell (2013) identified "semi-structured interviews, analysis of exam responses, and observations of classroom behavior" as common methods in threshold concepts research (p. 25), and Kathleen Quinlan et al. (2013) added "surveys, laboratory observations, grade distributions, and course feedback" to the list (p. 586). Although quantitative methods certainly figure in these lists, Barradell (2013) concluded "that conversation amongst teaching and learning stakeholders" characteristic of "transactional curriculum inquiry" are necessary for the identification of threshold concepts (p. 275). Quinlan et al. (2013) argued in favor of "tailored methodologies" used to research each of the different characteristics of threshold concepts. We suggest a similar approach for tracking changes in faculty thinking after faculty development experiences.

Narratives (Basgier & Simpson, 2019) and reflective practice (Flash, 2016) hold particular promise as tools for engaging faculty in the kinds of thinking about their knowledge that can engender changed conceptions. Storytelling and reflection give faculty members the opportunity to retain ownership of the ways they think about and talk about the teaching of writing in the disciplines. Narratives can also be leveraged as assessment mechanisms. When focused on learning and implementation of specific pedagogies germane to WAC, narrative and reflection can help WAC administrators gauge the extent of faculty members' changed thinking (Basgier & Simpson, 2020).

Moreover, narrative methods also complement the theory of threshold concepts. Land et al. (2016) expound on the idea that thresholds, including learning thresholds, are something one passes through. Although the metaphor of the threshold is a spatial one, the passing through also has a temporal dimension that can be plotted. The process of learning is messy and rarely linear, but we humans have a way of using narrative to make sense of what would otherwise be a messy stream of unbroken sensory experiences and mental phenomena. Through narrative methods, we can see how faculty encounter difficult WAC concepts, wrestle with them, test them, and (ideally) eventually internalize them as principled ways of thinking about disciplinary writing pedagogy. Still, as Creswell and Creswell (2017) point out, narrative methods can be labor-intensive and problematic for annual assessment reports due to their perceived lack of quantifiable data. Yet, there may be ways of capturing faculty learning through a quantitative instrument, for instance by Likert-type questions asking about the extent to which someone has changed a particular teaching practice in ways that align with different threshold concepts. As WAC continues working with threshold concepts as a framework for research and assessment into faculty learning, the field will need to identify innovative methodological tools that capture the integrative complexity of the conceptual terrain that characterizes teaching writing in the disciplines.

REFERENCES

Adler-Kassner, L. & Wardle, E. (Eds.). (2019). *(Re)Considering what we know: Learning thresholds in writing, composition, rhetoric, and literacy.* Utah State University Press.

Adler-Kassner, L., Clark, I., Robertson, L., Taczak, K. & Yancey, K. B. (2016). Assembling knowledge: The role of threshold concepts in facilitating transfer. In C. Anson and J. L. Moore (Eds.), *Critical transitions: Writing and the question of transfer* (pp. 17–47). The WAC Clearinghouse; University Press of Colorado. https://doi.org/10.37514/PER-B.2016.0797.

Adler-Kassner, L., Majewski, J. & Koshnick, D. (2012). The value of troublesome knowledge: Transfer and threshold concepts in writing and history. *Composition*

Forum, 26. http://compositionforum.com/issue/26/troublesome-knowledge-threshold.php.

Anson, C. M. (2015). Crossing thresholds: What's to know about writing across the curriculum. In L. Adler & E. Wardle (Eds.), *Naming what we know: Threshold concepts of writing studies* (pp. 203–219). Utah State University Press.

Baillie, C., Bowden, J. A. & Meyer, J. H. F. (2013). Threshold capabilities: Threshold concepts and knowledge capability linked through Variation Theory. *Higher Education, 65*(2), 227–46. https://doi.org/10.1007/s10734-012-9540-5.

Barradell, S. (2013). The identification of threshold concepts: A review of theoretical complexities and methodological challenges. *Higher Education, 65*, 265–276. https://doi.org/10.1007/s10734-012-9542-3.

Basgier, C. & Simpson, A. (2019). Trouble and transformation in higher education: Identifying threshold concepts through faculty narratives about teaching writing. *Studies in Higher Education, 45*(9), 1906–1918. https://doi.org/10.1080/03075079.2019.1598967.

Basgier, C. & Simpson, A. (2020). Reflecting on the past, reconstructing the future: Faculty members' threshold concepts for teaching writing in the disciplines. *Across the Disciplines, 17*(1/2), 6–25. https://doi.org/10.37514/ATD-J.2020.17.1-2.02.

Bazerman, C. (1988). *Shaping written knowledge: The genre and activity of the experimental article in science.* University of Wisconsin Press.

Berkenkotter, C. & Huckin, T. N. (1995). *Genre knowledge in disciplinary communication: Cognition/culture/power.* Lawrence Erlbaum Associates.

Brew, A. (2012). Teaching and research: New relationships and their implications for inquiry-based teaching and learning in higher education. *Higher Education Research & Development, 31*(1), 101–114. https://doi.org/10.1080/07294360.2012.642844.

Carroll, L. A. (2002). *Rehearsing new roles: How college students develop as writers.* Southern Illinois University Press.

Cordie, L. A. & Adelino, L. (2020). Authentic professional learning: Creating faculty development experiences through an assessment institute. *Journal of Transformative Learning, 7*(2), 19–33. https://jotl.uco.edu/index.php/jotl/article/view/283.

Creswell, J. W. & Creswell, J. D. (2017). *Research design: Qualitative, quantitative, and mixed methods approaches.* Sage.

Emig, J. (1977). Writing as a mode of learning. *College Composition and Communication, 28*(2), 122–128. https://doi.org/10.2307/356095.

Eodice, M., Geller, A. E. & Lerner, N. (2016). *The meaningful writing project: Learning, teaching, and writing in higher education.* Utah State University Press.

Fink, A. (2003). *The survey handbook* (2nd ed.). Sage.

Flash, P. (2016). From apprised to revised: Faculty in the disciplines change what they never knew they knew. In K. B. Yancey (Ed.), *A rhetoric of reflection* (pp. 227–249). Utah State University Press.

Fulton, B. R. (2018). Organizations and survey research: Implementing response enhancing strategies and conducting nonresponse analyses. *Sociological Methods & Research, 47*(2), 240–276. https://doi.org/10.1177/0049124115626169.

Herrington, A. J. (1981). Writing to learn: Writing across the disciplines. *College English, 43*(4), 379–387. https://doi.org/10.2307/377126.

Herrington, A. J. (1985). Writing in academic settings: A study of the contexts for writing in two college chemical engineering courses. *Research in the Teaching of English, 19*(4), 331–361. https://www.jstor.org/stable/40171066.

Keeler, L. C. (2006). *Student satisfaction and types of interaction in distance education courses* (Publication No. 305344216) [Doctoral dissertation, Colorado State University]. ProQuest Dissertations & Theses Global.

Lambie, G. W., Blount, A. J. & Mullen, P. R. (2017). Establishing content-oriented evidence for psychological assessments. *Measurement and Evaluation in Counseling and Development, 50*(4), 210–216. https://doi.org/10.1080/07481756.2017.1336930.

Land, R., Meyer, J. H. F. & Flanagan, M. T. (Eds.). (2016). *Threshold concepts in practice.* Sense Publishers.

London, J., Matthews, K. & Grover, V. (2017). On meaning and measurement: A review of content validity in IS. [Conference paper]. Twenty-third Americas Conference on Information Systems, Boston, MA, United States. Association for Information Systems. https://aisel.aisnet.org/amcis2017/AdvancesIS/Presentations/20/.

McCarthy, L. P. (1987). A stranger in strange lands: A college student writing across the curriculum. *Research in the Teaching of English, 21*(3), 233–265. https://library.ncte.org/journals/rte/issues/v21-3/15574.

Melzer, D. (2014). *Assignments across the curriculum: A national study of college writing.* Utah State University Press.

Meyer, J. H. F. & Land, R. (2005). Threshold concepts and troublesome knowledge (2): Epistemological considerations and a conceptual framework for teaching and learning. *Higher Education, 49*(3), 373–88. https://doi.org/10.1007/s10734-004-6779-5.

Meyer, J. H. F., Land, R. & Davies, P. (2008). Threshold concepts and troublesome knowledge: Issues of variation and variability. In R. Land, J. H. F. Meyer & J. Smith (Eds.), *Threshold concepts within the disciplines* (pp. 59–74). Sense Publishers.

Moon, A., Gere, A. R. & Shultz, G. V. (2018). Writing in the STEM classroom: Faculty conceptions of writing and its role in the undergraduate classroom. *Science Education, 102*(5), 1007–1028. https://doi.org/10.1002/sce.21454.

Murphy, C. A., Keiffer, E. A., Neal, J. A. & Crandall, P. G. (2013). A customizable evaluation instrument to facilitate comparisons of existing online training programs. *Knowledge Management & E-Learning: An International Journal, 5*(3), 251–268. https://doi.org/10.34105/j.kmel.2013.05.018.

Pratt, D. D. (1998). *Five perspectives on teaching in adult and higher education.* Krieger.

Quinlan, K. M., Male, S., Baillie, C., Stamboulis, A., Fill, J. & Jaffer, Z. (2013). Methodological challenges in researching threshold concepts: A comparative analysis of three projects. *Higher Education, 66,* 585–601. https://doi.org/10.1007/s10734-013-9623-y.

Rovinelli, R. J. & Hambleton, R. K. (1976). *On the use of content specialists in the assessment of criterion-referenced test item validity* [Conference presentation]. Annual

Meeting of the American Educational Research Association, San Francisco, CA, United States. https://files.eric.ed.gov/fulltext/ED121845.pdf.

Russell, D. (1995). Activity theory and its implications for writing instruction. In J. Petraglia (Ed.), *Reconceiving writing, rethinking writing instruction* (pp. 51–78). Lawrence Erlbaum Associates.

Russell, D. (2002). *Writing in the academic disciplines: A curricular history* (2nd ed.). Southern Illinois University Press.

Russell, D. R. & Yañez, A. (2003). "Big picture people rarely become historians": Genre systems and the contradictions of general education. In C. Bazerman & D. R. Russell (Eds.), *Writing selves/writing societies: Research from activity perspectives* (pp. 331–362). The WAC Clearinghouse; Mind, Culture, and Activity. https://doi.org/10.37514/PER-B.2003.2317.2.10.

Sireci, S. G. (1998). The construct of content validity. *Social Indicators Research, 45*(1–3), 83–117. https://doi.org/10.1023/A:1006985528729.

Thaiss, C. & Zawacki, T. M. (2006). *Engaged writers and dynamic disciplines: Research on the academic writing life*. Boynton/Cook.

Timmermans, J. A. & Meyer, J. H. F. (2017). A framework for working with university teachers to create and embed 'Integrated Threshold Concept Knowledge' (ITCK) in their practice. *International Journal for Academic Development, 24*(4), 354–368. https://doi.org/10.1080/1360144X.2017.1388241.

Turner, R. C. & Carlson, L. (2003). Indexes of item-objective congruence for multidimensional items. *International Journal of Testing, 3*(2), 163–171. https://doi.org/10.1207/S15327574IJT0302_5.

Walvoord, B. E. & McCarthy, L. P. (1990). *Thinking and writing in college: A naturalistic study of students in four disciplines*. The WAC Clearinghouse (originally published by NCTE). https://wac.colostate.edu/books/landmarks/thinkingwriting/.

CHAPTER 4.

STRENGTHENING THE CORE: DESIGNING AND IMPLEMENTING A NEW, SUSTAINABLE WAC/WID PROGRAM

Kimberly K. Gunter, Lindy E. Briggette, Mary Laughlin, Tiffany Wilgar, and Nadia Francine Zamin

Fairfield University

In the fall of 2019, after several years of intense negotiation and development, Fairfield University opened the academic year with a brand new core curriculum—its first in over 40 years. Titled the *Magis* Core, the new curriculum transformed the first-year writing requirement, introduced Fairfield's first-ever WAC/WID program, and brought a cohort of full-time, disciplinary writing faculty to campus. This chapter attempts to capture how we set and met goals throughout times of planned transition as well as during unforeseen and unprecedented challenges. It is our hope that this shared account of ongoing program-building inspires practical and adaptable growth-oriented strategies for other emerging WAC/WID programs. To that end, our chapter emphasizes three elements from the *Magis* Core transition:

1. The assembling of a disciplinary team to operationalize the Core Writing program's pedagogical agenda;
2. A strategic plan for building a coherent, assessment-driven campus writing culture; and,
3. The inaugural WAC/WID Workshop, a professional development—and public relations—success stemming from the aftermath of the COVID pandemic.

We hope that readers may find this chapter useful in launching new curricula, programs, and professional development initiatives and may join us in considering how to sustain these programs long-term.

DOI: https://doi.org/10.37514/PER-B.2023.1947.2.04

Gunter, Briggette, Laughlin, Wilgar, and Zamin

THE CORE WRITING PROGRAM'S TRANSITION: A NEW CURRICULUM, A NEW LABOR MODEL

Fairfield University is a private, Jesuit institution located in Fairfield, Connecticut; the student body numbers approximately 5,500 individuals, and the school is firmly rooted in traditions of humanistic inquiry. In 2014, Fairfield sought to revise its core curriculum due to a number of factors: Recent patterns indicated increasing enrollment in the professional schools, particularly the Dolan School of Business and the Egan School of Nursing and Health Studies. Due to school-specific external accreditation requirements, students majoring in programs such as engineering, nursing, and business had difficulty completing the core's required 60 credit-hours within four years; when necessary, core requirements were sometimes waived so individual students could graduate on time. In part to account for these enrollment shifts and to ensure that all students completed the same core, the university elected to revise its core curriculum.

As various core revisions were decided upon, the writing program also transformed. In the horse-trading needed to drop from a 60 credit-hour core to a 45 credit-hour core, the second of two required first-year composition (FYC) courses was eliminated. In the new core, students would enroll in one newly created FYC course that was to prepare them to complete three subsequent "writing intensive" courses. The three writing intensive courses constituted one "Signature Element" of the new core.

In 2017, Kim Gunter was recruited to Fairfield to develop this new FYC curriculum as well as what became known as the WAC/WID Signature Element. Invoking disciplinary language and best practices, Gunter made clear that WAC courses should not be classes where additional writing is simply *assigned*; instead, WAC classes should ask disciplinary faculty to *support* student writing. Gunter also proffered the addition of a WID option whereby students could complete WID sections of courses in a major and receive instruction on writing as scholars and professionals within their disciplines. This WID option added verticality to the Signature Element offerings and allowed any program on campus to participate in the newly imagined Core Writing program.

One of Gunter's priorities upon arriving at Fairfield was to create an FYC curriculum that aligned with contemporary knowledge and practices in the field. Previously, Fairfield's first-year writing program showed its age, with all students completing an expository writing class in their first semester (titled "Texts and Contexts I: Writing as Craft & Inquiry") and a writing-about-literature course in their second semester (titled "Texts and Contexts II: Writing about Literature"). While some campus constituents had assumed that the new FYC course would simply merge the previous two-course sequence into a single three-hour experience, Gunter instead proposed a new course (indeed, the *only* new course that emerged from core revision): ENGL 1001, "Introduction to Rhetoric and Composition." This course foregrounded five threshold concepts that are aligned with five key terms from the field: process, inquiry, rhetoric, genre, and transfer (we discuss this curriculum in more detail below).

Gunter also sought to underscore the fact that FYC would embody a new role on campus. Previously, "Texts and Contexts I" articulated directly to "Texts and Contexts II," and "Texts and Contexts II" then prepared students for their core literature classes. At this pivot point of core reform, however, Gunter messaged to all who would listen that ENGL 1001 was not designed to articulate to core literature classes but to *all* WAC/WID-designated courses on campus as well as upper-division rhetoric and composition courses in the rhetoric and professional writing (RPW) minor and the professional writing concentration of the English major. With FYC focused on rhetoric and composition and grounded in writing about writing approaches (Downs & Wardle, 2007; Wardle & Downs, 2013), pragmatic interpretation of "key terms" (Yancey et al., 2014), and introductory WAC/WID content (Melzer, 2014), the writing curriculum for the new *Magis* Core would foreground students' theoretical introduction to the discipline as well as a practical facility with composing knowledges and strategies.

To initiate this curricular shift, however, the Core Writing program's staffing model also required transformation. When Gunter arrived at Fairfield, 82.5 percent of FYC sections were taught by a cadre of part-time faculty, some of whom had never taken a graduate course in the field; also at that time, no WAC/WID program existed. As Gunter repeatedly advocated to administrators, it was not enough to hire a new Core Writing director, for one person does not make a program. At the same time, with savvy forethought, the emerging core proposal emphasized the importance of core courses being taught by full-time faculty. To align Core Writing to the values of the *Magis* Core and, more directly, to have the capacity to institute two new writing initiatives, Gunter argued for six new full-time rhetoric and composition hires. Additionally, Gunter began to illustrate to faculty across campus (including the provost, to whom she directly reported) that, while others had anticipated the need for full-time faculty to teach a new FYC course, they had not anticipated the professional development and support that current cross-disciplinary faculty would need in order to prepare for and succeed as WAC/WID teachers. Thus, part of Gunter's rationale for requesting six full-time positions was that all new full-time Core Writing faculty should receive reassigned time to provide support for the burgeoning WAC/WID Signature Element—a request that was eventually approved by Provost Christine Siegel. Before the first semester of the new *Magis* Core rollout, six new professors of the practice (POPs) had been hired, all holding terminal degrees in rhetoric and composition.

A few years have passed since those early discussions, and we've gained greater understanding of the nuances and challenges of our institutional ecology; particularly, we continue to recognize the benefits of a model that prioritizes expertise in the writing studies field. Namely, our labor model helps to build a stable cohort of full-time writing specialists capable of both introducing a disciplinary field to students and providing pedagogical guidance to WAC/WID colleagues. However, even while we celebrate the formation of a stable cohort of full-time writing specialists, we acknowledge that the implementation of this labor model was not without consequence for our adjunct faculty (Gunter, 2019). The move from a six-hour to a three-hour FYC requirement already meant that the need for adjunct labor in our program would be halved; the hiring of six full-time POPs (following two national searches) reduced that need even further. Adjunct faculty in Core Writing were welcomed to apply for the six full-time POP lines (and some did); however, given the disciplinary needs of the positions, none were ultimately hired into these new lines, which was a disappointment to several people across the campus community. We acknowledge the disappointment felt by some members of our community with regards to these hiring decisions, even as we as a team of disciplinary specialists move forward from a place of respectful regard.

In terms of seizing the moment of core reform in order to foster a new, robust writing culture across campus, we must also acknowledge that the remarkable support from our provost to hire a cohort of writing specialists has had far-reaching implications. As a result of this shift in labor models, in 2021, nearly 73 percent of students in our FYC course studied with a full-time faculty member who held a Ph.D. in the discipline (vs. less than 4 percent of sections being taught by faculty with the terminal degree in AY 2018). Additionally, all cross-disciplinary faculty have the opportunity to work one-on-one with a WAC/WID consultant in the development of writing pedagogies, activities, assignments, assessments, and courses. Without this support from the academic side of the university's administration, the current Core Writing program (both FYC and WAC/WID) would simply have been impossible, not to mention ill-prepared to meet the crisis of the pandemic.

BUILDING A CAMPUS WRITING CULTURE

Curriculum & Transfer

The newly hired POPs were tasked with forwarding pedagogical consistency within our campus writing culture. As instructors of the new FYC course as well as WAC/WID consultants who support cross-disciplinary colleagues, our

POP faculty were central in implementing disciplinary "threshold concepts," which became the necessary anchor for both our FYC student learning goals and outcomes *and* our mechanism for transfer of this knowledge into WAC/WID courses. Drawing from Jan H. F. Meyer and Ray Land (2003), a threshold concept operates like a portal that opens up new ways of thinking, providing transformation of an "internal view of subject matter, subject landscape, or even world view" (p. 1). While threshold concepts can be "troublesome" to learn, often because they conflict with pre-existing knowledge or understanding, once a threshold is crossed, so to speak, there is no going back.

In our ENGL 1001, five threshold concepts of writing were translated into the student learning outcomes built into the foundation of the course itself (see Table 4.1).

Table 4.1. Threshold Concepts and Student Learning Goals.

Threshold Concepts	Student Learning Goals in ENGL 1001
Writing is a process	Students will demonstrate understanding that writing is a collaborative, social, situated process and will demonstrate facility with the various tasks and habits of mind required by this process.
Writing is inquiry-driven	Students will join the academic community of ideas and scholarly inquiry by thinking critically, reading analytically, and writing supported, well-documented arguments.
Writing is rhetorical	Students will demonstrate sophisticated rhetorical knowledge.
All writing is genre writing	Students will demonstrate understanding of the concepts of genre and disciplinarity and their interplay.
Transfer is essential	Students will transfer previous literacies into the course and transfer course content from the course by fostering a sense of metacognition.

As we intentionally emphasized threshold concepts within the ENGL 1001 course, key terms became "conceptual anchors" (Yancey et al., 2014, p. 42), both in making our content visible *in* the classroom and facilitating transfer *outside* the classroom. For the variety of writing stakeholders in our own rhetorical ecology, key terms like "genre" and "rhetorical situation" operationalize threshold concepts and build consistency across FYC sections.[1] On our campus, key terms also serve a role (negotiated with our colleagues) in building a common vocabulary for conversations about written communication, and these terms

---

1   We differentiate between "key terms" and "threshold concepts" using guidance from Kara Taczak and Kathleen Blake Yancey (2015): "Key terms can demarcate a field and locate its historical origin: the key term of process, for instance, is often cited as a marker for the beginning of the field. But it does not make a claim about process; it has no predicate. Threshold concepts, in contrast, build claims from key terms" (p. 141).

are made visible for students and ENGL 1001 faculty via their appearance on syllabi, assignments, daily lesson plans, the public-facing Core Writing website, and our internal-facing faculty resource content.

Since they align with specific key terms from the field—process, inquiry, rhetoric, genre, and transfer—our five threshold concepts allowed us to build a curriculum that begins in our FYC course (ENGL 1001) and continues through the next three WAC or WID courses that students complete. These five threshold concepts are meant to translate directly to the learning goals that faculty who teach WAC/WID-designated sections also build into their courses. Our professional development work for WAC/WID faculty across campus is centered around these concepts, and our primary goals gesture toward two audiences: WAC/WID faculty *and* WAC/WID students. WAC/WID professional development showcases research and best practices from writing studies to our fellow faculty across the disciplines, and we aim to make the teaching of writing more meaningful and more successful for faculty while also making writing more meaningful and expectations more transparent for their students. In this way, the threshold concepts' integration into our curriculum cultivates a common writing language across campus; additionally, this language signals students' entry and ongoing participation in a larger campus culture of writing. Students first encounter the goals and outcomes of ENGL 1001, and, ideally, they later encounter similar writing-oriented goals, outcomes, and language in at least three WAC/WID courses (See Table 4.2).

A word about the role of transfer in WAC/WID may be useful here: While the need for disciplinarily-grounded attribution transfers across virtually all disciplines on campus and while we speak with our cross-disciplinary colleagues about FYC's teaching of attribution and documentation as rhetorical and transferable skills, we find that transfer is inherent and ubiquitous in the very existence of a WAC/WID program. Our work in building a WAC/WID program is the work of "placing discrete courses within broader contexts" (Moore, 2012, pp. 21–22) so that faculty across campus can see that the writing teaching/learning they are doing with their students is connected to the writing teaching/learning happening across campus. These articulations of transfer naturally inform our consultations with and designs of professional development for both FYC and WAC/WID faculty.

Over and over again, through our work with faculty and students in ENGL 1001 and our work with faculty who teach WAC/WID-designated courses, we strive to reiterate and foster these threshold concepts in order to strengthen a coherent writing culture across campus. This programmatic cohesion leads to more effective teaching of writing across all disciplines and, hopefully, to stronger student writers working in and emerging from all departments at Fairfield (where the achievement of the latter will be examined through our planned WAC/WID assessment activities, discussed below).

Table 4.2. Threshold Concepts, FYC Goals, and WAC/WID Goals.

Threshold Concepts	ENGL 1001 Goals	WAC/WID Goals
Writing is a process	Students will demonstrate understanding that writing is a collaborative, social, situated process and will demonstrate facility with the various tasks and habits of mind required by this process.	Students will respond to and use responses to drafts in revision, in this and other ways demonstrating metacognitive awareness about their writing.
Writing is inquiry-driven	Students will join the academic community of ideas and scholarly inquiry by thinking critically, reading analytically, and writing supported, well-documented arguments.	Students will use writing as an instrument of inquiry across a variety of writing situations, both formal and informal.
Writing is rhetorical	Students will make choices reflecting awareness of purpose, audience, and the rhetorical context in which they write.	Students will demonstrate sophisticated rhetorical knowledge.
All writing is genre writing	Students will engage in writing that responds to content or other texts in the discipline in ways that deepen student understanding of and facility with the genres of the discipline.	Students will demonstrate understanding of the concepts of genre and disciplinarity and their interplay.
Transfer is essential	Students will transfer previous literacies into the course and transfer course content from the course by fostering a sense of metacognition.	[All goals above apply to transfer as well as the final WAC/WID goal regarding attribution.] Students will use and cite texts and other sources of information in ways considered appropriate in the field.

PROFESSIONAL DEVELOPMENT RESOURCES

As our role in the new core took shape, we understood that concurrently building a new FYC curriculum *and* a new WAC/WID program required developing resources for students and faculty (both faculty who teach in rhetoric and composition and faculty who teach across the curriculum). While concurrently developing two programs was daunting, we also recognized the unique opportunity to support coherence across FYC and WAC/WID. Our first step toward doing so was to create a public-facing resource that could be used by students and faculty in rhetoric and composition courses and in WAC/WID classes as well. Thus, we created FairfieldCoreWriting.org.

We articulated several goals in creating this central website. Thereon, we seek to educate students and faculty about Fairfield's new writing curriculum, showcasing ENGL 1001, "Introduction to Rhetoric and Composition," as a foundational course for the WAC/WID classes that students will complete in their time as undergraduates. Additionally, we drill down into the curriculum, supporting students and faculty across the university in understanding threshold concepts, employing key terms, and practicing principles of rhetoric, writing, and disciplinarity. We also seek to make it easy for faculty to understand the learning goals for WAC/WID classes and the guidelines for applying for WAC/WID designations for their courses.

In creating this custom, in-house educational tool for our local context at Fairfield, though, our primary motivation is pedagogical. Our Fairfield Core Writing website functions as a teaching tool for both students and fellow faculty across the disciplines. For example, ENGL 1001 faculty can assign pages from the website for their students to read before discussing a concept like "genre" in class. Similarly, when a cross-disciplinary faculty member asks about genre (related to the WAC/WID outcome of "disciplinarity and genre"), we can point them to the same resource.

The website also includes a lexicon of key terms in rhetoric and writing studies, supporting our aim of fostering a common language across campus. We pitch this lexicon to faculty across all disciplines as language we use with students in the FYC course; if WAC/WID faculty use the same terms, we suggest, they can get to where they're going faster because the students will already be familiar with the term or concept. Not only does making use of this lexicon facilitate transfer, but it also nurtures a culture of writing on campus in which we are deeply invested. If transfer is "applied or adapted learned knowledge in new contexts" (Moore, 2012, p. 22) and rhetorical studies rests on the premise that words and rhetoric are "altering reality, not by the direct application of energy to objects, but by the creation of discourse which changes reality through the mediation of thought and action" (Bitzer, 1968, p. 4), then it stands to reason that a shared lexicon could create a common cognitive understanding about rhetorical concepts across campus that would facilitate transfer from "discrete courses within broader contexts" (Moore, 2012, pp. 21–22). We have attempted to make visible to both faculty and students that our lexicon, threshold concepts, and WAC/WID outcomes are all intertwined and recursively referential.

It's true that, to some extent, all of our work as Core Writing faculty and WAC/WID consultants helps to foster a culture of writing on campus, but the website offers a public-facing focal point to stabilize and reiterate foundational terms/concepts from the field. We use the website to establish the basics and set the tone for our programs, and we continually update it as our local needs, contexts, and practices change. In this way, the website becomes part of a feedback loop as we build, run, and assess the success of our initiatives.

WAC/WID Workshop Week

The above narrative is meant to capture the initial growth of our program as well as the challenges and opportunities of concurrently building two new, interlocked curricular initiatives (a new FYC course and a WAC/WID program). Here we'd like to pause to offer an example of our professional development—a workshop that unexpectedly took place in the early days of COVID quarantining and that has now become an annual event.

In May of 2020, we were scheduled to partner with our teaching and learning center and offer a two-day course design institute for faculty who were interested in creating WAC/WID courses. We realized, however, that traditional, in-person models of professional development would be impossible, and we seized a kairotic moment, proposing a new model for a workshop that would foreground WAC/WID scholarship while also providing a more pragmatic "how to" approach for faculty attempting to create and implement new writing courses. We asked ourselves: *What do faculty need from our WAC/WID program right now? What might a week-long workshop during a pandemic even look like? How can we re-see this moment as an opportunity to gain faculty buy-in as well as to foster long-term deployment of WAC/WID pedagogies across campus?*

When we first advertised what would become our annual WAC/WID Workshop Week, we saw more interest from faculty than we had anticipated. Keeping in mind the impact we could potentially have across various disciplines on our campus, we decided to scaffold writing studies scholarship along with best practices in WAC/WID pedagogy into a series of five half-day workshops. We began broadly with current theories in WAC/WID and progressively narrowed to more specific pedagogical practices (e.g., assignment development and sequencing, ideas for low-stakes writing-to-learn strategies that might support high-stakes writing-to-communicate genres, best practices in response to student writing, etc.). Given that many of our faculty found themselves teaching online for the first time, we also offered a workshop on teaching writing with digital tools, and our closing workshop gave faculty a chance to share their new course plans and "a-ha moments" from the week. We calculated that our week-long approach might allow workshop leaders and participants to better connect with each other as we navigated pandemic teaching and considered WAC/WID practices, and it would allow our colleagues to connect practical applications of writing studies scholarship to the needs of students in Fairfield's new WAC/WID Signature Element.

Over the course of that first WAC/WID Workshop Week, we watched as faculty from a range of departments tried on new pedagogical vocabulary (such as *scaffolding, assessment,* and *writing-to-learn*) and new key terms related to composing (such as *disciplinarity, genre,* and *rhetoric*), and we witnessed several epiphanies. It was a high point during the difficult context of the pandemic to hear faculty begin to meaningfully use rhetorical terms and WAC/WID concepts in reference to their own courses and assignments. Furthermore, going by concrete numbers, that first workshop week was even more impressive; our 22 participants successfully redesigned 29 courses using information and practices we covered in our various sessions. Our colleagues on the WAC/WID subcommittee, which vets new applications, even lauded the strengths of participants' courses versus the applications typically received from faculty who had not engaged in this professional development.

As June 2021 approached—with yet another pandemic version of end-of-semester rituals—we hosted the second iteration of our Workshop Week and were excited by similarly successful results. This time, after reviewing the courses submitted by 15 faculty participants, we gained 25 newly approved WAC/WID courses. And we were even more encouraged by participants' strikingly positive feedback. Anonymous comments from faculty participants in the June 2021 WAC/WID Workshop Week include:

- I really loved the myriad ways that through the workshop I am able to identify how writing is a continual process and included in all aspects of our lives.
- I hope that through including more varied writing opportunities students will come closer to identifying who they are, to seeing themselves in relation to a global society, continue to grow in their empathy and come closer to what it means to be human by expressing this through their work in the discipline of the class and through writing itself.
- My hope is that teaching a WAC/WID course will build a community of writers, rather than students and instructor.

Emerging here is the theme that writing is a social process that exists within a larger contextual system and an expansive community of writers. The articulation of that stance is in itself a big win for us and is but one example of the qualitatively different ways in which we now talk about writing with our cross-disciplinary colleagues.

Assessing Our Program

To explore how we use assessment to develop and sustain a new campus culture of writing, it is useful to briefly describe how we conduct assessment in our foundational course, ENGL 1001. The goal of assessment at this level is threefold: First, we use assessment to observe students' engagement with the course's student learning outcomes (SLOs). Second, we use assessment to regularize those self-reflective and self-assessing behaviors that can be so valuable when building, sustaining, and revising a program. Third, we use assessment practices at this level so that we can describe with evidence (to ourselves and other stakeholders) what is actually occurring in our classes.

The method of our programmatic assessment begins with appointing an assessment team of usually four to five full-time Core Writing faculty members. Whether we use direct or indirect assessment methods depends upon our priorities for the year. When we have conducted direct assessment, we have examined randomly selected samples of students' culminating course portfolios; when we have conducted indirect assessment, we have examined faculty artifacts from each section of ENGL 1001. We tackle student learning goals and outcomes for ENGL 1001 singly or in pairs and use an expert rater model; the assessment team norms ahead of each rating session, uses a shared rubric to guide rating scores, and rates artifacts' engagement with SLOs on a 5–6 point Likert-style scale.

Currently, we use four mechanisms to close the loop on our FYC assessment activities: (1) We regularly share our assessment findings and recommendations in program and departmental meetings; (2) we reinvest our assessment findings into the Core Writing program by incorporating findings into our faculty development programming; (3) we continue to refine and revise our assessment tools (including the rubric and selection of artifacts); and (4) our assessment activities and findings are reported to external stakeholders. We have been fortunate to work with various bodies on campus to further close the loop on our assessment activities, whether those initiatives take the form of conversations with campus librarians regarding information literacy across the disciplines or partnerships with faculty development handbook committees the leadership of which have asked us to lead well-attended, annual faculty development luncheons attended by perhaps one-third or more of all university full-time faculty.

Looking ahead, we have two main goals for assessment activities to further develop and sustain a culture of writing on our campus. The first focus for sustainable future assessment activities concentrates on an annual assessment institute comprised of full- and part-time faculty from the Core Writing program. In this institute, we would expand our direct and indirect assessment methods. For example, we hope to expand how we conduct indirect assessment and consider student and/or faculty reflections, focus groups, student surveys, and interviews. This avenue for program assessment offers largely collaborative opportunities for data analysis and the making of recommendations. Ideally, it would lead to an annual cycle of co-led faculty professional development. The second, broader focus for sustainable future assessment activities lies more directly in the WAC/WID program. Here, a WAC/WID assessment team consisting of both WAC/WID and disciplinary specialists from across the curriculum would be formed. This team would conduct annual cycles of assessment of WAC/WID SLOs via direct and indirect means, this work ideally leading to annual cycles of three professional development workshops (one to close the loop on the previous year's SLOs, one to support the current year's SLOs, and one to lay the foundation for the following year's SLOs). In the long term, it is our hope that both of these assessment initiatives might lead to longitudinal studies of students' composing and faculty's teaching of writing at Fairfield. In all of these efforts, our purpose is always to grow and support a coherent culture of writing on campus, in part by building architectures to sustain this work.

OPPORTUNITIES & CHALLENGES GOING FORWARD

As our campus tries to establish what a new normal might look like during a period that we hope soon to describe as "post-COVID," we find ourselves pausing to reflect on the last four years of enormous change, challenge, and success in Core Writing's FYC course and our WAC/WID initiative. In ENGL 1001, we have a new curriculum which our assessment activities suggest prepares students far more effectively for the writing that they do across campus, and we know that much of this success can be attributed to the faculty in our classrooms. We have gone from having 7.7 percent of our FYC sections taught by full-time faculty with a Ph.D. in rhetoric and composition in AY 2018 to 72.9 percent in AY 2021. We are also seeing our course caps decrease, with the cap in ENGL 1001 set at 17 for AY 2022, with a goal of 15 by AY 2024, and with the caps in WAC/WID-designated sections set at 20. Moreover, since our WAC/WID program officially launched in fall 2019, at least 20 percent of all full-time Fairfield faculty have now participated in at least one *multi-day* WAC/WID professional development workshop, with many others having attended our one-time events such as brown bags, drop-in sessions, or back-to-school consultations. Now in the midst of planning future workshops and having only just begun our third year of the new *Magis* Core, we are approaching our 175th WAC/WID-designated course, and with over 200 sections offered just this year, we find our ethos and our relationships across campus are strengthened.

We are not without challenges, however. Like most programs across the country, we face smaller budgets due to COVID's impact, and even before COVID, we found reassigned time for POP faculty receding. With ironic backlash now occurring perhaps in part due to our success, we sometimes face questions like, "Why do you continue to need so many resources when you now have so many WAC/WID-designated courses?" Thus, we find ourselves pausing to reflect and make deliberate decisions about just what the next four years will look like.

While growth of the program has been a driving force for the last four years—and not just for us but also for the administrators to whom we report—we find ourselves now asking not only how to grow the culture of writing at Fairfield but how to sustain and nourish it by maintaining faculty relationships, increasing student engagement, and building equitable, functional administrative systems. We seek to achieve long-term sustainability for the program not simply by considering practical matters (e.g., offering enough WAC/WID sections so that students can readily complete core requirements), though those matters are, of course, important. However, we find these day-to-day concerns no more important than considering what social justice (part of our university's mission) or sustainable labor conditions must look like in WAC/WID programs. We ask ourselves to anticipate and prepare for challenges that we foresee facing in our local conditions (e.g., will our resources continue to recede?) but also to leverage the privilege that we recognize that we have when compared to so many colleagues working in far less supported writing programs. In short, now that we have some successes and the momentum that comes along with them, we ask ourselves how we might effect, sustain, and build upon 50 years of WAC/WID scholarship—on our campus, in our community, and in our discipline.

REFERENCES

Bitzer, L. F. (1968). The rhetorical situation. *Philosophy & Rhetoric, 1*(1), 1–14. https://www.jstor.org/stable/40236733.

Downs, D. & Wardle, E. (2007). Teaching about writing, righting misconceptions: (Re)envisioning "first-year composition" as "introduction to writing studies." *College Composition and Communication, 58*(4), 552–84. https://www.jstor.org/stable/20456966.

Gunter, K. (2019). Advocacy, independence, and the painful kairotic moment for rhetoric and composition. *WPA: Writing Program Administration, 43*(1), 54–72. https://link.gale.com/apps/doc/A646110306/AONE?u=maine_oweb&sid=googleScholar&xid=b08ab21e.

Melzer, D. (2014). *Assignments across the curriculum: A national study of college writing*. Utah State University Press.

Meyer, J. H. F. & Land, R. (2003). Threshold concepts and troublesome knowledge: Linkages to ways of thinking and practising within the disciplines. In C. Rust (Ed.), *Improving Student Learning: Theory and Practice Ten Years* On (pp. 412–424). Oxford Brookes University.

Moore, J. L. (2012). Designing for transfer: A threshold concept. *The Journal of Faculty Development, 26*(3), 19–24. https://www.proquest.com/scholarly-journals/designing-transfer-threshold-concept/docview/1143304893/se-2.

Taczak, K. & Yancey, K. B. (2015). Threshold concepts in rhetoric and composition doctoral education: The delivered, lived, and experienced curricula. In L. Adler-Kassner & E. Wardle (Eds.), *Naming what we know: Threshold concepts of writing studies* (pp. 140–154). Utah State University Press.

Wardle, E. & Downs, D. (2013). Reflecting back and looking forward: Revisiting teaching about writing, righting misconceptions five years on. *Composition Forum, 27*(10). http://compositionforum.com/issue/27/reflecting-back.php.

Yancey, K. B., Robertson, L. & Taczak, K. (2014). *Writing across contexts: Transfer, composition and sites of writing*. Utah State University Press.

CHAPTER 5.

GROWING A WAC PROGRAM ALONGSIDE A NEW COLLEGE

Elizabeth Baxmeyer

California Northstate University College of Health Sciences

Rikki Corniola

California Northstate University College of Health Sciences

William Davis

Virginia Polytechnic Institute and State University

Gloria Poveda

California Northstate University College of Health Sciences

Christopher Wostenberg

California Northstate University College of Health Sciences

California Northstate University (CNU) began with the mission to advance the art and science of healthcare. As the university's undergraduate arm, the College of Health Sciences (CHS) was specifically developed to prepare students for careers in the health professions. From our college's first months of existence in 2015, we have implicitly and explicitly developed a curriculum with writing at its foundation. From life and physical science classes to arts and social science coursework, an emphasis on accurate, lucid written communication grounds our outcomes at all levels, including nearly every culminating course assignment rubric. To foster buy-in from our students regarding the importance of written communication—many students come to our college unaware of the significance of writing in all health professions—faculty and administrators first needed to ensure we shared compatible visions for writing in all undergraduate classes. Though it has required a shift in focus on the part of faculty, many of whom trained in distinct disciplines that champion publications but eschew direct writing instruction, our process has yielded successes and insights into ways to improve.

CHS combines a life and physical sciences curriculum that aligns with the humanities and social sciences to develop dedicated, lifelong learners possessing

DOI: https://doi.org/10.37514/PER-B.2023.1947.2.05

strength of character and interpersonal skills beyond any single discipline on which their education is based. To accomplish the goal of cross-discipline training for future health practitioners, CHS has developed a hierarchical scheme (Maher, 2004; Nusche, 2008) of learning outcomes (LOs) that students must master by graduation. Faculty incorporate writing to learn, writing to engage, and/or writing to communicate in CHS courses, lower and upper division, so graduates are prepared to demonstrate respect, empathy, and cultural competency toward the communities they are serving. LOs provide structure and expectations that faculty utilize when creating their courses to ensure comprehension of the unique content knowledge specific to disciplines while building the key skills that students need to be successful upon graduation. Student mastery of the LOs is monitored by the faculty throughout courses via quizzes/exams and signature assignments. Over the last six years, we have developed assessments aligned with Bloom's Taxonomy and, correspondingly, writing to learn, engage, and communicate. Following best practices in education research (van de Pol et al., 2010), faculty scaffold assignments to provide students multiple chances to improve and receive feedback from instructors prior to final assessments. As a demonstration of writing in the disciplines, first-year lab courses link each lab experiment with a specific section of a full lab report. By not requiring a full report for each lab, instructors focus on mastering specific elements of the report that, by semester's end, they can fully model. The guidelines for each lab report derive from criteria for peer review articles in the physical sciences, most notably the American Chemical Society, a physical and concrete reference for students. Writing in the disciplines supports information literacy and interpretation of data as they relate to a student's central hypothesis for the lab. Students build on these skills each semester so that, by their third year, they are writing undergraduate research proposals.

To maintain a cohesive, faculty-driven effort regarding overall curriculum design and development, CHS brings a team of faculty together as the college's Curriculum Committee. This committee is overseen by the dean of academic affairs but relies on members from all academic departments to provide critical feedback, address challenges, create innovative and student-centered experiences, and embed outcome-driven content. A separate faculty body, the Assessment Committee, sets the protocols for tracking student performance on the various LOs. Faculty receive instructions and guidance from beginning to end of course design through workshops and trainings. We have found that when faculty review and revise their course LOs alongside colleagues from other disciplines, discussions about assessment strategies, particularly regarding writing assignments, flourish. Beyond a better understanding of the kinds of writing needed for each course, faculty gain appreciation for the kinds of analytic and rhetorical skills students learn in other courses.

ESTABLISHING COLLABORATION AS A CORE CONCEPT

The founding faculty worked with administrators to create a collaborative environment where faculty become connected with courses across disciplines. At the start of our college, faculty in the same disciplines often worked together to co-develop and co-teach courses. Informal, cross-discipline discussions among faculty blossomed and, due to the close physical proximity of the faculty, the sharing of course documents, pedagogical approaches, and ideas for student support ensued. In recent years, we have increased faculty peer training on crafting assignments and rubrics that promote writing to engage, learn, and communicate. Students find consistent language across courses and disciplines in terms of assessments, expectations, and outcomes, and faculty see direct connections between their work and that of their colleagues. We are developing a connected teaching environment through innovative undergraduate curriculum design that crosses disciplines to encourage student assimilation of general education and pre-professional competencies into a cohesive knowledge core.

After our first year delivering classes, determined efforts to cross disciplinary boundaries led a group of science faculty to participate in a Course-based Undergraduate Research Experience (CURE) workshop to develop a project that could span disciplines. From the workshop, the faculty developed an Interdisciplinary Scientific Learning and Novel Discovery (ISLaND) project to link general biology and general chemistry lab courses across both first-year semesters. This format has allowed for scaffolding of assignments across multiple courses, ensuring students build upon concepts and ideas.

Additionally, multiple faculty could provide assessment of the same LOs. Eventually, further collaborations were made to include first-year English courses, tying together writing assignments. Whilst the first-year courses at CHS develop the writing skills undergraduates need to communicate their understanding of foundational concepts, it is in their final years that they effectively synthesize these skills to demonstrate their grasp of the scientific method as they write and present a research proposal and project. Their capstone project in research combines a literature review to formulate a novel research question along with a reasonable protocol to study their question. This culminates in a presentation of their work during CHS's annual Research Day to the college and invited guests from the wider community. Some students have even presented their work at the university, local, and/or national level. Such collaboration has provided critical preparation for students in their capstone scholarly project, which takes place over two semesters in their junior or senior year. Just as students are consistently assessed throughout their courses, the classes themselves are assessed in multiple ways. As mentioned, the first level of assessment involves the college's

Curriculum Committee when each course is proposed, followed by a review on a three-year cycle. Faculty revise their courses based on personal reflection, student evaluations, peer evaluations, and student performance. Student focus groups and graduating exit interviews and surveys assist in assessing individual course contributions to the overall CHS curriculum. The foundational structures developed to facilitate review and revision of courses have allowed for the implementation of innovations like rubric-based assessment and self-reflection portfolios, along with collaborations amongst faculty.

SUPPORTING WRITING THROUGH INTERDISCIPLINARITY

CHS began with few full-time faculty, directors, and deans, and as our student body has grown, so have faculty numbers. The growth has provided distinct challenges partly because our core full-time faculty must have expertise to teach a variety of classes that do not fit neatly into discrete job descriptions, especially in the humanities and social sciences. Our college's small size has distinct advantages in terms of student-professor ratios and engagement, and it also means many of us teach across disciplines. Because many faculty have interdisciplinary training, an instructor teaching composition courses might also teach music or philosophy courses; faculty leading communication courses could be asked to teach student success and leadership classes as well. In addition to a background and training in multiple disciplines, a mindset that embraces adaptation—to the needs of students and the college—is required. At CHS, we believe that effective healthcare requires practitioners with knowledge and techniques that transcend disciplines, so we are building a college that embraces and celebrates interdisciplinarity amongst the professoriate.

As our college expands, and we recruit academics with a passion for teaching that embraces ideas from multiple content areas, our returning faculty both mentor and learn from our new team members. Since our first semester delivering classes in 2015, we regularly engage in faculty development sessions led by other faculty so that, for instance, composition faculty can share methods for everything from assignment creation to evaluation. Our service learning faculty demonstrate how to incorporate content and methods from their courses to faculty across the college. When we all have a better understanding of the content of other courses at our college, we better demonstrate to our students the significance of the content they are learning in multiple contexts, thickening the strands that exist between seemingly disparate disciplines. CHS encourages a deep synthesis of the core values of each course in order to be most successful in the health professions. Students achieve this synthesis through completing reflections and projects that require a substantial amount of writing, no matter the subject. As faculty, communication and collaboration across courses is imperative to the success of student synthesis.

CHS faculty demonstrate the kind of interdisciplinary flexibility our students require and, as Catherine Lyall (2019) notes, an interdisciplinary mindset presents its own obstacles. At CHS, as at other institutions of higher learning, faculty aspire to achieve their own research interests and agendas while navigating institutional limitations: The scope of the research should meet the needs of the students and the college. Most of our faculty earned degrees in specific disciplines, and we trained alongside others with professional goals that often derived from a single discipline. CHS offers one undergraduate degree; however, it does not match the graduate degrees of our faculty, so we teach students who do not envision themselves working in the fields where we received our training. Thus, we connect our own research interests with the needs of our students and show them how the methods, skills, and knowledge we bring to our research also applies to their future work and careers. Though it is challenging to make a case for one's own field and area of research to the uninitiated, we are invigorated by the reminder that we are educating the next generation of healthcare practitioners: practitioners with a holistic training where no one discipline has natural prominence over another. Importantly, we are developing a new institution built upon the kinds of collaboration that, as Michael Crow and William Dabars (2015) call for, adapts to student needs as we create models and structures of knowledge creation and diffusion (p. 179).

As noted earlier, CHS prizes faculty that can teach beyond a narrow range of courses in part because we are a small cadre of academics seeking to learn from each other. When we take turns teaching the same course as other colleagues, we can share assignments, lesson plans, and advice on what worked in previous semesters. The course improves because of the input from the other faculty, and students benefit from a course infused with different perspectives on the same content. In the past year, we have begun designing courses collaboratively, where all faculty are encouraged to submit feedback to those leading the course's design. In some cases, like the re-design of our first-year experience course series, discussed in more detail below, the entire planning and implementation phases have included faculty from all disciplines at our college. We aimed to develop a course series that would respond to the needs of students from their first to their last semester, so all faculty were encouraged to participate and share information about the kinds of training students would need to enter their courses, to be attractive applicants for professional and graduate schools, and to be successful practitioners. Rather than working in distinct units/silos, we at CHS recognize that training future healthcare practitioners to be holistic, empathetic individuals attuned to the needs of their patients requires the synthesis of content from all our courses. To see the training of our students as a nested, collaborative process involving all of us, with no hierarchy of disciplines, faculty confront our own biases to establish an ethos of curiosity through empathetic communication. By encouraging respectful, open dialogue amongst our academic team about everything from content to assessment, we develop CHS courses rather than, say, philosophy or composition or sociology courses.

The cross-curricular inclusion we have established provides faculty with a better understanding of writing assignments in other courses. Recent research presented at the Fifteenth International Writing Across the Curriculum Conference by California State University Northridge's writing center has shown that transparency around how different faculty write and scaffold assignments creates more equitable opportunities for students to be successful (Payte et al., 2021). In addition, faculty members can reference one another in their own classes, strengthening the ethos between students and colleagues, and ultimately impacting students positively. Though there are some challenges to work out—learning how to assist, respectfully and professionally, in creating the kinds of assignments we would not normally teach, for example—CHS is dedicated to expanding its resources to create robust support systems that impact students' success in writing and communication across forums.

COURSE COLLABORATION TO LAY A WAC FOUNDATION

One course designed for the CHS experience is our first-year experience (FYE) series: College 100A and 100B. This year-long course was initiated as an interdisciplinary innovation to respond to student needs based on feedback from instructors at all levels in the student's health science undergraduate education. Having a largely interdisciplinary faculty base, especially in the humanities and social sciences through which foundational writing courses are created and taught, allows for the unique opportunity to build courses that are enriching and offer students the benefit of an interprofessional education beginning in their first semester. The aim is to prepare students to be successful in their undergraduate studies by teaching them strong study skills and self-management strategies. Originally, this course was one unit and taken as a stand-alone in the first semester. As with similar courses, it met some foundational needs of students, but student course surveys revealed that they did not always understand how the content connected to courses they would take in future years and to their future careers as health professionals. Thus, the faculty and administration determined that a course specifically designed for STEM and pre-med students could do more to meet the needs of ever-developing standards and requirements in healthcare education, such as: placing greater emphasis on empathetic communication, instilling a greater sense of responsibility to the community, and relaying the importance of the arts and humanities-based approaches to scientific problems. Achieving these goals requires significant, substantive, and critical writing, and we endeavor to include each of these elements in many of our classes—both STEM and humanities-based—by collaborating on course plans and inviting faculty across disciplines to engage with, and support, each other's content.

To design this new course series, faculty from different disciplines within the humanities and social sciences department, many with interdisciplinary backgrounds, formed a work group to identify topics, develop course plans, and devise assessments. Professors from the realms of psychology, music, English, leadership, student services, education, and philosophy (subjects with writing-intensive backgrounds) collaborated to create a two-semester version of the College 100 course—newly named: *First-Year Experience*—that included, in its fabric, deeper elements of critical self-reflection, ethical decision-making, and collaborative problem-solving. In addition, skills relating to self-organization, clear writing and reflection, communication, and collaboration were also emphasized. The intention was that this course would nurture the students' own approach to their education in a more holistic and long-lasting way and, in so doing, foster a sense of self-empowerment and act as a catalyst to motivate them to uphold the standards set by *First-Year Experience*. This approach is becoming widely adopted in graduate-level health profession programs and has been shown to benefit the practitioner when connecting and working with the community. Our very own CNU College of Medicine has a three-week leadership, humanities, and arts seminar course named the Wellness Elective, which addresses many similar components and supports students entering and exiting the medical school. Each year, more students sign up for the course and report feeling better prepared for the rigor of residency. Integrating standards and procedures from multiple disciplines also allows for more successful and productive engagement in interprofessional shared decision-making (Keshmiri et al., 2019), which is a large component of the process of learning at CHS.

To support this interdisciplinary approach to writing and learning, we have garnered robust and varied faculty participation in the Media and Communication Studio (MCS), CHS's version of a writing center. In the MCS, we emphasize the importance of cross-curricular, holistic learning by modeling effective collaboration as a writing community. One way we encourage buy-in from students and staff across programs is to invite faculty volunteers from all disciplines to participate as tutors and workshop leaders in the MCS. This work constitutes faculty service so is, in a practical sense, valuable time served for the professor. Many professors also comment on how rewarding and enjoyable the experience is because they get to know students they do not currently teach, and they learn how students engage with writing assignments in other courses and disciplines. It also, and perhaps more importantly, offers students a variety of perspectives regarding writing values, styles, and formats across genres and fields. As we are a health sciences-focused institution, supporting a diverse array of subjects in a cohesive and collaborative way is not only helpful, but also highly important for students to receive guidance from faculty in writing in the disciplines. Whether through one-to-one tutoring, or through small groups in workshops, students learn about writing in the disciplines from faculty trained in those fields, and they receive feedback from that same specialized community. All our students aspire to become health practitioners, professions in which one must collaborate frequently with specialists from many areas of expertise. In modeling this collaborative approach, we try to reflect the kinds of interactions our students may witness and have in the future, whilst emphasizing the importance of strong communication skills across disciplines to strengthen transdisciplinary learning.

In 2020, the MCS launched online tutoring and workshops through WC Online, a virtual tutoring platform. Student and faculty participation has risen significantly since we began offering online help, and both faculty and students have gained increased access to the resources provided by the MCS. Workshops cover topics ranging from common grammar pitfalls to research and source integration, and from timed writing assignments for medical school to developing a clear writer's voice. These workshops are held by faculty volunteers and Peer Assistant Learners, or PALs (students who are hand-picked by faculty and trained to help in the MCS) from both the humanities and core sciences departments, again instilling that writing is not only important in the expected courses, but of utmost significance in science classes, too. Students learn that if one cannot write or communicate effectively and equitably in the sciences, then perhaps core details that are important to the lay public regarding their own health may become lost in translation. As emerging research into comprehending complex information and public attitudes concerning COVID-19 demonstrates, this kind of conveyance of misinformation could have a detrimental effect on public safety (Melo & Cabral, 2020).

During the pandemic, students' health and sense of connection with the world has been a core focus for CHS. For much of 2021, most classes were delivered synchronously via Zoom so that students could follow health officials' recommendations for keeping a safe distance from others. In order to promote student engagement with each other and with real-world scenarios, despite students living in different cities and states and attending classes virtually, in January 2021 English faculty commenced a writing partnership with Lassen Volcanic National Park. Lassen gave us a wish list of roughly 150 prompts from over the last 20 years that they wanted to develop. These projects ranged from highly scientific to broadly educational, and covered issues and research goals specific to the park. We used these prompts to inform writing assignments in our second semester composition classes. We entered this partnership to give students opportunities to create authentic assignments for a truly public audience, and to practice a range of applied writing skills from literature reviews to project proposals and from media-based articles to visual texts. Students created projects that were substantial and useful to the park, and they learned new writing and media skills they had never used before. Through this form of assessment, faculty were also able to engage students on a level that served to contribute to their preparedness for their chosen career paths (Zilvinskis, 2015) by encouraging them to communicate effectively across audiences, be responsible for their research and proposed resolutions, and collaborate as a team to develop and synthesize expertise with the intention of benefiting the community. The projects offered an additional avenue of self-discovery and reflection, which the students found highly valuable and gratifying. In addition, many students said they felt happier through connecting more directly with the outside world and gained a more positive mindset in a socially difficult time (namely COVID-19 and lockdown). This experience solidified the concept that partnering with a national park and bringing that relationship into the classroom, especially during a public health crisis, helped students learn and apply vital communication skills—with the park and each other—whilst honoring a sense of self-care and empathy through writing. We intend to build upon this partnership, and others, and have started to collaborate with other disciplines across the college to help further students' understanding and appreciation for the impacts of public-focused research and writing, as well as community involvement.

REFLECTING ON SUCCESSES AND GROWTH

From our first year to now, our college's development has been guided by what we have learned from experience. Community engagement and collaboration across academic disciplines have taken shape by intentionally focusing on WAC and service learning (SL). At CHS, SL is an academic discipline, not an add-on to other courses. As far as undergraduate institutions, CHS is one of the only colleges designating SL as an academic discipline. Additionally, it is a requirement for graduation, and we have capitalized upon these opportunities to make writing an integral aspect of our SL curriculum.

While writing is not the main thrust of SL work outside our institution, it has taken a front-row seat in our curriculum design when creating assessment methods. One example is our signature project proposal (consisting of group work) where students write to investigate, prepare an action, reflect, demonstrate, and evaluate. This assignment, given in our Foundations of Service Learning class (COLL 210), assesses how well students understand, integrate, apply, and communicate the varying academic areas they are studying by writing about health and science topics anchored in SL concepts. SL concepts include warding against the server-served dichotomy while promoting teamwork, critical reflection in action, intercultural communication, professionalism, narrative writing, community research, narrative medicine, and knowledge transfer. Consequently, we rely on scaffolded writing assignments to guide our assessments.

Our partnership with Lassen Volcanic National Park (LVNP) gave the college access to the list of projects and research prompts LVNP shared. Distinct from how our English faculty used these prompts, our SL faculty saw an opportunity for students to develop a project proposal. Student teams investigate a chosen prompt from LVNP tailored for one of our community partners to be carried out during the subsequent course, COLL 220: Service Learning Practicum. In the end, each team delivers an in-depth, written project proposal based on the findings of their chosen prompt and an oral and visual presentation of that proposal to the class and community partners. Each prompt permits writing-to-engage activities crucial for critical engagement. For example, past prompts included an interactive fire lookout map and a three-day workshop on white-nose bat syndrome for K-5 students. Student team proposals are presented at the end of the Foundations of Service Learning course to the intended community partners. Ideally, the proposals are seamlessly carried out during the Service Learning Practicum in the subsequent semester. However, during the COVID-19 lockdown, we adjusted the delivery of the projects and relied on virtual platforms. For example, one group created an interactive map of fire lookouts that LVNP visitors could access through a QR code. This project was envisioned for a local elementary school to raise awareness of how LVNP keeps track of areas where fires are most common. Service learning students explained the chemical reaction of fire, the history behind each LVNP fire lookout, fire safety in parks, how to create QR codes, and how accessible they can be for disseminating information. Based on our work with LVNP, two emerging themes of teaching SL virtually involve: a) witnessing projects using QR codes, and b) following up with LVNP to see how QR codes could be utilized in SL. These two themes confirm that we are heading in the right direction for our young university by creating an educational environment that promotes innovation and leadership while modeling interdisciplinarity among faculty collaborations.

Since returning to in-person class delivery, we have continued to explore collaborations amongst faculty from distinct disciplines in courses that are traditionally taught by faculty in the life and physical sciences, like Course-based

Undergraduate Research Experiences (CUREs). In fall 2021, we launched CUREs team-taught by an SL faculty and a chemistry faculty, and another section taught by an interdisciplinary humanities and social sciences faculty. In these research-based courses, one student wove together computational drug discovery and service learning to generate a deliverable for a local community partner and a research presentation for the CHS campus. The collaboration provided students with feedback from experts that they might not normally consult, and it also afforded an opportunity to evaluate how faculty communicate about the projects and their assessments. As the semester progressed, the faculty recognized the need to revise assignments and the rubrics used to assess them. A greater emphasis needed to be placed on writing to learn and to engage rather than writing in the disciplines as the students first needed to prioritize communicating about the research and performing analysis. Though the final project poster's goal aligns with writing in the disciplines, too much too early was asked of students, and this stunted their learning as they were overwhelmed with trying to create texts that conformed to the conventions of the discipline.

Lastly, with our collective academic experiential knowledge, we are developing an educational portfolio assignment to use in SL and other courses. Our goal is to introduce students to the ePortfolio during the Foundations of Service Learning course and have them create a webpage through our learning management system. Our SL courses are at the 200 level (the range is 100 to 400), so students will have time to add content as they continue through their undergraduate education. We believe that the ePortfolio aligns well with our vision for a more holistic approach that embraces multiple academic disciplines and encourages creativity, innovation, and leadership with a focus on healthcare.

While there are numerous studies on the development and use of educational portfolios (e.g., Buyarski et al., 2015; Eynon, Gambino & Török, 2014; Slepcevic-Zach & Stock, 2018; Yancey, 2019), there are two general uses for educational portfolios we focused on: reflective and comprehensive portfolios (Roberts et al., 2014). In 2015, a national survey by the Association of American Colleges and Universities found that "93% of employers believe that a candidate's demonstrated capacity to think critically, communicate clearly, and solve complex problems is more important than his or her undergraduate major" (Hart Research Associates, 2015). We know that students have individual strengths and weaknesses. Still, it can be challenging to cater to each student and celebrate their uniqueness in a system often driven by LOs and assessments. We are learning more about how ePortfolios can represent each student in ways that end-of-course summative exams and assignments simply cannot. We are designing the ePortfolio with input from multiple academic areas to help students curate their online persona. Students will have autonomy to document and share their learning experiences through writing to engage. Using ePortfolios, students will highlight their critical thinking, communication, problem solving, and other skills through particular artifacts, e.g., service learning projects, Science Research Day projects, and writing assignments of their choice.

At a broader level, CHS faculty are devising a mechanism for students to develop an undergraduate work ePortfolio highlighting signature assignments across all their courses during their tenure at CHS. Through the ePortfolio, students will track their mastery of the various learning outcomes and showcase their achievements on professional school, internship, and job applications. The samples of written work from various courses provide insight into individual growth and strengths and help each student showcase their individual gains. CHS will encourage students to provide examples of interdisciplinary coursework as well as extra-curricular and co-curricular activities that display their application of skills acquired. Short self-reflection pieces connect the various sections and provide demonstrations of student learning that they can build upon in professional school. Through critical, written responses, students reflect on how the various parts of their undergraduate curriculum connect in achieving their goal of becoming a healthcare professional. Importantly, the ePortfolio enables them to communicate those gains to multiple audiences.

CONTINUED RESONANCE FOR WAC: SHAPING FUTURE HEALTHCARE PRACTITIONERS

Service learning and course-based research experiences for every student distinguish the CHS curriculum, and we use them to emphasize writing in courses across the disciplines. Our college trains faculty in building course learning outcomes and matching those outcomes to institutional and program outcomes. WAC directly connects writing to learn, to engage, and to communicate to Bloom's taxonomy, and we infuse that language into our trainings as well. Thus, all CHS faculty have shared tasks and goals: improving how students communicate their insights, their results, and their understanding, no matter the subject matter. CHS aims to empower students to apply critical thinking skills, as well as qualitative and quantitative methods, to one of the most complicated subjects: the intricacies of the human body and the human mind, and how both interact with as well as shape and are shaped by our environments.

REFERENCES

Buyarski, C. A., Aaron, R. W., Hansen, M. J., Hollingsworth, C. D., Johnson, C. A., Kahn, S., Landis, C. M., Pedersen, J. S. & Powell, A. A. (2015). Purpose and pedagogy: A conceptual model for an ePortfolio. *Theory Into Practice, 54*(4), 283–291. http://www.jstor.org/stable/43894476.

Crow, M. & Dabars, W. (2015). *Designing the new university.* Johns Hopkins University Press.

Eynon, B., Gambino, L. M. & Török, J. (2014). What difference can ePortfolio make? A field report from the connect to learning project. *International Journal of ePortfolio, 4*(1), 95–114.

Hart Research Associates. (2015). Falling short? College learning and career success. *Association of American Colleges and Universities.* https://www.aacu.org/research/falling-short-college-learning-and-career-success.

Keshmiri, F., Rezai, M. & Tavakoli, N. (2020). The effect of interprofessional education on healthcare providers' intentions to engage in interprofessional shared decision-making: Perspectives from the theory of planned behaviour. *Journal of Evaluation in Clinical Practice, 26*(4), 1153–1161. https://doi.org/10.1111/jep.13379.

Lyall, C. (2019). *Being an interdisciplinary academic: How institutions shape university careers.* Springer.

Maher, A. (2004). Learning outcomes in higher education: Implications for curriculum design and student learning. *Journal for Hospitality, Leisure, Sport and Tourism Education, 3*(2), 46–54.

Melo, C. & Cabral, S. (2020). Pandemics and communication: An experimental assessment. *RAP: Revista Brasileira de Administração Pública, 54*(4), 735–757. http://doi.org/10.1590/0034-761220200137x.

Nusche, D. (2008). Assessment of learning outcomes in higher education: A comparative review of selected practices. (*OECD* Education Working Papers, No. 15). https://doi.org/10.1787/19939019.

Payte, T., Filbeck, M., Huizar, L. & Ramirez, N. (2021, August 2–6). *The writing center as faculty resource for creating transparent assignments: A discussion of a CSUN writing center/faculty development collaboration* [Conference presentation]. Fifteenth International Writing Across the Curriculum Conference, Fort Collins, CO, United States. https://youtu.be/TH_1tYez9mQ.

Roberts, C., Shadbolt, N., Clark, T. & Simpson, P. (2014). The reliability and validity of a portfolio designed as a programmatic assessment of performance in an integrated clinical placement. *BMC Medical Education, 14*(1), 1–11. https://doi.org/10.1186/1472-6920-14-197.

Slepcevic-Zach, P. & Stock, M. (2018). ePortfolio as a tool for reflection and self-reflection. *Reflective Practice, 19*(3), 291–307. https://doi.org/10.1080/14623943.2018.1437399.

Van de Pol, J., Volman, M. & Beishuizen, J. (2010). Scaffolding in teacher-student interaction: A decade of research, *Education Psychology Review, 22,* 271–296. https://doi.org/10.1007/s10648-010-9127-6.

Yancey, K. B. (Ed.). (2019). *ePortfolio as curriculum: Models and practices for developing students' ePortfolio literacy.* Stylus Publishing.

Zilvinskis, J. (2015). Using authentic assessment to reinforce student learning in high-impact practices. *Assessment Update, 27,* 7–13. http://doi.org/10.1002/au.30040.

CHAPTER 6.
FURTHERING WAC INFLUENCE THROUGH STRATEGIC PARTNERSHIPS

Ming Fang, Kimberly Harrison, and Christine Martorana
Florida International University

Florida International University (FIU) is the nation's largest Hispanic-serving institution (HSI), located across two Miami campuses and serving approximately 58,000 students. It is also a relatively young institution—first welcoming students in 1972—with a dynamic, entrepreneurial culture and a national/international identity still in formation. The WAC program at FIU began as a provost's initiative in response to results from the National Survey of Student Engagement (NSSE) that indicated our students were not writing or revising as much as students in our peer institutions. In summer 2011, the vice provost formed a writing task force committee after the NSSE survey revealed that FIU students reported doing very little writing in their upper-division, major courses. One of the first actions of the task force was to consult with two nationally known WAC consultants—with one visiting campus twice to consult with stakeholders, including the provost, deans, and the task force and another hosting task force representatives at their home institution.[1] FIU's WAC program formally launched in 2012 with the goal of improving the institutional writing culture.

FIU's WAC program is a free-standing program, reporting to the Office of Academic Affairs. As WAC administration and consultants have always been writing program faculty, WAC is closely affiliated with the university writing program, housed in the English department; however, it is not a departmental program. Such independence brings both opportunities and challenges, and since its inception, our WAC program has had to be flexible and responsive to changes in upper administration, budgeting, and faculty needs. The program has gone through several iterations seeking the most effective, context-appropriate, and sustainable WAC model in response to these institutional changes. Right now, our WAC program is entering what we see as its third iteration. Initially,

---

1 Many thanks to Mike Palmquist and Terry M. Zawacki for their expertise and encouragement in our program's start-up period.

our program stemmed from a collaborative effort with our vice provost and resulted in a "school-based" WAC design, with WAC consultants housed in major schools such as the colleges of business and engineering and computing. This model transitioned to a program sustained largely through faculty grants; however, the funding to award faculty stipends for participating in WAC initiatives did not last. Given this reality, we have had to be creative with how we continue to build and sustain our WAC program with limited institutional resources, a common challenge faced by many WAC programs nationwide. Currently, our efforts focus on constructing cross-campus strategic partnerships, an approach that is proving promising as a strategy for sustaining the WAC program and keeping it institutionally relevant.

Our experiences suggest that building a strategic portfolio of partnerships can be a valuable and meaningful way to grow and sustain a WAC program. As a result of our cultivation of a varied portfolio of institutional partnerships in our urban, multilingual context, we have seen our program's reach expand and the interest among faculty for support in teaching effectively with writing grow. Based on our efforts, we offer *a taxonomy of strategic partnerships* that might serve other WAC programs in building their own sustaining partnerships and in interrogating current partnerships to understand their potential and limitations for program growth. We see this chapter as contributing to Michelle Cox, Jeffrey R. Galin, and Dan Melzer's 2018 call to theorize WAC program administration by presenting a classification of the types of strategic partners WAC programs can develop with the goal of sustaining WAC itself, while also contributing to a culture of transformational teaching and understanding of student writing.

CATEGORIZING AND DEFINING OUR STRATEGIC PARTNERSHIPS

In enacting a WAC sustainability strategy based on strategic partnerships, we recognize the importance of carefully considering and explicitly naming the types of partnerships being developed. This is because deliberately categorizing the partnership types invites us and others to more fully understand the unique nuances of each partnership: who is involved and in what roles, what each partnership entails, and how each one is sustained. As we will explain, while each partnership is not mutually exclusive, they do differ from one another in significant ways—and understanding these differences is key to curating a strategic portfolio of partnerships. To that end, we offer the following four categories to describe programmatic partnerships, a taxonomy that we developed to better understand, plan, and continue our programmatic sustainability efforts: invitational partnerships, imposed partnerships, supportive partnerships, and identity-building partnerships.

Furthering WAC Influence Through Strategic Partnerships

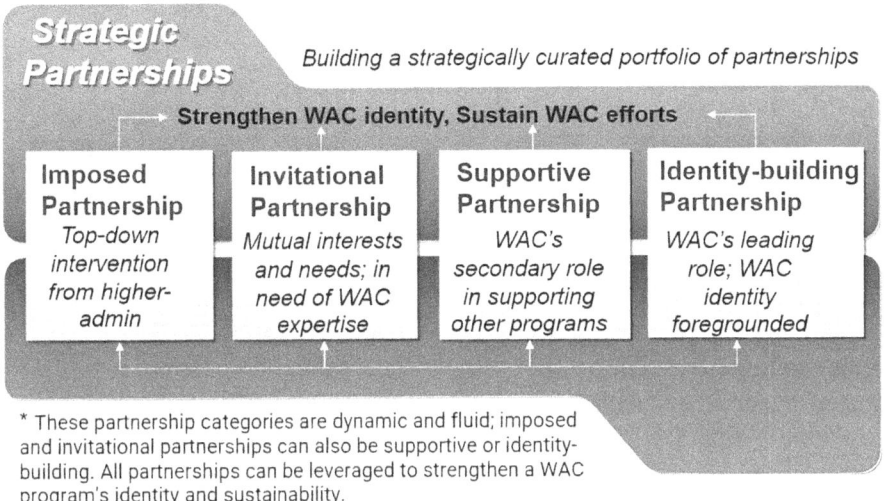

Figure 6.1. Four forms of strategic partnerships.

Invitational partnerships form out of mutual interests and needs between both parties. These partnerships are sparked by either WAC outreach to another university partner to offer programming and support or outreach by another program in need of WAC expertise. **Imposed partnerships** are those resulting from top-down intervention from higher administration. As made clear in WAC lore, these imposed relationships present challenges and require careful strategies for a productive partnership to form. Both invitational and imposed partnerships can be supportive or identity-building. We are calling **supportive partnerships** those in which WAC takes a supporting or secondary role, and the identity of the partner is forefront in programmatic efforts. In our experiences, these partnerships often occur when working with more established and better funded partners. **Identity-building partnerships**, on the other hand, occur when the partnership helps to foreground and build WAC program identity. In these collaborations, the identity of the partner may also be promoted, but not at the expense of our WAC program's identity. We use Figure 6.1 to illustrate these four forms of partnerships.

It is important to note that we have found all four forms of partnership valuable for keeping our WAC program institutionally relevant, and we advocate a multipronged approach that we have come to think of as building a strategically-curated portfolio of partnerships. In addition, although we present the partnership categories separately, we are not suggesting that the categories are mutually exclusive or unchanging. As Figure 6.1 shows, all four forms of partnership strengthen the WAC identity and sustain our WAC efforts. These partnership relations are not static, and in reality, the partnerships can and often do evolve and overlap over time. For example, the imposed partnerships that develop and become invitational are certainly successes, as are those supportive partnerships that evolve into more equal partnerships based on respect and effective outcomes. As the WAC program grows, what started as a supportive partnership may allow WAC's leading role to gradually emerge, thus moving a supportive partnership towards an identity-building partnership. Implicit in each strategic relationship developed is attention to transformative institutional change. Due to our identity as a WAC program within a large HSI, we are well-positioned to pay heed to Michelle Cox and Terry M. Zawacki's (2014) call to promote "a difference-as-resource academic writing culture rather than programs and pedagogical practices aimed at assimilating L2 students to Western culture and standard written English (SWE) norms" (p. 17). Such efforts entail encouraging and supporting faculty as they shift from the assumption that monolingual student writers are the norm and instead consider the more inclusive perspective that our multilingual, multicultural student body offers a distinct context for the teaching of writing.

In what follows, we share our experiences building a strategically-curated portfolio of partnerships with the goal of sustaining the institutional reach and relevance of our WAC program. Specifically, we describe within the framework of our taxonomy several of the partnerships we have cultivated and outline successes and challenges with such a programmatic approach. Finally, we provide reflective questions other programs might use to identify and/or strengthen productive strategic partnerships at their own institutions.

THEORIZING OUR STRATEGIC PARTNERSHIPS

Below we categorize some examples of the WAC partnerships we have developed at our home institution, indicating both benefits and drawbacks to our program's development and sustainability. We do so with the realization that each university's infrastructure differs significantly and that the partners we describe might be unique to our context. Still, our aim is that they serve to illustrate our partnership categories and to indicate that our proposed classification necessarily includes fluidity as relationships develop and shift.

Imposed Partnerships: As noted above, imposed partnerships are those that are initiated outside the partnership, often in efforts to accomplish an institutional goal. For example, in our program's early days, WAC consultants were assigned to specific schools by our provost's office to work with faculty to increase writing in their majors. WAC consultants kept office hours in the colleges such as education, engineering, and business with the goal of supporting faculty in teaching with writing. We further define this relationship as one that is *imposed/identity-building*, as WAC efforts were foregrounded. By agreeing to pilot WAC consultants in various schools, the WAC program gained funding for hires and course releases. Additionally, with the provost's office financial support, we hosted several well-attended WAC workshops and benefited from the expertise of national WAC consultants. The design of locating WAC consultants in schools, in the end, was not sustainable partially due to changes in school and provost office leadership. However, our program still benefits from gained resources and a number of the faculty who were participants in these partnership efforts are still active in WAC, so the relationship resulted in program growth.

Another imposed partnership is with the Center for Excellence in Writing (CEW), a unit that has a close relationship with our WAC program. Unlike at some other institutions where WAC is part of the writing center, at our institution, WAC and CEW are two separate entities with different operations and tasks. Still, we share the same mission of promoting a writing culture on campus, and the writing center staff are also our colleagues in the English department. Our collaboration with the CEW centers on the writing fellows program, which is housed in the CEW. The writing fellows program started before the formation of WAC, and we entered into the collaboration at the request of higher administration in our university who wanted to provide WAC training for faculty working with undergraduate student writing fellows to maximize their investment in the program. While the writing center trains writing fellows to work as peer writing mentors, our WAC team was tasked to focus on faculty development to best facilitate the effective use of the fellows in the courses within which they were embedded. We define this partnership as *imposed/supportive,* as our program was tasked to work with an established program housed in another unit. However, for our CEW colleagues, the partnership was an imposition that seemed to disrupt the work they had already been doing and the vision they had of the program, a vision that did not include systemized faculty development.

Since the fellows program predated the WAC program, it was somewhat challenging for their administration to see the value of WAC to their original programmatic operations, which focused solely on the training of writing fellows and not the faculty who participate in the fellows program. Therefore, the partnership has become one that is not systemized or coordinated. Instead, our WAC program offers support to the faculty who are assigned fellows, creating within the larger context of an imposed partnership opportunities for invitational partnerships for those faculty who choose to accept WAC support. We have had success with some faculty in this program who are receptive to our outreach. However, not all the faculty accept our invitation, and we struggle to persuade these faculty of our relevance. Additionally, we encounter some administrative challenges, such as the coordination of the respective WAC and CEW responsibilities while not stepping on each other's toes. This experience has also been an important learning experience for us in forming strategic partnerships. Communication about clear responsibility division and expectations for the collaboration should precede any concrete collaborative actions, especially for imposed partnerships, and any resistance from either side needs to be addressed or negotiated from the onset.

Invitational Partnerships: These partnerships develop from the initiative of one party in the partnership. One of our primary invitational partners is with the FIU Center for Advancement in Teaching (CAT), a collaboration motivated by our common interest in faculty pedagogical development across disciplines. We have collaborated on many workshops with common WAC topics and principles, such as giving effective feedback, alternative writing assessment, writing assignment design, and understanding and addressing plagiarism. In addition, as the need for hybrid and remote teaching rose on campus during the pandemic, we helped facilitate the CAT hybrid training and remote teaching training programs. As a result of this collaboration, our relationship with the center has been enhanced, and we have connected with more faculty across campus who have subsequently contacted us for additional pedagogical support and who have joined our program listserv and received our program newsletter.

Still, despite the ways in which our WAC identity on campus has grown as a result of our collaboration with CAT, our identity is also often overshadowed by CAT during the actual collaborations. This is due to the fact that CAT is a much larger entity on campus, complete with office space, staff, and a budget, resulting in wider and broader influence. Therefore, our collaborative workshops and other programming most often occur under the CAT moniker. In this way, this partnership functions mainly as an *invitational/supportive* partnership in which WAC takes a supporting role and CAT takes the lead. Even when we have taken the lead in a specific faculty development activity, we find that faculty participants still view CAT as the host due to the programming, advertisement, or sometimes location of the event. Recently, CAT's leadership acknowledged the importance of more intentionally building WAC identity through the collaboration, and we expect to explore ways of leveraging this partnership as an identity-building one.

Similarly, our partnership with FIU Online is one that is *invitational/supportive*. FIU Online is a well-funded and visible unit charged with preparing faculty across campus for online teaching and maintaining online courses as they run. The COVID-induced remote teaching context in the academic year 2020–2021 led to this new partnership. As a result of many faculty being rushed into remote teaching during the onset of the pandemic, FIU Online developed the Remote Teach Ready Badge (RTRB) and encouraged faculty to obtain the badge by attending a series of workshops on various remote teaching topics. FIU Online invited WAC to partner with them by offering a workshop as part of the requirement for the RTRB. We agreed to participate, and our workshop, which became a staple in the badge training sessions, focused on developing and facilitating online discussions. We identify this partnership as invitational and supportive, as we were providing WAC support in the university-wide initiative that was planned and executed by FIU Online. Through this collaboration, we were able to reach out to more faculty who may have not heard of WAC before, and we have also gained a new partnership—which we believe will lead to future collaborations, some with WAC taking a leading role.

Invitational/Identity-building partnerships are those in which WAC's identity is foregrounded from the start. This type of partnership is seen in the one we have with our faculty senate. While our state university system has a writing-intensive requirement, called the Gordon Rule Writing (GRW) requirement, our university had no mechanism for certifying or reviewing these courses until the development of WAC. Stemming from WAC outreach to the faculty senate chair to make the argument for such oversight, faculty senate established the Gordon Rule Oversight and WAC Committee to recommend university policies for the designation and recertification of GRW courses. WAC worked with the senate chair to establish a committee that included WAC directors and faculty members from various disciplines who had participated in WAC training or who were at least knowledgeable about our mission and values. Through this committee, we have established clear expectations for GRW courses based on WAC best practices.

The partnership with faculty senate that resulted in the Gordon Rule Oversight Committee was an invitational one; however, for some department chairs and faculty, the oversight committee can represent an imposed relationship. WAC encounters some resistance from departments and individual faculty who do not share the senate's felt need to have oversight of the GRW courses; they argue that faculty and departments are already under various accreditation oversight and such additional oversight adds unnecessary burden and workload. WAC works to redefine such relationships as more invitational by reaching out to departments and faculty to help clarify the GRW requirements and assist those faculty tasked with moving their department's courses through the approval process. Through such efforts, we have built sustained relationships. Also, working with the faculty senate offers additional benefits, including enhancing WAC's visibility on campus, supporting WAC's advocacy to the university upper administration, and boosting campus writing culture by making our WAC work known to the faculty representatives across disciplines in the senate.

Other *Invitational/ Identity-Building* partnerships are those we have formed with grant-supported initiatives. For example, FIU has a Mellon grant-funded program called the Humanities Edge (HE), which supports transfer students coming to FIU from the local transfer pathway partner college and majoring in the humanities. Given the HE's goal of supporting student success across the humanities, we approached HE leadership about how both of our programs might work together to support humanities faculty. They were excited to collaborate with the WAC program, and we view this relationship as an invitational partnership. One result of our collaboration with HE was a WAC Meet-n-Greet and Luncheon for humanities faculty held during the fall 2019 semester. As we started brainstorming with HE for this event, we worked together to identify the unique resources and strengths that both programs bring to the partnership; we then decided how to best structure this collaboration. As previously mentioned, our WAC program does not have its own source of funding; therefore, we agreed that the HE would offer their funding and outreach resources to invite faculty to the event and provide lunch for the attendees. WAC, in turn, would provide pedagogical resources to support the teaching of writing in the humanities and be present at the event to discuss such resources with the faculty. Since WAC took a visible lead during the event itself, we consider this partnership to also be identity-building. Not only did we share writing resources with many faculty for the first time, but the sign-in sheet for this event ultimately gave rise to our WAC email list, which we have since continued to build for outreach purposes.

Another Mellon grant-funded initiative at FIU is Project THINC: Teaching Humanities in the New Context. The overarching goal of Project THINC is to provide support around curricular development and scholarship for humanities faculty. One way Project THINC does so is by supporting a small number of humanities faculty in a course redesign based on learning-centeredness and inclusiveness. Upon hearing about this course redesign program, we recognized the potential for a strategic partnership in that our WAC program and Project THINC aim to support pedagogical growth and best teaching practices for our faculty. We therefore approached Project THINC about offering a workshop to support their course redesign plans, and our invitation was accepted. Since these initial conversations, we have worked with Project THINC to support two of their course redesign cohorts. Each time, Project THINC has connected us with their faculty cohort, and we have designed workshops to support the course redesigns. Beyond providing faculty contact information, Project THINC does not participate in the workshop plans or delivery; thus, faculty are fully aware that the workshops are designed and facilitated by WAC, and we therefore categorize this partnership as identity-building. This is not to say that Project THINC does not benefit as well. In reality, this partnership is mutually beneficial. With WAC's writing pedagogy expertise offered to Project THINC, their course redesign program is ultimately more robust, which makes it more beneficial for the faculty participants and also enhances the end-of-grant report Project THINC submits to the university and their funders.

SUCCESSES AND CHALLENGES OF THE STRATEGIC PARTNERSHIPS

Through these collaborative and strategic efforts, our WAC program aims to continue its broad mission of curricular and pedagogical changes with regard to writing, even in the face of fluctuations in funding and institutional support for our program. Our efforts in forming strategic partnerships clearly bear some successes. One major success is the increased reach and campus visibility of the WAC program. Through strategic partnerships, WAC served over 450 faculty last year compared to under 100 that were served at the height of our grant-funded efforts. As a result of this increased reach, we see evidence of shifts in faculty views of writing and writing instruction. Especially relevant to our institutional context in which 65 percent of our students identify as Hispanic and close to 60 percent report living in a household in which English is not the first language, we are seeing faculty more readily consider the potential for writing to support multilingual students' learning (IPEDS, n.d.). For instance, we recently hosted a WAC summit in partnership with the Humanities Edge. The theme of the summit was "Teaching Humanities with Writing in Urban, Multilingual Contexts," and around 40 FIU faculty attended the event to hear panels of humanities faculty share their approaches to teaching with writing. Much of the conversation focused on the ways in which faculty from various disciplines are designing writing assignments with the strengths and needs of our multilingual students in mind. One faculty member described a recurring journaling assignment where students are invited to communicate in multiple languages and with multiple modes, the purpose of which is to understand that writing can "be unfinished or inhabiting the gray space between two or more languages and materialities." Another faculty offered a similar sentiment in her discussion of the ways in which she encourages students to mix languages and dialects in low-stakes digital writing assignments. These assignments, she explained, show students "how linguistic choices can be used to leverage stronger connections to audience."

Additionally, we are seeing faculty interest grow in assessment practices that foreground issues of equity and inclusion. Our recent workshop on alternative assessments drew almost 40 faculty interested in practices such as specifications grading, collaborative rubrics, and contract grading. Throughout the workshop, we discussed the potential for alternative assessment practices such as these to create classrooms that are more inclusive and learner-centered. Faculty also commented on the need to "ungrade" and give students autonomy in the grading process. Following this workshop, several faculty asked for our help in reconsidering their approaches to assessment, and the Diversity, Equity, and Inclusion committee in the School of Social Work invited us to host a similar workshop for their faculty. We see that one workshop sometimes has a ripple effect in expanding and enhancing the transformative teaching practices that we advocate.

Not only have we seen a positive shift in faculty views, but we have also experienced increased trust with our campus partners, as evidenced by our ongoing work with CAT and the faculty senate. Our work with such well-known campus partners has led to more robust faculty buy-in across campus, as illustrated in increased faculty participation in WAC events and a greater number of faculty reaching out to WAC for individual support and consultations. We take this increased faculty interaction as a sign that our collaborations—even the ones that are initially imposed—have been fruitful in promoting WAC relevancy across campus. The increased trust also earns us more identity-building opportunities with current and new partners. Recently, for example, we formed a new partnership, after being invited to submit a proposal to the Office of Micro-credentialing in Academic & Student Affairs. The proposal was funded to support a WAC badging course and to compensate faculty who complete the badge. Faculty interest in the WAC badge is robust, with 57 faculty applying to our first badging course in the summer of 2022. Additionally, after partner events, we invite participants to subscribe to our WAC mailing list and are able to share our newsletter—which includes teaching tips, faculty spotlights, and promotions of upcoming events—with a much larger audience, further building WAC identity and faculty buy-in.

That said, while these partnerships have their strengths, they also have their challenges, the largest of which is that our WAC identity is overshadowed by that of the larger partner. Yet, due to our limited resources, our WAC program often needs to collaborate with larger campus partners with more resources and greater reach. As we have described, these partnerships have been voluntary, imposed, and supportive, and some of them have transformed into identity-building partnerships. However, when collaborations with these larger campus partners are only ever supportive, our WAC program identity is subsumed under the umbrella of these larger groups, which ultimately makes it more difficult to develop WAC as an independent campus program. It is important to maintain a strong WAC identity on our campus as one of our main reasons for establishing a WAC program was to centralize the teaching of writing across disciplines and challenge the marginalization of writing on campus. To advocate for WAC pedagogy and, more importantly, to be able to initiate changes in the institutional writing culture, our WAC program needs to sustain its independent identity and establish itself as a major voice in the institutional network.

The challenge of a subsumed WAC identity and less autonomy is a complex one to tackle. But as Cox, Galin, and Melzer (2018a) state, the resiliency of a WAC program depends on its ability to overcome challenges and obstacles (p. 81). To promote WAC as an independent campus program, we attempt to strike a balance between supportive and identity-building partnerships—that is, between supporting and working with larger campus partners while also maintaining a unique WAC identity and agenda. One way of doing so is by purposefully pursuing identity-building collaborations where the WAC identity and mission remain central. This does not mean that we forgo supportive partnerships with larger and/or more robust groups on campus; it just means that we think carefully about these partnerships, the events in which we participate, and how we market and promote these events. Importantly, we consider the strategic steps we can take to make sure our portfolio of curated partnerships includes a balance of supportive and identity-building collaborations.

A specific example of such strategic planning is how we position ourselves into an identity-building partnership with the Humanities Edge (HE) despite our limited resources. In reflecting on our partnership with the HE, we recognize that one reason they were willing to partner with us is that we offer mutually beneficial events that do not take much planning or facilitating on their part. Put simply, we need their institutional resources in order to offer compensation and reach a large number of faculty. They need our expertise with cross-disciplinary writing-intensive classes to provide pedagogical support to humanities faculty. The result of this partnership has been WAC-sponsored events made possible by the support of the HE, rather than HE workshops in which WAC participates. Although a subtle difference, we believe this is an important distinction, one that allows us to promote WAC as a fully-functioning, independent campus program. Importantly, the identity and mission of the WAC program remains central through the marketing, implementation, and follow-up of the events, which is significant in our efforts to balance working within the larger university context while maintaining a unique WAC identity and agenda.

BUILDING STRATEGIC PARTNERSHIPS IN VARIOUS INSTITUTIONAL CONTEXTS

In sharing our classification of and experiences with strategic partnerships, our hope is that other WAC programs will consider the potential for various campus partnerships to support and sustain their programs. Of course, each institution has its own context, and it is important for individual WAC programs to consider what a strategically-curated portfolio of partnerships might look like on their campus.

In an effort to help our readers identify their own strategic partnerships, informed by Cox et al. (2018b), we offer a series of questions that other WAC programs might ask themselves as they begin to curate their own partnerships. We developed these questions as we reflected on our experiences with varying partnerships, and they are the types of questions we ask ourselves as we move forward with future partnerships. Our hope is that these questions will spark meaningful reflection and discussion among other WAC programs interested in creating their own strategically-curated portfolio of partnerships.

IDENTIFYING POTENTIAL STRATEGIC PARTNERSHIPS:

- What are some of the initiatives on your campus that upper administration currently supports (i.e., your institution's strategic plan, recent grant-funded programs, etc.)?
- What are some of the most robust programs and/or centers on campus? (Here, you might list various campus programs and centers, thinking about "robust" in terms of campus and/or community outreach, monetary resources, and faculty/staff support.)
- Are there other campus groups or programs focused on teaching with and/or promoting writing on campus (i.e., a campus writing center, a digital writing studio, etc.)?
- What are the new programs/initiatives developing on campus, and how might these provide fruitful ground for new partnerships?
- What are the demographics of your student population, and what specific writing-related needs can you identify on your campus?

PLANNING FOR INVITATIONAL STRATEGIC PARTNERSHIPS:

- What collaborative projects can you imagine that would support WAC goals and mission?
- What collaborative projects can you and/or your partners imagine that would support the goals and missions of your partners?
- What collaborative projects might support the goals and missions of both your WAC program and those of your partner?
- What is the existing relationship between your WAC program and the programs you identified above? How might you leverage these relationships for further, mutually beneficial collaboration?

Developing Strategic Partnerships:

- What resources does your WAC program have at its disposal, and what resources does your WAC program lack (i.e., budget, full and/or part-time faculty, course releases, graduate and/or undergraduate student interns, mailing list, etc.)?
- In what specific partnerships, if any, is your WAC program already engaged? Are these partnerships invitational, imposed, supportive, and/or identity-building?
- Consider the potential fluidity of existing partnerships. For example, are there opportunities for WAC to take more of a leadership role in current supportive partnerships? Are there ways for imposed partnerships to shift toward invitational based on shared goals and priorities?
- In order to work with diverse partners, what specific types of partnerships might your WAC program pursue?

Sustaining Strategic Partnerships:

- How do the systems-level projects with larger campus partners lead to enduring changes on the campus culture of writing?
- How do micro-level projects (working with individual faculty) create opportunities for systems-level projects?
- How can your WAC program communicate regularly with various campus partners to maintain relevance and visibility (i.e., website, newsletter, campus committees, WAC signature events, etc.)?
- How can your WAC program monitor progress with and assess your partnerships so that your partnership portfolio continues to grow and includes a variety of partnership types?
- What steps can your WAC program take to help move supportive partnerships into identity-building partnerships in future collaborations?

Although this list of questions is certainly not exhaustive, we hope that it offers a helpful framework for how WAC programs might consider and pursue strategic partnerships within their specific institutional contexts. We have experienced firsthand the value of forming strategic partnerships on campus for building and sustaining a relevant WAC program. The four forms of strategic partnership we have cultivated all have enhanced our WAC work on campus and our WAC visibility, which supports our WAC program's sustainability. Looking forward, as Christopher Thaiss stated in his opening plenary speech for this IWAC conference, "There is no sustainability without adaptability" (Rutz & Thaiss, 2021). While we know very clearly we would like to sustain WAC faculty development practices and expand WAC's outreach and influence through our strategic partnerships, changes happen every day, every semester, and every year. Therefore, what we hold on to and what adaptations we make are perennial considerations. We offer our experiences with and categorizations of partnership-building in an effort to provide a heuristic for establishing and developing institutional partnerships as new situations arise.

REFERENCES

Cox, M., Galin, J. & Melzer, D. (2018a). Building sustainable WAC programs: A whole systems approach. *The WAC Journal, 29*, 64–87. https://doi.org/10.37514/WAC-J.2018.29.1.03.

Cox, M., Galin, J. & Melzer, D. (2018b). *Sustainable WAC: A whole systems approach to launching and developing writing across the curriculum programs.* NCTE.

Cox, M. & Zawacki, T. M. (2014). Introduction. In T. M. Zawacki & M. Cox (Eds.), *WAC and second language writers: Research towards linguistically and culturally inclusive programs and practices* (pp. 15–40). The WAC Clearinghouse; Parlor Press. https://doi.org/10.37514/PER-B.2014.0551.1.3.

IPEDS Data Collection System. (n.d.). Retrieved March 19, 2023, from https://nces.ed.gov/ipeds/datacenter/institutionprofile.aspx?unitId=133951&goToReportId=6.

Rutz, C. & Thaiss, C. (2021, August 2–6). *Opening plenary: WAC fearlessness, sustainability, and adaptability over five decades* [Conference presentation]. Fifteenth International Writing Across the Curriculum Conference, Fort Collins, CO, United States. https://youtu.be/UJ9p8q-xZNo?list=PLGneEQPQbvyLsWkkRLtvQSAgCDYb9bEoG.

SECTION 2. PEDAGOGICAL CONSIDERATIONS

In the second section of this collection, we focus on the generative and collaborative spaces of WAC classrooms and writing centers to investigate issues of pedagogy, including those that promote diversity, equity, inclusion, and justice (DEIJ). The chapters included in this section explore how faculty are teaching writing through critical reflection and creative nonfiction. They consider the implications of algorithms that structure our engagement with student work, from learning management systems to disciplinary genres, and they propose and describe innovative theories and curricula that support students in learning and growing as writers. The authors in this section provide valuable reflections on the past, present, and future of WAC approaches to instructing and engaging student writers.

Opening this section, **Julie Birt** and **Christy Goldsmith** consider the definition of critical reflection as it is taught through the writing-intensive (WI) courses at their institution. They mention how the 2015 University of Missouri student protests and the 2016 presidential election prompted them to think critically about their dataset of WI course proposals and, specifically, the role that writing can have in (re)shaping cultures of teaching and learning. In an analysis of assignment prompts and instructor reflection, their research examines the varying ways reflective writing is defined and used in writing-intensive courses as well as ways to leverage reflective writing to promote inclusive teaching across the disciplines. Birt and Goldsmith's chapter matters as WAC continues to ask how writing can impact the changing conditions of teaching and learning on our college campuses. For example, they observe how WI course proposals favored argumentative writing over reflection. We find their observation notable because, at a time of social and political unrest, they recognized within the course frameworks how arguing without reflection can be a missed opportunity for students to grapple with their own experiences, knowledges, and beliefs including the ways in which their arguments are shaped. Birt and Goldsmith's chapter reminds us of what reflective writing can do in strengthening student learning across the disciplines because it is an asset for students to evaluate the processes underlying the conversations they join.

Continuing the theme of reflective composing, **James P. Austin** argues for incorporating elements of creative nonfiction (CNF) into our pedagogical approaches in order to encourage student learning in the disciplines by writing from a personal disposition. Drawing from his teaching experience in Egypt, Austin's chapter identifies opportunities for creative writing approaches in the transfer of learning by using CNF to support students' understanding of their own learning processes and themselves within their learning processes. This work is important to consider as WAC examines innovations in teaching and learning that include what it means to value the assets, resources, and experiences of all students as they engage writing in the disciplines through multiple modes of writing.

Using personal narrative to convey their varied and various experiences within educational contexts, particularly in writing centers, **William J. Macaulay, Jr.**, **Pamela B. Childers**, and **Brandall C. Jones** reflect on the critical role that writing centers have and can continue to play in creating equitable learning environments. Macaulay et al. recognize how writing centers—often safer spaces that promote diverse discourses across campus—are also where WAC work happens. In this chapter, Jones describes his high school writing center, which was directed by Childers, as "the space that welcomed my unique self" (p. 130), and he acknowledges the role of this space in his own personal development, leading him to an accomplished career in the arts. The authors end by offering concrete suggestions for how to take an antiracist and inclusive approach to WAC-based writing center work. They use narrative to chronicle a welcome yet unexpected outcome of their IWAC 2020–21 collaboration: getting to know each other's perspectives on a deeper level.

Shifting focus to the digital spaces in our classrooms, **Kathleen Daly Weisse** addresses the use of big data in higher education for measuring student learning and questions the problematic ways in which learning management systems (LMS) assess student participation. In her chapter, Weisse critiques the use of these "digital traces," particularly in Canvas, and makes a powerful argument for WAC practitioners: "the problem is that assessing learning with these technologies demands that learning itself be re-defined and reconfigured so as to be measurable by such a tool" (p. 145). She cautions that faculty need to think twice before relying on prescribed indicators of learning. Her critiques are significant to WAC because they reveal the assumptions related to participation that can be consequential to learning assessment and student outcomes. As WAC seeks to lead discussions and practices of pedagogical innovation, addressing assumptions of student participation that can be framed by digital learning platforms will become increasingly important for how we discuss assessment at our colleges and universities.

In conversation with Weisse, **Angela J. Zito** concludes this section with an exploration of how disciplinary genres function similarly to LMS algorithms, thereby influencing our pedagogical practices and assessments. Using the literary analysis essay as a case study, Zito interviews English instructors and interrogates how teaching of these conventions leads to the perpetuation of inequitable, racist, colonial assessment practices. This chapter illustrates how "disciplinary genre conventions can conceal as well as reveal aspects of student learning" (p. 166) and must be used carefully and thoughtfully when used to assess non-writing student learning outcomes.

CHAPTER 7.
ACCESSING CRITICAL REFLECTION TO PROMOTE INCLUSIVITY IN WRITING INTENSIVE COURSES

Julie Birt and Christy Goldsmith
University of Missouri

More than a century ago, John Dewey (1910) introduced the term "reflective thinking," describing a systematic action wherein the "successive portions of reflective thought grow out of one another and support one another" (p. 3). In his succeeding pages, Dewey develops a theory of intellectual thought that favors a balance of product and process, evidence-based choice making, and thoughtful inference—an iterative process we'd call "critical thinking" in our modern parlance. Similarly, in "Defining Reflection: Another Look at John Dewey and Reflective Thinking," Carol Rodgers (2002) revisits Dewey's foundational work and concludes, "Over the past 15 years, reflection has suffered from a loss of meaning. In becoming everything to everybody, it has lost the ability to be seen" (p. 843).

This loss of meaning is illustrated in the varied definitions of "reflection" across disciplines and contexts. In the sciences, reflection is sometimes defined through its metacognitive functions—namely, thinking about thinking or "self-understanding" and thinking about process or "self-regulation." (Brown, 1987). Other theorists focus on the social purpose of reflection in higher education with its goal to "transform practice in some way, whether it is the practice of learning or the practice of the discipline or the profession" (Ryan, 2011, p. 103).

Extending the conversation to adult learning communities, Stephen Brookfield (1996) developed a theory of *critical* reflection that is activated via experiential learning and requires adult learners to "question and then replace or reframe an assumption [by] recognizing the hegemonic aspects of dominant cultural values" (p. 376). However, though these pedagogues have been writing about reflective thinking for nearly a century, as Kathleen Blake Yancey (1998) writes, even in composition classrooms, "reflection has played but a small role in [the] history of composing" (p. 7).

Our exploration of reflection in writing intensive (WI) classes at our university began amidst the social and political turmoil following the 2015 University of Missouri student protests and the 2016 presidential election. While we were engaging in real time discussion and reflection on our campus, we noticed that our dataset—i.e., WI course proposals—contained much about *argument* but little about *reflection*. Of course, the disparity in representation of these genres is not surprising. The trend echoes James Britton et al.'s (1975) findings about transactional versus expressive language in secondary writing and mirrors Dan Melzer's (2014) wide-reaching study of postsecondary writing assignments. However, while Melzer laments how infrequently students are required to "relate course content to personal experiences and interests, use personal experiences to develop and support their arguments, or reflect on their own learning" (p. 33), he also highlights the unique position of WAC programs to continue to increase writing variety, including reflective writing. As WAC administrators, we saw the local and national discussions about racial equity, justice, free speech, and the facade of neutrality as a catalyst (Seltzer, 2018). This intersection of context and research provided us with an opportunity to investigate the current state of reflective writing in WI courses, and it allowed us to consider the possibilities of reflective writing to produce more inclusive teaching across the disciplines.

In this chapter, we examine how reflective writing emerges in WI course design for various disciplines at our institution. We overview our established WAC program, use grounded theory methodology to create a definition, examine the qualities of reflective writing described by WI instructors, and suggest ways reflective writing can be incorporated in writing courses as inclusive pedagogy.

RESEARCH CONTEXT

Situated at a large flagship and land grant university with a robust WAC program, our study drew on a comprehensive data set. Each semester a WI course is taught, the instructor must submit a proposal for approval to meet the WI guidelines. This WI proposal includes responding to the question: "Explain briefly the nature of the assignment(s) which address(es) a question for which there is more than one acceptable interpretation, explanation, analysis or evaluation." For this study, we analyzed the responses to this question in 351 WI course proposals equally situated across the natural and applied sciences (n=116), humanities and arts (n=117), and education and social science courses (n=118).

Data Analysis

We used grounded theory analyses to position our study in the "social, historical, local, and interactional context" of our institution and program (Charmaz, 2014, p. 322). In our previous study (Goldsmith, Birt & Lannin, 2019), we broadly categorized the instructors' responses (n=351) into six types of writing assignments that engage students in complex problems in their discipline. For this study, we focused on the category with the fewest instances: critical reflection (n=26).

Our first round of analysis centered on developing a final definition for critical reflection. We had originally created an initial definition that forefronted individual positionality: "Writing assignments that ask students to think critically about their own positionality while reflecting on course material or course experiences." During this round of analysis, we investigated ways in which the identified responses either agreed or disagreed with our initial definition for critical reflection. However, as we focused only on the assignments we collectively coded as "critical reflection," we found that our previous definition of reflection was too limited. Our new definition of critical reflection, which incorporated those responses that disagreed with our original definition, then became:

> writing assignments where instructors do more than ask students to turn inward, they ask students to deepen their disciplinary learning by thinking critically about any (or all) of the following: their own positionality, the choices made in their project, the audience of their work and/or the course material.

We created this broader definition of reflection before moving into deeper analyses of the specific characteristics of reflection.

Next, we reviewed the critical reflection instructor responses and categorized seven qualities identified in the data through open coding using the constant comparative method (Charmaz, 2010). For example, Julie developed the *subjective with no right answer* code, which included responses such as "not necessarily the 'correctness' of ideas" and "their unique response is celebrated rather than questioned." Christy created the *to uncover something hidden or ignored* code, which included responses such as "uncover hidden meaning, and explore underlying assumptions" and "explore own belief system and moral compass." During research team meetings, we reached agreement on codes and further condensed these seven categories based on commonalities across both researchers' codes to generate the final findings described below. We recorded individual and team interpretations and categorizations of the data in memos for record-keeping of the data analysis process.

FINDINGS

Our broader definition of reflection, which included asking students to think critically beyond themselves, helped to sketch a clearer picture of the qualities and types of reflective writing in WI writing assignments, expanding the possibilities for including reflection in WI classes.

Finding #1: Qualities of WI Reflective Writing

We found that, in WI courses, critical reflection included three overarching qualities: responding subjectively, moving from personal to social, and contemplating contextually-bound problems.

Responding Subjectively

Within the reflective writing activities, we see a focus on the "room" or "space" for individual student experiences. In many instances, instructors expect students to respond subjectively to a writing prompt, which is often a departure from more traditional content-first approaches in the disciplines. For example, one instructor describes an assignment requiring students to "adapt forms from readings to accommodate their own autobiographies."[1] Another instructor assigns reading responses to "invite students to take passages from the readings and critique, question, and connect to their own lives." In a theater course, students analyze screen plays, "based primarily in phenomenology, with students first noting their subjective response to a work and coming up with an essence for that work, bracketing out any received wisdom, so that their unique response is celebrated rather than questioned." These types of assignments illustrate how instructors allow students space to integrate, and even celebrate, their own experiences while learning the content of the course.

Moving from Personal to Social

Instructors also ask students to consider how their individual experiences interact with the larger social environment and even reflect that backwards on themselves. In one course, students reflect on "their own personalities and biographies

---

1 Unless otherwise noted, all quotes are taken from individual course proposals, which were categorized as an example of reflection.

and bring these into conversation with questions of global citizenship and planetary responsibility." Another instance prompts film students to "first . . . read and write about the opinions of others. Then . . . begin with their own reactions and evaluations of film work."

Students may also be expected to consider their own life experiences before analyzing the experiences of a culture outside of their own. One instructor plans writing assignments that "involve a personal side which is up to the individual's experience in terms of how they respond and draw parallels with the Amish." In another instance, students are asked to move from being one scholar/student to consider the larger research community. In all of these instances, students must acknowledge their subject position and negotiate the course content—and often the social aspect of the topic—to produce a unique interpretation for the writing prompt.

Contemplating Contextually-Bound Problems

Overall, we established that these reflective writing assignments take place in context—whether it is the context of the classroom, course content, or an individual student's prior experiences. We first noted context as important in the data via an assignment that asks students "to bring their individual experiences with service into the context of the classroom and texts." This assignment led us to notice context in many other assignments. For example, in another course, students tackle "sensitive and challenging issues on which there may be considerable disagreement (e.g., purpose of Black Lives Matter movement, ban on refugees from Muslim-majority countries, etc.)."

WI instructors also make clear to their students that context can affect their writing. This focus on contextual writing is shown more explicitly in one reflective writing assignment from the social sciences: "Leadership concepts, to a large extent, are influenced by contextual factors and perceptions of leaders and followers, based upon their unique situation. The instructor embraces the notion that students will have different experiences and multiple perspectives regarding interpersonal interactions." Thus, there are multiple ways instructors leverage context to provide a place for students' reflective writing.

These overarching characteristics speak to the ways reflective writing activities can deepen disciplinary learning while also engaging students' experiences and knowledge. The qualities present in reflection—responding subjectively, moving from personal to social, and contemplating contextually-bound problems—emphasize the power of language to support examination of individual beliefs and taken-for-granted assumptions.

Finding #2: Specific Types of WI Reflective Writing Assignments

Through creating metaphorical buckets in which instances of WI reflective writing could be placed, our second finding categorized specific types of reflective writing in our dataset. *Traditional* reflective writing tasks focus the students' reflection inward while *reflection for metacognition* and *reflection to grapple with belief systems* require students to critically analyze the learning process and explore belief systems outside of their own.

Traditional Reflective Writing

We found the more novel reflection assignments—the ones that spoke to our expanded definition of critical reflection—to be the most interesting, but we must acknowledge that our dataset also contained traditional reflection tasks (Calderhead, 1989; Farrah, 1988; Gore & Zeichner, 1991), asking students to wrestle with their own viewpoints. In these assignments, students often consider an evocative situation and interrogate their own positionality. In a humanities class, students must "write beyond 'the reading made me feel . . .'" In a social sciences class, students might be required to "focus [their] attention on an aspect of our social lives we tacitly agree to ignore." In these instances, students perform individual, isolated reflection that has the capacity to get them to think more deeply about their learning or positionality (Elbow, 1991; Greene, 2011; Lawrence, 2013; Yancey, 1998) but which does not foster inclusion as powerfully as the other two categories of reflective writing assignments: *reflection for metacognition* and *reflection to grapple with belief systems*.

Reflection for Metacognition

Reflection for metacognition requires students to think beyond their individual reaction and move towards action, often requiring revision of previous writing/thinking or motivating different choices for the future. Assignments in this category of critical reflective writing might require students to "evaluate their own learning in the context of the themes [the class] proposes," or instructors might ask students to "[go] back, [review their] decisions, and [not make] the same mistake twice." Xiang Huang and Calvin S. Kalman (2012) describe this type of reflective writing that asks students to work in a "hermeneutical circle" by going back and forth between the textbook and their experiences, all while considering their own understanding of the course concepts. In short, these metacognitive reflective writing tasks engage students in writing with the goal of impacting their future course performance and disciplinary decision-making. In contrast to more traditional reflection tasks that ask writers to only consider their individual viewpoint, metacognitive reflection tasks ask writers to negotiate both their own positionality and their content learning.

Reflection to Grapple with Belief Systems

We were especially interested in one instructor who used the verb "grapple" to characterize their reflective writing assignment. This literature professor required students to "describe [their] response to a specific literary work from class, to explain what it is about the work that evokes that response, and then to 'grapple' with that response in some way." We see this particular assignment as a bridge between more traditional reflective writing (which focuses on the self) to our more expansive definition of reflection that explores broader social concepts. In this category—*grapple with belief systems*—students must reflect on concepts by applying belief systems outside their own.

We define "belief systems" broadly to mean not only religious or political beliefs but also beliefs about the ways we *do* certain disciplines—i.e., composing a journalistic piece or completing an engineering model. For example, one task requires that "students examine the consequences of the use of nuclear weapons from the perspective of those in the target area." Another instructor asks students to identify their own perspective in one discussion board post and then "take the opposite position [of] their initial post in reply to another student's post." In this category, WI instructors require students not only to be aware of their individual choices within the context of the discipline; they require students to interrogate the ways in which disciplines are constituted.

From the traditional writing tasks that ask students to analyze their positionality to the more active tasks where students have to negotiate their learning, the diversity of approaches reflected in our data reveal multiple entry points into reflective writing available to instructors.

IMPLICATIONS: REFLECTION AS AN INCLUSIONARY PROCESS

Through our iterative analysis process, we expanded our focus to encapsulate all applications of reflective writing that we saw in our WI course assignments. We believe our particular findings speak to the powerful connection between an expansive view of critical reflection and inclusive WI teaching. In their article arguing to legitimize reflective writing in the Scholarship of Teaching and Learning (SoTL), Alison Cook-Sather, Sophia Abbot, and Peter Felten (2019) write, "The genre of reflective writing constitutes a kind of brave space; it does not promise to protect and exempt people from the challenge that real learning and growth require" (p. 19). We echo their words and suggest that broadening what counts as reflection in undergraduate education has the potential to produce more inclusive WI classes. In the following discussion, we define inclusion through the lens of our university, create a model of critical reflection for use in faculty development sessions, and conclude by considering the impact of reflective writing across contexts.

Defining Inclusion

The Inclusive Excellence Framework at our university provides the following definition of inclusion:

> The active, intentional, and on-going engagement with diversity—in people, in the curriculum, in the co-curriculum, and in communities with which individuals might connect—in ways that increase one's awareness, content knowledge, cognitive sophistication, and empathic understanding of the complex ways individuals interact with and within systems and institutions. (Office of Institutional Equity, 2022)

We contend that the reflective writing qualities and types we detail here meet the components of inclusion in our institution's Inclusive Excellence Framework. Through reflective writing, instructors support students as they explore complex and varying viewpoints while also furthering content learning in disciplinary courses. Specifically, critical reflective writing assignments are a way for instructors to draw on the unique experiences of the diverse set of students in their classrooms. For example, the negotiation required in metacognitive reflective writing is an active process, often calling for students to reevaluate and/or navigate their learning with peers. Through critical reflection, students are invited to explore, consider, and analyze a variety of viewpoints that reveal the "complex ways individuals interact with and within systems and institutions" (Office of Institutional Equity, 2022).

In his review of the reflection and inclusion literature in K-12 schools, Mark Minott (2019) found that a combination of reflective writing characteristics deepen the possibilities for inclusive learning. We heartily agree, but we are also cognizant that critical reflective writing, especially, might be a new endeavor for university instructors. Our analysis also reminded us that powerful reflective writing activities can take many forms—informal or formal, low or high stakes—and serve a variety of purposes, highlighting personal or social experiences, spurring thought or action. If we view these reflective writing activities as fluid and interconnected, we open up multiple entry points for disciplinary faculty to engage with reflective writing in their courses. Faculty can capitalize on the disciplinary discourse practices around the actual term "critical reflection" to make the practice more approachable for instructors who may be hesitant. If, for example, engineering instructors (such as those in our program) already include reflection for metacognition in their courses, a discussion of the other types of reflective writing might give them gentle encouragement to experiment with new reflective writing activities, which can become a low-stakes way to support students' engineering planning and design (Runnel et al., 2013).

A Reflection Continuum Toward a More Inclusive WI Pedagogy

We see the reflective writing assignments identified here not as a hierarchy—i.e., one type of reflective writing isn't necessarily "better" or "more inclusive" than others—but rather as a continuum (see Figure 7.1).

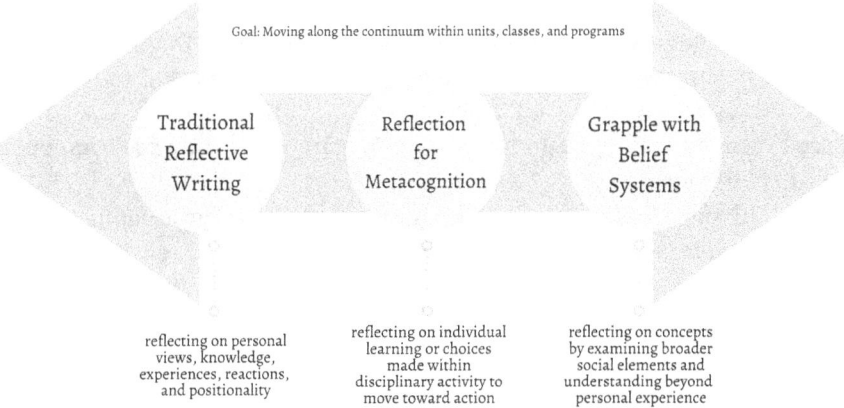

Figure 7.1. Continuum of Reflective Writing. This continuum moves from more traditional (left) to more complex (right) reflection practices.

We situated each type of reflective writing horizontally to highlight the fluidity of movement possible between the category with a brief definition below the category name. The variety of outcomes indicated in this continuum—reflecting on personal views, individual learning, and broader social understanding—are outcomes we see in nearly all undergraduate majors in our WAC program. This continuum allows multiple entry points of engagement, and it highlights our eventual aim or endpoint: to move towards more inclusive WI classes via the integration of critical reflection where students use writing to grapple with belief systems in all disciplinary literacy courses.

As we can see from these writing elements and assignments, including critical reflection in any form serves to push against simplistic binary views of complex disciplinary issues and reveals that there is no universal process for learning. The more traditional reflective writing assignments are a way for instructors to draw on—and value—the unique experiences of diverse sets of students in their classrooms. The more complex forms of critical reflection ask students to interrogate disciplinary, social, or belief systems. Further, these assignments provide a relatively low-stakes way to write toward and beyond the content, asking students to grapple with this complexity without adding additional time for planning or grading.

As instructors design activities to move students along the critical reflective writing continuum, they create a space for critical thinking around new or contrasting ideas and highlight the value of exploring multiple pathways toward a solution. Rafael Otfinowski and Marina Silva-Opps (2015) demonstrate the possibilities that accompany thoughtful reflective writing exercises in the science classroom. Through explicit modeling of reflective writing in their biology course, they found that students were able to expand their critical thinking with greater confidence to challenge existing scientific concepts. Finally, by increasing opportunities for free writes, quick writes, and other informal writing activities, reflective assignments add value to writing-to-learn, an already key component of WAC philosophy.

We think these findings about WI critical reflective writing assignments have significant implications for the WAC/WID field. Most importantly, our findings begin to answer Brookfield's (1996) call for "more attention to how making meaning [and] critical thinking . . . are viscerally experienced processes" (p. 379). For students, learning can feel like a simple input (e.g., lecture or textbook reading) to a final output (e.g., exam or essay). Critical reflective writing activities make the learning process more complex for students, upending the simple input/output model and producing the "visceral experience" that Brookfield describes. Reflection highlights the ways learning is connected to values and prior knowledge, and it helps students see learning as something experienced through a process. Importantly, critical reflection extends learning even after the content is mastered or the project is completed.

If we return to the context with which we began this investigation, we are reminded of the ways the social and institutional climate impacts classroom learning. For example, on our campus during the 2015 student protests, some instructors made space for discussion and reflective writing to help students process their experiences *before* or even *while* they were engaging with course content. Abraham H. Maslow (1981) reminds us that students are unable to focus on cognitive learning if they don't feel a connection to their learning communities. Incorporating more reflection can provide students with that connection. If we expand reflective writing to go beyond the person and beyond metacognition—and if we encourage a variety of applications for critical reflection—we produce deeper learning and more inclusive WI classes. Further, this expansion has the possibility to increase student engagement and sense of belonging as students feel seen for their experiences and existing knowledge (Otfinowski & Silva-Opps, 2015). This sense of belonging is both a central tenet of our university's strategic plan and a core value of our WAC program.

Further highlighting the impact of the institutional climate, like many universities, budget considerations on our campus necessitate a direct connection between our WAC program's value and the mission of our university. Our analysis of the varied uses of critical reflection in WI classes has reaffirmed the value of reflection for us as WAC administrators and reminded us that, as Dewey (1910) wrote, reflective thinking has the quality to "grow" and "support" students' disciplinary thinking. The reflective thinking categories we establish here push Dewey's definition further, creating possibilities for inclusive WI classes rich with content learning *and* space for students to consider experiences, solutions, and identities outside of their own.

REFERENCES

Britton, J., Burgess, T., Martin, N., McLeod, A. & Rosen, H. (1975). *The development of writing abilities*. Macmillan.

Brookfield, S. (1996). Adult learning: An overview. In A. C. Tuijnman (Ed.), *International Encyclopedia of Adult Education and Training* (2nd ed.). Pergamon Press.

Brown, A. (1987). Metacognition, executive control, self-regulation, and other more mysterious mechanisms. In F. E. Weinert & R. H. Kluwe (Eds.), *Metacognition, motivation, and understanding* (pp. 60–108). Lawrence Erlbaum Associates.

Calderhead, J. (1989). Reflective teaching and teacher education. *Teaching and Teacher Education, 5,* 43–51. https://doi.org/10.1016/0742-051X(89)90018-8.

Charmaz, K. (2010). Grounded theory: Objectivist and constructivist methods. In W. Luttrell (Ed.), *Qualitative educational research: Readings in reflexive methodology and transformative practice* (pp. 183–207). Routledge.

Charmaz, K. (2014). *Constructing grounded theory* (2nd ed.). Sage.

Cook-Sather, A., Abbot, S. & Felten, P. (2019). Legitimating reflective writing in SoTL: "Dysfunctional illusions of rigor" revisited. *Teaching and Learning Inquiry, 7*(2), 14–27. https://doi.org/10.20343/teachlearninqu.7.2.2.

Dewey, J. (1910). *How we think* [Project Gutenburg e-book, 2011]. (Part I, pp. 1–56). http://www.gutenberg.org/files/37423/ 37423-h/37423-h.htm.

Elbow, P. (1991). Toward a phenomenology of freewriting. In P. Belanoff, P. Elbow & S. Fontaine (Eds.), *Nothing begins with n: New investigations of freewriting* (pp. 189–213). Southern Illinois University Press.

Farrah, H. (1998). The reflective thought process: John Dewey re-visited. *Journal of Creative Behavior, 22*, 1–8. https://doi.org/10.1002/j.2162-6057.1988.tb01338.x.

Goldsmith, C., Birt, J. & Lannin, A. (2019). *Engaging complexity in WAC/WID assignments: Against a dichotomous approach to argumentation in the disciplines* [Google slides]. Council of Writing Program Administrators.

Gore, J. & Zeichner, K. (1991). Action research and reflective teaching in preservice teacher education: A case study from the United States. *Teaching and Teacher Education, 7*, 119–136. https://doi.org/10.1016/0742-051X(91)90022-H.

Greene, K. (2011). Research for the classroom: The power of reflective writing. *The English Journal, 100*(4), 90–93. https://www.jstor.org/stable/23047788.

Huang, X. & Kalman, C. S. (2012). A case study on reflective writing. *Journal of College Science Teaching, 42*(1), 92. https://www.jstor.org/stable/43748411.

Lawrence, H. (2013). Personal, reflective writing: A pedagogical strategy for teaching business students to write. *Business Communication Quarterly, 76*(2), 192–206. https://doi:10.1177/1080569913478155.

Maslow, A. H. (1981). *Motivation and personality*. Prabhat Prakashan.

Melzer, D. (2014). *Assignments across the curriculum: A national study of college writing*. Utah State University Press.

Minott, M. (2019). Reflective teaching, inclusive teaching, and the teacher's task in the inclusive classroom: A literary investigation. *British Journal of Special Education, 46*, 226–238. https://doi.org/10.1111/1467–8578.12260.

Office of Institutional Equity. (2022). *Inclusive excellence framework*. University of Missouri. https://diversity.missouri.edu/our-work/inclusive-excellence-framework/.

Otfinowski, R. & Silva-Opps, M. (2015). Writing toward a scientific identity: Shifting from prescriptive to reflective writing in undergraduate biology. *Journal of College Science Teaching, 45*(2), 19–23. https://doi.org/10.2505/4/jcst15_045_02_19.

Rodgers, C. (2002). Defining reflection: Another look at John Dewey and reflective thinking. *Teachers College Record, 104*(4), 842–866. https://doi.org/10.1111/1467-9620.00181.

Runnel, M. I., Pedaste, M. & Leijen, Ä. (2013). Model for guiding reflection in the context of inquiry-based science education. *Journal of Baltic Science Education, 12*(1), 107. https://doi.org/10.33225/jbse/13.12.107.

Ryan, M. (2011). Improving reflective writing in higher education: a social semiotic perspective. T*eaching in Higher Education, 16*(1), 99–111. https://doi.org/10.1080/13562517.2010.507311.

Seltzer, R. (2018, September 12). Missouri 3 years later: Lessons learned, protests still resonate. *Inside Higher Ed.* https://www.insidehighered.com/news/2018/09/12/administrators-students-and-activists-take-stock-three-years-after-2015-missouri.

Yancey, K. B. (1998). *Reflection in the writing classroom*. Utah State University Press.

CHAPTER 8.
USING CREATIVE NONFICTION TO INFLUENCE STUDENT DISPOSITIONS TOWARD WRITING TRANSFER AND DEVELOPMENT: PEDAGOGICAL OPPORTUNITIES FOR WAC

James P. Austin
Central Connecticut State University

Years ago, when I sat in fiction workshops in my MFA program, I often asked myself a simple but important question: How does one learn to write literature? The creative writing workshops offered little in the way of actual writing instruction; instead, I would write, submit, and listen, twice each quarter, to the erudite critiques of my fellow MFA students. At that point, at least in my experience, the challenge of how to solve the various problems and shortcomings pointed out in critiques was mine alone. Some of my fellow MFA students appeared to have a feel for how to develop their writing under these conditions, and they thrived. However, for this writer, the structures and strictures of the graduate MFA workshop—that the writer must remain silent while their work is under free-ranging, personality-driven discussion; that the writer must sift through the mountains of feedback delivered primarily in written, formal critiques for which there was no instruction—left me with no sense of how to get better at discussing my peers' work, or writing critiques that would help them, and me, to improve in writing through such feedback. In many ways, my voice was silenced as I sat silently waiting for peers, many of whom had the same amount of experience as I did, to pass their judgment upon my work.

Felicia Rose Chavez (2021) has noted a racialized dimension to workshops that silence marginalized writers while favoring white voices and white writers; as a white man who attended an MFA workshop, I do not share the same experiences she narrates in her book, but I am sympathetic to its thesis and have felt, in my own way, as though I did not belong at the workshop table. I often felt out of step with the focus of the conversations—an assiduous rejection of context and a fastidious attention to the text on the page. While this approach can bring many benefits, in my MFA workshops, the absence of context limited the kinds of comments we were able to make, and as a result, some voices became more prominent than others. For me, I felt that some outside context could help me evaluate a workshop draft and could even enrich the kind of strict textual reading and analysis preferred by so many workshops. It might have helped me better understand the themes of a text written from outside my privileged perspective. Instead, context and text analysis often were situated in opposition to one another. At the conclusion of a workshop, we had provided (or received) significant oral and written feedback. But what to do with it all—how to actually revise a workshop submission for the better—was opaque in the feedback. This was, as I understood, the writer's job to figure out. None of this made sense to me.

There are many creative writers who publish books on craft, ranging from the free-spirited approaches advocated by writers like Natalie Goldberg and Anne Lamott (heroes of my undergraduate years) to how-to textbooks by writers like Janet Burroway. When it came time for me to teach creative writing, first in graduate school and later at a transnational university in Egypt, I did not use either sort of text. I wanted to build a pedagogy that at least addressed my own past confusion; I also wanted students to have a tangible sense of themes and sentence types typical of the genre to guide their development as readers into creative writers. I came to understand by teaching creative nonfiction (CNF) in Egypt that students needed to learn and practice some of the different kinds of sentences that built traditional CNF essays: narrative, figurative, and reflective. Together, these sentence types could help undergraduate writers create CNF essays that focused on an individual's journey and that were told from a perspective of greater wisdom, which allowed for reflection that attaches significance to narrated events. In so doing, I adapted some of my composition pedagogies to the teaching of CNF by showing students how different types of sentences could be composed and orchestrated to accomplish the work of CNF writing.

My perspective changed, however, when I began my doctoral program, and I was introduced to literacy studies, which focused my attention on the social-cultural aspects of communication and which caused me to reflect upon the social-cultural aspects of the CNF writing produced by my students in Egypt. The focus on context and history was a counterpoint to the experiences I described in my MFA writing workshops. Because of this new training, I became aware that my cosmopolitan Egyptian students had been writing about topics, and expressing attitudes about these topics, that were not typically present in Egyptian public discourse: sex, alcohol use, terminal illness, endemic sexual harassment, poverty, religious uncertainty, and more. I realized that these particular students could address these topics in the personalized ways expected of them in CNF: through narration and reflection from a vantage point of greater wisdom and maturity. This led me to see creative writing, and CNF in particular, as a form of western-based literacy with culturally-bound ideologies. I also had discovered that it could be taught and learned *in context*—Egyptian students in Egypt would utilize this literacy in context-specific ways.

Such an insight not only completed a long journey from my ponderous MFA student days but also initiated a new one: considering the unique ways in which CNF (and creative writing generally) is not so different from other literacies we learn in higher education. Such a realization might be anathema in the workshops of many graduate creative writing programs, yet it rang true for me. This understanding has brought opportunities for writing pedagogy relevant to both composition and WAC, which I discuss in this chapter. Given the personal nature of such writing and its cache with many students I have worked with through the years, I argue that CNF can be used in many kinds of writing courses to scaffold WAC, especially when we frame it as a form of literacy, with all the characterizing (and limiting) ideologies germane to literacy.

The questions driving this chapter are: How do we define CNF? What is the benefit of conceptualizing CNF as a form of literacy using a New Literacy Studies framework? How can CNF's unique qualities as a kind of literacy inform WAC pedagogies, particularly transfer and student attitudes toward literacy learning? What opportunities and challenges are presented through teaching western-based CNF literacies in non-western contexts, especially as they pertain to WAC?

I respond to these questions, first by defining CNF through the lens of literacy studies and then present new approaches for using CNF to achieve WAC-based goals. I reflect on my own teaching to suggest connections between CNF, composition, and WAC. Next, I describe a pedagogy that employs CNF to encourage students to see the value in transfer. Following that, I reflect on my use of CNF in basic writing courses to scaffold student understanding of sentence types used in CNF and, eventually, academic writing. This supports their writing development in academic and CNF genres. Finally, I consider how CNF, when deployed in other global regions with attitudes about public discourse and critical engagement different from that of the west reveals great potential as a dynamic pedagogical tool appropriate for WAC. In my conclusion, I consider how these approaches may be used in WAC to support student writing development moving forward.

DEFINING & CONCEPTUALIZING CREATIVE NONFICTION THROUGH THE LENS OF LITERACY STUDIES

New Literacy Studies, as an interdisciplinary field, ranges from education studies to the social sciences to English studies. As Brian Street (2003) writes, an "ideological" perspective sees literacy as "a social practice, not simply a technical and neutral skill [. . .] rooted in conceptions of knowledge, identity, and being [. . .] embedded in social practices, such [that] the effects of learning that particular literacy will be dependent on those particular contexts" (p. 78). This definition is a useful way to reframe CNF and clarify what makes it a social practice based in western conceptualizations of identity and insight. For example, Robert Root, Michael J. Steinberg, and Sonya Huber (2005) describe the common elements of CNF as that of a writer making subjective statements about reality with a focus on self-discovery and self-exploration through a use of literary techniques. Philip Lopate (1995) writes that the personal essay seeks connections between individual experience and universal connection using tonal intimacy, sincerity, candor, honesty, and, importantly, "a certain unity to human experience" (p. xxiii). Brenda Miller and Suzanne Paola (2004) add in their introduction to *Tell It Slant* that CNF involves "a close, if not intimate, relationship with the reader, a relationship that demands honesty" (p. 3). Chavez (2020), meanwhile, argues that white voices are given special preference in the canon, in the stories created within writing programs, and even in the power structures that hierarchize the creative writing classroom. She suggests, among other things, realigning traditional power structures and creating a "living archive" of writing by writers from many backgrounds to create and maintain a space where many writers can thrive.

TRANSFER & DISPOSITIONS: CONNECTING CNF TO WAC

Through teaching, I encourage students to develop discursive practices that can exist usefully beyond first-year writing and, therefore, to gain meta-abilities that can weather the switch from composition to disciplinary writing. Developing approaches to writing transfer has been an ongoing challenge. Mike Palmquist (2020) pointed out that much of WAC focuses on writing in the disciplines (WID) and writing to learn (WTL), noting that WID focuses on higher-order concerns in disciplinary writing, while WTL focuses on lower-order disciplinary concerns. The result: a gap within WAC that Palmquist believes can be addressed through writing to engage. For me, his articulation of the different levels of WAC also reveals opportunities to consider relationships between WAC and first-year writing that involve both transfer and student dispositions—*valuing* transfer as a form of engagement. I suggest that writing to engage should begin in first-year writing and can be taken up through engagement initiatives in WAC.

The promise and problems of transfer have bedeviled others through the years. Lucille Parkinson McCarthy (1987) in her study of classroom contexts noted that

> as students go from one classroom to another they must play a wide range of games, the rules for which [. . .] include many conventions and presuppositions that are not explicitly articulated [. . .] writing in college is viewed as a process of assessing and adapting to the requirements in unfamiliar academic settings. (p. 234)

J. Paul Johnson and Ethan Krase (2012) in their mixed-methods study noted that students are rarely engaged in first-year composition (FYC) to WID transfer, despite sometimes utilizing adapted forms of peer review in their WID courses. They note that when students "perceive FYC as a trial space for learning discursive strategies, they can then later adapt these practices to the demands of upper-division courses" (p. 8). To that end, John H. Whicker (2022) found that students who engaged in writing about writing (WaW) activities in FYC developed meta-knowledge useful for successful transfer into WAC and beyond.

Other scholars have identified student dispositions or attitudes as a key factor influencing transfer from FYC into other domains of college literacy development. Elizabeth Wardle (2007), in her longitudinal study of seven first-year writing students, claimed that the students "did not perceive a need to adopt or adapt most of the writing behaviors they used in FYC for other courses" (p. 76), even when they clearly could benefit from doing so. Wardle focused on problems with writing assignments and suggests ways for these assignments to be engaging, inductive, inclusive of student interests, and more (pp. 77–78)—recommendations that reflect many of the priorities of this chapter. Ryan T. Roderick (2019) noted writing transfer scholars have discovered that "knowledge about writing is not enough to fully explain how some writers succeed and others fail to adapt to new or unfamiliar situations" (p. 412). He further questions the effectiveness of transfer-based approaches to help students adapt to unfamiliar writing situations. Indeed, rhetorical, genre, and writing knowledge, as well as understanding that transfer *can* benefit one's writing, is not enough to *assure* transfer.

I maintain that writing students and instructors must *value* transfer, and that writing instructors can help students recognize transfer and value it from one kind of writing context to another. I argue that CNF offers an effective way to use curricular interventions to engage learning through the insight students gain from reflecting on their learning experiences, which can in turn encourage students to recognize principles in writing development that can transfer to other kinds of writing situations.

To illustrate, I adopt an approach to dispositions developed by Dana Lynn Driscoll and Jennifer Wells (2012), who argue that dispositions influence "students' sensitivity toward and willingness to engage in transfer" and can be positive or negative, context-specific, or generalized. Significantly, these scholars ask the following questions pertinent to my own:

- What is the role of curricular interventions in shifting dispositions?
- Can we teach students in a way that encourages transfer-oriented and generative dispositions? (Driscoll & Wells, 2012)

CNF represents a potentially powerful tool for a WAC-based pedagogy in response to these questions. Novosel (2018) argues that CNF's focus on reflection can be used to develop a pedagogy encouraging metacognition in academic writing. I add that CNF is a form of literacy at once disciplined and personal that can be used by WAC practitioners to help students learn the elements of not just CNF but academic writing and narrate and reflect key experiences that can assist with social belonging and inculcation into academic disciplines.

In any discipline, the ability to reflect upon one's writing process and to develop the meta-knowledge necessary to increase ability and self-efficacy is critical. As we will see below, the types of sentences present in CNF can be used to help students narrate their writing and thinking, develop metaphors that can suggest new ways of thinking about writing, and comment on what matters most or what has proven to be most valuable or enduring in their work. This, in turn, can deepen students' meta-knowledge, an important aspect of writing development from the first year into the disciplines.

REFLECTIONS ON TEACHING

Praxis in First-Year Writing with Relevance to WAC

When teaching composition courses at Central Connecticut State University, I often include "Coming into Language" by Jimmy Santiago Baca (2014) early in the class. The text is an effective and relevant example of CNF by a person who learns to read and write against great odds. In my basic writing classes, I use Baca's piece in two ways: to engage students in thinking about telling a personal story while also showing them how Baca uses different sentence types/segments to accomplish his goals. The types I point out to students are narration, figurative language, and reflection. I want students to recognize that writing is a creative and generative act and I want to engage them on a personal level. There is no better literacy for this than CNF, in my view, and Baca's evocative piece has proven an especially effective example.

After students read Baca, I introduce a worksheet based on the essay that underscores the sentence types I wish to emphasize in a paragraph. I point out the color-coded sentence types: blue represents narration, yellow is for figurative language, and green is for reflection. This illustrates the different types of sentences used to accomplish different tasks expected of CNF literacies. It also shows that a writer is thinking differently throughout an essay, using sentence types to orchestrate the completion of a writing task that asks the writer to think and process information in multiple ways. For example, Baca's piece narrates his journey to literacy learning in prison; students see how he builds the story in chronological order, and how he skips past entire years and focuses an entire paragraph on single moment. They observe his use of florid metaphors to help emphasize his state of mind; they also see his insight and commentary when he brings mature perspectives to events that were exciting and life changing. This work manifests in his essay through different kinds of sentences. Then I invite students to identify sentences from another paragraph that has yet to be coded. I read each sentence out loud and elicit responses from the class.

I teach Baca in this way not because I am trying to turn students into nonfiction writers but because I want them to understand and identify the kinds of sentences that can accomplish different goals according to the expectations of a genre and the ways a writer will need to communicate to meet those goals. I find that students in basic writing can be unfamiliar with what different sentences accomplish individually, much less how they work together in paragraphs and essays. Using CNF, and Baca in particular, is an effective way to encourage them to approach writing in this way. This sets up transfer into academic writing assignments later in the course, especially when we examine different academic paragraphs (introduction, body, conclusion) and identify how different sentence types are used to help build those paragraphs. By starting with CNF, I have witnessed enhanced student engagement with the concept of sentence types and can more readily transfer that knowledge to other genres with different sentence types.

Pedagogically speaking, this is a straightforward activity that draws upon students' engagement with Baca's nonfiction piece to introduce them to the general concept of sentence types. This is useful in first-year writing; however, this activity would seem especially useful for WAC, in that it uses engaged reading to pivot students toward a cross-curricular concept without asking students to sacrifice their enjoyment of CNF.

This exercise on Baca's work often precedes an assignment wherein students write a narrative that spans three generations of their family—an adapted version of Ray McDermott's (2004) cross-generational narrative. The generational narrative also tends to deepen students' appreciation for the literacy experiences of prior generations, which brings stories of immigration, language challenges, and upward mobility through education. In this respect, the assignment helps place the students in a familial literacy context that focuses on the successes, challenges, and agendas for literacy learning and education. I have adapted this approach for upper-division courses as well and find that students value understanding family agendas that connect their interests to the people and places that helped bring them into a university classroom. While this may not seem like a strict "applied" form of WAC, I think it is important to use narrative writing, and models of this genre, to encourage students to connect themselves and their backgrounds to their academic interests, goals, and agendas.

Finally, students in basic writing write brief, quarterly journals focused on aspects of metacognition, ranging from describing to evaluating their writing process on specific assignments. By narrating their writing experiences, students can begin to gain some of the metacognitive knowledge so critical to their developing writing processes. Asking students to "narrate" their metacognition is significant, or it keeps with the narrative focus of aspects of the class and introduces an approach to metacognition that can be adapted across the curriculum—telling the story of their own writing development.

Expanding International Considerations

As a form of literacy, CNF is culturally bound and tends to express western-based values through its epistemology. Not all cultures would support public writing that challenges, for example, familial and cultural norms. Likewise, concepts like self-discovery and self-exploration are important western values, particularly American values, and they may not always be accepted in other parts of the world. Likewise, the epistemological statement by Lopate (1995) that CNF "presupposes a certain unity to human experience" (p. xxiii) tends to ignore the western bias of CNF. Indeed, CNF exists within certain cultural-geographic spaces, despite claims of universal applicability.

Still, many writing studies scholars who study the Middle East-North Africa (MENA) note keen student interest in western-based creative literacies, either in class or through literacy events like poetry readings. Lynne Ronesi (2017) writes about the enthusiastic response to a spoken word poetry event at the American University of Sharjah, while Amanda Fields and Melanie Carter (2015) explore the political-expressivist usage of selfies for a classroom assignment. Lisa R. Arnold et al. (2017) describe a transnational partnership between students in Michigan and Beirut that involved peer interviews among students in a project that includes reflective writing and analysis of literacy narratives. These studies discovered an interest in creative literacies among MENA students and began to consider how these students as novice practitioners may adapt creative literacies to explore priorities of their own.

Jonathan Alexander's (2018) focus on the "active nature" of literacy learning underscores that students are the shapers of literacy learning, not simply passive vessels, and CNF is a particularly apt example of such. When teaching CNF at a transnational university in Egypt, my MENA students were comfortable using a so-called western-based literacy like CNF to explore topics that were not typically addressed in public discourse, thereby revealing how CNF, or any form of literacy, is shaped more by those who use it than cultural or geographic points of origin. Indeed, Emily Golson and Lammert Holdijk (2012) from the American University in Cairo (AUC) found that CNF "tapped into a hidden need for attention to creative expression" (p. 185) among AUC students. While conducting IRB-approved research during my doctoral study following my 2010 return from Egypt, I interviewed a CNF teacher in Egypt who shared a story about a student's personal essay on his atheistic beliefs. Initially concerned that she was going to have to "protect" the student from critique by his Muslim and Coptic Christian classmates, some of whom were devout, she observed instead the seriousness and curiosity of these students during discussion, which focused on the merits of the writing and the often-unacknowledged presence of religious doubt.

To the instructor, this experience indicated that these young Egyptians were eager for opportunities to acknowledge and discuss complex religious, ideological, and cultural dilemmas not always addressed publicly in Egyptian society. In the small public venue of a CNF workshop, it was brave of the student to write about atheism in a region where atheism is not readily accepted in public society. This student writer had started a conversation about Egypt and was not simply perpetuating western values through CNF. This so-called western literacy was redirected by a young Egyptian to reflect their interests and needs. This is a critical example of the unique possibilities presented by CNF as it touches on the disciplined and the personal. The western boundedness of literacy is not deterministic, for in the hands of an Egyptian writer, topics and attitudes germane to the nation found a public outlet. This example also reveals potential in developing student attitudes toward writing transfer.

To illustrate, upon reflecting on my own CNF teaching in Egypt, I recall many students wrote stirring CNF accounts on diverse topics: parental illness and cultural stigma, the fallout within a friend group when one of them came out as gay, endemic sexual harassment, and, notably, the cultural dissonance of visiting Mecca followed by socially permissive housing compounds that allowed smoking, alcohol, and bikinis. These topics and the reflections students had on their experiences seemed to have few, if any, public outlets in Egypt. The student writers used western-based CNF literacy as a launching point to address the desire for public discourse in a culture that often prefers to acquiesce to cultural norms. The characteristics of CNF—the narrative aspects, the personal story, the public audience—reveal how this form of literacy offers students the tools to explore topics and assume critical stances in unique ways. Not only is this beneficial in a course specifically designed to improve upon a student's CNF literacy abilities, such as a creative writing course, but CNF writing has the potential to connect one's personal interests, motives, and critical commentary to the wider contexts that incorporate academic disciplines.

Narrating personal experiences along with academic topics can improve critical engagement, and though no known studies have investigated this type of engagement (yet), I posit that the cognitive and social processes of writing CNF are different from academic writing. This difference, therefore, can allow students to approach their academic interests, developing disciplinary identities and writing processes, in novel ways. These "meshed" literacies, both academic and CNF, may also reconfigure students' understanding of how disciplines articulate and respond to exigencies and can alter their motivations to pursue academic literacies. Likewise, it can set the stage for post-graduation writing, for, as Alexander et al. (2020) note in their introduction of the concept of "wayfinding," writing beyond school involves recalibrations of "anticipated knowledge" imported from college writing, often influenced by growing knowledge of how writing situations and genres "intertwine" in ways not typically addressed in higher education writing curriculum (p. 123).

Thus, CNF with its unique characteristics offers dynamic possibilities for student writing development in social, cognitive, and motivational ways. Allowing students to write or integrate aspects of CNF can cultivate the expansive possibilities of personal engagement within the context of a disciplined form of literacy, to accelerate and potentially alter disciplinary genres and the ethos of developing writers. It is also possible that CNF approaches can lead to genre innovation in the form of blending: narrative openings to standard disciplinary genres or new "researcher narrative" genres that establish the motivation and genesis behind research projects.

CONCLUSION

I conclude this chapter by reflecting upon my experiences using CNF to scaffold academic literacy development from basic writing to creative writing. This kind of writing has deepened student writers' understanding of family literacy and educational agendas while also scaffolding academic reading and writing development, thereby creating possibilities for academic genre innovation. I have found that student writers tend to be more amenable to transfer, writing development, and deep engagement and reflection when CNF is incorporated into the curriculum. CNF's themes, approaches, motives, and sentence types can deepen student engagement with learning the basics of academic paragraphs, reflecting on family literacy narratives, considering the value in transferring from one genre of writing to another, engaging topics and expressing views that may elude traditional social-cultural constraints, and reflecting upon inculcation into disciplinary episteme in dynamic ways. There is much experimentation, research, and reporting yet to come among WAC teachers and administrators around the globe that could include CNF to explore writing in multiple disciplines across the curriculum.

REFERENCES

Alexander, J. (2018). Editorial comment: Desiring literacy. *College Composition and Communication, 69*(3), 529–533. https://www.jstor.org/stable/44784942.

Alexander, J., Lunsford, K. & Whithaus, C. (2020). Toward wayfinding: A metaphor for understanding writing experiences. *Written Communication, 37*(1), 104–131. https://doi.org/10.1177/0741088319882325.

Arnold, L. R., DeGenaro, W., Iskandarani, R., Khoury, M., Willard-Traub, M. & Sinno, Z. (2017). Literacy narratives across borders: Beirut and Dearborn as twenty-first century transnational spaces. In L. R. Arnold, A. Nebel & L. Ronesi (Eds.), *Emerging writing research from the Middle East-North Africa region* (pp. 219–240). The WAC Clearinghouse; University Press of Colorado. https://doi.org/10.37514/INT-B.2017.0896.2.10.

Baca, J. S. (2014, March 3). *Coming into language.* Pen America. https://pen.org/coming-into-language.

Chavez, F. R. (2021). *The anti-racist writing workshop: How to decolonize the creative classroom.* Haymarket Books.

Driscoll, D. L. & Wells, J. (2012). Beyond knowledge and skills: Writing transfer and the role of student dispositions. *Composition Forum, 26.* https://compositionforum.com/issue/26/beyond-knowledge-skills.php.

Fields, A. & Carter, M. (2015). Selfie. *Community Literacy Journal, 10*(1), 100–109. https://doi.org/10.25148/clj.10.1.009279.

Golson, E. & Holdijk, L. (2012). The Department of Rhetoric and Composition at the American University in Cairo: Achievements and challenges. In C. Thaiss, G. Bräuer, P. Carlino, L. Ganobcsik-Williams & A. Sinha (Eds.), *Writing programs worldwide: Profiles of academic writing in many places* (pp. 181–188). The WAC Clearinghouse; Parlor Press. https://doi.org/10.37514/PER-B.2012.0346.2.16.

Johnson, J. P. & Krase, E. (2012). Coming to learn: From first-year composition to writing in the disciplines. *Across the Disciplines, 9*(2), 1–24. https://doi.org/10.37514/ATD-J.2012.9.2.02.

Lopate, P. (Ed.). (1995). *The art of the personal essay: An anthology from the classical era to the present.* Anchor.

McCarthy, L. P. (1987). A stranger in strange lands: A college student writing across the curriculum. *Research in the Teaching of English, 21*(3), 233–265. https://www.jstor.org/stable/40171114.

McDermott, R. (2004). Putting literacy in its place. *Journal of Education, 184*(1), 11–30.

Miller, B. & Paola, S. (2019). *Tell it slant.* McGraw Hill Professional.

Novosel, N. E. (2018). *Teaching them to fish: Creative nonfiction as a toolkit for transfer* (Order no. 10959601) [Doctoral dissertation, Bowling Green State University]. Proquest.

Palmquist, M. (2020). A middle way for WAC: Writing to engage. *The WAC Journal, 31.* https://doi.org/10.37514/WAC-J.2020.31.1.01.

Roderick, R. T. (2019). Self-regulation and rhetorical problem solving: How graduate students adapt to an unfamiliar writing project. *Written Communication, 36*(3), 410–436. https://doi.org/10.1177/0741088319843511.

Ronesi, L. (2017). Students running the show: Performance poetry night. In L. R. Arnold, A. Nebel & L. Ronesi (Eds.), *Emerging writing research from the Middle East-North Africa region* (pp. 265–288). The WAC Clearinghouse; University Press of Colorado. https://doi.org/10.37514/INT-B.2017.0896.2.10.

Root, R., Steinberg, M. & Huber, S. (Eds.). (2011). *The fourth genre: Contemporary writers of/on creative nonfiction.* Longman.

Street, B. (2003). What's new in New Literacy Studies. *Current Issues in Comparative Education, 5*(2), 77–91. https://www.tc.columbia.edu/cice/pdf/25734_5_2_Street.pdf.

Wardle, E. (2007). Understanding "transfer" from FYC: Preliminary results of a longitudinal study. *WPA: Writing Program Administration, 31*(1/2), 124–149. http://162.241.207.49/archives/31n1-2/31n1-2wardle.pdf.

Whicker, J. H. (2022). "Types of writing," levels of generality, and "what transfers?": Upper-level students and the transfer of first-year writing knowledge. *Across the Disciplines, 18*(3/4), 284–304. https://doi.org/10.37514/ATD-J.2022.18.3-4.05.

CHAPTER 9.

WAC AND WRITING CENTERS: FINDING SPACE TO WORK ON INSTITUTIONAL DIVERSITY, EQUITY, AND INCLUSION

William J. Macauley, Jr.
University of Nevada, Reno

Pamela B. Childers
The McCallie School

Brandall C. Jones
Kenny Leon's True Colors Theatre Company

When we began working on our presentation for the IWAC conference, we knew little of one another's individual life stories. One-hour Zoom sessions invariably ran into twice that time as we learned those stories. After submitting our proposal and being invited to the conference, we set aside many evenings to Zoom what was happening as the conference and our lives were impacted by a pandemic, unemployment, fires, floods, hurricanes, BLM marches, #MeToo, and LGBTQ+ and immigration concerns, as well as our own worries. We talked in depth about the *1619 Project* (Hannah-Jones et al., 2021), educational challenges with hybrid classes, mental health issues, and how Harvard treated Cornel West.

We discussed Nikole Hannah-Jones' choice to turn down UNC-Chapel Hill's tenure offer and go to Howard. Was she rejecting making a difference at UNC and instead continuing the HBCU tradition of Howard? We wanted to know the details of how and why she made that decision and what impact it would have on both universities. In fact, we were practicing exactly what we had done in WAC writing centers throughout the process of proposing, sharing, collaborating, revising, questioning, and editing what we would finally present. Because we explored those comparisons, we share a narrative here: WAC writing centers can function as spaces for diversity, inclusion, and equity.

DOI: https://doi.org/10.37514/PER-B.2023.1947.2.09

INTRODUCTION

Writing centers have long been sites for discursive diversity, for negotiating among registers, codes, and the value systems they represent. Can writing center culture and WAC theory/practice combine to support diversity and inclusion[1] in cultural and social terms, as well as in disciplinary and generic ones? The issues of racism raised in Asao B. Inoue's (2019a) CCCC Chair's Address, Isabel Wilkerson's (2020) *Caste*, and Ibram X. Kendi's (2019) *How to Be an Antiracist* are complicated by "white fragility" that seems to remove majority academics and academic institutions from responsibility for their own racism (DiAngelo, 2018). Because education in the US grew out of, continues to represent, and preserves white privilege, even/especially in codified discourses, it must be deliberately involved in responding to the inequities it perpetuates. Critical pedagogy, particularly Freirean models, argues that the oppressed must free themselves and their oppressors, but even this liberatory perspective does not relieve education and its proctors of responsibility.

So, how can this be done? Writing centers are increasingly understood as WAC centers because they promote and support diverse disciplinary discourses, work with individuals as well as disciplinary communities by advocating in both directions. As "WACtivist" sites, writing centers could arguably promote diversity, equity, and inclusion for all. In doing so, they facilitate an inclusive awareness based on WAC's student-centered priorities. Could principles of WAC be deployed in post/secondary writing centers as guiding principles for growing DEI beyond disciplinary considerations?

White fragility is a significant obstacle to diversity and inclusion based on the racism that is foundational to American education. This new effort must be handled with trusted, informed, and reliable educators. We must support both individuals and this larger effort. Writing centers can be essential and uniquely suited to both kinds of work because so much good WAC work is already being accomplished through writing centers.

What will it take for all writing centers to develop into diversity, equity, and inclusion (DEI) centers? Educators and consultants must become learners before they can be anything else. They must be comfortable making mistakes

---

1   We use the terms diversity, equity, and inclusion and their collective acronym, DEI, throughout this piece. When we say diversity, we mean that we value difference. When we say equity, we are advocating fairness and consistency. When we say inclusion, we mean that this is not about appearances but about full engagement that makes the most of difference by welcoming all on equal terms and footings. For further information on our interpretations of these terms, please visit the "Higher Education Today" blog, where we think you will find an apt clarification and valuable information: https://www.higheredtoday.org/2021/01/13/refocusing-diversity-equity-inclusion-pandemic-beyond-lessons-community-practice/.

and learning from them in an environment characterized by a growth mindset (Dweck, 2016) and double-loop problem-solving (Argyris, 1976). They have to take risks, overcome much of their own fragility, and be supported in doing so, like any good WAC-aware writing center would do. But they also have to support focused and collaborative problem-solving, keeping it manageable for all involved. WAC-based writing centers provide a model for this work and an opportunity for low-risk, safe, and nonjudgmental learning. They create options in comparative safety and temper them with responsibility and community. WAC writing centers become microcosms of how these collaborative communities can be started and are scalable from there. In a 2019 discussion of the CCCC Committee for Change and Review's work, Inoue emailed that the committee could be mined for structure and process in accomplishing these ends. We argue that WAC writing centers refine the 'ore' of that mining.

In the narratives below, we share stories of learning and growing through WAC writing centers, impacting work beyond those writing centers. Story and narrative, beyond being basic to human meaning-making, are now more accepted as research methodologies and objects of study and, more importantly, as means of researching, studying, and understanding. Certainly, these practices create opportunities for more diverse ways of knowing and learning, and inclusive means of building research and scholarship, as evident through work like Norma González, Luis C. Moll, and Cathi Amanti's (2005) *Funds of Knowledge: Theorizing Practices in Households, Communities,* and even earlier through scholarship like *Women's Ways of Knowing: The Development of Self, Voice, and Mind* by Mary Field Belenky, Blythe McVicker Clinchy, Nancy Rule Goldberger, and Jill Mattuck Tarule (1997). This chapter will articulate these arguments and responses through our narratives of actual work that has been done and can be done.

FROM A HIGH SCHOOL WAC PROGRAM TO ARTS DIRECTOR: A FORMER WRITING FELLOW SHARES HIS STORY–BRANDALL'S STORY

To be the "other" is rarely a pleasant experience, and this unpleasant truth applies to writing centers, as well. To feel invited to be one's full self is essential to the development of the young mind.

As a Black boy from a working-class family, I was able to attend the private, expensive, and predominantly white all-boys McCallie School in Chattanooga, Tennessee. This opportunity was made possible because of wealthy, white benefactors that my parents worked for, as well as the many long hours labored by my determined parents. My skin color inherently made me into a pariah in such an environment, but there was another non-physical trait that created distance: I was, and of course remain, gay. In such a deeply religious and largely homogenous environment, these traits, at times, created great tension and a sense of not belonging.

After completing McCallie's middle school, I entered McCallie's high school, and it was there that I discovered a connection with the arts: singing in all four choruses and eventually performing in the plays and musicals as well. This experience was the spark for my career to come.

In my junior year, what began as an independent study in prose to prepare for college application essays became much more, including an additional independent study in poetry during my senior year. At that time, the Caldwell Writing Center was directed by Dr. Pamela Childers, whom I now call "Pam," and those independent studies were central to finding my authentic voice, shaping the proud Black, gay man that I am today.

At a school that did not provide a cultural connection for a Black boy and certainly lacked any clubs or support groups for gay students, the writing center was the space that welcomed my unique self. An elective on African history that the instructor focused on the American Civil Rights Movement and an all-white production of "Dreamgirls," presented by McCallie in partnership with a local all-girls school, are two examples of McCallie's environment at that time.

In numerous ways, Pam created a welcoming, judgment-free zone in the writing center, in which my unique identity was celebrated instead of diminished. Rather than creating exercises centered on the literary works of individuals with no connection to my identity, Pam's approach of listening to my needs allowed me to co-create exercises with her, often heavily focused on journaling and self-analysis, based on my personal interests. This approach made me feel that I had something to contribute and that my voice, my opinion, mattered. And by utilizing a one-to-one teaching style, peer scrutiny was eliminated, which was necessary at a time when I was exploring personal areas that my peers may not have understood. This is not to suggest that there were no opportunities for peer-to-peer teaching and collaboration but, instead, that such opportunities were selected to ensure that all involved could contribute fully without fear of personal exposure.

Through a guided exploration of my own curiosity, which is Paulo Freire's (2018) approach to teaching, Pam introduced me to Walt Whitman's *Leaves of Grass* (1855) and incorporated Ralph Ellison's *Invisible Man* (1952) into my studies. In confronting reflections of myself through works such as these, Pam often encouraged me to reach for "more," to "dig deeper," to continually ask questions for further investigation in order to prevent merely surface writing or surface conclusions. This approach remains with me today.

After McCallie, I pursued studies in the performing arts and eventually focused on arts administration. In my career as an arts administrator, the skills that I learned in the writing center have, most importantly, helped me to become an effective communicator. With my personal mission "to uplift the overlooked through the arts," my career has centered on community engagement and removing barriers to accessing the arts, primarily for low-income communities of color. I have developed and implemented programs at a number of organizations, currently serving as Connectivity Director for Kenny Leon's True Colors Theatre Company in Atlanta, Georgia. True Colors focuses on sharing stories of the African diaspora, which has made our productions and programs timelier during this current racial awakening.

Over the past few years, I have found opportunities to become a more outspoken advocate for overlooked communities, and some of these opportunities have involved Pam. We remained connected since my time at McCallie, and we have collaborated on meaningful projects, such as writing letters to push for equity and a safe environment at McCallie for LGBTQ students and faculty. McCallie has a history of not being a space in which its LGBTQ students have been able to learn without harassment and discrimination, and Pam and I felt that our connections with the school could make a difference. Although there is still much work to be done and we continue to advocate with other brave voices, as of this publication, the school has amended its policies to include LGBTQ identities and has formed a club for the LGBTQ students. Progress. I also use the Community Conversations/ True Talks series, a program through True Colors, as a form of advocacy by bringing together leading voices to hopefully inspire tomorrow's leaders. One such conversation took place in the spring of 2021, through "Art Meets Activism: John Lewis, C.T. Vivian, and The Baptism" (Arts ATL, 2021). This special event honored the legacies of John Lewis, C.T. Vivian, and other contemporary artists for the 56th anniversary of Bloody Sunday, presented in partnership with the Lincoln Center, Emory University, and the MLK Collection at Morehouse College.

In my work as a producer and arts administrator, I realize that I directly apply Pam's approach in the writing center by listening, co-creating programs with the communities I serve, and creating spaces in which those communities are valued, just as I experienced many years ago. The skills I learned in the writing center have undoubtedly impacted my effectiveness as a communicator, whether pitching proposals to partners and sponsors for new community-serving programs, negotiating contracts with artists, or leading teams for special collaborations. I am constantly communicating through writing, and my years in the writing center with Pam taught me how to communicate in a way that is true to my unique, authentic voice.

AWARENESS OF DIVERSITY, EQUITY, AND INCLUSION IN THE CLASSROOM AND WAC-BASED WRITING CENTERS–PAM'S STORY

My work with Brandall began long after I started my teaching career. However, from student teaching in English and biology, I had begun taking risks across disciplines, trying to create safe learning environments and engaging diverse students, faculty, and administrators. In 1966, I started teaching at a public school in New Jersey. At the end of my first day, I knew the students in my last period 9th grade English class were an apathetic mix of low-income, ESL, minority, and repeat students. Unlike my college prep classes, this one met in an old science classroom, so I decided not to stand behind the stationary lab table and instead walked down the rows looking each student in the eyes and asking them how they wanted to meet the requirements of the course. After a few stunned moments, Kenny, an African American senior who needed one more semester of English to graduate, spoke up. "No one ever asked us that question before. I'd like to try my hand at teaching a grammar lesson so I can understand what I failed last time." Students who had never spoken up or had been given derogatory nicknames took his lead, and we all congratulated Kenny when he successfully completed that semester. This class taught me that something in the system needed to be changed.

A history colleague, who was teaching many of the same students, agreed to team-teach English and history as a double period the following year to the lowest scoring incoming 9th graders from several school districts. Our new principal thought such a program would give him some positive publicity, and we even invited some of the students to pick their textbooks before the school year began. That was my start of rattling cages (Childers, 2017). That pilot expanded to a four-year program, and I followed the initial group to graduation. My colleagues in both departments discovered how to engage students in learning, and realized ALL students show more improvement when someone cares about them!

At night, I taught and counseled Adult Basic Education (ABE) to those who had never graduated high school and ESL classes to new Americans. Some had immigrated from Mexico, South America, Cuba, Caribbean islands, Greece, Vietnam, and even Russia. All came to classes after long hours of work, with the hope of a better life for themselves and their families. We made learning a joy, a social connection, and a dignified commitment by adding celebratory social events with certificates of attendance. Together we learned about a variety of cultures and about one another, from people of various professions, nationalities, and education who were there for the same reason. We all took pride in one another's successes.

By the mid-1970s the new Red Bank Regional High School for grades 9–12 brought together for the first time students from three diverse school districts. I had completed a graduate degree and became aware of WAC through studies of James Britton (1975) and Nancy Martin (1976), taken a course with colleagues across disciplines at Rutgers, and contemplated how to improve the writing of ALL students. Through a Northeastern University Summer Writing Institute, Lil Brannon introduced me to the idea of a writing center, and I began studying the works of Janet Emig (1971; 1983), Donald Murray (1968; 1984), Peter Elbow (1973), and Mike Rose (1989). I distinctly remember my first NCTE conference in 1981 where Murray talked about moving in front of his desk to finally writing with his students. He gave me permission to do what I had tried years before, to engage all students in learning and responding to the writing of others. That's when I decided to propose a WAC-based writing center as a pilot program involving my cross-disciplinary colleagues.

Teaching American literature one day, I realized I wanted to create a space to accommodate what Whitman called "The Great Equalizer." A writing center could create that opportunity, serving students from diverse socio-economic and multi-ethnic communities, with varying academic preparations with BIPOC, multilingual, and LGBTQ identities. We moved into larger spaces with trained student volunteer reader-responders and faculty participants. Students who would never encounter one another because of tracking were now interacting during free periods in the writing center or coming with their whole class to participate in a cross-disciplinary writing workshop. At the same time, the school also became a state-designated school for the Performing Arts. I was assigned to design a county-wide audition process for students, select those who would attend as creative writing majors the following year, and create the curriculum I would teach. These new students added energy and financial assistance from their school districts that enabled us to expand the writing center with this new program. We could attend one-day conferences, publish literary calendars and magazines, have poetry readings, participate in master classes through the Geraldine R. Dodge Foundation, and allow all students in the school to become part of this "great equalizer."

In 1990, I accepted a new endowed chair position at an independent boys' college preparatory day/boarding school in Chattanooga, Tennessee. NCTE had just published *The High School Writing Center* (Farrell, 1998), and I realized this perfect opportunity to make a difference at another educational institution. I reflected on what I had learned from starting that first WAC-based writing center: creating a safe space for all writers, encouraging writers to take risks with drafts, learning how to really listen in dialogic exchanges, offering challenges to critical thinking skills, being able to laugh at oneself (Sherwood & Childers,

2014), developing collaborations among various groups across disciplines, and setting the tone of acceptance in a student-centered environment.

Art Young and Toby Fulwiler's (1986) WAC work reinforced student-centered learning; Frank Smith (1998) reminded me of the joy of learning; and Stephen D. Brookfield and Stephen Preskill's (2005) *Discussion as a Way of Teaching* helped me discover how to involve students and faculty in designing a program and participating in special writing activities across the curriculum. I posted an invitation on the writing center door that said, "Welcome to the Writing Center, a low-risk environment where there is a reverence for writing." Brandall saw that sign when he entered McCallie. Little did I know that invitation would open the door for many other disenfranchised students.

My work with science teacher Michael Lowry turned into team teaching a new senior science seminar called *Oceans: Past and Present* in a landlocked state of Tennessee and many WAC projects with other science classes through the writing center (Lowry & Childers, 2016). We expanded to offer independent study courses across disciplines like the ones Brandall took (Baker et al., 2007; Childers & Straka, 2004; Grant et al., 1997) and created a writing fellows program. Students taught computer science courses after school for teachers and students (Davis & Childers, 2006); and presented Diversity Day workshops, such as the one writing fellows led viewing "The Motorcycle Diaries," with questions to begin discussion of the social, cultural, and health issues the young Che Guevara experienced on his journey, then focusing on Guevara's later life and death. Students also published collaborative work (Childers, et al., 1998), offered online grammar lessons, taught poetry to 9th graders (Mooney et al., 2010), and presented at IWAC and CCCC conferences. Besides my own classes, I sometimes taught research and writing units in AP biology, Bible, and AP American history. Students saw me out of the writing center, learning with and from them in other disciplines. One history teacher told his students, "Take your paper to the writing center and talk with Dr. Childers; she hates history and will question anything you haven't explained to her clearly." I even began teaching graduate courses in the teaching of writing, so K-12 teachers could learn how to value WAC in their classes.

These experiences in two very different secondary schools had similarities. Both offered Advanced Placement, specialized, and developmental courses for students from diverse racial, religious, academic, gender orientation, and economic backgrounds; included wealthy students and students on full or partial financial assistance; and included a smorgasbord of international students. Many students were discovering and struggling with their own sexuality and gender identity. Brandall was not alone, and others at both institutions were just as brave to find a safe place in the writing center to discuss those concerns. What the institutions and administrators allowed through WAC and writing center programs were opportunities for students to engage in the joy of learning, to collaborate with one another, teachers, and even globally with people from other institutions or careers.

I want to return to Kenny, who taught me to engage students by making the class student centered and trusting them to know what they needed to succeed. And, Whitman, whose idea of the great equalizer influenced my idea of a writing center where students at both schools could discover their passions. I learned the dignity of each of us as individuals, worthy of being heard, questioned, respected, and challenged to discover the best that we can be. Yes, writing can be a great equalizer, like a writing center, and Kenny was one of my best teachers.

IS AGENCY ENOUGH? THE POWER AND PERIL OF INDIVIDUALISM IN SYSTEMIC RACISM—BILL'S STORY

I was moved to the Midwest at eight. More than one kid there couldn't play with me because I was Catholic. I wasn't. I was an idol worshiper because that's what they said Catholics did. Wasn't and didn't. One kid called me an "idolater." Neither of us could say what an idolator was, but we both knew what rejection was. There, in America's heartland, my parents didn't notice right away their being shown homes in only Black and Latinx neighborhoods. What stung once they did notice was that choice being made about and for them. I understood then that school had to become a way out.

I tried college in '79 and hated it, as I did most of the jobs I wandered through then. School was not specific or welcoming, but it had to be better than factory work. My blue-collar background meant that no one I knew could really say what college would do. Even so, it beat factory work. Not unlike my folks eventually buying their one and only home, it was a good thing and a lot of money and very poorly understood. I knew what would happen if I didn't go to school. I saw what my folks had; Dad didn't finish ninth grade and Mom couldn't use her full-ride Regent's Scholarship. We had a blunt belief in education and going beyond high school rejected my workaday home culture for something unknown (Finn, 2009). "What are they teaching you over there, anyway" seemed innocuous enough at the time, but it never really was.

In college, I took studio art classes and experienced incredible autonomy and community. More than in my major. This perpetuated continuing extremes for me: status quo/certainty/jobs versus other options/uncertainty/breathing room. My 30+ years in writing centers since provide my greatest sense of professional community because it's all options and uncertainty. Every student who walked through the doors was working on something unique, something that could be their own. As a director, there was never any end to the possibilities of where my writing centers could go, what they could do, what new options they could explore. There was no shortage of collaborators on writing. It's the writing *with* (Deans, 1998) and the shared experiences (Ryan & Zimmerelli, 2015) that most engaged me.

My studio-focused dissertation propelled my career forward. Since then, agency and self-efficacy via social psychology, brain development, and young adult psychology have amplified my study of writer empowerment. Over the past four years, I've studied Oxford University's tutorial pedagogies, an elite pedagogy to be sure, which safely assume competence and capability. Each student could be exceptional, enhanced through mentoring and challenge (Palfreyman, 2019). These studies have led to mindful writing that emphasizes awareness of the writer, the writing, and the written. This has become a rich context for empowering student writers.

These interests and work resonate with DEI work now, too, because I have to step back from controlling any writing I encounter. I have to be open to perspectives that may not be familiar. And I have to respect that others' ways will not be my own and see the value in their purposes and processes. That said, across these contexts, I find a consistent complication: Neophytes are expected to adapt, to be agents of change in extant classism, racism, ageism, ableism, sexism, even while they are reminded always that 'you are welcome here as long as you assimilate' (Inoue, 2019b).; 'you are welcome here, as long as you assimilate' seems to be the message. For example, TAs in writing studies acclimate quickly to conflicting roles and responsibilities. Systemic flaws and challenges are freely acknowledged in the literature, but scholars' solutions are almost always laid at the feet of TAs, not unlike the burden of responding to racism put on our BIPOC brothers and sisters described in Robin DiAngelo's (2018) *White Fragility*. Those empowered by these systems expect victims of those systems' to fix them.

Freire (2018) says the oppressed must free themselves and their oppressors. I understand that oppressors creating new systems, even with the best intentions, sustains the powers that oppress. It just seems like a lot to ask of those already dealing with being oppressed.

Writing centers can be thought of as exceptions here. Stephen M. North (1987) famously wrote that writing centers make better writers. 'Give the writer control' is writing center dogma. Do writing consultants have that power? If so, aren't they then oppressive in caste if not in practice? Are writing centers really to decide who writers should be? Writing center staff are usually trained in what is called "nondirectivity" as a way to respect writer autonomy. Nondirectivity can oppress when done poorly, becoming a weird game of "guess what I'm thinking." Writers then chase right answers because nondirective tutors won't tell them what those answers are. Choosing "nondirection" is power, as is denying the power in that choice.

The challenge in DEI work, as it is in training writing center staff and working directly with student writers, is to be available not only to the activity but to the differences, the valuations, the appropriateness of unfamiliar or "other" ways of making and expressing meaning. Where curricula can provide articulated paths to identified goals, writing centers and writing tutors cannot because they deal with so many variations, individuals, and disciplines. That work has to be done through inquiry, not decision. It has to be done through context *and* episode, not through reliance on the status quo. While a writing center can be "directive" about its purposes and practices, neither a writing center nor a writing tutor can be effective if they attempt to homogenize their practices or the writers who seek their help.

When Vershawn Young and other scholars use varying registers, dialects, and codings, strong professional community responses follow, many less than positive. Writing teachers and centers work to facilitate academic discourses. Students can think that othered discourses have little or no academic value. What happens when family or neighborhood logics aren't allowed in school? When students start to sound different at home? Don't choose academic discourses?

Think about Cornel West and his recent bid for tenure at Harvard. His mind and discourse make him a most recognizable public intellectual. But, when it came to permanent employment at a prestigious institution he had already been serving, something changed. Too much agency? Sounds too Black? Why deny him his earned seat at the high table now?

It seems what made Hannah-Jones attractive to UNC confounded her tenure bid. UNC eventually offered her tenure, grudgingly and under public pressure, but something clearly changed. Is it that people of color can be agentive, just not too agentive? Are diversity, equity, and inclusion marketing concepts rather than real interests? Sheryl I. Fontaine and Susan Hunter (1993) write:

> Real changes in the way the story is unfolding, then, will not come from our simply being included or alluded to in the current narratives. To become heard does not mean to become part of the center or to move away from the borders [. . .] the voices gathered together here may not be raised again next year [. . .] And then again some may be. As we write ourselves into the story [. . .] our unheard voices will not necessarily become tomorrow's heard voices. There's no guarantee. (p. 15)

So, how might WAC writing centers, with such promise, move the needle on confounding systemic racism in higher education? Larry Ward (2020) tells us that this work will take "deeper education, skillful introspection, and wise cultivating of the seeds of compassion for self and all relations" over a "bridge of mercy" (p. 89, p. 95). Doing this work includes self-compassion and post-traumatic growth, deploying "help now" strategies, reflecting on our own humanness, cultivating resources for resilience, making room for the work, and learning to hold suffering with clarity and grace (Ward, 2020). There are more specific tools available to us, too.

Coming to these discussions, we can:

- Choose deliberately among Kendi's (2018) options: separatist, assimilationist, or antiracist;
- Use Freire's (2018) ideas of every person having their own word and respecting those words;
- Use Thich Nhat Hanh's (2017) ideas of listening lovingly and speaking compassionately.

Participating in these efforts, we can:

- Remember West's (2021) acknowledgment: "Do you have a fingerprint? Then you have a voice!" Use it;
- Use DiAngelo's (2018) "reasonable roles and reasonable expectations";
- Use Carol S. Dweck's (2016) "growth mindset" to make room for productive mistakes;
- Ground our teaching/tutoring in González, Moll, and Amanti's (2005) "funds of knowledge";
- Use Ronald A. Heifetz's (2009) differentiation between "technical problem-solving" (here's a problem, here's a solution) and "adaptive change" (broader work and unfamiliar responses).

To grow from these experiences, we can:

- Avoid what Amy Lombardi (2021) calls our habit of "hyper-macro-izing" difficult topics, forgetting that people are directly impacted by our work or lack of it;
- Assume the Oxford tutorial premise that everyone is more than competent and possibly exceptional (Palfreyman, 2019);
- Use Chris Argyris' (1976) double-loop problem-solving to ask why *toward* finding solutions;
- Remember Alina Tugend's (2012) revealing our discomfort with error: we have to get comfortable with making mistakes and being wrong sometimes.

WAC-based writing centers are especially well positioned for this important work (Waldo, 2004). We do work like this every day with student writers making their ways into diverse disciplinary ways of knowing and communicating. Acknowledge that power; use that privilege! Extend quality WAC writing center work by carefully developing practices for diversity, equity, and inclusion. Prepare centers for this work. West, DiAngelo, Freire, Ward, Hanh, Dweck and so many others will help. Will we let them?

OUR REFLECTIONS

Each of us changed what we had originally intended to write because of a question, idea, or experience with the other two. All three of us had worked hard at a variety of jobs to pay for our own educations with support from scholarships, grants, and loans, so we had a connection to the socio-economic concerns of others as well as discriminatory experiences tied to race, gender, sexuality, class, and educational backgrounds. It has been exhilarating as we have gone from three unique individuals with totally different backgrounds to discovering commonalities, changing some of our own ideas, taking risks, accepting new perspectives from what we had read or observed, challenging one another to "dig deeper," and supporting one another's efforts. In real time, we practiced the theme of this conference by "Celebrating Successes, Recognizing Challenges, Inviting Critiques and Innovations."

REFERENCES

Argyris, C. (1976). Theories of action that inhibit individual learning. *The American Psychologist, 31*(9), 638–54. https://doi.org/10.1037/0003-066x.31.9.638.

Arts ATL. (2021). *Art meets activism: John Lewis, C.T. Vivian, and the baptism.* ARTS ATL.

Baker, W., Conney, A., Jones, B., Mullens, D. & Murnan, S. (2007). Independent studies in writing based in the writing center. *Southern Discourse, 10*(3), 6–7.

Belenky, M. F., Clinchy, B. M., Goldberger, N. R. & Tarule, J. M. (1997). *Women's ways of knowing: The development of self, voice, and mind* (10th Anniversary ed.). Basic Books.

Britton, J. (1975). *The development of writing abilities.* National Council of Teachers of English.

Brookfield, S. D. & Preskill, S. (2005). *Discussion as a way of teaching: Tools and techniques for democratic classrooms* (2nd ed.). Jossey-Bass.

Childers, P. (2017). Rattling cages to make a difference. *JAEPL: The Journal for the Assembly for Expanded Perspectives on Learning, 22*(1). https://trace.tennessee.edu/jaepl/vol22/iss1/12/.

Childers, P., Laughter, J., Lowry, M. & Trumpeter, S. (1998). Developing a community in a secondary school writing center. In C. P. Haviland, M. Notarangelo, L. Whitley-Putz & T. Wolf (Eds.), *Weaving knowledge together: Writing centers and collaboration* (pp. 28–57). NWCA Press.

Childers, P. & Straka, J. (2004). Developing lifelong language skills in a writing center. *The Writing Lab Newsletter, 28*(10), 5–6.

Davis, M. H. & Childers, P. B. (2006). Compass points: Practicing what we preach. *Southern Discourse, 9*(1), 10–11.

Deans, T. A. (1998). *Community-based and service learning college writing initiatives in relation to composition studies and critical theory*. ScholarWorks@UMass Amherst.

DiAngelo, R. (2018). *White fragility: Why it's so hard for white people to talk about racism*. Beacon Press.

Dweck, C. S. (2016). *Mindset: The new psychology of success* (Updated ed.). Ballantine Books.

Elbow, P. (1973). *Writing without teachers*. Oxford University Press.

Ellison, R. (1952). *Invisible man*. Random House.

Emig, J. (1971). *The composing processes of twelfth graders*. National Council of Teachers of English.

Emig, J. (1983). *The web of meaning: Essays on writing, teaching, learning, and thinking*. Heinemann.

Farrell, P. B. (1998). *The high school writing center: Establishing and maintaining one*. National Council of Teachers of English.

Finn, P. J. (2009). *Literacy with an attitude: Educating working-class children in their own self-interest* (2nd ed.). State University of New York Press.

Fontaine, S. I. & Hunter, S. (Eds.). (1993). *Writing ourselves into the story: Unheard voices from composition studies*. Southern Illinois University Press.

Freire, P. (2018). *Pedagogy of the oppressed* (50th Anniversary ed.). Bloomsbury Academic.

González, N., Moll, L. C. & Amanti, C. (2005). *Funds of knowledge: Theorizing practices in households, communities, and classrooms*. Lawrence Erlbaum Associates.

Grant, T., Murphy, A., Stafford, B. & Childers, P. (1997). Peer tutors and students work with assessment. *The Clearing House, 71*(2), 103–105. https://www.jstor.org/stable/30192094.

Hanh, T. N. (2017). *Happy teachers change the world: A guide for cultivating mindfulness in education*. Parallax Press.

Hannah-Jones, N., Roper, C., Silverman, I. & Silverstein, J. (Eds.). (2021). *The 1619 project: A new origin story*. One World.

Heifetz, R. A. (2009). *Leadership without easy answers*. Harvard University Press.

Inoue, A. (2019a). CCCC committee for change update. CCCC@NCTE.org.

Inoue, A. (2019b). How do we language so people stop killing each other, or what do we do about white language supremacy? *College Composition and Communication, 71*(2), 352–69. https://www.jstor.org/stable/26877937.

Kendi, I. X. (2019). *How to be an antiracist*. Random House.

Lombardi, A. (2021, April 26). *Thoughts from a grad student* [Email distribution list post]. WPA-L. http://lists.asu.edu/archives/wpa-l.html.

Lowry, M. J. & Childers, P. B. (2016). Bridging the gap through frameworks: Secondary school science and writing center interactions to form good 'habits of mind'. In R. McClure & J. P. Purdy (Eds.), *The future scholar: Researching and teaching the frameworks for writing and information literacy* (pp. 179–204). Information Today.

Martin, N. (1976). *Writing and learning across the curriculum.* Boynton/Cook.

Mooney, D., Mullins, T. J., Ray, K. & Childers, P. B. (2010). Compass points: The value of indirect classroom teaching. *Southern Discourse, 14*(1), 6–7.

Murray, D. (1968). *A writer teaches writing: A practical method of teaching composition.* Houghton Mifflin.

Murray, D. (1984). *Write to learn.* Holt McDougal.

North, S. M. (1987). The idea of a writing center. *College English, 46*(5), 433–446. https://doi.org/10.2307/377047.

Palfreyman, D. (Ed.). (2019). *The Oxford tutorial: Thanks, you taught me how to think.* [Independently published.]

Rose, M. (1989). *Lives on the boundary: The struggles and achievements of America's underprepared.* Free Press.

Ryan, L. & Zimmerelli, L. (2015). *The Bedford guide for writing tutors* (6th ed.). Bedford/St. Martin's.

Sherwood, S. & Childers, P. (2014). Mining humor in the writing center: Comical misunderstanding as pathways to knowledge. *The Writing Lab Newsletter, 38*(7–8), 6–9. https://www.wlnjournal.org/archives/v38/38.7-8.pdf.

Smith, F. (1998). *The book of learning and forgetting.* Teachers College Press.

Tugend, A. (2012). *Better by mistake: The unexpected benefits of being wrong.* Riverhead Books.

Waldo, M. L. (2004). *Demythologizing language differences in the academy: Establishing discipline-based writing programs.* Lawrence Erlbaum Associates.

Ward, L. (2020). *America's racial karma: An invitation to heal.* Parallax Press.

West, C. (2021, January 3–5). *Where do we go from here? Chaos or community?* [Conference keynote]. Writing and Well-Being and 2nd UNR Crossings Conferences. Reno, NV, United States.

Whitman, W. (1855). *Leaves of grass.* Self-published.

Wilkerson, I. (2020). *Caste: The origins of our discontents.* Random House.

Young, A. & Fulwiler, T. (1986). *Writing across the disciplines: Research into practice.* Heinemann.

CHAPTER 10.

WHEN LEARNING OUTCOMES MASK LEARNING, PART 1: THE PROMISES AND PITFALLS OF LEARNING ANALYTICS

Kathleen Daly Weisse
New Mexico State University

In 2006, the U.S. Commission on the Future of Higher Education released a report interrogating and criticizing American universities for failing to adequately prepare students for the demands of their future careers. The report's authors claimed, "As other nations rapidly improve their higher education systems, we are disturbed by evidence that the quality of student learning at U.S. colleges and universities is inadequate and, in some cases, declining" (Spellings, 2006, p. 3). They noted that this is a crisis, not just of learning, but of institutional transparency, explaining that the current "lack of useful data and accountability hinders policymakers and the public from making informed decisions and prevents higher education from demonstrating its contribution to the public good" (Spellings, 2006, p. 4). University administrators across the U.S. have since scrambled to collect and analyze student data that could be used as evidence of the educational rigor of their programs and thus demonstrate that students at their institutions are achieving desired learning outcomes.

Compiling the data necessary to analyze an entire institution's educational outcomes is a large, complex endeavor requiring significant labor and resources. To make this a more manageable, affordable, and efficient endeavor, many administrators turned to learning analytics (LA), a type of educational Big Data that includes "the measurement, data collection, data analysis, and reporting of data about learners and their contexts" (SoLAR). LA refers to any tools and/or methods for using automated algorithms to make meaning from large and complex sets of data generated from user activities in digital learning environments.

To deploy LA at the institutional level, universities needed educational data. And not just demographic data or enrollment data; they needed data generated in the classrooms themselves. Fortunately, for many universities, administrators already had access to a trove of educational data, specifically data mined from

DOI: https://doi.org/10.37514/PER-B.2023.1947.2.10

the institution's learning management system. Learning management systems (LMSs)—also known as course management systems—are online learning systems and platforms designed to create and host digital learning environments for both face-to-face and online courses (Salisbury, 2017). Because LMSs are typically designed for university-wide implementation and are thus used in courses across disciplines and colleges, more often than not, a university's LMS is also its largest and most comprehensive repository of educational data. So while LMSs aren't the sole place where LA can be deployed, they are certainly an attractive host of these operations.

LMSs became popular in the 21st century, when open-source LMSs with internal networks, like Moodle™ and then BlackBoard™, were introduced onto the higher education marketplace. For administrators, the introduction of LMS technology offered new (albeit expensive) opportunities for streamlining educational and institutional operations using data-driven decision-making. According to Hamish Coates et al. (2005), equipped with the data infrastructure afforded by an LMS, administrators could "reduce course management overheads, reduce physical space demands, enhance knowledge management, unify fragmented information technology initiatives within institutions, expedite information access, set auditable standards for course design and delivery and improve quality assurance procedures" (p. 24). Essentially, LMSs promised to empower university administrators with "a hitherto undreamt-of capacity to control and regulate teaching" (Coates et al., 2005, p. 24). In doing so, LMSs provide the structure for a top-down model where the institution is able to make decisions without necessitating student involvement.

The most popular LMSs among higher education institutions today are those that are pitched by developers and educational associations as state-of-the-art, data-powered mechanisms for helping administrators, educators, and students increase educational accessibility and foster student success while simultaneously streamlining course management and data mining efforts. As recent scholarship critiquing the Big Data boom in higher education has shown, however, once such programs are integrated, LMSs almost always fall short of their initial promise (Crawford et al., 2014; McKee, 2011; Reyman, 2010).

In much of the research on data-driven assessment technologies, the limitations of LMS-based LA are framed as temporally-bound problems that will be solved once technology inevitably progresses. By focusing criticism on the limitations of today's technology or the improper application of LMS programs, however, we as teachers and administrators in higher education leave unquestioned the assumption that these assessment technologies actually have the capacity to accurately and adequately measure student learning (Aguilar et al., 2021). In this chapter, I critically interrogate the promise at the heart of LA—namely, that it will make learning more personalized while simultaneously holding institutions accountable to concrete standards—and argue that such a promise is necessarily unfulfillable. The underlying algorithmic structures for analyzing data are simply incapable of accounting for the complex and multi-faceted realities of student learning.

THE (UNFULFILLABLE) PROMISE OF LEARNING ANALYTICS

How do learning analytics (LA) work? Essentially, LA is an algorithmic process that relies on data mined from user activities on a platform or from student-generated data to assess and make predictions about student learning. The algorithm processes data from course materials like assignment submissions, exam and quiz answers, and online activities such as page views, clicks, and timestamps. Specifically, these machine learning algorithms sift through data to identify traces of "student learning" that can be aggregated across assignments in a course, across many students in a single course, and/or across many courses in an institution and then used as evidence of individual learning performance.

LA is methodologically contingent upon the belief that an objective measure of student effort and learning can be gleaned from digital traces. In 2012, the U.S. Department of Education released the report "Enhancing Teaching and Learning through Educational Data Mining and Learning Analytics," claiming that LA could "predict" students' chances of success by comparing data said to represent a student's digital engagement with predetermined standards for what a successful or unsuccessful student's individual digital engagement should look like: "Using these measures, teachers can distinguish between students who are not trying and those who are trying but still struggling and then differentiate instruction for each group" (Bienkowski et al., 2012, p. 20). This claim assumes educational data that have been mined and analyzed not only can be but are wholly representative of an individual student's experience and engagement with digital material.

Such an assumption presents obvious gaps and problems of representativeness. For instance, the data points and patterns that the algorithm privileges and identifies as evidence of learning do not clearly map onto disciplinary understandings of what learning looks like. Further, the programs and data infrastructures undergirding learning analytic systems cannot account for students or educators whose activities do not register as digital signals. The problem here is not that there is not enough data, or that the analysis is not sophisticated enough, or that these systems are just preliminary attempts to use tools that will eventually, with greater refinement, accomplish the tasks set before them. Rather, the problem is that assessing learning with these technologies demands that learning itself be re-defined and reconfigured so as to be measurable by such a tool. Although the initial promise of LA is grounded in rhetorics of personalized learning, this promise comes with the caveat that the mechanisms through which LA are deployed place constraints around what can be counted as learning. While all methods for assessment require that learning be reshaped to fit the assessment model, the process of reshaping learning can be more exaggerated when using LA for assessment of data-driven learning outcomes and less clearly connected to common learning goals like critical thinking and deep reading. To put this into perspective, I want to reiterate the examples that the authors of the U.S. Department of Education report provide of the types of data points that are collected by learning software: "minutes spent on a unit, hints used, and common errors" (Bienkowski et al., 2012, p. 20).

Just as instructors have to reshape their pedagogical approaches and materials to fit within the predetermined structure of their institution's LMS or any other LA-based application, students also have to adjust how they approach the learning process. These patterns of refitting and reshaping learning to meet the demands of an LMS's predetermined structure creates a feedback loop. Over years of continued use and refinement of educator and student behavior to meet its constraints, the system creates data that motivates those behaviors most amenable to the data generation and analysis functions it has been designed to fulfill. Importantly, the system never re-aligns itself with the student learning outcomes that the system was originally intended to measure and refine (Kuh & Ewell, 2010). Data thus become an end unto themselves.

To more clearly illustrate what qualifies as learning in LA contexts, and thus more clearly illustrate the risks that these systems pose for how we understand learning, I want to turn to a discussion about the data infrastructure and instructional practices behind the most popular and fastest-growing LMS for higher education in the US: Instructure's Canvas.

LEARNING ANALYTICS IN THE CANVAS LMS

Developed and launched in 2011 by for-profit company Instructure, Canvas™ is a cloud-based LMS marketed for use in both K-12 and higher education contexts. What distinguished Canvas from other LMSs early on was that it operated as a Software as a Service (SaaS), a subscription-based and centrally hosted model of software licensing and development. The SaaS model means that users can access the Canvas software online, rather than through a downloaded, offline program. Similar to other SaaS like Google Drive and OneDrive, both of which operate via the cloud as well, Canvas's infrastructure makes its program easy for users to access and for developers to update. While Canvas is not currently the only SaaS-operated LMS on the market, it was the first to offer cloud-based services capable of conducting large-scale data analytics and harnessing educational data to assess student learning. In the years following Canvas's release, while other LMS providers struggled to integrate similar data functionality into their services, Canvas was able to make its way to the forefront of LMS technologies and gain a significant advantage in the marketplace early on. As of 2021, Canvas is used by over 38 percent of higher education institutions in the US and is the fastest growing LMS on the market ("LMS Data," 2021).

One of Canvas's premiere features is the advanced set of tools it provides for data analytics. Literally marketed as being "like Moneyball for student success instead of baseball"—referencing the wild success of the Oakland A's data-driven roster in 2002—Canvas's analytics are designed to serve a number of different functions aimed at bettering the quality of student education ("Improving Learning," 2019). In explanations of the potential benefits that universities can reap from using Canvas's analytics, the feature that Instructure emphasizes most is the LMS's capacity to help identify "at risk" students, which the program defines as "at risk of dropping out of a course, program, or institution" ("Glossary," 2019).

The main mechanisms through which instructors using Canvas are supposedly able to identify "at risk" students are the "Course Analytics" feature, which includes compilations of data from all of the students in a single course and/or all of the students in multiple sections of the same course, and the "Student Analytics" feature, which includes data from individual students enrolled in each course. Both the course analytics and the student analytics rely on user-generated data, which are presented to instructors as data visualizations (mis)representing student engagement and progress.

Canvas's data visualizations largely take the form of bar charts and line graphs. While the course and student analytics are largely similar in their graphical representation, Canvas also offers a student "Context Card," which includes a more simplistic view of an individual student's analytics. In addition to providing the student's current grade, number of missing and complete assignments, and grades on the three most recent assignments, it includes a section titled "Activity Compared to the Class." As the graphic in Figure 10.1 shows, these "activities" are represented as two, three-star rating visualizations that show the individual student's page views and participation data in comparison to their classmates:

Both of the minimalist, star-rating data visualizations are offered to instructors without any details as to what exactly these visualizations mean. They provide no evidence of the mechanisms, data, or methods used in their production. The data used to construct the "Page Views" visualization is relatively straightforward in terms of what is being rated and compared (i.e., the number of discrete page views from each student's account, which are also made available to instructors in more detail via a timestamped log of each time a student has accessed the Canvas course page). The data that the "Participation" visualization is meant to represent, however, are not implicitly clear for instructors using the context card feature.

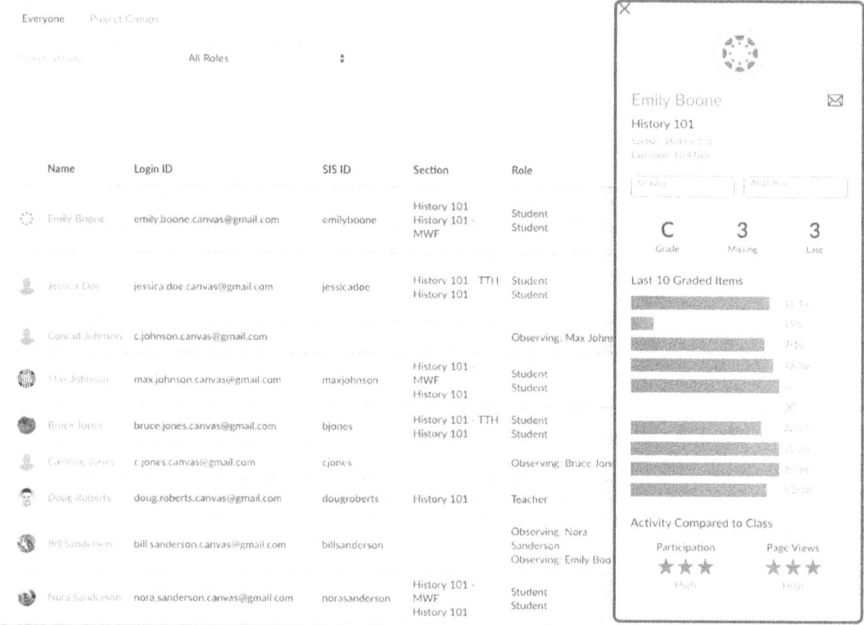

Figure 10.1. Graphic context card.

Despite the lack of explanation or context, the familiarity and clarity of the star-rating system grants the data visualization rhetorical power, encoding a particular kind of student success as a nudge to instructors. What counts as success and how it is represented in the context card is contingent on what is encoded into the algorithm. While Instructure does not provide an explanation of the context card mechanism on the Canvas portal, the Canvas Community website describes it as a "simplified overview of a student's progress" that is based on grades and "standard page view and participation activity in course analytics" (Canvas Doc Team, n.d.).

To create participation scores, Canvas's system compares the data that each individual student's account activity generates with the equivalent data from their classmates' accounts. The user actions that generate the data upon which these visualizations are based include: commenting on an announcement, submitting an assignment, submitting a quiz, initiating a quiz, joining a web conference, creating a wiki page, posting a discussion comment, and loading a collaboration page. Once data have been generated, they are then aggregated and fed into an algorithm that scores student participation in relation to their peers. The resultant participation scores are presented to instructors in the form of a three-star rating system labeled "Participation."

The explanation provided on the Canvas Community website also includes an important qualifier as to the quality of the data represented in the context card feature: Canvas's mobile app is not configured to collect data generated by student activities and actions (Canvas Doc Team, n.d.).[1] In other words, because the algorithm used to create student analytics cannot account for the mobile app's limited data functionality, for those students who mainly use the Canvas mobile app, their student analytics will be skewed. Importantly, a student might use a mobile device as their primary means for accessing Canvas for a number of reasons, including individual learning preferences or having limited access to WIFI, a laptop, or a desktop. For those students, in the space where student-generated data should appear, there will instead be potentially significant gaps in logged activity. When their data are run through Canvas's predictive models, these students can potentially receive lower participation and page view ratings than their peers whose activity data have been successfully harvested via the Canvas website. While instructors could theoretically account for these gaps in some other way, for instance, by asking students which type of device they use to access Canvas and then taking the device-type into consideration when assessing participation, this correction is unlikely given that these issues in data quality are not made readily apparent to instructors using the course and student analytics functions on their Canvas course page. It is also worth pointing out that, by posting this explanation of the context card on a page external to the Canvas website, developers are working against their own narratives that LMSs are self-contained systems. Even if instructors were able to find and access the information that is posted on the external Canvas Community website, they would be hard pressed to find detailed explanations about how Canvas's LA work.

Just as Canvas's analytics fail to account for data generated via the mobile app, they also inevitably fail to account for non-digital activities. If, for instance, a student downloads the course assignments and syllabus, or prints out a PDF of course materials, perhaps for accessibility reasons, they may return to that printed or downloaded document many more times throughout the semester. However, because their page view and participation data will only show that they have visited the page once, Canvas's analytics will rate that student's activities as being less than, say, another student in the course who accesses course material just as frequently, but via a web browser.

These largely unaddressed issues with the quality and equity of student data are problematic, especially considering that Canvas posits its course and student analytics features as capable of predicting and preventing "at risk" students. Consider the following hypothetical example: An instructor using Canvas notices that a student has been automatically flagged by the system's course and student

---

1 "Mobile data is not included unless a user accesses Canvas directly through a mobile browser, or if a user accesses content within the mobile app that redirects to a mobile browser."

analytics features as potentially "at risk" (for instance, by highlighting their name in red in the gradebook). The instructor clicks on the student's context card and sees that, according to the system's analytics, the student has a low page view ranking (one star out of three), a low participation ranking (two stars out of three), and has not submitted anything for an assignment that is now overdue. If the course is small enough in terms of student enrollment, and if the semester is far enough along that the instructor knows the student personally, the instructor might realize that the student has not shown up to class for the past few sessions. Wanting to investigate further, the instructor checks the student's activity records and finds that the student has not generated any new data for two weeks. Assuming the student has not recently logged onto the course Canvas site, the instructor could then triangulate that perhaps the student is experiencing some distress and send a follow-up email. If the class is large or it is early in the semester, and the instructor is not familiar with the student, however, the likelihood of them recognizing this student as being at risk drops significantly. Now, imagine that there is a student who has been regularly attending class, but experiences perpetual anxiety about her performance, leading her to check the course's Canvas page frequently. Because she has generated a lot of data on the Canvas website, she is not flagged by the system. Her high participation and page view rankings mask the difficulty she's having, preventing the same kind of outreach more "obviously" struggling students would receive.

There are a number of factors that could contribute to a false positive or negative in Canvas's analytics: mental health, technical difficulties or limitations, group work, or offline ("analog") work. Identifying and correcting a false positive or negative is difficult, however, given how opaquely Canvas's Course and Student Analytics are structured. While analytics for individual students are made available to instructors, those same analytics are not available within the student view. In other words, students cannot see the data that they themselves have generated. On the one hand, opacity could be a benefit because students are less likely to game the system by artificially manipulating their data. However, it poses an even larger ethical dilemma: Without disclosing the types of assessment mechanics of the Canvas website to students in the course syllabus, for example, students may not be aware of how (or even *that*) their digital behavior is influencing not only their instructor's perception of them but potentially their course grade as well. Leaving students unaware of how their activity is being represented to instructors renders them unable to address inconsistencies, errors, or gaps that may arise across their own Canvas data.

The idea of tracking student activity for assessment purposes resonates with a movement in writing assessment toward labor-based contract grading. At their most basic level, labor-based grading contracts are a form of writing assessment that privileges student work, or labor, done for the course (i.e., reading, writing, reflecting, discussing, assessing) over subjective judgements from instructors and peers as to the quality of student writing. Essentially, the more labor that students do for the course, the better their grade will be. Scholarship from Asao Inoue (2019) frames labor-based contract grading as a powerful tool for antiracist writing assessment. Inoue (2019) argues that, because labor-based contracts count all labor as equally valuable when determining student grades, they help "build equity among diverse students with diverse linguistic competencies since it is a grading system that does not depend on a particular set of linguistic competencies to acquire grades" (p. 132).

Mapping the ideas central to labor-based contract grading onto the LMS learning analytic model, we can see a number of parallels emerge. Both LA and labor-based contract grading are framed rhetorically as pedagogical tools for making classroom environments more inclusive and for helping empower student learners to achieve course learning goals. Further, both assessment practices use records of student activity to gauge student progress toward course learning goals.

While both models of assessment are built upon the same promise—namely, that they can help instructors teach more equitably and effectively—their underlying methodologies reveal stark differences: When constructing a labor-based grading contract, instructors and students have a significant degree of agency to decide what counts as labor. When using course and student analytics on an LMS like Canvas, however, students are granted no agency to decide what data count as effort or labor, nor can they intervene in their own assessment. Returning to the notion of using LA as a lens into students' affective experience, we can see how LMS might then create risky learning environments wherein individual students, coded as users, are compared and assessed.

DATA QUALITY AND THE FUTURE OF DATA ANALYTICS

Over the past few years, some schools have begun using their LMS software as a tool to detect cheating retroactively by using data mined during exams and without student consent. New York Times contributors Natasha Singer and Aaron Krolik (2021) have investigated Dartmouth's use of Canvas for detecting academic dishonesty. They found that Dartmouth's Medical School had accused 17 students of cheating with evidence that had been identified using automated systems for gathering user activity data. Singer and Krolik (2021) explain,

> While some students may have cheated, technology experts said, it would be difficult for a disciplinary committee to distinguish cheating from non-cheating based on the data

snapshots that Dartmouth provided to accused students. And in an analysis of the Canvas software code, The Times found instances in which the system automatically generated activity data even when no one was using a device.

Questions about the quality of data are rarely at the forefront of institutional discussions around LMS adoption. This lack of attention toward the Big Data end of Canvas is in part a product of the way that data privacy policies get configured in LMS software. For students, informed consent with respect to LMS data practices and policies becomes tacit upon enrollment. When universities subscribe to a particular LMS, they are not only giving consent for their own institutional data to be harvested, but they are also granting consent on behalf of their staff, faculty, and students. This practice of granting consent-by-proxy raises important ethical issues around data practices, especially in terms of what data are made visible and for whom. These issues are compounded when we consider the issues with data quality illustrated earlier: Many students and instructors are unaware of the data being collected.

It is important to recognize that, while not all instructors are currently using LA to track and assess students' learning progress (and while these features may not yet be perceived as critical to the system's functionality), there continues to be more widespread uptake among educators of features like the student context card, especially in the wake of the pandemic as instructors become more familiar with the Canvas platform and gain experience facilitating more of their teaching via the Canvas LMS. As high-enrollment courses and online-only courses become more prevalent on college campuses (a parallel change that is also a result of increased demands for greater efficiency and access in higher education), instructors may find themselves ever more inclined to use Canvas's LA to gauge their students' progress and effort. Their assessments will be (whether they know it or not) tied directly to the capacity of the LMS to track and analyze student data.

LA will soon be (if they aren't already) knocking on the door of WAC practitioners around the nation. As Mike Palmquist (2020) notes, "It seems likely that we will see a significant emphasis on the development of analytics tools that draw on data from student writing, their other behaviors in their courses, and their academic and demographic backgrounds" (p. 64). It's critical that WAC practitioners pay attention to these developments and anticipate the ways in which they will impact the writing classroom. It is our responsibility to investigate how LA function at our own institutions and to learn how (and what) student data gets packaged and presented to instructors so that we can engage in critical conversation with faculty about the digital contexts within which they are teaching and students are writing. When talking to faculty about responding to and evaluating student writing, for instance, WAC leaders should create space to discuss the ways that their institution's LMS shapes the assessment process, including LA functions like Canvas's context card.

LMSs are not pedagogically neutral technologies, but rather, through their very design, they influence and guide teaching. Data-driven learning assessment, and LA more broadly, necessitate that higher education agencies, including instructors, students, and administrators, try to normalize not only what success looks like in the classroom and university, but also how students can move across educational spaces and how instructors can engage with students. The standards of success built into LMSs and other LA-equipped platforms are grounded in subjective claims with real material consequences. As Trevor Pinch (2008) argues, "Standards are rarely simply technical matters; they are powerful ways of bringing a resolution to debates that might encompass different social meanings of a technology. Standards are set to be followed; they entail routinized social actions and are in effect a form of institutionalization" (p. 473). Not only does this limit the visibility of non-digital actors, but it simultaneously promotes a fabricated perspective of student experience because the algorithmic outputs of the system are always already contingent on subjective agencies that produced the parameters for data interpretation.

Despite the myriad conveniences LA platforms afford instructors (especially in terms of streamlining the management and distribution of course materials), the reliance on algorithmic structures for analyzing data will always fail to account for the complex and multi-faceted realities of student learning. Far from revealing the realities of student learning, LA creates and deepens blind spots around how instructors can best "see" student learning, all while fostering misconceptions about what counts as learning in the writing classroom. As a mode of assessment, LA—with its reliance on predetermined standards for assessing learning and opaque methods for surveilling student work—ends up constraining rather than empowering student learners.

REFERENCES

Aguilar, S. J., Karabenick, S. A., Teasley, S. D. & Baek, C. (2021). Associations between learning analytics dashboard exposure and motivation and self-regulated learning. *Computers and Education, 162*, pp. 1–11. https://doi.org/10.1016/j.compedu.2020.104085.

Bienkowski, M., Feng, M. & Means, B. (2012). Enhancing teaching and learning through educational data mining and learning analytics: An issue brief. U.S. Department of Education, Office of Educational Technology. https://tech.ed.gov/wp-content/uploads/2014/03/edm-la-brief.pdf.

Canvas Doc Team. (n.d.). *Canvas LMS Community*. Retrieved June 26, 2019, from https://community.canvaslms.com/docs/DOC-12709-4152698664.

Canvas the Learning Management Platform. (2019). *Canvas*. https://www.instructure.com/canvas.

Coates, H., James, R. & Baldwin, G. (2005). A critical examination of the effects of learning management systems on university teaching and learning. *Tertiary Education and Management, 11*, 19–36. https://doi.org/10.1007/s11233-004-3567-9.

Crawford, K., Gray, M. L. & Miltner, K. (2014). Critiquing big data: Politics, ethics, epistemology. *International Journal of Communication, 8*(10). https://ijoc.org/index.php/ijoc/article/view/2167/1164.

Glossary. (2019). *Canvas*. https://learn.canvas.net/courses/1208/pages/glossary-basic-analytics-terms?module_item_id=161592.

Improving Learning. (2019). *Canvas*. https://www.instructure.com/canvas/higher-education/empowering-faculty/improving-learning.

Inoue, A. B. (2019). *Labor-based grading contracts: Building equity and inclusion in the compassionate writing classroom*. The WAC Clearinghouse; University Press of Colorado. https://doi.org/10.37514/PER-B.2019.0216.0.

Kuh, G. D. & Ewell, P. T. (2010). The state of learning outcomes assessment in the United States. *Higher Education Management and Policy, 22*(1), 1–20. https://doi.org/10.1787/17269822.

LMS Data, Spring 2021 Updates. (2021, June 21). Edutechnica. https://edutechnica.com/2021/06/21/lms-data-spring-2021-updates/.

McKee, H. A. (2011). Policy matters now and in the future. Net neutrality, corporate data mining, and government surveillance. *Computers and Composition, 28*(4), 276–291. https://doi.org/10.1016/j.compcom.2011.09.001.

Palmquist, M. (2020). Learning analytics in writing instruction: Implications for writing across the curriculum. In L. E. Bartlett, S. L. Tarabochia, A. R. Olinger, A. R. & M. J. Marshall (Eds.), *Diverse approaches to teaching, learning, and writing across the curriculum: IWAC at 25* (pp. 55–72). The WAC Clearinghouse; University Press of Colorado. https://doi.org/10.37514/PER-B.2020.0360.

Pinch, T. (2008). Technology and institutions: Living in a material world. *Theory and Society, 37*(5), 461–483. https://www.jstor.org/stable/40345597.

Reyman, J. (2010). *The rhetoric of intellectual property: Copyright law and the regulation of digital culture*. Routledge.

Salisbury, M. (2017, April 9). Big hopes, scant evidence. *The Chronicle of Higher Education*. https://www.chronicle.com/article/big-hopes-scant-evidence/.

Singer, N. & Krolik, A. (2021, May 9). Online cheating charges upend Dartmouth Medical School. *The New York Times*. New York Times Company. https://www.nytimes.com/2021/05/09/technology/dartmouth-geisel-medical-cheating.html.

Society for Learning Analytics Research. (2022). *What is learning analytics?* SoLAR. https://www.solaresearch.org/about/what-is-learning-analytics/.

Spellings, M. (2006). *A test of leadership: Charting the future of U.S. higher education*. U.S. Department of Education.

CHAPTER 11.

WHEN LEARNING OUTCOMES MASK LEARNING, PART 2: PROBING ASSUMPTIONS ABOUT ASSESSMENT VIA DISCIPLINARY GENRES

Angela J. Zito
University of Wisconsin-Madison

Kathleen Daly Weisse's interrogation of learning analytics' (LA) unfulfillable promise in Chapter 10 opens an introspective space for us to reflect on the promise at the heart of WAC—that teaching with writing can deepen student learning in and across disciplines.[1] In this critical space, I ask: To what extent might disciplinary genres posit "algorithmic" assessments of their own? That is, to draw out the analogy in full, is it all that far-fetched to consider some of the prescribed conventions of disciplinary writing as themselves arbitrary indicators of student learning outcomes (SLOs), somewhere along the same spectrum as page views and timestamps? The significance of this question lies less in the exactness of the analogy than in the stakes that its comparison makes apparent: If we take seriously the concerns Kathleen raises about LA's capacity to capture the complex realities of student learning, we must also consider how the gap between student learning in the disciplines and student *writing* in the disciplines might likewise obscure or delegitimize some forms of learning and, in so doing, perpetuate inequities in higher education.

Consider, for instance, Asao Inoue (2015; 2019) and colleagues' (Inoue & Poe, 2012) demonstrations of how constructs like disciplinary convention can house white racial habitus and white language supremacy to the persistent exclusion of students of color. Further, as Dan Melzer (2014) reports in his study of assignments across the disciplines, even where instructors emphasize

---

1 This chapter was conceived and written prior to OpenAI's public release of ChatGPT in late 2022. I encourage readers to consider, now, how the training of such generative artificial intelligence renders genre literally (not analogically) algorithmic, and how such generic reproduction affects student learning and writing in the disciplines.

"critical thinking" in their course learning outcomes, their evaluative focus often targets students' performance of academic writing—what Inoue refers to as students' performance of white English, or what Jamila M. Kareem (2020) refers to as students' performance of "linguistic respectability." Importantly, Kareem also reminds us that the expectation for such performance exceeds linguistic patterns and perpetuates exclusion on cultural levels, too. "A focus on disciplinary conventions is critical to current WAC principles," she writes, "yet without exploring or critiquing the cultural epistemologies embedded within the conventions, programs remain assimilationist" (2020, p. 304). Again, the algorithm analogy serves to underscore the stakes of assessment via disciplinary genres: Where LA codify digital behavior (e.g., page views) as indicators of learning, genre conventions codify linguistic behavior as indicators of learning. Assimilation of digital behaviors to fit LA assessment tools may not pose serious concerns to some, but assimilation of linguistic and cultural behavior to fit the assessment tool of formal academic writing should be more clearly problematic to all.

There is simply more to be said about WAC's role in prompting faculty to critically examine their use of disciplinary genres to assess student learning. This is especially true where course learning outcomes do not prioritize professionalization in the discipline, as in many introductory level undergraduate courses. While such courses' learning outcomes might include something like "clear academic writing," more often they will identify foundational knowledge and skills in disciplinary ways of thinking, reading, and researching. However, as observed by IWAC colleagues who attended my and Kathleen's panel presentation at the Fifteenth International Writing Across The Curriculum Conference, these latter outcomes often become "coded" in particular features of writing anyway. As one conference participant put it: "a piece of writing functions sort of like Canvas analytics—a potentially reductive extrapolation." Another chimed in, saying, "It's so easy for the assessment itself (the essay, the genre, etc.) to become the learning goal. They tend to subsume the teacher's hopes & dreams for the course" (Weisse & Zito, 2021).

In this chapter, I report findings from my scholarship of teaching and learning (SoTL) in literary studies that contribute to such a conversation in WAC. I discuss how a group of English literature instructors independently but universally agree on a core SLO for introductory level courses—"reading for complexity"—and how they use a disciplinary genre (the literary analysis essay) to assess student learning toward that outcome. My analysis reveals a pattern among some of these instructors to assume that student writing provides a transparent reflection of student thinking, such that the complexity of a student's writing serves as a proxy for their "reading for complexity." I argue that a student's development of disciplinary reading practices (or research practices or thinking practices) is not necessarily transparent in their performance of discipline-specific genres, and that, as such, genre conventions are insufficient (if not exclusionary) as indicators of some SLOs. I propose that WAC practitioners might adopt a phrase like *writing ~~reading~~* as a theoretical shorthand for this concept.[2] For example, while the literature instructors in my study identified *reading* as the core SLO in their introductory courses, some focused their assessment of this SLO solely in formal academic *writing*, which ignores or omits other indicators of effective disciplinary reading (thus, *writing ~~reading~~*). In other contexts, WAC professionals might help faculty identify ways in which disciplinary genre conventions conceal as well reveal student achievement of thinking-oriented SLOs (*writing ~~thinking~~*) and research-oriented SLOs (*writing ~~research~~*) as well as reading-oriented SLOs.

STUDY CONTEXT AND METHODS

This IRB-approved study, conducted at the University of Wisconsin-Madison, focused on the assessment practices of introductory literature course (ILC) instructors. ILCs are general education literature courses open to all undergraduate students with no prerequisites. At this institution, they are offered in both high-enrollment lecture and small seminar formats. All the instructors interviewed as part of this study taught ILCs in the lecture format, which are taught by a combination of faculty (who design course assignments and facilitate lecture) and graduate teaching assistants (who design small discussion lesson plans and grade student papers). Enrollment can be anywhere from 50 to 200.

As part of a grounded theory approach, I conducted intensive semi-structured interviews with 18 ILC instructors, including five faculty (two assistant and three full professors), three faculty administrators (full professors who also hold administrative posts within the department), and ten graduate teaching assistants (TAs). The semi-structured design of my interview protocol promoted flexibility in these conversations, allowing them to develop around participants' perspectives, experiences, and reflections. Conversation generally moved from instructors' broad views about the purpose of ILCs toward increasingly specific considerations of their own goals and practices. I purposefully designed this conversational movement—from broad purpose to SLOs to means of assessment—in order to elicit participants' reflections on disciplinary, institutional, and departmental influences on their goals and practices.

---

2   The visual representation of this phrase includes a line struck through the word *reading*, such that it is simultaneously legible and obscured.

I used a combination of process and *in vivo* coding in my initial analysis of interview transcripts (Saldaña, 2013). As I grew more familiar with the data and could see how smaller coded units coalesced into larger categories, my focused coding began the work of "raising concepts" (Charmaz, 2014, p. 247). One of the theoretical concepts developed through this iterative analysis I termed *writing reading*. The following sections of this chapter elaborate on the genesis of this concept and, more importantly, its implications for WAC.

IDENTIFYING "READING FOR COMPLEXITY" AS A DISCIPLINARY LEARNING OUTCOME

My analysis yielded six categories of SLOs that participating instructors identified for their ILCs: read literature, read the world, participate in academic discourse, participate in collective life, find pleasure (in literature and the humanities), and gain confidence (in personal capacities). Reading, in its complementary permutations as "read literature" and "read the world," is unique among these categories in its universal identification among participating instructors. The phrases "read literature" and "read the world" are in vivo codes that I used to track and categorize patterns in instructors' descriptions of reading-focused learning outcomes. The "world," in my coding, refers to any text identified as not literature by the interviewee, including texts like personal experience (e.g., "[students] themselves"), interpersonal relations (e.g., "situations in real life"), larger sociocultural phenomena (e.g., "social and cultural landscapes"), popular media (e.g., "things [students] see online"), and academic writing (e.g., "history texts," "psychology texts").

The remaining SLO categories ("participate in academic discourse," "participate in collective life," "find pleasure," and "gain confidence"), while not necessarily posited as vehicles for reading, were typically presented alongside reading literature and reading the world. I interpret this particular co-occurrence not as a hierarchy but as a continuum of outcomes (see Figure 11.1).

Conceptualizing instructors' desired learning outcomes in this way enables us to perceive various circuits through the continuum, highlighting some outcomes while keeping the others "in view," so to speak. This might mean, for instance, that one instructor traces a circuit among the outcomes "read literature," "participate in academic discourse," "read the world," and "gain confidence." Within this circuit, the instructor might expect that students will learn to write in academic prose appropriate to the literary studies discourse community ("participate in academic discourse"), specifically so that they might demonstrate their abilities to "read literature" and "read the world." I will return to this prioritization of outcomes in the following section.

When Learning Outcomes Mask Learning, Part 2

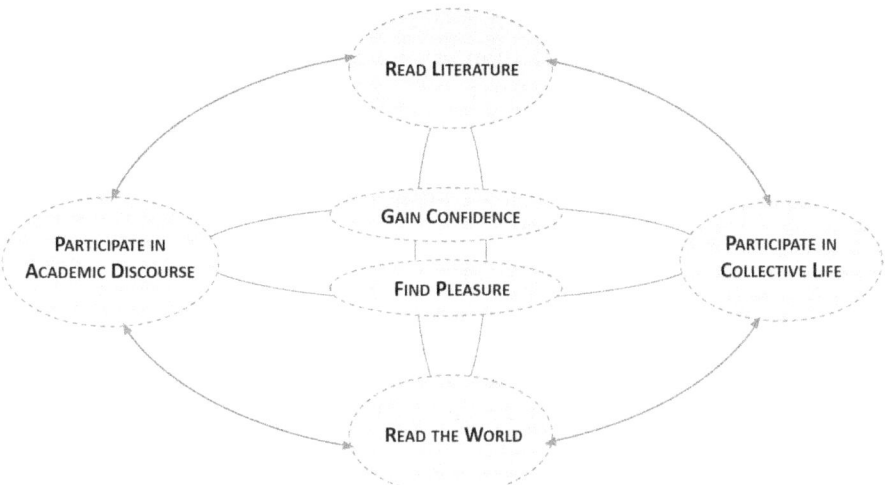

Figure 11.1. Continuum of student learning outcomes for introductory literature courses.

First, let me concede that it is unsurprising that reading would figure so prominently in these interviews—one naturally expects students to read in literature courses. What's interesting is that participating instructors emphasize not only *what* is read but *how*. The *how* of reading ties the two outcomes together in that instructors claim—vehemently—that one can and should read the world just as one would read literature. For example, faculty ILC lecturer Cameron says, "I'm teaching [students] to read the world by exploring and practicing methods of analysis in some of the most complex and sophisticated forms of cultural expression we can encounter. You get good at that, you get good at reading the world." The "methods" of reading taught in ILCs, Cameron implies, remain intact when transferred across objects of reading, be they worldly or literary. Within this hypothesis of transfer, Cameron and others seem to identify one particularly salient outcome of literary learning: Students will become better readers of whatever they encounter by practicing the methods of analysis unique to literary study.

The potential for transfer of reading methods between worldly and literary texts, as instructors perceive it, positions these kinds of texts as separate from one another. For many literary scholars, though (including those I interviewed), hard boundaries separating the world from literary imaginings of it are blurry if not specious. To account for this, I've attempted to capture both the close relation and distinction between reading *literature* and reading *the world* in their orientation on the continuum illustrated in Figure 11.1. The circular formation of and dotted lines around all the outcome categories are meant to visualize the fluid and provisional boundaries between them, as each is defined at least in part by its relation to the others. "Read literature" and "read the world" mirror one another, each described by interviewees as some combination of "close reading skills," "critical reading skills," and "critical thinking skills."

The only real difference, it would appear, is *what* is being read. For many instructors, however, this difference contains within it a distinct sameness. For instance, one faculty instructor, Jesse, proposed that literature allows, invites, or otherwise prepares students to *also* read the world (conceptually separating the two objects), but then went on to suggest that it is the substance of literature and not just how it is read that makes it best suited to build this connection—specifically, because the substance of literature creates the *illusion* that it and not the world is being read (conceptually combining the two objects). Jesse said:

> [Literature] gives a little cushion to what you're talking about. [. . .] We're not talking about what's going on in your life, we're talking about [a fictional world]. I mean, it's a little disingenuous, but I think it's like the problems in literature that we discuss are life problems, and life problems are connected to literature. So, it is a bit of an illusion that it's a cushion, but I think that it becomes easier to talk about issues when we have a fictional world as the point of our discussion.

By figuring literature as an illusory "cushion" between the reader and the "real" world implicated in the fictional text, Jesse posits that these two objects of reading are simultaneously the same and different. "Reading literature" and "reading the world" are distinct but inextricable categories that define the reading practices characteristic of literary study.

Reading is thus theorized in these instructor interviews as a continuous oscillation between navigating complexity in literature and navigating complexity in the world, such that engaging in one practice either reflects or anticipates the other. *Reading for complexity*, as I articulate this shared learning outcome, requires the navigation of diverse perspectives, the exploration of many possible interpretations, and the active construction of meaning with (not merely of) the text. This learning outcome is consistent with what research in SoTL and writing in the disciplines (WID) has identified as the characterizing features of disciplinary reading in literary studies (Chick et al., 2009; Tinkle et al., 2013; Wilder, 2012; Wolfe & Wilder, 2016). This includes the analogous relation literary scholars draw between literature and the world through the shared traits of complexity, ambiguity, multiplicity, and difficulty (Bruns, 2011; Linkon, 2011; Rosenblatt, 1995; Salvatori & Donahue, 2005; Zunshine, 2006).

Though "reading for complexity" was not stated explicitly in their course syllabi or writing assignments, this learning outcome clearly informed what participating ILC instructors taught, how they taught it, and how they designed their assessments. However, the disciplinary practice that defines successful reading for complexity (i.e., the conscious oscillation between reading literature and reading the world) can become obscured through the major genre used to evaluate it.

THE LITERARY ANALYSIS ESSAY; OR, WHERE STUDENT READING BECOMES (IN)VISIBLE

When asked how they can perceive and evaluate student learning in their courses, all participating instructors identified writing assignments as the primary means. They located evidence of students' reading for complexity most frequently and in most detail within a specific genre of writing: the literary analysis essay. The prevalence of this genre suggests that these ILC instructors perceived it to be their most effective assessment tool. What strikes me as more important still is that the majority of instructors did not identify the literary analysis essay as a disciplinary genre, nor as a genre chosen specifically to assess students' reading for complexity. Rather, most discussed students' literary analysis essays as "writing" generally, the assessment of which would simultaneously evaluate students' capacities to read for complexity and to write those readings out.

WID scholar Laura Wilder (2012) reports similar trends in her conversations with literature professors who use the literary analysis essay to assess students' acquisition of "domain knowledge" in literary reading practices. "The demonstration of this knowledge in writing," she reports, "is presented as a transparent transition: discover an understanding of literature and then 'show' that understanding in writing" (p. 71). Wilder also notes that, though her interviewees described their assignments as having some commonalities with the literary analysis they write professionally, "they do little to clarify the specific rhetorical purposes and strategies of this genre by insisting to students that the 'good writing' they seek defies genre and disciplinary contexts" (p. 63). Wilder's observation echoes those made in previous WAC research (for example, Thaiss & Zawacki, 2006).

Contrary to her interviewees' beliefs, Wilder (2012) characterizes literary analysis *as* a disciplinary genre by analyzing its rhetorical strategies, which she demonstrates are foundational to the construction of knowledge within the literary studies discourse community.[3] In undergraduate contexts, the literary analysis essay is an approximation of the literary criticism published

---

3   See Wilder's (2012) discussion of special topoi in literary analysis.

by scholars in the field. The genre is argumentative in nature, making claims about the meaning of a text by using characteristic rhetorical strategies and supporting those claims through analysis of the text's formal, linguistic, and contextual features.

While the rhetorical strategies Wilder identifies work to categorize literary analysis as a discipline-specific genre, the structural similarities between literary analysis and other academic writing allow it to be categorized more generally as what John Bean and Dan Melzer (2021) term "closed-form, thesis governed writing" (p. 74). They observe that this kind of writing is "prototypical" for most academic prose (p. 74) and identify the following characteristic features:

- An explicit thesis statement, usually in the introduction;
- Clear forecasting of the structure to follow;
- Unified and coherent paragraphs introduced by topic sentences;
- Clear transitions and signposts throughout (in some cases facilitated by various levels of headings); and
- Coherently linked sentences aimed at maximum clarity and readability (p. 48).

Bean and Melzer describe this kind of writing as "closed" because its structural features promise a reading experience with no digressions, gaps, or other surprises. "Because its structure and style aim for maximum clarity," they write, "the value of closed-form prose rests on the quality of the ideas it presents. The closed-form structure aims to make those ideas as clear and transparent as possible" (p. 48).

This assumption that closed-form writing provides a clear view into student learning and thinking is strikingly similar to Wilder's observation about the "transparent transition" her interviewees assumed take place in students' literary analyses. Here we begin to see the potential for disciplinary genre conventions—or the structural expectations of closed-form academic writing more broadly—to pose problematic "algorithms" for the assessment of student learning. An algorithmic approach to assessment uses a prescribed set of variables to indicate the quality of students' ideas or the advancement of their learning. Compare the characteristics of closed-form prose listed above (e.g., explicit thesis statement, clear transitions) to learning analytics data (e.g., page views, time per page). What train of logic connects the prescribed indicator to the intended learning outcome? What assumptions must we make to expect that an effective topic sentence will indicate a student's ability to read for complexity?

In my own interviews, ILC instructors often connected the kinds of reading they were looking for to similar structural indicators in students' literary analysis essays. Specifically, instructors identified "sophistication of analysis" as evidence of reading for complexity. The way many of them described the kinds of sophistication they hope to see in student writing echoes how they characterized literary reading. For instance, Jaime, an assistant professor, perceived evidence of student learning in the increasingly nuanced questions students ask of texts over the course of multiple literary analysis assignments:

> [S]tudents often start [by] asking questions that are universalizing: "How does this text say something about what it means to be a good mother? Or what it means to live a good life?" Instead, they later start to ask questions like, "How does this [text] provide a variety of ways of understanding responses to environmental crisis?" They start asking questions that are more historically focused, and actually more interesting for that. [. . .] You can [also] start to see students do more generous analyses. Initially, most students want to take one of [two] polarizing approaches: they either buy into the ideology of a [text] completely—and so they are trying to make a convincing case for why the most messed up ideologically bad elements of a text are good—or they're complete ideology readers—they're like this whole text is evil, and it's evil to its core, boom. You can tell that students are becoming more [skilled readers] when they begin to really engage with the fine-grained nuances of a text as itself being contradictory, having multiple ideologies operate at once, and doing different things for different viewers. Like, you can just see that in the analysis.

What Jaime looks for in student writing is evidence of a reading process that precedes and reemerges through the student's process of composition. Students' pursuit of more advanced, nuanced questions evinces a mindset that expects and seeks to parse complexity in the text, and students' increasing engagement with paradox ("a text as itself being contradictory") evinces a process of rereading and exploration of multiple possibilities for making sense of the text. Through these aspects of students' development across multiple literary analyses, Jaime sees artifacts of students reading for complexity.

However, how instructors use the term "analysis" to describe what they look for in student writing seems split: Some instructors tie together sophistication *of thought* and sophistication *of expression* under the term "analysis," whereas others seek to extricate the two. For instance, TA instructor Riley seems to use the terms "argument," "analysis," and "belief" interchangeably when describing where she wants to see students' heightened sophistication as evidence of their literary reading: "Something that I look for is a shift or some sort of development in sophistication in the ways that [students] make arguments, or the sophistication of the analysis that goes into coming to that position, or that belief, which you can definitely see in their writing." While sophistication in "the ways that [students] make arguments" might suggest a facility for articulating thesis statements and topic sentences, sophistication of "the analysis that goes into coming to that [. . .] belief" points to the process of actively exploring several "positions" before identifying a particularly compelling interpretation around which to articulate a thesis.

Scott, another TA participating in this focus group interview, more explicitly values sophistication of thought over sophistication of expression, leading others in the group to ascribe value to the level of difficulty students' analyses achieve:

> SCOTT: It's really difficult, these sorts of learning goals that we're talking about [i.e. reading for complexity]. They're ones that even we still are kind of learning, right? And, so, it's the idea that first starting to grapple with it— Even if the student stumbles, so long as they made the effort and are living sort of within the text itself, I'm happy with that. Even if the reading is kind of goofy.
>
> RILEY: Yeah, I definitely will value sort of quirkiness and grappling—very highly actually.
>
> JENNY: It's like in gymnastics or whatever, the difficulty points. Yeah, I give huge points for difficulty.

These TAs want to see their students push beyond their initial understandings of a text by "grappling" with increasingly sophisticated ideas in and derived from the text. They recognize these increasingly sophisticated ideas as evidence of successful reading for complexity (through "difficulty points"), even where the expression of those ideas is not yet itself sophisticated (the "reading" as it is presented in writing is "kind of goofy").

Those instructors who located "sophistication of analysis" in quality of expression as well as ideas did so by pointing to logically organized and evidence-based argumentation as the primary indicator. As such, sophistication of expression included adherence to the structural conventions of closed form, thesis-governed writing, as well as to the linguistic conventions of standard edited American English. For example, Marion, a TA, posited that sophistication in written expression leads to and/or exemplifies sophistication in thinking. "Those things function together," she said, and continued:

> No matter how great your ideas are, if you can't communicate them effectively no one will know what they are, and you'll

> never be able to share them with anyone. So, the idea is that if you get good at one you'll get good at the other, right? If you don't feel like you have great big original ideas, if you just practice at crafting a specific enough argument you'll learn how to come up with those ideas. Or, if you feel like you have lots of great ideas, if you work at crafting/explaining them well those ideas will get better and better.

By positing that writing and rewriting arguments leads not only to the generation but the increased sophistication of ideas, Marion seems to imply a process of reading and rereading for complexity as well. Marion suggests that students' logically organized, evidence-based argumentation serves to guide, support, and ultimately visualize reading for complexity—whether that is rereading their own writing with an eye toward "communicating more effectively" (i.e., by observing the structural and linguistic conventions of the assignment's genre) or rereading the literary text with the conventions of literary argumentation in mind (i.e., by sifting through passages that might better support an interpretive claim).

Lee, a full professor, proposes a similar theory about the reciprocal nature of sophistication in thought and expression—practice one (i.e., writing within disciplinary conventions) and get better at the other (i.e., reading for complexity). Lee describes reading for complexity as "an ability to step back from one's own ideological assumptions and look at one's own culture with more analytic perspective." When asked how such an outcome might be assessed, Lee replied:

> Most of the grading reflects written work, and good writing requires clear thinking, and it requires logical thinking and logical presentation of ideas, and if you can get students to make headway in effectively organizing paragraphs and effectively organizing arguments, you really have changed their thinking skills. [. . .] I think [stepping back from one's own ideological assumptions] would be reflected in the analytic work that students did. But it's not as easy to [pause] I think it's easier to just look at a paragraph and say, "Look at the flow, does this logically follow from this, has this been defended?" [. . .] Whereas this kind of conceptual growth— It's going to be there in the sophistication of the thinking, but harder to pinpoint.

Lee proposes a transparent transition between students' reading for complexity and the sophistication with which that reading is expressed. The structural features of the genre—thesis statement, topic sentences, systematic quotation and analysis—are presumed to be the best available means of assessing students' ability to read for complexity.

Reading for complexity requires students to wrestle with unfamiliar language, investigate multiple interpretive possibilities, and contend with worldviews significantly different from their own. When instructors frame the disciplinary writing done in ILCs as general "academic" writing, these reading practices become more difficult for students to perceive (hence, *writing ~~reading~~*). Further, when instructors adopt structural and linguistic features of student writing as indicators of their engagement with textual complexity, *writing assessment* can easily and tacitly displace writing as an *assessment of reading* (also, *writing ~~reading~~*).

IMPLICATIONS FOR WAC AND (IN)EQUITY IN STUDENT LEARNING

Kathleen's discussion of LA illuminates the necessity of interrogating our systems of assessment so that we think twice before relying on prescribed indicators of learning. I propose that WAC practitioners and the instructors they work with exercise similar caution when adopting the prescribed conventions of disciplinary genres. Used as an assessment of non-writing SLOs, disciplinary genre conventions can conceal as well as reveal aspects of student learning. Of greater concern, by assuming that students' performance of closed-form, thesis-governed writing provides a transparent indicator of their thinking, we risk perpetuating the exclusion of already marginalized students by expecting—and rewarding—assimilation into dominant (i.e., White, colonial, ableist, etc.) discourse.

WAC provides a critical venue for wrestling with these issues of assessment. When consulting with instructors on course design and scaffolding writing assignments to assess course SLOs, WAC professionals might discuss the limitations of using disciplinary genre conventions as a default measure of student learning. A phrase like "writing ~~reading~~" or "writing ~~research~~," with the non-writing SLO partially obscured with a strikethrough, might serve as a shorthand reminder of these limitations. WAC practitioners can describe how an instructor's evaluative focus on students' formal academic writing skills can actually obstruct their perception of whether and how well students achieve their target SLOs. Instructors might then be encouraged to make more conscious, purposeful decisions about what disciplinary genres or genre conventions (if any) to adopt as indicators of non-writing learning outcomes. Or, those non-writing learning outcomes might be more intentionally woven into these consultations, encouraging faculty to consider how an SLO like reading or research is approached in their course as a disciplinary practice, how it is scaffolded alongside other course content, and how it is assessed.

Of course, individual consultations aren't the only way in which concerns about equity in assessment might be broached. Angela Glotfelter, Ann Updike, and Elizabeth Wardle (2020) make a strong case that cross-disciplinary conversations among faculty—more so than being lectured at by WAC consultants—can lead to increased awareness of how deeply connected academic genres are to disciplinary ways of thinking. From their program assessment of such a WAC faculty seminar, Glotfelter et al. (2020) report that faculty began to break large writing assignments into smaller parts, provide more scaffolding, and allow more time for students to write. For example, one faculty survey respondent shared that, "While I used scaffolded writing in the past, I have increased the number of low-stakes assignments, and become more deliberate in tailoring them to specific, initially limited objectives" (p. 182). Participants' increased intentionality in aligning assignments and outcomes shows a movement away from "algorithmic" structures of assessment. In other words, by engaging in cross-disciplinary conversation with other faculty, these instructors began to more carefully *select* indicators ("tailoring [assignments] to specific, initially limited objectives") rather than uncritically adopt those indicators prescribed in disciplinary genres.

More important still, WAC—as a profession and as a community of individual practitioners—might choose to enact Culturally Sustaining Pedagogy (CSP) in the ways Kareem (2020) suggests. Incorporating CSP into WAC would mean, according to Kareem, "resist[ing] practices that aim to assimilate the blackness and brownness out of students and instead see raciolinguistic diversity as a strength" (p. 295). Further, she writes, "CSP affords the means to study, understand, and learn to use writing in disciplines through the lens of complex discursive practices of communities of color, by decentering Eurocentrism in the curriculum" (p. 299). In this way, CSP perhaps offers a framework for instructors (for literature instructors, especially) to "read for complexity" the texts of their discipline—that is, to navigate diverse perspectives, explore many possible interpretations, and actively construct meaning with (not of) their students.

REFERENCES

Bean, J. C. & Melzer, D. (2021). *Engaging ideas: The professor's guide to integrating writing, critical thinking, and active learning in the classroom* (3rd ed.). Jossey-Bass.

Bruns, C. V. (2011). *Why literature? The value of literary reading and what it means for teaching.* The Continuum International Publishing Group.

Charmaz, K. (2014). *Constructing grounded theory* (2nd ed.). Sage.

Chick, N. L., Hassel, H. & Haynie, A. (2009). Pressing an ear against the hive: Reading literature for complexity. *Pedagogy, 9*(3), 399–422. https://doi.org/10.1215/15314200-2009-003.

Glotfelter, A., Updike A. & Wardle E. (2020). "Something invisible . . . has been made visible for me": An expertise-based WAC seminar model grounded in theory and (cross) disciplinary dialogue. In L. E. Bartlett, S. L. Tarabochia, A. R. Olinger & M. J. Marshall (Eds.), *Diverse approaches to teaching, learning, and writing across the curriculum: IWAC at 25* (pp. 167–192). The WAC Clearinghouse; University Press of Colorado. https://doi.org/10.37514/PER-B.2020.0360.2.10.

Inoue, A. B. (2015). *Antiracist writing assessment ecologies: Teaching and assessing writing for a socially just future*. The WAC Clearinghouse; Parlor Press. https://doi.org/10.37514/PER-B.2015.0698.

Inoue, A. B. (2019). How do we language so people stop killing each other, or what do we do about white language supremacy? *College Composition and Communication, 71*(2), 352–369. https://library.ncte.org/journals/CCC/issues/v71-2/30427.

Inoue, A. B. & Poe, M. (Eds.). (2012). *Race and writing assessment*. Peter Lang.

Kareem, J. M. (2020). Sustained communities for sustained learning: connecting culturally sustaining pedagogy to WAC learning outcomes. In L. E. Bartlett, S. L. Tarabochia, A. R. Olinger & M. J. Marshall (Eds.), *Diverse approaches to teaching, learning and writing across the curriculum: IWAC at 25* (pp. 293–308). The WAC Clearinghouse; University Press of Colorado. https://doi.org/10.37514/PER-B.2020.0360.2.16.

Linkon, S. L. (2011). *Literary learning: Teaching the English major*. Indiana University Press.

Melzer, D. (2014). *Assignments across the curriculum: A national study of college writing*. Utah State University Press.

Rosenblatt, L. M. (1995). *Literature as exploration* (5th ed.). Modern Language Association of America.

Saldaña, J. (2013). *The coding manual for qualitative researchers*. Sage.

Salvatori, M. R. & Donahue, P. (2005). *The elements (and pleasures) of difficulty*. Pearson.

Thaiss, C. & Zawacki, T. M. (2006). *Engaged writers and dynamic disciplines: Research on the academic writing life*. Boynton/Cook.

Tinkle, T., Atias, D., McAdams, R. M. & Zukerman, C. (2013). Teaching close reading skills in a large lecture course. *Pedagogy, 13*(3), 505–535. https://doi.org/10.1215/15314200-2266432.

Weisse, K. D. & Zito, A. J. (2021, August 6). *When learning outcomes mask learning: Probing assumptions about writing assessment in the age of learning analytics* [Conference presentation]. Fifteenth International Writing Across the Curriculum Conference. Fort Collins, CO, United States. https://youtu.be/bbWy3jz1_nA?list=PLGneEQPQbvyLsWkkRLtvQSAgCDYb9bEoG.

Wilder, L. (2012). *Rhetorical strategies and genre conventions in literary studies*. Southern Illinois University Press.

Wolfe, J. & Wilder, L. (2016). *Digging into literature: Strategies for reading, analysis, and writing*. Bedford/St. Martin's.

Zunshine, L. (2006). *Why we read fiction: Theory of mind and the novel*. The Ohio State University Press.

SECTION 3. INSTITUTIONAL CONSIDERATIONS

The third and final section of this collection focuses on some of the more macro-level issues relevant to WAC: how programs evolve over time, how WAC coordinators are trained in diverse institutional contexts, and how global/international contexts align (or do not). This section works to situate WAC within larger cultural, historical, and institutional contexts, reminding us that understanding our histories is as much about propelling us forward as it is reflecting on what has been. Furthermore, as we examine the histories of our programs, there is value in taking up what it means to leverage our histories toward programmatic sustainability on our college campuses. For example, Fabrizio et al. discuss how WAC fellows develop problem-solving skills at two colleges within the City University of New York (CUNY), which support how organizational units address complex problems related to student learning. This demonstrates the ways in which WAC programs can not only recognize but leverage their strengths amid institutional challenges.

Moreover, learning from the past aids us in navigating forward through new terrain. It engages with questions of the responsibilities of WAC as a field—to its students and its practitioners. Chapters in this section explore important questions, such as: How is English as the primary language for WAC scholarship inhibiting our collective understanding of global contexts, of evolving and adapting into more inclusive programs? How are we supporting the next generation of teachers, administrators, and scholars? What is the future of WAC?

Andrea Fabrizio, Linda Hirsch, Dennis Paoli, and **Trudy Smoke** open this section with a historical perspective on the complex CUNY WAC Program, contrasting the models implemented at Hostos Community College and Hunter College in particular, both of which are Hispanic-Serving Institutions (HSIs). Fabrizio et al. reflect on the successes and challenges of these programs as they have matured, highlighting the values of a partnership between the two colleges that led to the sharing of ideas and practices for more sustainable programming. In Fabrizio et al., WAC coordinators in two different institutions describe the way that they learned their roles as an evolving collaborative process, which is crucial to negotiating "the challenges of local program building while navigating CUNY policies" (p. 175). The chapter can be generative for readers who seek to examine the intricacies of sustainability and how programs navigate and adapt through institutional changes and challenges of funding, staffing, faculty development, and curricular reach.

Following this exploration of programming and professionalization, **Mandy Olejnik, Amy Cicchino, Christna M. LaVecchia,** and **Al Harahap** consider the development of WAC coordinators from the perspective of graduate students and new WAC coordinators. The chapter represents a roundtable discussion of the possibilities for graduate students to engage in professional development. Olejnik et al. argue that growth in administrative and professional support of WAC administrators needs to occur in tandem with growth of programmatic initiatives. In their chapter, which is adapted from their roundtable session at the Fifteenth International Writing Across the Curriculum Conference, the authors ask important questions of the WAC community regarding support for graduate students, early career scholars, and other faculty placed in positions of managing WAC programs. Their chapter also extends conversations of access.

Further extending the conversation to spaces outside of the United States, **Estela Ines Moyano's** chapter highlights the importance of instruction locale and disciplinary learning by making a powerful argument about the radical nature of writing pedagogy relevant to the WAC community and especially to WAC scholars in the region of Latin America. Some may take it as a given that writing will be taught as a general education requirement and even within a specific major or discipline. However, the teaching of writing in a Latin American educational context via WAC can be seen as an innovative idea in strengthening student persistence—which more people, including college and university administrators, are starting to embrace. Because of what writing can mean and what it can do to support student learning (e.g., moving from writing to master textual comprehension to writing that strengthens disciplinary learning through meaning-making), we see this embrace as significant especially given the fight that countries in Latin America and others around the world have made and are making to preserve their democracies. This chapter teaches us that writing programs can enrich students' processes of learning in academic and political networks that, as Moyano suggests, allow for progress and growth within research, community-oriented work, and students' development in their future professions. Even though Moyano does not explicitly mention writing for democracy and social change, her work adds to the momentum of what writing can mean for students and faculty across disciplines who navigate various social, political, and professional contexts related to critical reflection and disciplinary learning. Her work welcomes an expansive readership to this very collection.

Similarly, **Alena Kačmárová, Magdaléna Bilá,** and **Ingrida Vaňková's** chapter addresses questions of whose languages are privileged in scholarly publishing and the sustainability of these practices. While WAC work is often focused on educational locales, we also must take into consideration how our scholarly practices are communicated and disseminated, and how those choices limit access to scholars whose languages are not English. In their chapter, Kačmárová et al. examine the conflicts at play specifically between Anglo-American and Slovak writing conventions, and they offer insights into the implications of this dissonance, especially for Slovak scholars.

This chapter is followed by a deep reflection by **David R. Russell** on the history of WAC's endurance and sustainability, which is significant to our understanding of how writing has shaped educational reforms. By examining WAC's impact through a comparison and contrast approach with other "across-the-curriculum" movements, Russell's chapter positions readers to further understand the reach and scope that WAC has had in higher education. It is through this history and an "across-the-curriculum" lens that we not only come to understand and appreciate WAC's impact on higher education, but how writing is mobilized in various networks of learning.

As we aim to assess the impact of our programs and communicate to our institutions their significance, this history can be vital in highlighting not only what writing is but what it does at our colleges and universities. For example, Russell mentions how "WAC is often supported by—and supports—a large network of writing centers, with a long history of service to the wider university community, whereas mathematics tutoring centers typically do not have that campus-wide history or outreach" (p. 240). In the example, we observe collaborative practices through WAC's involvement in supporting learning and university service—practices that are further exemplified by Macauley, Childers, and Jones within this proceedings. These practices might be shared with broader institutional stakeholders to show how WAC is integral to teaching and learning.

Furthermore, Russell reflects on the issues that we continue to grapple with including how we support teaching and learning through writing and communication. He argues that the future of WAC should involve collaboration with other related "across-the-curriculum" programs, specifically communication across the curriculum (CXC) and quantitative reasoning (QR) across the curriculum. He also calls for more collaboration between WAC and the current movement for general education reform. We see this as crucial especially as colleges and universities review their general education curricula and the role of writing in the digital age.

Concluding this section and collection is a revision of the third plenary session given by **Al Harahap, Federico Navarro, and Alisa Russell**. In this chapter, the authors examine both how and what it means to position our programs toward decolonial, equitable, antiracist, and socially just futures. We learn that striving toward such futures is not in addition to WAC sustainability, but vital to achieving it. We know that our student populations continue to shift, and this is a trend we see in the United States and in countries like Chile where students once classified as "non-traditional" are now in the majority. They have disrupted a script that has historically aimed to reserve educational access to a select few —one that secures itself through dominant deficit discourses of writing. However, Harahap, Navarro, and Russell remind us that the challenge we face is how we will embrace what it means to position ourselves as connectors of writing on our college campuses. How will we re-create our identities and innovate our programs toward equitable and socially just futures? Through a crowdsourced document of action items they collected, we learn that being more aware and deliberate of our work as a discipline can be messy, but it is an ongoing and necessary process if we are to enact changes that are not only framed by our reflections but our actions. This work is not only a way of knowing but a way of being and this can shape how we embody WAC on our campuses both now and in the future.

Through these last two chapters and this collection, we can also understand the immense task before us in not only continuing WAC's momentum but addressing the challenges before us and moving forward with an urgency for innovation and adaptability. It is vital that we continue to shape how the field adapts and works through the changes, challenges, and opportunities that are evident in higher education both now and in the future.

CHAPTER 12.
BUILT TO LAST: TWO DECADES OF SUSTAINING WAC PROGRAMS AT CUNY

Andrea Fabrizio
Hostos Community College, City University of New York

Linda Hirsch
Hostos Community College, City University of New York

Dennis Paoli
Hunter College, City University of New York

Trudy Smoke
Hunter College, City University of New York

When in 1999 the City University of New York (CUNY) created a university-wide Writing Across the Curriculum (WAC) program, WAC programs of varied sizes and ambitions had already existed throughout the country for several decades (Condon & Rutz, 2012; Cox et al., 2014). The principles of WAC pedagogy were generally determined, if still practically debated, and disseminated in journals of composition studies and collections of case studies, and singular features and measures of WAC Program assessment were in development relative to local initiatives.[1]

Program sustainability, however, in theory and measure, was nascent and inchoate, though the issue gained visibility as programs at some institutions stalled, waned, reorganized, or were discontinued. David R. Russell (1997) could still find the success of WAC over the previous 27 years "surprising" (p. 3); Neal Lerner (2001) would soon re-issue the old warning against the pitfalls menacing WAC efforts. Now, over two decades later, eminent academic voices (Palmquist et al., 2020) celebrate 50 years of WAC, its "longevity and reach"

---

1   Cf, e.g., Fulwiler & Young, *Programs That Work* (1990); Yancey & Huot, *Assessing Writing Across the Curriculum* (1997); and Anson, *The WAC Casebook* (2002), the "scenes" in which had been developed and collected over years; and, of course, Bean's *Engaging Ideas*, first published in 1994 and now in its third edition.

DOI: https://doi.org/10.37514/PER-B.2023.1947.2.12

(p. 9) and its "sense of identity" (p. 5). When the question is posed if WAC will continue to flourish, continuity is a given and WAC's potential is now one of continuous growth.

The CUNY WAC initiative, beginning as a university mandate, still exists. What features of the program's founding framework and the related local structures adopted at the university's individual colleges proved fundamental to their persistence as programs? What operational changes over time tempered and energized programs, or challenged and compromised them? This chapter examines how the CUNY WAC Program and representative programs at two of its institutions, Hostos Community College and Hunter College, sustained their services and institutional structures and how the profiles of these programs and their histories conform to and comment on the models of sustainability offered by Michelle Cox, Jeffrey R. Galin, and Dan Melzer (2018b) in *Sustainable WAC: A Whole Systems Approach to Launching and Developing Writing Across the Curriculum Programs* and Cox and Galin (2019) in *Tracking the Sustainable Development of WAC Programs Using Sustainability Indicators: Limitations and Possibilities*.

WAC AT CUNY: IN THE BEGINNING

CUNY is the largest urban public university in the country, with 25 affiliated degree-granting community colleges, senior colleges, and graduate schools located throughout the city's five boroughs. Over 275,000 students attend courses yearly across the system. Sixteen of CUNY's colleges are Hispanic-serving institutions (HSIs).

When the Board of Trustees (BoT) passed the resolution that established the university's WAC program, CUNY exemplified the cultural conflicts of the late 1990s (Cooper, 1998; Holdstein, 2001; McLeod & Miraglia, 2001). The university and its individual colleges faced public and private criticism stemming from a decades-old open admissions policy and the influx of students judged in the press and political rhetoric as ill-prepared for college work, particularly in relation to writing. The CUNY BoT, many of them political appointees, pressed for and ultimately imposed change.

Contemporaneous with the 1999 CUNY WAC mandate was a reorganization of the university to relocate remedial/developmental programs from the senior colleges to the system's community and comprehensive colleges. This reorganization also instituted a university-wide reading/writing/quantitative analysis test, the CUNY Proficiency Exam (CPE), as a graduation requirement for an associate degree from the community colleges and for continued progress at the senior colleges.

In a top-down dynamic, CUNY set the university-wide goal of improving student writing proficiencies for future academic and professional work, a goal common to all stakeholders, but the variety of cultures and climates among CUNY's then 18 campuses led to diverse implementation models. Critically, the university initiative provided the flexibility necessary for the features and framework of local campus programs to be rooted in and reflect campus culture, shaped by the individual college's institutional structure and resources.

College programs would be led by campus WAC coordinators appointed by their colleges who would report to a university dean. Tasked with building the programs on their campuses, the first college WAC coordinators in 1999, in most cases from English departments, knew each other from professional organizations, conferences, and university-level committees, if they did at all. Understanding what it meant to be a WAC coordinator, including how to negotiate the challenges of local program building while navigating CUNY policies, was an evolving collaborative experience. Under the auspices of the university's central administration, the university dean convened five coordinators' meetings a year to share strategies for meeting program responsibilities—budget, staffing, housing and visibility, pedagogy, assessment, faculty interaction, release time—and to air concerns.

To support and staff the campus WAC programs, the BoT resolution also mandated the creation of and funding for a two-year CUNY writing fellowship for graduate students from the CUNY Graduate Center. Six CUNY writing fellows from various disciplines were recruited by each college to facilitate the efforts of campus WAC programs. According to CUNY recommendations, writing fellows could support local faculty development programs at the colleges, provide instruction on a supplemental basis to student writers, and offer writing support services to departments and college administrations, such as research and curricular development. As terms of their fellowship, writing fellows could not teach classes, grade papers, assist in non-WAC-related research, or provide personal services. The writing fellow, as created, was a liminal position, advised to partner with faculty in WAC activities, and even participate in WAC-related faculty development, but who would not adopt traditional faculty roles or professional responsibilities (Hirsch & Fabrizio, 2011).

A project of foundational importance to the CUNY WAC program was the professional development of the writing fellows, which began in 2000 with a CUNY-wide week-long late-summer institute for fellows and faculty. Though most graduate students have taught in their discipline, they rarely experience professional development in writing pedagogy and WAC. To address this need, WAC coordinators collaborated on the planning, direction, and implementation of the fellows' professional development, primarily through readings, information sessions, and workshops on WAC principles and methods (e.g., assignment design, responding to student writing, tutorial methods, ESL/ELL issues, reading across the curriculum). Fellows also received continued professional development in WAC principles and best practices under local conditions from the coordinators on their assigned campuses.

Perhaps the most strategic and decisive project of the CUNY WAC program proceeded from the university's directive that where possible the individual colleges create writing intensive (WI) courses and graduation requirements. Several CUNY colleges already had WI courses in their curricula, but most CUNY schools subsequently heeded the university's recommendation and instituted WI courses and requirements. Two models emerged: professional development programs to certify faculty as versed and accomplished in the principles of WAC pedagogy, who then designed and taught WI courses, and the certification of WI courses by college governance systems without a corresponding certification of faculty.

The programs at Hostos Community College and Hunter College provide both strikingly similar and starkly different program models in distinctly diverse local contexts (Hirsch & Paoli, 2012).

WAC AT HOSTOS COMMUNITY COLLEGE: BUILDING THE PROGRAM

Hostos Community College is an urban, bilingual college of 7,000 students serving New York City's South Bronx community, one of the poorest in the country. An HSI, Hostos enrolls an ethnically and linguistically diverse student population. Ninety-nine percent of students receive some form of financial aid. At the time of the WAC program's inception, over 75 percent of the incoming student body required some form of developmental education and/or ESL/ELL instruction (Hirsch & DeLuca, 2003; Hirsch & Fabrizio, 2011).

Before the CUNY WAC mandate was enacted, Hostos, though struggling with the developmental math and English needs of its students, had successfully enacted a FIPSE-funded project that provided some of the first quantitative and qualitative evidence of the effectiveness of WAC principles with post-ELL students (Hirsch, 1988). An earlier "Needs Assessment Survey" identified faculty attitudes and concerns about student writing: Faculty bemoaned the state of student writing, and most saw the English department as bearing responsibility for student writing abilities. Responding to the BoT mandate, Linda Hirsch, the WAC Ccoordinator at Hostos (a Professor of English with an expertise in ESL/ELL instruction), formed a WAC advisory committee with representatives from each department (mostly chairs) to include diverse disciplinary perspectives and establish WAC goals unique to the campus.

A key component of WAC at Hostos has been the development of specially-designed WI sections of multi-section courses that provide opportunities for both formal and informal writing. Students must complete two WI sections to graduate. The WAC program established a certification model for faculty developing WI sections by running faculty professional development workshops throughout the year, assigning writing fellows to work with faculty to incorporate WAC practices into their pedagogy, and certifying faculty to create and teach WI courses at the college. The WAC program established itself at Hostos by creating its first WIs with faculty who were most interested in doing so. It assigned them a writing fellow to collaborate with, paid them a stipend, capped class enrollment at 25, and provided ongoing professional development. Each successive year more faculty worked to create WI sections.

Early on, the WAC program recruited a WI task force of faculty, separate from the WAC advisory committee, to review WI course syllabi and recommend them for WI designation to the Hostos college-wide curriculum committee. Expanding faculty responsibilities for WAC policies as well as participation in its practices created a greater understanding among faculty of the value of WAC and helped change the campus attitude in relation to student writing and writing instruction.

WAC AT HUNTER COLLEGE: BUILDING THE PROGRAM

Founded in 1870, Hunter College, one of CUNY's senior colleges, is located in Manhattan and enrolls over 20,000 students, of which some 16,000 are undergraduates, from all five of the city's boroughs. The student body is majority ethnic-minority, and over half of the school's students work while attending the college. An HSI and Asian American and Native American Pacific Islander-serving institution (AANAPISI), Hunter has a large multilingual student population and commonly counts speakers of over 50 different languages among its enrollees. The schools of education, nursing, and social work are the most prominent of the college's graduate programs.

Until 1999, Hunter had multi-tiered developmental reading and writing course sequences as well as freshman and advanced composition courses, but after the university reorganization that included the creation of the CUNY WAC program, composition at Hunter, still siloed in the English department, offered no remedial component. Many professors did not feel prepared for or interested in teaching writing in disciplinary content courses. The campus mood at Hunter around academic writing was much the same as that at Hostos: Students should have learned how to write by the time they reached 200-level courses, and if they did not, it was the fault of composition courses, and they should go to the writing center.

With little administrative support, the WAC coordinator, Trudy Smoke, also the director of freshman composition and an expert in linguistic and ESL/ELL issues, worked with faculty and departments that already had a commitment to writing, though many departments viewed WAC and writing requirements as a violation of academic freedom (Smoke, 1998). To help WAC make its way into those departments, Smoke reached out to Dennis Paoli, the coordinator of Hunter's Rockowitz Writing Center (RWC), which serves student writers across the curriculum at every level, to pool their institutional knowledge and plan the best options for WAC services (Harris, 2002). In 1994, Hunter's freshman composition program and writing center had collaborated to host a "Writing at Hunter" college conference with multi-disciplinary faculty participation; now the partnership of freshman composition and the writing center would continue in the creation of a WAC co-coordinatorship.

Two years into the CUNY WAC initiative, Hunter passed a graduation requirement for three "Significant Writing" WI courses. The W-designated class requirements were minimal: At least 50 percent of the grade must be based on writing; due dates must allow for "faculty feedback"; English 120 (Freshman Composition) must be at least a co-requisite; and the course must be regularly offered. Once Significant Writing became a graduation requirement, nearly every department in the college wanted to offer WI courses at the 100- and sometimes 200-level. Departments reviewed their courses and sought W-designation for those that reasonably met the skeletal requirements. W-designations were certified by the college senate's Course of Studies Committee, on which WAC co-coordinator Smoke served.

After courses had been W-designated, the college had little to say about who would teach them. Instruction was the province of the individual departments. Unlike Hostos, Hunter did not have a faculty certification program. As they evolved, W-designated courses were often taught by graduate students and part-time adjunct faculty who were rarely given smaller class sizes or paid for the additional hours necessary to develop the writing aspects of their courses. As contingent faculty were frequently hired late, they sometimes did not know they were teaching WI courses until the RWC notified them offering tutorial services and informing them that the WAC program could provide copies of John Bean's *Engaging Ideas* to help them develop their pedagogy. In the best cases, when departments or individual instructors requested help in developing writing-to-learn pedagogy for their W-designated courses, the WAC program, when possible, offered the assistance of a writing fellow.

The fellows came to play a pivotal role in WI course development, often working with newly hired graduate students to help them design assignments and assessments and incorporate WAC practices into their syllabi and instruction.

Writing fellows provided services for departments as diverse as biology, chemistry, economics, English, health sciences, history, philosophy, psychology, romance languages, and sociology, among others. They worked with department chairs, senior and junior faculty, adjuncts, teaching grad students, and students; participated in and led voluntary workshops for full- and part-time faculty on a variety of WAC topics (e.g., Building a W Course, The Digital Future of Academic Writing, Is Writing a Safe Space?, Ungrading, etc.); did research on ESL/ELL instruction, freshman year programs, and multi-section course instruction; consulted on departmental and course-specific writing issues, including assessment and curricular reform; represented the WAC program at meetings of the college's faculty professional development program, the Academic Center for Excellence in Research and Teaching (ACERT); and provided services to courses, including student tutorials and workshops on discipline-specific writing features (Nicolas, 2008).

CHANGES AND CHALLENGES: THE SECOND DECADE

Policy and structural changes over the years following the BoT resolution rippled through the university's WAC program. The second decade of WAC at CUNY saw two substantial program changes at the university level that presented significant challenges to the campus programs.

Funding

Early in its second decade, WAC at CUNY was repositioned administratively under the university's office of the dean of undergraduate education and funded through that office's Coordinated Undergraduate Education (CUE) program. The major impact of this change was funding. From their creation, college WAC programs had been directly funded by the university. After the administrative reorganization of WAC, CUE funds were disbursed to the college administrations, which determined locally what funding the college WAC program would receive. Campus WAC programs found themselves competing with other college initiatives for funding, and those not as institutionally visible and/or stable were disadvantaged. Previously, coordinators had been able to appeal as a group for WAC's importance as a pedagogy and program directly to a university dean who understood WAC as a movement as well as a line item. This new situation put pressure on coordinators, including those at Hostos and Hunter, to advocate individually with college administrators, which often meant educating them in WAC pedagogy and history as well as in the features and benefits of their WAC programs, an extra, crucial task in an expanding role.

STAFFING

A restructuring of the CUNY Graduate Center's funding for doctoral students necessitated a change in the University's Writing Fellowship, from a two-year competitive award to the single final year in a five-year Chancellor's Fellowship awarded to students upon entry to the Graduate Center. The decision to reorganize the financing of graduate education at the Center resulted in downstream programmatic changes at the university and local campus levels in the recruiting, professional development, and managing of the redesignated CUNY WAC fellows. A one-year, as opposed to a two-year, term of service to a WAC program proved a less rich experience for the fellow, deducted a year per fellow of experienced service to the colleges from the previous level, and increased the yearly demand for professional development.

Ironically, the university's continued funding of the fellowship that furnished staffing for campus WAC programs at no cost to the colleges afforded some college administrations the option to essentially defund WAC. In some cases, the WAC fellows were, with the coordinator, the entire staff of the local WAC program. This change at the top led to greater turnover in program staff, more intensive training, instances of compromised motivation, more vigilant management of fellows on the campuses, and reorganization of program services—issues that pertained and responsibilities that fell to the coordinators. At some sites, WAC program offerings and operations suffered cutbacks and/or college administrations assumed a greater role in directing services and remapping WAC to reframed local organizational structures and initiatives.

ANSWERS AND ADAPTATIONS

The work of CUNY WAC fellows with faculty, whether in a certification program or a less formal collaboration, amplifies the professional development to redound to both parties (Falchikov, 2001). WAC fellows, especially those recruited to the system's community colleges where they did not get a chance to teach as graduate students, gain experience in writing instruction for ESL/ELL students from the professional development efforts of the coordinators *and* from their own efforts participating in the professional development of faculty. In the over two decades of the CUNY WAC program, many of those fellows—upwards of 2,000—have progressed to become faculty themselves at CUNY, across the country, and internationally.

Andrea Fabrizio was a writing fellow at Hostos Community College from 2003 to 2005; Linda Hirsch was, as she had been from the beginning of the university's WAC initiative and continues today, the campus coordinator. As fellows are in a liminal state in relation to faculty, so are coordinators in relation to fellows, being both managers and mentors. In providing the fellows at Hostos with program structure and organization, modeling for them appropriate communication, demonstrating transparency while directing and conducting their on-campus professional development, and being dependably available to them when needed, Hirsch not only supervised the fellows but instilled in them the values of WAC practice. In working with faculty, Fabrizio not only gained experience in academic collaboration, problem-solving, and the reciprocal learning inherent in the work, but she engaged with disciplinary structures and ideologies outside her previous acquaintance, found cross-disciplinary channels and overlays, and discovered the range of faculty and student preparation for and predisposition toward writing in a discipline (history) other than her field of study (Hirsch & Fabrizio, 2011).

Given the significance of that experience, Fabrizio came to appreciate the professional development opportunities offered by the university and the local program as practical lifelines and occupational learning. When her fellowship ended in 2005, she was hired as an adjunct lecturer at Hostos, a substitute instructor from 2005–2007, and, upon completion of her Ph.D. in 2008, an assistant professor of English. The vocational trajectory from fellow to WAC-ready faculty member demonstrates a continuity that has scaffolded CUNY's WAC program, a trajectory that reaches to institutions and programs both nationally and globally.

In the continuity of Hirsch's coordinatorship there accrued additional value. What Fabrizio gained from Hirsch's mentoring was not only a grounding in WAC principles and expertise in its practices, but a host of leadership skills: advocacy, authority, community-building, delegating, goal-setting, and managing multiple perspectives, among numerous others. When funding and fellowship changes at the university level brought pressures to bear on the local programs, the response at Hostos was already at hand: Fabrizio had joined Hirsch as co-coordinator of the WAC program in 2009. As a team, they have effectively met the challenges of the expanded responsibilities of WAC program management and administration.

At Hunter, the response to the budgetary and staffing challenges was program expansion—expanding the number and the curricular reach of the WAC fellows. Having one of the largest and most interdisciplinary programs in romance languages in the university, Hunter was serviceable as an assignment for WAC fellows from the Graduate Center's programs in French, Latin American, Iberian, and Latino Cultures, and comparative literature with an Italian doctoral specialization and for international students from those linguistic backgrounds who otherwise might be difficult to place in suitable programs. The already popular services fellows provided became more widespread and visible across Hunter's curriculum, supporting a specialized certificate program in translation and organizing a student writing conference in Spanish. The enhanced prominence of the fellows burnished WAC's image at the college and helped buttress the program's arguments for its stability and future.

THE WHOLE SYSTEMS APPROACH: BUILDING SUSTAINABLE WAC PROGRAMS

To capture the ambitious scope and dynamic of CUNY WAC, the authors of this chapter adapted and applied Michelle Cox, Jeff Galin, and Dan Melzer's (2018a; 2018b) "Whole Systems Approach." Their methodologies yield applicable heuristic models: the whole systems methodology for transformative change (in which stakeholders develop and transform a program through the recursive stages of Understand, Plan, Develop, Lead); the WAC anthrosphere (applying critical perspectives on WAC programs as Human/Social, Support/Economic, and Natural/Institutional systems); and the DPSIR Framework for Problem-Solving (recognizing *Driving Forces, Pressures, State Indicators, Impacts,* and *Responses* that determine program reactions to emergent needs) (Cox & Galin, 2019). These methods help stakeholders identify Sustainability Indicators (SIs) that in turn aid faculty, students, and administrators in determining and addressing the sustainability of a local WAC program or project.

WAC Program Sustainability at CUNY/Hostos/Hunter

Appearing near a milestone year for the CUNY WAC program, the *Whole Systems Approach* presented itself as an opportunity for the CUNY and college programs to gauge their progress and staying power. Mapping onto certain features of the heuristics was immediate and obvious. For example, "involving stakeholders" in the Whole Systems Approach Planning stage of WAC at the university, given the size of the institution and the tradition of faculty expertise in composition studies, was dealing from one of CUNY's strengths, as it was at Hostos when Hirsch recruited a WAC Advisory Committee. Accumulated local "lore" and shared theoretical perspective were operationalized in the creation of the position of CUNY WAC coordinator (North, 1987). Together early cohorts of coordinators engaged collaboratively to "Understand" WAC in the complex, interwoven contexts of CUNY and their local campuses and "Plan," i.e., define their roles and envision their programs, which they would then "Develop" (Cox et al., 2018a; 2018b).

Mapping onto the sustainability model's "WAC Anthrosphere," the CUNY initiative built and sustains itself as a "Human/Social system" by empowering coordinators to return to campuses and create WAC as an institutional system within the curricula of their colleges. Additionally, it empowers coordinators to advocate for their programs with administrators who constitute the local campus economic system. When Smoke recruited Paoli to co-coordinate the program at Hunter, the coalition with the writing center not only expanded the local social system of WAC but also bolstered the "Support/Economic system" by securing space (infrastructure) for meetings and services (space is scarce on a Manhattan campus) and connected WAC with a stable and amenable "curricular ecology and resource system" with which it shared principles and mission, establishing a "pedagogical footprint" as a "Natural/Institutional system" (Cox & Galin, 2019).

In relation to any program goal or stressor, at any stage in the Whole Systems Approach or from any of the WAC Anthrosphere's perspectives, multiple Sustainability Indicators (SI) can be identified. Cox and Galin (2019) caution that any list of possible SIs be qualified and ultimately selective to ascertain the key SIs to track. WI courses, especially as meeting a requirement, are historically a key SI for WAC, and were a critical project in the Develop stage of the CUNY WAC program. As an example of meeting a goal, Hostos currently offers over 130 WI sections representing a wide range of disciplines and levels. Unlike senior colleges, which might require that WI courses be upper-level, Hostos permits students to enroll in select WIs if they are taking a developmental writing course. Each department and academic program offers WI sections taught by the primarily full-time faculty who created them. Sustainability is indicated by few waiver requests, which is evidence that enough courses exist to meet demand. As an example of addressing a stressor, without benefit of a certification process contingent faculty were often thrust into teaching Hunter's WI courses, which created an opportunity for WAC outreach, fellow placement, and professional development workshops.

The DPSIR heuristic applied to the CUNY WAC program reveals a fundamental dynamic of the model: The *Driving Force* behind several of the most crucial problems is budgetary and created at the university level; the *Pressure* created by those forces is felt locally on campus programs; the *State Indicators* are numerous and include less CUNY-level fellows professional development, less local program funding, and more group interviews during fellow recruitment; the *Impacts* include increased responsibilities for coordinators, some of them passed on to the WAC fellows; and the *Response* is almost always the increased commitment and labor of the coordinators and the fellows.

As an example of a response driven by a local force, turnover in a college's upper administration over the course of a decades-long program requires renewed, often redundant, educating and advocacy efforts by WAC coordinators. The possibility of a difference in vision for the program proceeding from the provost's or vice president's office can require re-examination of institutional ties and collaborations, inquiry into areas of possible negotiation, re-focused data collection and ally recruitment, or resignation (in both senses). Over the course of twenty years, there have been 14 associate provosts, deans, and assistants to the president overseeing WAC at Hunter College, the constant adjustment to new administrators and agendas applying pressure to the program, especially since 2012, when the program budget became part of the packaged CUE budget to be allocated by the college administration. This revolving-door reporting structure, particularly in the context of the falling-off from the program's collaborative relationship with a WAC-friendly dean, resulted in dire impacts, particularly to WAC program budgets, which grew smaller and were assigned later. The Hunter WAC program's response to the instability of administrative structure was continuity. The co-coordinators remained steadfast, advocating from shared principles, maintaining partnerships with departments and academic programs, which in turn advocated for WAC.

In an extraordinary global example of the DPSIR dynamic, the driving force of COVID-19 exerted many urgent pressures on higher education, proliferated negative state indicators, caused severe impacts, but as evidence of its maturity, the WAC program at Hostos was able to respond and sustain its faculty WI certification model by adapting a modality already in place, expanding use of an online certification platform for adjunct faculty, facilitated by WAC fellows, to certify all faculty during the pandemic.

KEY SUSTAINABILITY INDICATORS FOR THE CUNY/HOSTOS/HUNTER WAC PROGRAMS

Dan Melzer, in discussing sustainability and WAC in an interview, noted:

> My own career reinforces for me that a WPA identity is less about individual roles or individual personality and more about building structures and working collaboratively . . . [and the reforms] had a lot to do with changing the structure of the system and very little to do with my own identity. (Polk, 2020, p. 90)

While agreeing with Melzer that the importance of collaborative work cannot be overstressed, the authors of this chapter maintain that the personality of the coordinators does matter (Condon 1997, as cited in Holdstein, 2001). The CUNY writing fellow and WAC programs were seeded by the mandate but were sustained by commitment and care. WAC coordinators must be aware, committed, creative, persistent, and stubborn as well as flexible. They must be present and put in the time. Newly assigned WAC coordinators take on the role like deer in the headlights—eyes open to the opportunity but stunned by the magnitude and significance of the responsibility and the consequences of program failure. Meetings of WAC coordinators have evolved to become a fostering environment and a major factor in the sustainability of the college programs. The two programs featured here have grown into WAC ecologies that are sustainable, dynamic, and able to surmount multiple challenges, and bear witness to leadership as a key SI for WAC programs (Basgier et al., 2020; Palmquist et al., 2020; Thaiss & Porter, 2010; Walvoord, 1996; Walvoord, 2018).

When Smoke and Paoli recently retired, they were fortunate to recruit a faculty member in the philosophy department, Daniel Harris, who had been a WAC fellow at LaGuardia Community College, to be coordinator of Hunter's WAC program. Harris has taken the program digital, prioritized fellow experience, scheduled fewer but longer campus professional development meetings, and grown the demand by faculty and departments for the services of the fellows. Absent certification, Hunter's WI requirement has claim to integrity and sustainability primarily through faculty appreciation of the efforts of the college's cohorts of WAC fellows (Fodrey & Mikovits, 2020; Polk, 2020). As the success of Harris and Fabrizio (now chair of the Hostos English department) demonstrates, the engagement of graduate students in professional development and the provision of WAC program services is another key indicator in the sustainability of CUNY's WAC program.

The structure and location of CUNY facilitates the close collaboration of coordinators and WAC fellows, and from this collaboration flow many of the various programs' local projects. WAC programs at colleges without these advantages might profitably seek collaboration with WAC program coordinators through site visits and online platforms. Schools without graduate programs might create administrative positions in WAC for contingent faculty with WAC experience. If the CUNY model cannot be adopted, it may be adapted relative to its key components.

Prominent among the key indicators is CUNY's Board of Trustees' mandate that there be a university-wide campus-based WAC program. In solving problems and surmounting obstacles at the college level, in arguing for resources or exhorting faculty and fellows to embrace WAC pedagogy, coordinators have always been able to point to the mandate, to the university's vision of itself as a progressive institution at which students learn by writing. As WAC enters upon its next generation of practice and practitioners at CUNY, that vision endures.

REFERENCES

Anson, C. (2002). *The WAC casebook: Scenes for faculty reflection and program development*. Oxford University Press.

Basgier, C., Cox, M., Falconer, H. M., Galin, J., Harahap, A., Hendrickson, B., Melzer, D., Palmquist, M. & Sheriff, S. (2020). The formation of a professional organization for writing across the curriculum. In L. E. Bartlett, S. L. Tarabochia, A. R. Olinger & M. J. Marshall (Eds.), *Diverse approaches to teaching, learning, and writing across the curriculum: IWAC at 25* (pp. 33–43). The WAC Clearinghouse; University Press of Colorado. https://doi.org/10.37514/PER-B.2020.0360.

Bean, J. C. (2011). *Engaging ideas: The professor's guide to integrating writing, critical thinking, and active learning in the classroom*. Wiley.

Condon, W. & Rutz, C. (2012). A taxonomy of writing across the curriculum programs: Evolving to serve broader agendas. *College Composition and Communication, 64*(2), 357–382. https://www.jstor.org/stable/43490756.

Cooper, S. E. (1998). Remediation's end: Can New York educate the children of the "whole people"? *Academe, 84*(4), 14–20. https://doi.org/10.2307/40252307.

Cox, M., Chaudoir, S., Cripps, M., Galin, J., Hall, J., Kaufman, O. B., Lane, S., McMullen Light, M., Poe, M., Redd, T., Salem, L., Thaiss, C., Townsend, M. & Zawacki, T. M. (2014). *Statement of WAC principles and practices*. https://wac.colostate.edu/principles/.

Cox, M., Galin, J. R. & Melzer, D. (2018a). Building sustainable WAC programs: A whole systems approach, The *WAC Journal, 29*. https://doi.org/10.37514/WAC-J.2018.29.1.03.

Cox, M., Galin, J. R. & Melzer, D. (2018b). *Sustainable WAC: A whole systems approach to launching and developing writing across the curriculum programs*. National Council of Teachers of English.

Cox, M. & Galin, J. R. (2019). Tracking the sustainable development of WAC programs using sustainability indicators: Limitations and possibilities. *Across the Disciplines, 16*(4), 38–60. https://doi.org/10.37514/ATD-J.2019.16.4.20.

Falchikov, N. (2001). *Learning together: Peer tutoring in higher education*. Routledge Falmer.

Fodrey, C. & Mikovits, M. (2020). Theorizing WAC faculty development in multimodal project design. *Across the Disciplines, 17*(1/2), 42–58. https://doi.org/10.37514/ATD-J.2020.17.1-2.04.

Fulwiler, T. & Young, A. (1990). *Programs that work: Models and methods for writing across the curriculum*. Boynton/Cook.

Harris, M. (2002). Writing center administration: Making local, institutional knowledge in our writing centers. In P. Gillespie, A. Gillam, L. Falls Brown & B. Stay (Eds.), *Writing center research: Extending the conversation* (pp. 75–89). Lawrence Erlbaum Associates.

Hirsch, L. (1988). Language across the curriculum: A model for ESL students in content courses. In S. Benesch (Ed.), *Ending remediation: Linking content and ESL instruction in higher education* (pp. 676–689). TESOL.

Hirsch, L. & DeLuca, C. (2003). WAC in an urban and bilingual setting: Writing-to-learn in English y en Español. *Language and Learning Across the Disciplines, 6*(3). https://doi.org/10.37514/LLD-J.2003.6.3.09.

Hirsch, L. & Fabrizio, A. (2011). The writing fellow/faculty collaboration in a community college: Paradigms of teaching and learning across the curriculum. In J. Summerfield & C. Smith (Eds.), *Making teaching and learning matter: Transformative spaces in higher education* (pp. 145–170). Springer.

Hirsch, L. & Paoli, D. (2012). The City University of New York: The implementation and Impact of WAC/WID in a multi-campus US urban university. In C. Thaiss, G. Bräuer, P. Carlino, L. Ganobcsik-Williams & A. Sinha (Eds.). *Writing programs worldwide: Profiles of academic writing in many places* (pp. 439–454). The WAC Clearinghouse; Parlor Press. https://doi.org/10.37514/PER-B.2012.0346.

Holdstein, D. H. (2001). "Writing across the curriculum" and the paradoxes of institutional initiatives. *Pedagogy, 1*(1), 37–52. https://doi.org/10.1215/15314200-1-1-37.

Lerner, N. (2001). A history of WAC at a college of pharmacy. *Language and Learning Across the Disciplines, 5*(1), 6–19. https://doi.org/10.37514/LLD-J.2001.5.1.03.

McLeod, S. H. & Miraglia, E. (2001). Writing across the curriculum in a time of change. In S. H. McLeod, E. Miraglia, M. Soven & C. Thaiss (Eds.), *WAC for the new millennium: Strategies for continuing writing-across-the-curriculum programs* (pp. 1–27). National Council of Teachers of English.

Nicolas, M. (2008). *(E)Merging identities: Graduate students in the writing center.* Fountainhead Press.

North, S. M. (1987). *The making of knowledge in composition: Portrait of an emerging field.* Boynton/Cook.

Palmquist, M., Childers, P., Maimon, E., Mullin, J., Rice, R., Russell, A. & Russell, D. R. (2020). Fifty years of WAC: Where have we been? Where are we going? *Across the Disciplines, 17*(3/4), 5–45. https://doi.org/10.37514/ATD-J.2020.17.3.01.

Polk, T. (2020). Something larger than imagined: Developing a theory, building an organization, sustaining a movement. *The WAC Journal, 31.* https://doi.org/10.37514/WAC-J.2020.31.1.04.

Russell, D. R. (1997). Writing to learn to do: WAC, WAW, WAW—Wow! *Language and Learning Across the Disciplines, 2*(2), 3–8. https://doi.org/10.37514/LLD-J.1997.2.2.02.

Smoke, T. (1998). Collaborating with power: Contradictions of working as a WPA. *WPA: Writing Program Administration, 21*(2/3), 92–100. http://associationdatabase.co/archives/21n2-3/21n2-3smoke.pdf.

Thaiss, C. & Porter, T. (2010). The state of WAC/WID in 2010: Methods and results of the U.S. survey of the international WAC/WID mapping project. *College Composition and Communication, 61*(3), 534–570. https://www.jstor.org/stable/40593339.

Walvoord, B. (1996). The future of WAC. *College English, 58*(1), 58–79. https://doi.org/10.2307/378534.

Walvoord, B. (2018). Foreword. In Cox M., Galin, J. R. & Melzer, D. (Eds.), *Sustainable WAC: A whole systems approach to launching and developing writing across the curriculum programs* (pp. ix–xi). National Council of Teachers of English.

Yancey, K. B. & Huot, B. (1997). *Assessing writing across the curriculum: Diverse approaches and practices.* Ablex.

CHAPTER 13.

BLURRED BOUNDARIES: SUSSING OUT THRESHOLDS BETWEEN WAC AND WPA IN ADMINISTRATIVE PROFESSIONALIZATION

Mandy Olejnik
Miami University (Ohio)

Amy Cicchino
Embry-Riddle Aeronautical University

Christina M. LaVecchia
University of Cincinnati

Al Harahap
Queens College, CUNY

Over the past 50 years, the field of WAC has increasingly shifted from discussions of starting programs to efforts of sustaining programs (Cox, Galin & Melzer, 2018). Similarly, WAC pedagogical support has moved from the one-off workshop model of "writing-to-learn" pedagogy (Walvoord, 1996) to other models of effecting long-term change with faculty (Glotfelter, Updike & Wardle, 2020; Martin, 2021). Alongside these programmatic and pedagogical trends, we argue that WAC administrative support and professionalization need to similarly grow. To work toward sustainability as a field, we need to (re)consider the professionalization of WAC administrators—both in graduate school and throughout their careers.

The need for WAC-specific preparation is heightened by the prevalence of WAC practitioners moving into WAC work by institutional circumstance or, even if by choice, then without knowing explicitly what they've signed up for. Something is needed to better prepare and support those who do this work. Yet, the blurry and idiosyncratic nature of WAC work itself makes generalizable "training" a complex task. And while general WPA preparation is relevant to and overlaps with WAC administration, WAC work is positioned differently and requires relationships with institutional units that necessitate different sets of skills. Currently, few formal resources exist for WAC WPA professionalization, apart from the graduate organization WAC-GO (which relies on the labor of volunteer graduate students), the WAC Summer Institute (which can only serve a limited number of WAC WPAs and can be costly to attend), and the Association for Writing Across the Curriculum (AWAC), which was created in 2017 to "support and grow WAC as a global intellectual and pedagogical movement" (AWAC, n.d.). These developments, while generative for all involved, are not yet systematic in the mainstream writing studies zeitgeist and are also geared more toward those *already* in WAC positions or connected to the WAC community. Taken together, these conditions leave a present need for WAC-specific discussions about professionalizing WAC administrators.

In this chapter, we capture the spirit of our IWAC 2020 roundtable as we extend conversations from broader WPA scholarship on administrative professionalization (Charlton, 2009; Charlton et al., 2011; Elder, Schoen & Skinnell, 2014; Foley-Schramm et al., 2018; Latterell, 2003) to frame approaches to WAC-specific development for new-to-WAC WPAs, early career WPAs, and gWPAs. In the following sections of this chapter, we share the main discussion of our roundtable, with each heading representing a question discussed during the roundtable and each presenter given space to share their insight in subsequent sub-headings separated by name. In all, we view this chapter as the beginning of an ongoing dialogue about how we could and, perhaps importantly, *should* professionalize new and upcoming WAC administrators into the field given its current (more established) standing and robust history.

WAC PROFESSIONALIZATION AND PREPARATION

WPAs often enter WAC positions with minimal or mis-matched preparation (Cox, Galin & Melzer, 2018; Townsend, 2016). Our own preparation has been non-linear (or even "patchwork") and varied in its levels of formality and informality. As a group, we hold a range of positions, including a fourth-year Ph.D. candidate (Mandy), a WPA in a 12-month administrative NTT faculty role (Amy), a WPA in a 9-month NTT faculty appointment (Christina), and a faculty member who does WAC work at his local institution through ad hoc programs, like faculty and student learning communities (Al).[1] We have a range of prior experiences,

---

1 These positions were those we held at the time the "IWAC 2020" roundtable was first presented, in August 2021 (delayed a year from its intended delivery date because of COVID-19). For more on our transitions to new positions, see the Coda.

too, that we consider as having prepared us for WAC work; for instance, all of us had WPA training in graduate school, which typically prepares graduate students for a variety of administrative work after graduation (Elder, Schoen & Skinnell, 2014). Moreover, some of these experiences taught us how to speak to audiences outside the discipline; for example, all of us have worked in writing centers and found supporting writers across disciplines to be formative for cross-disciplinary conversation (Pemberton, 1995) with various kinds and degrees of complexities (Soliday, 2005). Christina further notes that an "alt-ac" (alternative academic) postdoc in a healthcare research unit taught her how to be not just the only rhet/comp specialist in the room but the only *humanist* in the room and helped her better understand writing needs outside of English (LaVecchia & Ramírez, 2020).

A noteworthy point of variance lies in how intentional (or not) our preparation for WAC work was (Maurer, Matzker & Dively, 2021). Some of us (Mandy, Amy) identify as "GenAdmin" (Charlton et al., 2011), having trained explicitly through assistantships to enter administrative work—an orientation that shapes our identities as administrator-scholar-teachers and our decisions to seek out administrative positions immediately following graduation. Some of us trained toward WAC work explicitly as graduate students. Mandy, for example, began as a consultant and later an assistant director of a business writing center, working with faculty on how to teach writing before moving into her school's WAC program proper, where she would soon be working full-time as a staff member. Al took WAC-specific units of coursework, served as a classroom-embedded writing fellow in writing-intensive courses at two different institutions, and conducted WAC-related research while administering a writing center. Meanwhile, some of us (Amy, Christina) received training in WPA work broadly as graduate students, but not in WAC explicitly—indeed, not every university has a WAC program and some of us were thinking more broadly about plans to be a WPA in other contexts such as a first-year composition program or writing center. While general WPA preparation is relevant for WAC administrators, it is nonetheless adjacent to administering WAC/WID programs, leaving a present need for WAC-specific discussions about professionalizing WAC administrators.

We also define WPA preparation capaciously. Most of us took WPA-focused coursework (Mandy, Amy, Al) or developed an exam list in graduate school on WPA work (Christina, Amy, Al); for some of us, there was an opportunity to focus that work on WAC administration specifically (Mandy, Al). Prior WPA work has also given us transferable skills: doing faculty development as a department chair in a K-12 context (Amy), or performing outreach to and collaborating with content-area faculty as associate director of a writing center (Al), or assisting in the administration of FYC as a gWPA (Amy, Christina). And all four of us have been active in national organizations like the CWPA and WPA-GO.

These diverse experiences, which all led us to practice WAC administration, have prompted us to reconsider the professionalization of WAC administrators—both in graduate school and throughout their careers.

VISION AND STRATEGIES FOR WAC PROFESSIONALIZATION

Despite calls for more situated WAC preparation (LaFrance & Russell, 2018), our experiences and those of the attendees at our IWAC 2020 roundtable were of uneven WAC preparation. The minimalist form of WAC preparation we and our attendees often experienced was having a "WAC week" in a composition theory or writing program administration course (a seemingly common experience yet largely not recognized as an issue in the literature). One roundtable attendee mentioned a professor adding WAC week to a seminar syllabus only after learning she had an interest and background in WAC, meaning that in other iterations of the course, WAC was totally absent. As well, a number of attendees were able to use their qualifying exams to focus on WAC scholarship, but this still positioned WAC work as a special topic or special interest one could pursue on their own. Even these opportunities to engage with readings on WAC, however, leave a major gap in WAC application and practice, gaps that AWAC, IWAC, and WAC-GO cannot necessarily fill.

When those of us with uneven preparation later came to take on WAC WPA positions, we experienced imposter syndrome (Robinson, 2021) and had to juggle learning on the job with practicing WAC work in new local contexts (LaFrance & Russell, 2018). Because so much WAC work is conceptual and relates to shared principles about writing development and disciplinary writing, new WAC WPAs are vulnerable when they do not feel that they have the expertise to mitigate faculty resistance and support their efforts with scholarship and evidence-based practices from the field (Mahala & Swilky, 1994). Many roundtable attendees noted that after being "thrown into WAC" they similarly grasped for WAC resources that could both teach them about conversations in WAC and also have practical application in their local contexts. While graduate students who could read about—but not practice—WAC experienced one form of uneven preparation, new-to-WAC administrators without opportunities to read about WAC theories or research experienced a different kind of underpreparedness.

MANDY

As a field, we should embrace and understand that WAC is a form of WPA work with specific expertise. It should be formally studied in WPA classes. Even if one doesn't have a WAC program on their campus, programs should at least expose students to it and help them learn more about it. There's a certain tension in WAC work overall with this idea of WAC being a very practical sub-discipline. WAC work is in some ways also very responsive—WAC is responding in-the-moment and personally to issues that faculty have, but it's also academic and scholarly. WAC work is not "scullery," as Elaine P. Maimon (1980) says about all administration and writing studies work. It's thus important to expose students to what that work looks like, what it can be, and help them explore it in a more intellectual way.

Christina

When we talk about preparation for WAC work, I think that on-the-job learning is not only somewhat inescapable, but also shouldn't be seen as secondary or inferior to theoretical preparation. As I see it, WPA studies has been shaped by the desire to prepare future WPAs, both practically and theoretically, so they're not stuck figuring things out haphazardly on the job (e.g., Brown, Enos & Chaput, 2002; Malenczyk, 2016; Myers-Breslin, 1999). But I think that preparatory orientation risks giving graduate students the impression that they need to be fully ready to go on day one and that, if they read enough, they won't make mistakes once they get into the position—and that clearly can't ever be the case.

There were many things that I knew intellectually when I came into my position directing a WAC program, but nonetheless, I still experienced a learning curve when applying them in practice. For instance, I knew intellectually that the institutional culture I was heading into was different from the one I was coming from—that a large, public R1 was going to be different from a small, private Catholic institution that is very teaching-heavy and service- and mission-focused. Yet, I still made missteps because I had to learn the culture of my new institution firsthand. About two days after my own new faculty orientation, my dean asked if I would address the faculty on Welcome Back Day as the new WAC director. In my desire to rise to the occasion, I made a speech about writing as an act of inquiry and articulated this philosophical vision of writing for the WAC program. But what people actually wanted and needed to hear was, "Hey, it's scary to teach writing for the first time! A bunch of you are being thrown into these new writing-intensive courses this year, and if you need practical help with designing assignments, teaching students how to write reflection essays, or grading papers, come talk to me." But I had to figure that out through doing the work and making these kinds of small missteps.

While WAC administration and general WPA work are not fully equivalent, I also believe—and Amy will touch on this more later —that much of the training that we've had from WPA contexts is transferable to WAC roles. Deciding how much top-down uniformity to impose on a program versus giving individual instructors or programs agency, navigating power dynamics and structures—those concerns all still apply. (They just don't make up the totality of our work in WAC contexts.) Overall, I found that both my preparation in WPA studies as well as on-the-ground learning (experienced both in the early days of directing my program and in my previous role, which I'll further discuss later on) have been really important for my growth.

WAC PROFESSIONALIZATION WITHOUT ACCESS TO WAC PROGRAMS

Questions of access repeatedly arose throughout our roundtable, with both presenters and attendees coming together from vastly different WAC contexts. At the time, both Amy and Mandy, for example, were working within WAC programs housed in the provost's office, completely separate from English; Christina, meanwhile, ran both the WAC program and the first-year writing sequence (despite the title Director of Writing Across the Curriculum), creating some different kinds of blurred boundaries. Still others in attendance came from institutions that didn't *have* WAC programs, and they had to seek out WAC opportunities either at other schools or by conducting research across campus. When preparing for either current or future WAC roles, access to WAC-related work is crucial.

Mandy

One important aspect of learning more about WAC work is visibility and access. AWAC as an organization has helped WAC grow because, prior to AWAC, we didn't have a central hub for people who are interested in WAC work to gather and collaborate. I think this is especially important for people coming into new WAC director roles. Finding resources and places like AWAC that can offer mentoring, visibility, and exposure to different WAC scholarship and methods is beneficial to WAC scholars and practitioners. These connections and opportunities are important for graduate students, too. I work a lot with WAC-GO, and as part of our mission, we're trying to help graduate students simply learn more about what WAC is and connect students with others who study and work in it.

Christina

One of the most useful things we can do, in addition to the strategies that Mandy has mentioned, is to learn about writing and knowledge-making outside of our discipline and outside of the humanities. My out-of-field experiences are largely what the hiring committee saw as preparing me for and qualifying me for directing WAC, and I would say my experiences teaching and collaborating on scientific writing is some of the most useful preparation that I've had.

These experiences helped me to destabilize my ideas of what good writing is and to let go of the idea that writing has to look a certain way or that the writing process has to unfold in a certain way. And I think this outlook lets me come in with more trust for the programs and faculty that I work with and also has been really useful for setting a foundation for what our WAC program should look like, do, and achieve.

Amy

Like Christina, I was not explicitly prepared in WAC but had preparation in WPA work. When one doesn't have a WAC program, I recommend two strategies for learning about WAC. First, consider how what we are currently doing has the capacity to be adapted into WAC contexts. There are some programmatic tasks that transfer across the type of program: budgets, scheduling, communicating a program's purpose succinctly to others, curricular design, data collection, assessment, and doing WPA-focused research. Gain experience in those common and transferable WPA skills. There are also other places to go within the institution to see WAC-like work. Where are those larger institutional conversations about writing and writing instruction happening? Learn about the work done in writing centers, teaching and learning centers, summer bridge programs, writing in the disciplines programs (e.g., business writing, agricultural communications), and academic support offices.

Second, we can still learn about concepts, challenges, and services that are specific to WAC by talking to WAC WPAs and professionals at other institutions. Even without a local WAC program, we can still participate in the WAC community more broadly by joining and participating in global conversations about WAC. Join WAC-GO and AWAC. These organizations offer opportunities to engage with the WAC community. If conference funding is available, attend IWAC, but if not, consider AWAC's virtual workshops, join AWAC writing groups, and apply for WAC research support. Read the *WAC Journal* and *Across the Disciplines* and explore resources on the WAC Clearinghouse site. If you are feeling isolated and without other WAC folks, consider sending a cold-call email to a potential WAC mentor. WAC folks are notorious for their friendliness. If, after reading an article or chapter on WAC, you want to hear more about the author's experience, email them. Do not be discouraged if that email never yields a response, although I wouldn't be surprised if authors did respond and offer to set up a time to chat.

WAC mentorship is also important to consider. For those of us who have graduated from a program without WAC, we can still identify WAC mentors through conferences and other professional networks. Given the labor issues that are already present in WPA and higher education, finding other WAC professionals who can offer advice and guidance is vital to feeling like we are part of a larger community of WAC practice. AWAC's Board of Consultants and mentoring events offer one potential place to make such connections while the WAC SIG at the Conference on College Composition and Communication offers another. I have often relied on the generosity and kindness of WAC mentors who did not know me before we met at a conference, over email, or from serving on an AWAC committee together.

PLACE AND BOUNDARIES OF WAC PROFESSIONALIZATION

Our roundtable discussion continually circled around the delineations between WAC work, WPA work, and rhetoric and composition. While the differences felt meaningful to those of us who had made transitions to WAC administration, outside of our discipline the delineations are less visible. Institutions, and especially small schools, do not know (or have the resources) to prioritize WAC-specific professionalization or might ask a WPA of another program to take on WAC work in addition to the position they were originally hired for. Quickly, the "writing person" could become the "WAC person": for instance, the National Census of Writing (2017) reports only 44 percent (74 out of 166 reporting) of WAC programs at four-year institutions have a dedicated WAC administrator. In many other cases, administrators of the writing program, first-year writing program, or writing center also take responsibility for WAC work, and there may or may not be much formal support for such blended roles.

All WAC work is also WPA work, given their overlap in faculty development, supervision and mentorship, and curriculum development. Yet, the ability to work with disciplinary faculty requires different administrative strategies, which can be emotionally draining. Further, WAC WPAs might find other areas related to teaching and learning attached to their WAC programs: technology and instructional design, research support, or teacher development. Put differently, there is a need to balance multiple goals and hats in WAC roles. These differences demand further teasing out so we can parse the superficial differences from those that require WAC-specific preparation and development.

Mandy

I'd like to go back to Christina's discussion of transfer. I think that it might not be so much that we have a lack of preparation to do WAC work, but there might be a lack of *framing* around it. As preceding sections have covered, certain skills and rhetorical dexterities around how to talk with people about writing, how to talk about teaching, and how to scaffold writing all apply in WAC as much as in first-year composition or other WPA contexts. Those connections, however, might not be made as visible, which leads to an important question to discuss: Is there really a transfer problem happening? Is there a way that we can make more visible these connections between the different arms of WPA work? Is there a way that we can introduce these connections in our courses and in our day-to-day work? Where can we move forward to make more visible the work that we all do as administrators?

Christina

Another idea relevant to this conversation is that even if the field has a pretty firm idea of what we think WAC work is, as distinct from the rest of WPA work, not every institution makes a clear delineation between them. For instance, my (now former) institution's WAC program includes the first-year writing sequence, and at some schools it includes the writing center. So, as much as we talk about the boundaries, those boundaries aren't always necessarily present in titles and job duties. There's a lot of permeation happening in actual practice at various institutions.

Amy

To agree with Mandy and Christina, this demarcation between WAC and non-WAC WPA work seems problematic and superficial. In fact, I want to lean even more dramatically into the pro-WAC professionalization argument because it is highly likely that WPAs who have a strong foundation in composition (and even some English faculty without any experience in composition) can find themselves doing WAC work. Institutional stakeholders do not realize the nuance in how folks with our backgrounds are professionalized at the graduate level. As noted above, we might quickly become "the writing person" and inherit the job of starting a WAC program at our institutions. Until we can attend to this dilemma, it's not appropriate for us to say only folks who know they are destined to be WAC WPAs should be professionalized in WAC. WAC preparation should be a part of WPA professionalization and WAC needs to become a part of how we talk about writing in rhetoric and composition. If those conversations aren't already happening in graduate programs, we need to push to begin them. Graduate students need opportunities to go out into the institution and learn about how writing functions in other disciplines because it very much could be a reality of their professional life, whether or not they imagine that at this moment.

However, even if they do receive WAC training but never take on WAC work, a knowledge of WAC principles in WPA professional development would only benefit WPAs in achieving a more holistic understanding of writing across the institution. If tomorrow I were to wake up as director of a first-year composition program, my WAC knowledge would still help me communicate with different stakeholders, discuss how first-year composition relates to disciplinary and professional goals for writing, and know the campus partners I could reach out to for collaboration (e.g., academic support, athletics, teaching and learning center, library services, etc.). WAC should be a part of well-rounded WPA professionalization, and WAC should be included in how we discuss the ways writing works across the institution.

Christina

All of this said regarding the permeable boundaries between WAC and WPA work, I'm not discounting the value of WAC-specific preparation. In fact, I spent much of the summer before I began my WAC position talking to WAC people and reading WAC conversations—reading lore, reading theoretical pieces, reading practical advice on assessment and faculty programming (Condon et al., 2016; Cox, Galin & Melzer, 2018; Fulwiler, 1989; Zawacki & Rogers, 2011).

Through this reading, I found helpful strategies for founding a new program and building relationships with faculty (Bastian, 2014; McLeod & Soven, 2000), all of whom had high teaching loads and underprepared, at-risk students. And so one challenge I faced was that faculty, even those who had shown a real interest in pedagogical professionalization, didn't often have the time to come to my workshops or even to consult with me individually. Reading WAC literature helped me to find other ways of reaching them. For example, the literature suggests that faculty writing instruction—so faculty writing groups or workshops where they get to work on their own writing—can help faculty to learn more about the writing process and how to coach it, as well as help them to better empathize with student writers (Faery, 1993; Fassinger, Gilliland & Johnson, 1992). And I found that faculty writing support helped me reach different segments of the faculty population, namely the folks who are less likely to come to the teaching workshops but more likely to be interested in working on their own writing (Anson, 2013).

I don't want to suggest that WAC-specific preparation isn't useful, because clearly I found it so. That said, I also don't want to suggest a binary view of preparation, where we see ourselves as either "qualified" or "not qualified" for WAC work based on whether we undertook the exact "right" training. I think we can find our way to WAC work through multiple paths, as my own story shows. Ultimately, to move beyond a binary view of WAC preparation, we must better identify the qualities that signal our potential for WAC leadership, such as the ability to work with content faculty from varying fields, the ability to persuade audiences with differing priorities for writing, the ability to mediate differing perceptions of writing, and so on. By focusing on an asset model of WAC preparation (i.e., what qualities does this person possess that are WAC transferable?) over a deficit model of WAC preparation (i.e., this person didn't have access to a WAC program in graduate school or didn't take WAC-specific coursework and is therefore unqualified), we can embrace multiple pathways to WAC work.

RESPONSE FROM AL

Overall, I feel that we all still have some difficulty, or perhaps hesitance is the more appropriate word, in articulating WAC professionalization as its own distinct exigency, as many of us both within writing programs as well as in other academic units are always already trying to do some WAC-like work. I would imagine very few units aren't still under the influence of Merrill Sheils' 1975 *Newsweek* article "Why Johnny Can't Write," which has created a recursive moral panic in academia that has been difficult to shake off. So the opportunities for WAC work are out there if we look hard enough for the right opportunities and interested stakeholders.

The problem, if we want to call it that, is that these professionalizing opportunities aren't as intentional or structured. WAC, compared to more generic WPA work, FYW administration, or writing center work, is institutionally elusive by nature, with vague boundaries. So WAC administrators, both intentional and circumstantial, must also be trained and develop astute institutional perception for these opportunities. Even when we identify them, we often find ourselves in a position of having to be agents, diplomats, mediators between various, sometimes competing, pedagogies and values when it comes to discussions such as: "What is good writing?" "What is a good writing assignment?" "What is effective writing assessment?" etc., all of which have been institutionally and culturally constructed in different ways in different fields. And it requires a WAC administrator or agent to have a whole other skillset to negotiate all these issues with other academic communities, especially when oftentime the administrators who do this relational groundwork are contingent faculty, graduate students, and others who are not necessarily imbued with the perceived ethos of the tenure track. The differences in these power dynamics then necessitate various kinds of other mental and emotional labor, which also translates into the time, energy, and material conditions of the WAC administrator.

Yet, as an area with the vague boundaries I mentioned earlier, these pockets of WAC work are also porous enough for exploration. What may be a source of struggle may also be an opportunity in that WAC work has the distinct trait of being able to move fluidly throughout the institution beyond typical writing program or writing center parameters and limitations. We can interact and collaborate with colleagues in other academic units. What's at stake here is how willing we are to defer authority, not just in content and pedagogy, but in professionalization itself. What does it mean or look like to have a WAC professionalization that includes our content colleagues? After all, we don't want to just replicate what Susan Miller (1991) described as being the menial laborers in service to the literary arms of the English department, just now to the rest of the institution, and inviting them to be a part of WAC professionalization would share that labor. What we may need to do in our professionalization is more deliberate studying, referencing, and disseminating of previous case studies doing this work, such as Chris Anson (2002), Christopher Thaiss and Terry M. Zawacki (2006), and Anne E. Geller and Michele Eodice (2013).

CONCLUSION

We and our roundtable attendees struggled to create a clear definition of what it means to be a WAC WPA (or WAC gWPA). In part, this difficulty returns to transfer and framing our work: Which parts of WAC program administration are specific to WAC and which reflect more general administrative duties? Our discussion with attendees briefly identified some tasks that emphasize the blurred boundaries we have articulated between general WPA work and WAC-specific WPA duties:

- Promoting student writing and student work;
- Defending writing as a meaningful part of the learning process;
- Asserting the need to teach disciplinary and professional writing expectations explicitly;
- Leading discussions about teaching writing across campus, including conversations about teaching writing in various contexts (e.g., online writing instruction) or teaching in general;
- Becoming de facto teaching and learning centers on campus (particularly at small schools where those centers may not exist): Once

relationships are built, we often advise on non-writing-related teaching topics such as technology, instructional design, etc.;
- Empathizing with faculty on the challenges of writing instruction, like the labor needed to give meaningful feedback, being graceful as students acquire and practice new writing knowledge, and the difficulty of trying and refining new writing assignments;
- Helping faculty find solutions to their problems by curating and translating research and theories from WAC so that they are accessible and applicable for faculty at our local institutions;
- Supporting faculty as writers and researchers by helping them reflect on their own writing processes and guiding them in researching writing in their courses and programs;
- Articulating the mission and vision of a program to institutional stakeholders; and
- Developing flexible processes for assessing writing across various local contexts, programs, and services.

While incomplete, this list illustrates a set of tasks that WAC WPAs frequently perform; indeed, especially at institutions without a formal WAC program, this list could effectively serve as the specialized objectives for a WAC WPA job description. A similar, more formal list specific to WAC WPAs—à la CWPA's official position statement, *Evaluating the Intellectual Work of Writing Administration*—would offer a valuable resource for those hoping to prepare graduate students for WAC work and WAC administrators as they document the need for support and resources from institutional stakeholders.

As this chapter demonstrates, a major tension surrounding the work of WAC is not only what it is and how to sustain it but also how to prepare professionals for this work. WAC has a long and storied history, celebrating 50 years of growth, expansion, and writing innovation across disciplines. As we enter our next 50 years and beyond, we'd do well to more clearly and explicitly define our roles, make visible our labor, and advocate for ourselves as WAC WPAs with the resources and support to carry out our missions.

CODA

Since drafting this chapter, all four authors have moved positions and, in most cases, institutions. Mandy took a year-round Assistant Director staff position in the WAC program at her institution. Amy left her WAC program, joining a Center for Teaching and Learning Excellence at another institution as a year-round

Associate Director staff member embedded in the college of business. Al took on a lecturer position in an English department at a different institution. Christina left her faculty WPA position to take on an Assistant Professor position specializing in discipline-based education research at another institution.

Mandy is the only author whose current job explicitly engages a WAC program; however, the three other authors still engage in WAC-like work. More specifically, our WAC preparation informs how we craft professional development opportunities for colleagues across the disciplines, participate in institutional conversations about writing, design research projects that study student learning and development, or teach writing or writing-enriched courses. In other words, we have discovered that there is a lot of room to engage in WAC-like work outside the confines of administrative roles and, further, that our WAC-shaped perspectives are both useful and highly valued in many other university contexts.

REFERENCES

Anson, C. (Ed.). (2002). *The WAC casebook: Scenes for faculty reflection and program development*. Oxford University Press.

Anson, C. (2013). Beyond the curriculum: Supporting faculty writing groups in WAC programs. In A. E. Geller & M. Eodice (Eds.), *Working with faculty writers* (pp. 21–37). Utah State University Press.

Association for Writing Across the Curriculum. (n.d.). About AWAC. Retrieved June 1, 2021 from https://wacassociation.org/about-awac/.

Bastian, H. (2014). Performing the groundwork: Building a WEC/WAC writing program at The College of St. Scholastica. *Composition Forum, 29*. https://compositionforum.com/issue/29/st-scholastica.php.

Brown, S. C., Enos, T. J. & Chaput, C. (Eds.). (2002). *The writing program administrator's resource: A guide to reflective institutional practice*. Taylor & Francis Group.

Charlton, J. (2009). The future of WPA professionalization: A 2007 survey. *Praxis: A Writing Center Journal, 7*(1). https://doi.org/10.15781/T2SQ8R050.

Charlton, C., Charlton, J., Graban, T. S., Ryan, K. J. & Stolley, A. F. (2011). *GenAdmin: Theorizing WPA identities in the twenty-first century*. Parlor Press.

Condon, W., Iverson, E. R., Manduca, C. A., Rutz, C. & Willett, G. (2016). *Faculty development and student learning: Assessing the connections*. Indiana University Press.

Council of Writing Program Administrators. (1998). *Evaluating the intellectual work of writing administration* [Position statement]. Council of Writing Program Administrators. http://wpacouncil.org/aws/CWPA/pt/sd/news_article/242849/_PARENT/layout_details/false.

Cox, M., Galin, J. & Melzer, D. (2018). *Sustainable WAC: A whole systems approach to launching and developing writing across the curriculum programs*. National Council of Teachers of English.

Elder, C. L., Schoen, M. & Skinnell, R. (2014). Strengthening graduate student preparation for WPA work. *WPA: Writing Program Administration*, *37*(2), 13–35. https://digital.library.unt.edu/ark:/67531/metadc505760/.

Faery, R. B. (1993). Teachers *and* writers: The faculty writing workshop and writing across the curriculum. *WPA: Writing Program Administration*, *17*(1–2), 31–42. http://162.241.207.49/archives/17n1-2/17n1-2faery.pdf.

Fassinger, P. A., Gilliland, N. & Johnson, L. L. (1992). Benefits of a faculty writing circle—Better teaching. *College Teaching*, *40*(2), 53–56. https://doi.org/10.1080/87567555.1992.10532266.

Foley-Schramm, A., Fullerton, B., James, E. M. & Morton-Aiken, J. (2018). Preparing graduate students for the field: A graduate student praxis heuristic for WPA professionalization and institutional politics. *WPA: Writing Program Administration*, *41*(2), 89–103. https://link.gale.com/apps/doc/A646110340/AONE?u=anon~15e0ab73&sid=googleScholar&xid=3b20de1e.

Fulwiler, T. (1989). Writing workshops and the mechanics of change. *WPA: Writing Program Administration*, *12*(3), 7–20. http://162.241.207.49/archives/12n3/12n3fulwiler.pdf.

Geller, A. E. & Eodice, M. (2013). *Working with faculty writers*. Utah State University Press.

Glotfelter, A., Updike, A. & Wardle, E. (2020). "Something invisible . . . has been made visible for me": An expertise-based WAC seminar model grounded in theory and (cross) disciplinary dialogue. In L. E. Bartlett, S. L. Tarabochia, A. R. Olinger & M. J. Marshall (Eds.), *Diverse Approaches to Teaching, Learning, and Writing Across the Curriculum: IWAC at 25* (pp. 167–192). The WAC Clearinghouse; University Press of Colorado. https://doi.org/10.37514/PER-B.2020.0360.2.10.

LaFrance, M. & Russell, A. (2018). Preparing writing studies graduate students within authentic WAC-contexts: A research methods course and WAC program review crossover project as a critical site of situated learning. *The WAC Journal*, *29*, 207–229. https://doi.org/10.37514/wac-j.2018.29.1.10.

Latterell, C. (2003). Defining roles for graduate students in writing program administration: Balancing pragmatic needs with a postmodern ethics of action. *WPA: Writing Program Administration*, *27*(1), 23–39. http://associationdatabase.co/archives/27n1-2/27n1-2latterell.pdf.

LaVecchia, C. M. & Ramírez, C. (2020). The versatility of a rhetoric and composition degree: Tales from former postdocs outside the field [in Connecting: On "showing up" in teaching, tutoring, and writing: A search for humanity, C. I. Wenger (Ed.)]. *The Journal of the Assembly for Expanded Perspectives on Learning*, *25*, 193–99. https://trace.tennessee.edu/jaepl/vol25/iss1/5.

Mahala, D. & Swilky, J. (1994). Resistance and reform: The functions of expertise in writing across the curriculum. *Language and Learning across the Disciplines*, *1*(2), 35–62. https://doi.org/10.37514/lld-j.1994.1.2.03.

Maimon, E. P. (1980). Cinderella to Hercules: Demythologizing writing across the curriculum. *Journal of Basic Writing*, *2*(4), 3–11. https://doi.org/10.37514/jbw-j.1980.2.4.02.

Malenczyk, R. (Ed.). (2016). *A rhetoric for writing program administrators* (2nd ed.). Parlor Press.

Martin, C. (2021). *Facilitating institutional change through writing-related faculty development* [Doctoral dissertation, Miami University]. Electronic Theses and Dissertations Center. http://rave.ohiolink.edu/etdc/view?acc_num=miami161796149420 7509.

Maurer, K. T., Matzker, F. & Dively, R. L. (2021). The graduate teaching assistant as assistant WPA: Navigating the hazards of liminal terrain between the role of student and the role of authority figure. In W. J. Macauley, Jr., L. R. Anglesey, B. Edwards, K. M. Lambrecht & P. Lovas (Eds.), *Standing at the threshold: Working through liminality in the composition and rhetoric TAship* (pp. 85–109). Utah State University Press.

McLeod, S. H. & Soven, M. (Eds.). (2000). *Writing across the curriculum: A guide to developing programs.* The WAC Clearinghouse. https://wac.colostate.edu/books/landmarks/mcleod-soven/. (Original work published 1992 by Sage.)

Miller, S. (1991). *Textual carnivals: The politics of composition.* Southern Illinois University Press.

Myers-Breslin, L. (1999). *Administrative problem-solving for writing programs and writing centers: Scenarios in effective program management.* National Council of Teachers of English.

National Census of Writing. (2017). 2017 four-year institution survey. National Census of Writing. https://writingcensus.ucsd.edu/survey/4/year/2017?question_name=s4y2017wac19&op=Submit#results.

Pemberton, M. A. (1995). Rethinking the WAC/writing center connection. *The Writing Center Journal, 15*(2), 116–133. https://doi.org/10.7771/2832-9414.1283.

Robinson, R. (2021). *"I've fooled them all!": Imposter syndrome and the WPA* (Publication No. 28417830) [Doctoral dissertation, Michigan State University]. ProQuest Dissertations & Theses Global.

Sheils, M. (1975, December 8). Why Johnny can't write. *Newsweek, 86*(23).

Soliday, M. (2005). General readers and classroom tutors across the curriculum. In C. Spigelman & L. Grobman (Eds.), *On location: Theory and practice in classroom-based writing tutoring* (pp. 31–43). Utah State University Press. https://digitalcommons.usu.edu/usupress_pubs/151.

Thaiss, C. & Zawacki, T. M. (2006). *Engaged writers and dynamic disciplines: Research on the academic writing life.* Boynton/Cook.

Townsend, M. A. (2016). What are writing across the curriculum and writing in the disciplines? In R. Malenczyk (Ed.), *A rhetoric for writing program administrators* (2nd ed., pp. 115–128). Parlor Press.

Walvoord, B. (1996). The future of WAC. *College English, 58*(1), 58–79. https://doi.org/10.2307/378534.

Zawacki, T. M. & Rogers, P. M. (2011). *Writing across the curriculum: A critical sourcebook.* Bedford/St. Martin's.

CHAPTER 14.
A WAC/WID EXPERIENCE IN ARGENTINA: WORKING FOR A HIGH DEGREE OF INSTITUTIONALIZATION

Estela Ines Moyano
Universidad Nacional Guillermo Brown

This chapter addresses the experience of a Writing across the Curriculum/Writing in the Disciplines (WAC/WID) program in Argentina at the Universidad Nacional Guillermo Brown. This university has created a Program of Professional and Academic Discourse Skills (Programa Competencias en Discurso Profesional y Académico) as part of its academic structure with a high degree of institutionalization. This institutionalization is manifested in different domains:

- First, the program is financed by the university, considering it as part of its budget, and is installed along the curriculum of all the degrees under an administrator that is a tenured professor;
- Second, it was installed by the university Organizer President from the beginning of the functioning of the institution in 2019, and then, after a period of intensive work, confirmed in 2022 by the Superior Council, which is the higher body of the university government;
- Third, it has the support of the academic area of government of the university in the organization of the work of each semester; and
- Fourth, it has political support that allows its progress as it grows in activities that enrich it, including research and community-oriented work.

The WAC/WID experience at Universidad Nacional Guillermo Brown consists of the introduction of reading, writing, and orality regarding multimodal texts in several subjects along each degree and across the curriculum. This means that a language professor works in several subjects of the degree, teaching students how to resolve the writing or oral activities that their subject professors ask them to do. This design includes two intensive writing subjects in the first semester of each degree; one in the second, third, and fourth semesters; and one per year in the rest of the curriculum of each degree.

The program is considered part of the WAC tradition because it is conceived as an initiative inside the specific subjects of a degree, different from separated composition courses (Bazerman et al., 2005). It is also considered as a WID program because it is oriented to teach the particularities of the discourse of each discipline in order to favor not only the competencies of mastering texts but especially the learning of the disciplinary contents (Bazerman et al., 2005; Thaiss & Porter, 2010). To do this, the professors that work in the program conduct research in the schematic structure of the genres at play and the characteristics of the discourse in the different disciplines in order to teach them to the students. This research is based in linguistic development, as will be explained later in this chapter.

This chapter justifies the necessity of teaching literacy across the university curriculum, presents the theoretical perspective that sustains the work developed, and explains the pedagogical proposal implemented. The program itself is described and some results are shown to demonstrate the evolution of the students in writing an instance of a genre in two disciplines. The work shows the achievements of the program design, its implementation, and its high degree of institutionalization.

CONTEXT

Public university education in Argentina is not only free of tuition and fees but it also doesn't demand any kind of admission exams. This means that the requirement for entrance to the university is only having finished secondary studies. Those candidates who have not completed secondary studies can have access to a university education if they are more than 25 years old and have professional experience in the field of the selected degree. All of these dispositions are interpreted as democratization of university studies and are socially considered of great value.

However, some scholars have called attention to the conditions of access to university studies as problematic. Ana María Ezcurra (2011), for example, considers it an "exclusive inclusion" that is socially conditioned. The "exclusive inclusion" refers to the fact that the success of each student in the process of university education depends on their cultural capital, according to Pierre Bourdieu (Tovillas, 2010). This position resonates with Basil Bernstein (1990), who states that success in education is conditioned by differences between restricted and elaborated codes, which are socially distributed. In fact, there is as a consequence a great percentage of attrition of students during the course of each degree.

It is necessary to suggest, then, that universities must propose creative solutions to the high attrition rates that affect the whole student population. One solution consists of deciding what to teach in order to reduce the breach between students, guaranteeing them the possibility of continuing and completing their degree. Teaching academic and professional literacy across the curriculum and along the different degrees emerges as an important resource so that students can complete their studies.

THEORETICAL FRAMEWORK

The university is a social space in which students begin their new educational experience. This social space demands working with new genres, understood as staged, goal-oriented social activities realized through language (Martin & Rose, 2008). These new genres, then, imply new social purposes, new schematic structures (i.e., discourse organization in stages), and the use of new language resources, specially created to produce disciplinary knowledge (Christie & Martin, 1997; Halliday, 2004a; Halliday & Martin, 1993). These genres are specialized social activities that the students face for the first time in their educational trajectory. Hence, new processes of learning are necessary.

Students need to learn specific contents in different disciplines by managing their language and genres. According to Michael Halliday (1993), accessing new resources in the general system of language allows students to learn new knowledge; the developing of language is at the same time the developing of learning content. Language, as the most sophisticated semiotic system created by humans, is the condition and the resource by which the experience is transformed into knowledge. This conceptualization from systemic functional linguistics resonates with a long tradition, including proposals in philosophy, socio-historical psychology, and educational psychology, which argue that language is the means to constructing knowledge (Moyano & Blanco, 2021). Systemic functional linguistics proposes that language is the means to constructing the world (field), social activities, relations between participants (tenor), and resources of texture, i.e., construe text (mode) (Halliday, 1982). Pedagogically speaking, it is important *to teach language* in order to learn the resources to construct meaning; *to teach about language*, to systematize these resources and make them conscious; and *to teach through language*, in order to learn contents of different disciplines (Halliday, 2004b). Consequently, teaching language in these different aspects means that teaching how to produce a text involves all these approaches to language, which opens the door to produce new knowledge through writing. This practice of teaching is done inside the subjects of the different degrees, not separately.

Therefore, learning new genres and the language used to instantiate them in texts allows students to improve their performance at the university and, in the future, in their professions. To do this, the students also need to learn the processes of reading and writing to achieve autonomy in accessing and producing disciplinary contents. Estela Ines Moyano and Nestor Blanco (2021) have shown the progress of university students in producing new knowledge through the improvement of text construction in a process of a genre-based learning, based on the developments of Jim Martin and his colleagues in the frame of systemic functional linguistics (Martin, 1999; Rose & Martin, 2012) and adapted by Moyano (2007).

The question then becomes: What do students need to know in order to develop disciplinary knowledge as well as academic and professional communications skills? First, the context of the sphere of production and circulation of the genre is at stake. Second, the genre itself—its social purpose, its schematic structure, and the specific language resources at play in the discipline—needs to be considered. Third, a procedure for approaching and producing new genres, which will give students independence in this process after their university experience, needs to be in place.

This position goes beyond WAC/WID traditions in respect to teaching language (Bawarshi & Reiff, 2010). The genre-based proposal presented here is implemented to teach not only the schematic structure but also the specific resources of language that characterize a genre to favor knowledge construction. This decision has been taken after a long experience with teaching reading and writing based in the concept of genre, register, and discourse developed by Martin and his colleagues (Eggins & Martin, 2003; Hao, 2020; Martin, 1992; Martin & Rose, 2007; 2008; Martin & White, 2005; Moyano, 2016; 2021a; 2021b, among others in a long tradition). This experience has taken place at different institutions in Argentina and has been communicated in different publications (Moyano, 2007; 2010; 2017; 2018, among others).

A PROPOSAL FOR TEACHING GENRES ACROSS THE CURRICULUM AND ALONG EACH DEGREE

In this section, I will approach different aspects of the proposal for the Program of Professional and Academic Discourse Skills at the Universidad Nacional Guillermo Brown in Argentina. First, I will expound the logic of organization across the curriculum and along the degrees. Second, I will present the pedagogical design we apply repeatedly in each intervention. Third, I will discuss the strategy we use to work along the degrees. Finally, I will show two examples of the results obtained in the process of teaching genres.

Teaching Genre-Based Literacy across the Curriculum and along Each Degree

In 2019, after two attempts of organization as part of the process of creation, the Universidad Nacional Guillermo Brown started its functions. One of the innovative initiatives pursued in this period was the creation of what was called an "Area of Professional and Academic Discourse Skills" (Área de Competencias en Discurso Profesional y Académico). This area, integrated by language teachers and researchers, proposed the institutionalization of a process of academic and professional literacy across the university curriculum and along each degree.

The initiative consisted of designating several subjects as intensive writing throughout each degree's plan. The implementation included the participation of one professor of the created area in each of these subjects, as it will be described later, applying the pedagogical proposal presented in the next section. The subjects were selected in each degree in accordance with the contents to be developed, proposing as part of the minimum contents of the syllabus the inclusion of genres that are appropriate to them. This decision means that teaching academic literacy is mandatory in these subjects.

In the first proposal, the selection of subjects with intervention of the area was made intensively along each degree: two in the first semester (one common to all the degrees and one specific to each of them), and one subject per semester in each year until the end of each degree plan. This decision allowed students to learn different genres and macrogenres (Martin & Rose, 2008), as in the example described by Cecilia Serpa (2021) and in the cases shown by Moyano and Blanco (2021). It also gave students the chance to learn a procedure to write new genres independently, in other subjects or in the future, when working in their professions. This procedure comprises the three stages of the pedagogical proposal, including the negotiation of the field and the reflection on other variables of the context. The students are able to learn this process due to the explicit teaching (Bernstein, 1990) implemented in each subject.

The purpose of this initiative was teaching reading and writing in order to promote skills in producing new knowledge inside the disciplines. Managing resources of language to produce different types of meaning (the construction of the world and relationships plus the design of a text that deploys these meanings), as well as teaching different genres understood as social activities realized by language comprising those meanings, allow for the construction of new knowledge and the participation in different areas of social activity (Martin, 1993; Moyano & Blanco, 2021).

After the first implementation, and in light of the results obtained, some of the disciplines' professors posed the question about what to do in order to teach reading and writing when they are not accompanied in their courses by a professor of the Area of Professional and Academic Discourse Skills. This question led to a design proposal for an online course oriented to disciplinary professors. This course reflects on the theoretical justification of implementing the mentioned area and the reason why students benefit from learning academic and professional literacy. It also presents the pedagogical proposal of the area and suggests activities derived from it that a non-specialist in language can assign to students in order to work with reading, writing, and oral activities related to texts that instantiate relevant genres in the subject they teach. These practices allow the possibility of creating a sort of "big team" of professors at the university, guiding the students in gaining experience in literacy skills.

In 2022, the area was transformed into a program with a modification. After four semesters of teaching in teams, one subject per year of the degree (from the third year until the final) is selected for intensive writing. In this second part of the degree, the professor in charge of teaching academic or professional genres is discipline specific. To do this job, this professor has to take and complete a course taught by the professors of the Professional and Academic Discourse Skills program and receive supervision during the programming and implementation of the classes of teaching literacy. This kind of work redistributes responsibilities at the end of each degree.

Genre-Based Pedagogical Proposal: Reading and Writing to Know (RWK)

The genre-based pedagogical proposal applied in the work of the program (Figure 14.1) has been developed and adapted (Moyano, 2007) from the Sydney School's Teaching Learning Cycle (Martin, 1999; Rose & Martin, 2012). Recently, it has been named Reading and Writing to Know (RWK). In the central column of Figure 14.1, the three stages of the process are deployed: Deconstruction, Construction, and Editing. The Construction stage is preceded by a sub-stage, Text Design. As seen in the third column, every stage is initiated by a joint work between teachers and students[1] and then completed by groups of students to finally reach an independent product. This process is done in order to model the work in each stage and to provide scaffolding for the students' transition from heteronomy to autonomy. All of the stages suppose a negotiation of the field, as shown in the first column of Figure 14.1. This negotiation is understood as the topic of the text taken as model and the one elaborated and edited by the students. Then a reflection about the tenor, which comprise the relationships between interactants, and the mode, as the construction of text as ancillary or constitutive of the activity.

---

1   When the pedagogical proposal is applied to the tertiary level, the Construction stage is not fulfilled by joint work between teachers and students, except when special kinds of resources are taught, e.g., the use of grammatical metaphor (Hao, 2020) or resources of engagement with other voices (Martin & White, 2005).

Field Negotiation	Deconstruction		* Joint reading * Joint reading in small groups * Individual reading
Negotiation of Tenor and Mode	Text Design	Construction	* Joint writing * Joint writing in small groups * Individual writing
		Editing	* Joint edition * Joint edition in small groups * Individual edition

Figure 14.1. Genre-based pedagogical proposal: Reading and Writing to Know (RWK) (adapted from Moyano, 2007).

The stage called Deconstruction consists in jointly determining the genre at play, identifying the stages of its schematic structure realized by language in the text analyzed as a model, contributing to the purpose of the genre and the relevant linguistic resources utilized to create meaning. Before doing this, the professor has to research instances of the genre at play to identify these characteristics and select what to teach to the students. This research is made on the ground of the developments of the Sydney School on genre, register, and discourse (Eggins & Martin, 2003; Hao, 2020; Martin, 1992; Martin & Rose, 2008; 2007; Martin & White, 2005; Moyano, 2016; 2021a; 2021b, among many others).

In the Construction stage, the professors and the students at the university level work with the joint design of the new text, proposing the use of all kinds of schemas for planning, taking into account the field and the contents that will be distributed in the schematic structure of the genre. Then, the students produce the first version of the new text either in groups or individually and deliver it to the professor.

After a brief global commentary made by the professor, the students learn in a class dedicated to joint Editing how to use a guide to edit their own texts. This guide is constructed by the language professor following what has been taught in the Deconstruction stage. The subject professors may add some requests of disciplinary content to the guide. Finally, the students edit their texts following the guide and make the final delivery of the second version of the text. The evaluation of the two different versions is performed with a rubric made *ad hoc*. This rubric considers the different aspects of the texts that have been taught to the students—the schematic structure and the resources of language at different levels of the text (discourse, grammatical, and graphic resources)—and may include the disciplinary content aspects added. Although both versions are evaluated to construe statistics, only the second version of the text is marked.

STRATEGY FOR TEACHING ALONG THE DEGREE

As introduced above, the program includes two intensive writing subjects in the first semester of all the degrees: one in the second, the third, and the fourth semester, and then one per year in each degree. Once the subjects in each degree have been selected, the strategy applied to teach how to write an instance of a genre during the two first years of instruction (four semesters) consist of a teaching association of a literacy professor and the professor of the discipline in which the process of teaching literacy takes place (Figure 14.2).

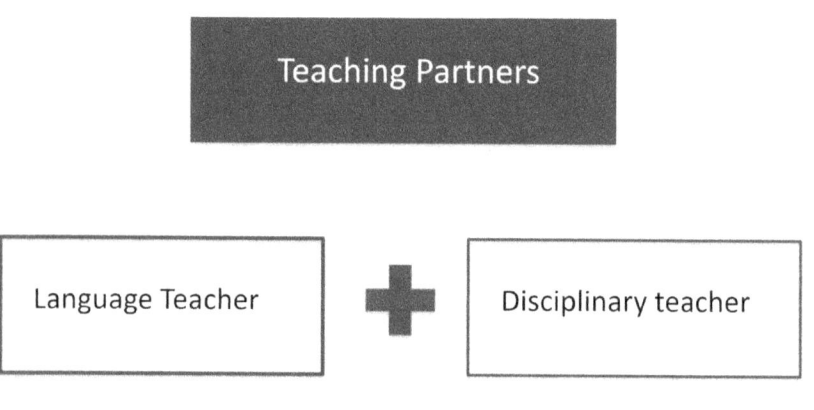

Figure 14.2. Integration of teaching teams (Moyano, 2010; 2017; 2018).

These actors have different roles in the classroom as shown in Figure 14.3. The literacy professor is in charge of teaching the different stages of RWK, which consists of a process of learning new genres that the students need to incorporate for independent use in the future. The role of the discipline professor is to discuss the social context of the genre and the interpersonal interactions that take place through it as social activity as well as to reflect and discuss different aspects of the field of the text at play. This collaborative work enriches the process of reading and writing, giving the students the possibility of consciously associating the literacy process with knowledge construction.

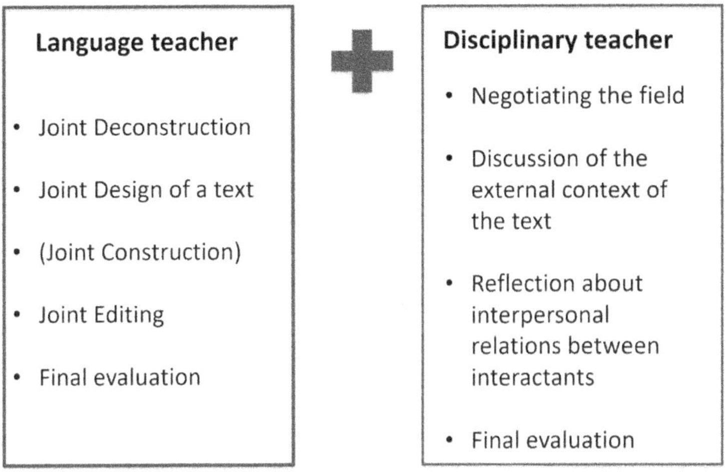

Language teacher
• Joint Deconstruction
• Joint Design of a text
• (Joint Construction)
• Joint Editing
• Final evaluation
Disciplinary teacher
• Negotiating the field
• Discussion of the external context of the text
• Reflection about interpersonal relations between interactants
• Final evaluation

Figure 14.3. Distribution of the roles of teaching (Moyano, 2010; 2017; 2018).

From the third year until the end of the degree, the instruction is the responsibility of the disciplinary professor guided by a literacy professor (Figure 14.4). To do this, they need to complete a course dictated by the team of the Program of Professional and Academic Discourse Skills. Their job with the students is also supervised by the more experienced professors of the program.

Science of Language Professor
Course oriented to Discipline Professors (second level)
Acompanying Discipline Professors in the implementation of RWK
Discipline Professor
RWK implementation

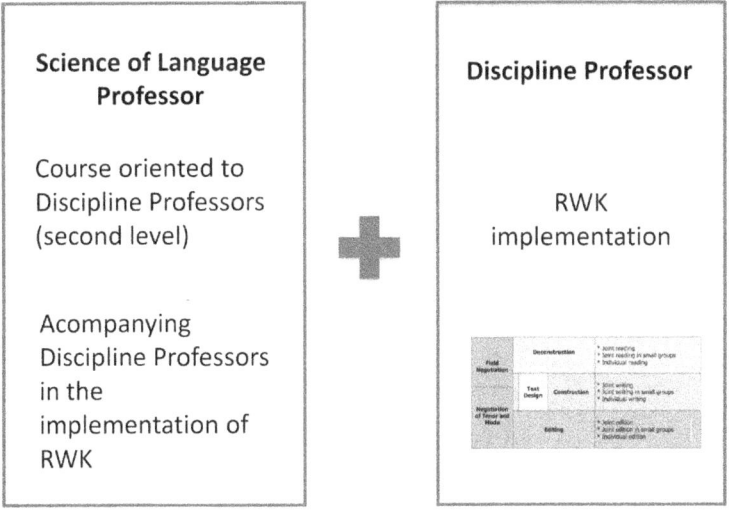

Figure 14.4. Second stage of the implementation of the program (since 3rd year of the degree).

RESULTS OBTAINED

In this section, I will show two examples of results obtained in different subjects with the methodology of intervention described.

Figure 14.5 shows the evolution in the grade obtained (represented by numbers in the scale from 0 to 10 in the vertical axis) by individual texts (represented by numbers in the horizontal axis). The texts, instances of scientific of technological projects, were produced in two different versions (the first as a draft, the second as an edited text) by students in a subject called Science, Technology and Society. This is a subject located in the first semester of the first year of all the degrees at the university. The figure shows the achievements of the first version of the text (light gray bars), influenced by the Deconstruction stage of the pedagogical proposal. The dark gray bars represent the second version of each text, after a process of Editing. The figure shows that all of the texts have improved, some of them in a considerable dimension (e.g., texts 11, 18, and 28). It is important to highlight that even the best texts have improved (e.g., 1, 3, and 32). These results imply that the students have made progress in managing the text and quite possibly mastering the genre. It is possible to say this from previous experience in which the students had to engage the same genre more than once (Moyano, 2007).

Figure 14.6 shows the results obtained in another first-year subject, Epistemology and History of Mathematics, this time in a degree of a complementary cycle oriented to give a university degree to teachers of mathematics. The texts produced by the students (displayed along the horizontal axis) were instances of an analytical exposition (Martin, 1989) and were produced in small groups. The light gray bars represent the first version of the texts, and the dark gray bars the second, after a process of Editing. As in the case presented before, the students' texts improved with the editing, as shown on the vertical axis, which represents the grade. In many cases, this improvement is considerable, and it is probable that the students have learned the genre after this careful production. This figure also shows a reduction in the breach between groups.

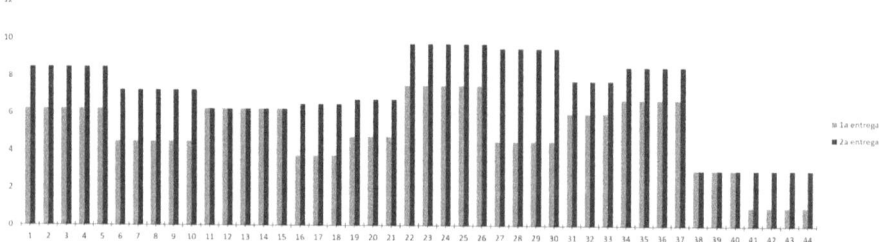

Figure 14.5. Results of the evolution of instances of a project in Science, Technology and Society, a subject of the first year of all the degrees at the university.

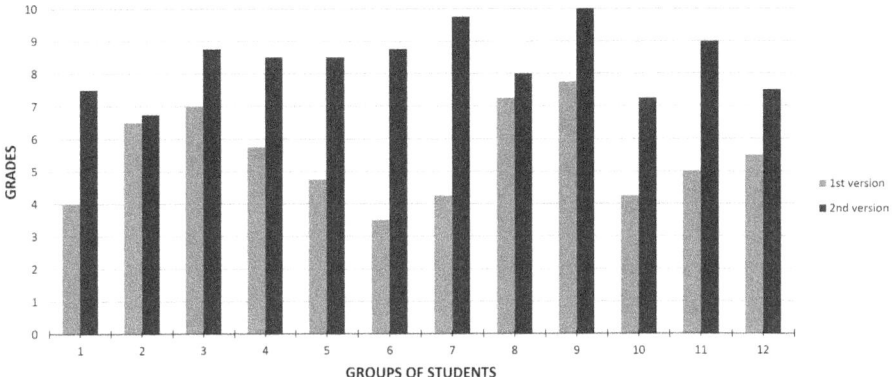

Figure 14.6. Results of the evolution of instances of the genre analytical exposition (Martin, 1989) in Epistemology and History of Mathematics, in a degree oriented to complete the university cycle of mathematics teachers.

Moyano and Blanco (2021) have shown from a qualitative analysis of one example of each of these cases that the evolution of improving the texts has impacted the evolution of knowledge construction in the selected field.

FINAL REMARKS

The main aim of the WAC/WID program at the Universidad Nacional Guillermo Brown is to help students to develop skills in reading and writing academic texts in order to increase their knowledge construction along the plan of the degree they have chosen. This goal is a gateway to achieve success in their path through the university and their graduation. More than that, the work with academic and professional discourse competencies with the explicit pedagogical device utilized through the process of teaching in each of the designated subjects gives the students resources for accessing new genres in the future.

To achieve the purposes of the Program of Academic and Professional Discourse Skills, the commitment of a group of professors is not enough. The success of the pursued goals is a matter of institutionalization. When the institution is committed to the aims proposed by the program, which is based on a theoretical, pedagogical, and strategically oriented proposal, its functioning and positive results are almost guaranteed. This is why institutionalization is so relevant.

The institutionalization of a program is shown by various actions that can be summed up into features such as financial, academic, and political support. This support ensures that the authorities of different levels, such as coordinators of degrees, are also engaged with the program, which influences the disposition of the professors of the subjects at the beginning of the process. After the first experience of working in teams with the language professors and in light of the results obtained by the proposal, professors of the specific subjects of different degrees are, for the most part, notably committed to the program and involved in its goals and processes. Slowly, other discipline professors start to be curious about how to help students to increase their reading and writing skills and decide to enroll themselves in the course that the Discourse Skills program has prepared for them.

The main achievements of the program are the progress the students show in the development of reading and writing specific academic and professional genre skills as well as their consequent progress in knowledge construction in each subject. The students get accustomed to the program activities due to the frequency of the intensive writing subjects along the degree. They make a thorough work following the instructions given through the pedagogical proposal described here, and their texts show important progress from the first to the second version they write. The process with each genre is a new start, but they learn how to proceed as long as they revisit the process of accessing them (i.e., the RWK design). Knowledge about genres and disciplinary language is critical for students to progress in their autonomy. After that intense process of teaching and learning, they are aware of the main resources provided by their own language (Spanish) to construe texts as instances of academic or professional genres when they have a model to explore. This is an important accomplishment for the future when as professionals they will need to access new genres by themselves.

REFERENCES

Bazerman, C., Little, J., Bethel, L., Chavkin, T., Fouquette, D. & Garufis, J. (2005). *Reference guide to writing across the curriculum.* Parlor Press; The WAC Clearinghouse. https://wac.colostate.edu/books/referenceguides/bazerman-wac/.

Bawarshi, A. & Reiff, M. J. (2010). *Genre. An introduction to history, theory, research, and pedagogy.* Parlor Press; The WAC Clearinghouse. https://wac.colostate.edu/books/referenceguides/bawarshi-reiff/.

Bernstein, B. (1990). *Class, codes and control: The structuring of pedagogic discourse* (Vol. 4). Routledge.

Christie, F. & Martin, J. R. (Eds.). (1997). *Genre and institutions: Social processes in the workplace and school.* Continuum.

Eggins, S. & Martin, J. R. (2003). El contexto como género: Una perspectiva lingüístico-funcional. *Revista Signos, 36*(54), 185–205. https://doi.org/10.4067/s0718-09342003005400005.

Ezcurra, A. M. (2011). *Igualdad en educación superior: Un desafío mundial.* Universidad Nacional de General Sarmiento.

Halliday, M. A. K. (1982). *El lenguaje como semiótica social*. FCE.
Halliday, M. A. K. (1993). Towards a language-based theory of learning. *Linguistics and Education, 5*, 93–116. https://doi.org/10.1016/0898-5898(93)90026-7.
Halliday, M. A. K. (2004a). *The language of science*. In J. Webster (Ed.), *The collected works of M.A.K. Halliday* (Vol. 5). Continuum.
Halliday, M. A. K. (2004b). Three aspects of children's language development: Learning language, learning through language, learning about language. In J. Webster (Ed.), *The language of early childhood: Collected works of M.A.K. Halliday* (Vol. 4, pp. 308–326). Continuum.
Halliday, M. A. K. & Martin, J. R. (1993). *Writing science: Literacy and discursive power*. University of Pittsburgh Press.
Hao, J. (2020). *Analyzing scientific discourse from a systemic functional perspective: A framework for exploring knowledge building in biology*. Routledge.
Martin, J. R. (1989). *Factual writing: Exploring and challenging social reality*. Oxford University Press.
Martin, J. R. (1992). *English text: System and structure*. Benjamin.
Martin, J. R. (1993). A contextual theory of language. In W. Cope & M. Kalantzis (Eds.), *The Powers of literacy: A genre approach to teaching literacy* (pp. 116–136). Falmer (Critical Perspectives on Literacy and Education); University of Pittsburgh Press (Pittsburg Series in Composition, Literacy, and Culture).
Martin, J. R. (1999). Mentoring semogenesis: "Genre-based" literacy pedagogy. In F. Christie (Ed.), *Pedagogy and the shaping of consciousness: Linguistic and social processes* (pp. 123–155). Cassell (Open Linguistics Series).
Martin J. R. & Rose, D. (2007). *Working with discourse: Meaning beyond the clause*. Equinox.
Martin J. R. & Rose, D. (2008). *Genre relations: Mapping culture*. Equinox.
Martin, J. R. & White, P. P. R. (2005). *The language of evaluation: Appraisal in English*. Palgrave.
Moyano, E. I. (2007). Enseñanza de la lectura y la escritura basada en la teoría de género y registro de la LSF: Resultados de una investigación. *Revista Signos, 40*(65), 573–608. https://doi.org/10.15645/alabe.2012.5.1.
Moyano, E. I. (2010). Escritura académica a lo largo de la carrera: Un programa institucional. *Revista Signos, 43*(74), 465–488. https://doi.org/10.4067/s0718-09342010000500004.
Moyano, E. I. (2016). Theme in English and Spanish: Different means of realization for the same textual function. *English Text Construction, 9*(1), 190–220. https://doi.org/10.1075/etc.9.1.10moy.
Moyano, E. I. (2017). Diseño e implementación de programa de lectura y escritura en el nivel universitario: Principios y estrategias. *Lenguas Modernas, 50* (segundo semestre), 47–72. https://doi.org/10.53673/th.v2i8.156.
Moyano, E. I. (2018). La enseñanza de la lectura y la escritura académicas mediante programas a lo largo del curriculum universitario: Opción teórica, didáctica y de gestión. *DELTA, 34*(1), 235–267. https://doi.org/10.1590/0102-4450748962 74115057.

Moyano, E. I. (2021a). La función de Tema en español: Sus medios de realización desde la perspectiva trinocular de la Lingüística Sistémico-Funcional. *Revista Signos, 54*(106), 487–517. https://doi.org/10.4067/s0718-09342021000200487.

Moyano, E. I. (2021b). Metodología para la descripción de géneros en el marco de la lingüística sistémico-funcional: Su adaptación al español. *Revista Organon, 35*(71), 257–279. https://doi.org/10.22456/2238-8915.113374.

Moyano, E. I. & Blanco, N. H. (2021). Function of language in learning and knowledge construction. *Revista Signum, 24*(3), 93–115.

Rose, D. & Martin, J. R. (2012). *Learning to write, reading to learn: Genre, knowledge and pedagogy in the Sydney School*. Equinox.

Serpa, C. (2021). La enseñanza de la escritura en el campo de la programación: Exposición y análisis de una experiencia en torno al macrogénero descripción de flujograma. *Revista Íkala, 26*(1), 77–96. https://doi.org/10.17533/udea.ikala.v26n01a02.

Thaiss, C. & Porter, T. (2010). The state of WAC/WID in 2010: Methods and results of the US survey of the international WAC/WID mapping project. *College Composition and Communication, 61*(3), 524–570. https://www.jstor.org/stable/40593339.

Tovillas, P. (2010). *Bourdieu: Una introducción.* Quadrata.

CHAPTER 15.
ENGLISH AS A LINGUA ACADEMICA IN SCHOLARLY PUBLISHING: THE CLASH OF ANGLO-AMERICAN AND SLOVAK WRITING STYLE CONVENTIONS

Alena Kačmárová, Magdaléna Bilá, and Ingrida Vaňková
Prešov University, Prešov, Slovakia

In recent years, scholarly publishing has expanded in volume predominantly because the transfer of knowledge and research findings has become a necessary part of a scholar's responsibilities.[1] Scholars need to submit research reports to international scholarly journals registered in databases, which automatically presupposes publishing in English. When we consider the share of published research by countries/cultures, we realize that Slovak authors represent the minority in humanities research journals; anecdotal evidence allows for estimation of about 3 percent of published papers authored by Slovak scholars. Slovak authors may be discouraged from submitting to journals due to viewing a language as a barrier. Two scenarios can occur. In order to assure a quality text, an author can submit either the English text to have it proofread or a Slovak text to have it translated, all in good faith that the final version will be a good quality text. However, neither a proofreader nor a translator will alter macrostructure (the big picture), mezzostructure (paragraphing), and microstructure (bulkiness of the language) due to lack of powers or lack of linguistic expertise. Either may derive from their unawareness of the concept of English as a lingua franca in opposition to English as a lingua franca of science (hereinafter used as lingua academica to differentiate between general lingua franca and lingua franca of science).

We adhere to the view that there is a fundamental difference between English as a lingua franca and English as a lingua academica (Bilá & Kačmárová, 2021, p. 22). English as a lingua franca, i.e., a language conveying meaning in

---

[1] This study is part of research activities conducted within the research grant project KEGA 007PU-4/2019 "Defining a writing style of scholarly papers written in English vs. Slovak/Slavic lingua-culture conventions."

communication between interactants with different mother tongues, is more of a "code" than a "language," as it is void of history and culture and is typified by a situation-bound lexicon or various levels of grammatical accuracy. The meaning is negotiated during conversation. We dare venture that English as a lingua academica is rightfully tagged a "language," as this term embraces history and culture (or lingua-culture). It is associated with written production and Anglo-American writing style employed in expert journals. This presupposes higher requirements on the language standards. The purpose of academic usage of a language is more than just negotiating meaning while neglecting form; it is the usage of the language in accordance with conventionalized routines of text composition on all levels, from macrostructure to microstructure, which is embodied in the concept of a writing style.

In an effort to understand the concept of a writing style, we turn to the classification of writing styles offered by Johan Galtung (1981). In general, his typology includes four writing styles: Anglo-Saxon, Germanic, Gallic, and Nipponic. Geographically, these styles align with the countries of the UK/USA, Germany, France, and Japan, respectively. Previous studies (Bowe & Martin, 2007; Chamonikolasová, 2005; Clyne, 1994; Čmejrková, 1996; Dahl, 2004; Galtung, 1981; Walková, 2014) describe the four cultural styles in terms of type of information, text layout, organization of ideas, and the nature of discourse. Adopting a more general perspective, we uncover a conceptual dichotomy of the outlined features (Bilá, Kačmárová & Vaňková, 2020). Based on the discrepancies, we can establish two types of styles: Saxonic style and other-than-Saxonic style. The former includes Anglo-American writing tradition and style; the latter includes German, French, and Japanese traditions and writing styles. It is interesting that Galtung's classification lacks the category and/or writing style of Slavic lingua-cultures. Světla Čmejrková (1996) observes that "when Johan Galtung (1981, 1985) compares saxonic, teutonic, gallic, and nipponic intellectual styles, he notices that Eastern Europe, including the former Soviet Union, found itself under the influence of the teutonic intellectual style due to a long historical tradition" (p. 140; lower-case letters for styles in the original). The discrepancies within the outlined features have been identified by Čmejrková (1996), as well as through personal observation (see Table 15.1).

Presently, we feel pressure imposed on scholars to draft a text intended for translation into English; this necessitates bringing a new concept: "writing-for-translation stylistics." Thus, the present chapter aims to identify what is at the core of the Slovak approach to writing academic papers and how it differs from the Anglo-American approach so that the writing-for-translation stylistics can be established and in due time introduced into curriculum design. This experience directs our attention to the distinctiveness of a linguistics tradition and training in approaching writing tasks, which makes Slovak authors unaware of possible failure when publishing in English. The present chapter offers both conceptual and empirical research. The conceptual research provides for the understanding of how a Slovak author's mindset is programmed through years of schooling and how the linguistics tradition is communicated in Slovak language classes. The empirical research materializes problems encountered by Slovak authors in composing a text to be translated and supposedly included in the concept of writing-for-translation stylistics. The present chapter identifies the main clash between Slovak and Anglo-American writing styles and in doing so intends to raise interest in researching discrepancies between Anglo-American and other writing styles.

Table 15.1. The table illustrates the differences between Saxonic and other-than-Saxonic writing styles.

	Saxonic writing style	Other-Than-Saxonic writing style
type of information	empirical in nature	theorizing in nature
text layout	research-problem-based	literature-mention-based
organization of ideas	introducing the purpose up front	delaying the purpose in the paper (if present at all)
the nature of discourse	linear → → ß → → dialogic precise discourse reader-friendliness observed	non-linear monologic vague discourse reader-friendliness neglected

CONCEPTUAL RESEARCH

METHODOLOGY

The conceptual analysis is conducted in two steps: conceptualizing the Slovak academic writing style based on the analysis of the Slovak linguistics tradition, and defining the parameters that distinguish Saxonic (for geopolitical reasons, hereinafter labeled as Anglo-American) from Slovak academic writing. The employed method is the conceptualization scheme consisting of four steps (Kačmárová, Bilá & Vaňková, 2018). In this scheme, a term is not treated in isolation but rather as a textual unit, accounting for the target recipient and context. This approach reflects the cooperation or interlinkage of hermeneutics, salience, and conceptualization. The four steps embody four concepts: frame establishment, encoding or pre-understanding, salience, and code configuration. In other words, we treated the Slovak stylistics terminology as follows:

1. Frame: We set the frame, i.e., the identification of the field into which the term concerned falls, and which represents the setting for the definition and exemplification to be provided (hereinafter referred to as "frame").
2. Definition: We supplied the definition or explanation of what the concept of the term stands for in the language of origin, the conventionalized definition presently available in scholarly literature and teaching materials (hereinafter referred to as "definition").
3. Exemplification: We searched for contextualized examples (hereinafter referred to as "exemplification").
4. Translation: We suggested functional translation or the term implying lingua-culture-specific understanding (hereinafter referred to as "translation").

As a result, we offer the conceptualization of academic writing as conventionalized in the Slovak linguistics setting. This should serve as an explanation of the clash between Slovak and Anglo-American writing styles.

Findings

In the Slovak linguistics tradition, any treatment of writing styles seems to be part of stylistics. However, neither the formal nor the semantic representation of what academic writing stands for in Anglo-American lingua-culture is present in Slovak stylistics. The notion of writing and speaking in Slovak linguistics is rather tradition-based, building upon the prominent Slovak linguist Jozef Mistrík (1997) and his quite complex classification. The classification draws on three underlying notions (in Slovak "štýl," literally "style"; "slohový útvar," literally "form of composition"; and "slohový postup," literally "procedure of composition") and their subclassification. As a matter of fact, these are more theoretical constructs than performance-based notions. They draw on a language-system-based approach pertaining to the Slovak setting; contrariwise, we view the Anglo-American approach more "parole"/speech-oriented (in the Saussurean sense).

We consider it necessary to discuss the compatibility of Slovak and English terminology as this may shed light on lingua-culture-specific insight into writing. It follows that English renderings of Slovak concepts are not easily provided. Thus, in order to understand the level of compatibility between Slovak and English terms, we have to consider their content analysis, and we can do so through adopting the conceptualization scheme (Kačmárová, Bilá & Vaňková, 2018). The following analysis provides the conceptualization of the key Slovak terminology and its renderings into English.

Source Term 1: 'štýl' (semantic translation: style)

1. Frame: Stylistics/Writing
2. Definition: The notion is defined as the selection and arrangement of language based on the author's intention.
3. Exemplification: The notion represents the typology of seven items. These terms are considered culture-specific items, as their literal translation may cause misunderstanding. Table 15.2 provides the Slovak term, its literal (semantic) translation based on the term's surface structure, and its functional translation based on the term's deep structure. Adopting a bottom-up approach, a native speaker of English does not conceptualize the third column of Table 15.2 as a style, rather as a text type.
4. Translation: The suggested English equivalent of the Slovak term "style" is "text type."

Source Term 2: "slohový postup" (semantic translation: the procedure of composition)

Table 15.2. The table provides semantic (literal) and functional translations of Slovak terms.

Slovak term	Semantic translation	Suggested functional translation
náučný štýl	educational/scientific style	academic texts
administratívny štýl	clerical style	business writing
publicistický štýl	journalistic style	journalistic writing
rečnícky štýl	oratorical style	a speech
esejistický štýl	essay style	belletristic rhetoric
hovorový štýl	colloquial style	vernacular language
umelecký štýl	artistic style	belle-letters text

1. Frame: Stylistics/Writing
2. Definition: The notion comprises information on how to approach a topic, i.e., what vocabulary is used and how sentences are structured. Succinctly, microstylistics is the focus.
3. Exemplification: The present concept includes five categories: informative, narrative, descriptive, explanatory, and reflectionist. The terms imply the function of the text; e.g., the text is intended for giving information, creating or reproducing a story, describing characters, providing explanation, or reflecting one's subjective stance. This is in sharp contrast to the term "postup" (literally meaning "procedure"), as the Slovak term suggests instructions will be given; however, the opposite is the case. The practice shows that in schooling the mere procedure of writing, argument development, and paragraph development are not taught.
4. Translation: The suggested translation is writing technique/strategy/method.

Source Term 3: "slohový útvar" (semantic translation: "form of composition"; form meaning product/category)

1. Frame: Stylistics/Writing
2. Definition: The present notion is traditionally defined as the end-product generated through the employment of a particular writing technique.
3. Exemplification: It includes numerous items, e.g., email, dialogue, report, announcement, order, editorial, story, fable, description, travelogue, lecture, article, review, commentary discussion, or a speech.
4. Translation: Based on the provided examples, the suggested translation is genre.

In the search for the affiliation of academic text in Slovak stylistics, we need to interlink a text type (source term 1) and a genre (source term 3). Table 15.3 below exemplifies genres for specific text types. The table indicates that even though at first sight academic text is missing in the typology, it is implied in the term "náučný štýl," which can be literally translated as educational or scientific style (see the boldface type in Table 15.3).

Pondering further, we realize that "academic *text*" is merely a product not involving a process. In the search for "academic *writing*" in the Slovak typology, we find it absent, and to identify it, we need to interlink all three underlying notions. It follows that the Anglo-American term "academic writing" is not classified as a single concept in Slovak. We identify its presence only as an intersection of the three notions (see Figure 15.1). In Slovak, the alternative of Anglo-American academic writing is hence represented by the overlap of the concepts indicated by the boldface type in Table 15.4.

Table 15.3. The table identifies genres that represent particular text types in Slovak stylistics (based on Mistrík, 1997).

Text type	Genres
academic texts	thesis, dissertation, scholarly paper, essay, lecture, discussion, commentary, review, instructions, encyclopedias, dictionaries, anthologies, synopses
business writing	minutes, protocol, contract, certificate, regulation, statute, notice, statement, notification, summary, notice/letter, appeal, claim, invitation, form
journalistic writing	report, interview, announcement, advertisement, poster, editorial, commentary, gloss, review, comment, discussion, debate, caricature, pamphlet column, feature story, news, report
speech styles	political speech, court trial speech, lecture, conference speech, tourist guide speech, speech during discussion, sermon, public speeches on festive occasions, opening speeches, closing speeches, speeches during family gatherings, toast
belletristic rhetoric	belletristic essay
vernacular language	story, chat, dialog, phone calls, private letters/emails, child's language, youth's jargon
belle-letters text	poetry/prose/drama genres

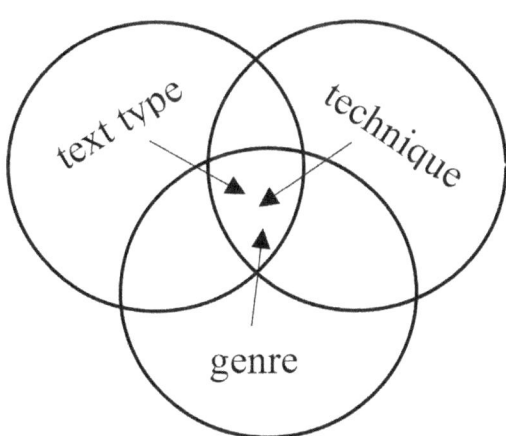

Figure 15.1. *The figure illustrates that academic writing in Slovak stylistics is the outcome of the intersection of three Slovak stylistics notions.*

Table 15.4. The table demonstrates Slovak understanding of text-type-genre-technique interlinkage and the boldface type highlights the case of academic writing (Hybenová & Saganová, 2012; Mistrík,1997).

Strategy/Method/Technique	Text type	Genre
Informative	• vernacular language • business writing • journalistic writing	• email, dialog, chat • report, announcement • order, column
Narrative	• vernacular language • belle-letters text	• story, narration • fable, fairy tale, novel
Descriptive	• vernacular language • academic text • belle-letters text	• description • instructions, report • travelogue, prose genres
Explanatory	• academic text • journalistic writing • speech styles	• paper, lecture, thesis • report • public/political speeches
Reflectionist	• academic text • journalistic writing • speech styles • belle-letters text	• reflection, review • editorial, commentary • discussion, speeches • poetry/prose/drama genres

This is to say, a report, a paper, a lecture, a thesis, a review, etc. fall within academic text and can utilize descriptive, explanatory, and/or reflectionist strategy/method/techniques. They are interpreted as variations of a specific text type used in the scholarly, educational environment, and characterized by accuracy and objectivity of information. Based on the conducted analysis, our understanding is that the Slovak approach is quite prescriptive, though making an impression of being descriptive. Despite the classifications present, the definitions present, and the process-based approach implied in the term "slohový postup" (literally procedure of composition), an author lacks exposition to the process of writing or step-by step instructions on how to draft a text.

The Anglo-American understanding of academic writing involves a process-oriented treatment, which is hinted at through presence and meticulous practice, for instance, paragraph development. Slovak schooling adopts the following strategy: Microstructure (sentence structuring, vocabulary choice, stylistic appropriateness) is introduced and practiced; macrostructure (the function of the text, the layout, organization of the text) is introduced but not trained; and mezzostructure (paragraphing, paragraph development) is neither introduced nor attended to.

The concept of mezzostructure is not even recognized in Slovak stylistics. If a term is not included in the lexicon, it is obvious that the concept is non-existent. Slovak stylistics lacks terms like a thesis statement, topic sentence, support, and the like.

As a result (based on our research, see below), a Slovak author's paragraphs are either underdeveloped or overdeveloped, or they do not follow the thread of ideas—whether we consider interparagraph relations or intraparagraph relations (see the following section for exemplification). Slovak authors lack awareness of mezzostructure. When publishing in their mother tongue in domestic settings, this is not a problem. However, when a paper in English is submitted, a style (i.e., macro-mezzo-micro synergy) is automatically expected to be part of the submitted piece. We consider it necessary to build awareness in the authors of the dialectal relationship between language and style (let us call it 3M synergy), which can be done through the establishment of writing-for-translation stylistics and further modification of the curriculum design (in doctoral studies) in that this discipline will be included as a compulsory item.

EMPIRICAL RESEARCH

The empirical research involves analyses on three levels that in our view make the core of the concept of writing style: macrostructure, mezzostructure, and microstructure.

Research into Macrostructure

Methodology

We understand macrostructure in terms of type of information and text layout. The former can represent a text that is empirical, theoretical, or theorizing in nature. An empirical text is based on empirical research; a theoretical text is based on research advancing a theory or contributing a new paradigm; and a theorizing text is mere compilation of what is known of a particular issue. It follows that the first two clearly state a research problem, research aim, and methodology; the third one lacks some or all elements mentioned. This is reflected in the text layout in that the first two have sections typically following the Introduction-Method-Results-and-Discussion (IMRAD) principle; the third one is either not divided into the sections or, for obvious reasons, most elements of the IMRAD principle are missing.

We conducted research to identify the prevailing type of information and text layout in papers written in English by non-native speakers. We selected a scholarly journal, compiled a corpus of 30 papers, examined the papers, and interpreted the results. Out of them, one was written by a native speaker of English; it supplied all four pieces of information, so this study was excluded from further analysis. Twenty-nine papers were authored by non-native speakers of English from 13 countries, falling within the group of other-than Saxonic lingua-cultures. The criterion for deciding whether or not the paper is empirical/theoretical or theorizing in nature is the explicit verbalization of four items: a research problem, research aim, research question or hypothesis, and methods. We understand the four items to mean the following (Bilá, Kačmárová & Vaňková, 2020):

1. a research problem is an issue worth exploring so the existing knowledge can be expanded;
2. an aim is the verbalization of why research is conducted;
3. a research question and/or hypothesis need not be used in tandem—a research question is typically associated with qualitative research; a hypothesis is typically associated with quantitative research; and
4. research methods need not be explicitly named, but at least they should be indicated through the research procedure or plan.

Findings

The findings (Bilá, Kačmárová & Vaňková, 2020) pointed at two important facts: First, the author's style met the objectives of the Saxonic style in 51 percent of submissions; and second, the publisher tolerated the interference of the native lingua-culture. The toleration of interference means that the publisher allowed a paper to be published even though some items were missing or improperly expressed (i.e., did not correspond with the four above definitions; e.g., the aim resembled a method rather than proper aim). The research problem was present in 48 percent of submissions, the research aim in 55 percent of submissions, the research question or a hypothesis in 43 percent of submissions, and methods in 60 percent of submissions. These statistics are, however, mere presence of the four items. The statement of aim, for instance, was expressed appropriately only in 28 percent of submissions; in 17 percent of papers, it was missing; in 55 percent of papers, it was expressed inappropriately—it named either a method or a topic, i.e., it answered the question "what" rather than "why":

> [1] The aim of the paper is to explore/compare/analyze/examine . . .
>
> [2] The paper focuses on . . . / deals with . . .

We managed to identify some good examples of aim statements, though:

> [3] The paper offers argument in favor of . . . and proves that . . .
>
> [4] I demonstrate how . . . is a shortcoming for . . .

Research into Mezzostructure

Methodology

Mezzostructure, in our view, means organization of ideas, paragraph arrangement, internal structuring (understood as presence of topic sentence, support, and closing sentence), length of paragraphs, and homogeneity of ideas (vs. multiple standpoints) in a paragraph. We compiled a corpus of 20 papers submitted for translation to the present chapter authors. The papers fell in the fields of social work, history, aesthetics, media studies, and Slovak studies. Their authors were Slovak natives, non-professional users of English. The procedure consisted of semantic translation, functional translation, and meta-analysis of a translator's choices in order to identify lingua-cultural conventions.

Findings

With regard to paragraphing, we observed a disorderly approach whether to the number of paragraphs, structure of a paragraph, number of topics, or multiple standpoints (in some papers, it looked like a spiral development of topics—moving and coming back). This resulted in the underdevelopment or overdevelopment of a paragraph. Example 1 below presents a sample in which a change in font type (alternatively regular font type and italics) means a shift to a new topic, and generally lack of internal structure:

> **Example 1 Multiple standpoints and topics.**
>
> Intercultural differences (as a result of globalization) are becoming an area where only able managers succeed. When entering the international market, we also encounter differences in communication, thinking, and behavior of people from different cultural backgrounds. *It is necessary that we accept these differences and are able to adapt to them, especially in an environment where people work in international teams. An integral part of success is therefore, first and foremost, tolerance, understanding, and acceptance of the culture.*
>
> According to Leung et al. (2014) and Caputo et al. (2018), cultural aspects are important in the field of international trade, of which management is a part. *We are talking above all about the European Union communities, which are mixed and created by the migration of the population, which brings, above all, multiculturalism affecting social and cultural change.*
>
> In international trade, the intercultural competence of managers is essential, as well as knowledge of the culture of the country

with which the business is closed. Intercultural aspects can greatly influence the behavior of business partners (Barner-Rasmussen et al., 2014; Caprar et al., 2015; Del Giudice et al., 2017).

The cultural aspect includes economic, social, and family life, religion, sports, food and arts. The emphasis is on what people are doing at a certain time and in a certain place. Each person is a part of a certain social group composed of several levels of mental programming.

Example 2 below evidences a paragraph (by a prominent Slovak linguist) consisting of two sentences (change in font type means a start of a new sentence) with ostentatious syntax within the paragraph:

Example 2 Ostentatious syntax within a paragraph.

The relationship of symmetry and asymmetry between form and content in language has become (as indicated in point 1) a basic stimulator of two central semiotic essences, "bases", "tonalities", "messages" of the language system at its origin and is fully reflected in the development and the current "happening" of its elements. *It is an iconic-symbolic - with symmetry between form and content (form is part of the reflective surface of the sign)—and arbitrary (with "inherited" symmetry, but dominantly with asymmetry between form and content; form is not part of the reflective surface of the sign) semiotic principle, which closely—especially through their elements, signs—cooperate, complement each other and regroup within each other (this fact is also documented by the neurophysiological basis of speech: these are dominant functions—developmentally earlier—right and left cerebral hemispheres, as confirmed by basic types of aphasia—suppression of the relation of similarity, or the relation of adjacency, i.e. metaphorical versus metonymic principle—Jakobson, 1991, p. 87 n.), creating overlapping sets of such binary oppositions in the language system (from to-date research of ours, cf. XY 2007a, 2007b, 2008, 2011, 2016, etc.), to which belong the following (the first symptom is dominantly applied in the "zone" of the iconic-symbolic principle, for the second the dominant semiotic background is the arbitrariness principle): associativeness (e.g. in the style-forming process, it is the phase of selection of thematic elements) and linearity (e.g. in the generation of text in different communication situations this "factor" guarantees lingual-syntactic processing of thematic elements; it is thus the axis of composition).*

The two samples are semantic translations of the original Slovak versions. The research shows that the Slovak mindset is such that the paragraph arrangement is a tool of pursuing author's voice, and the length of a paragraph or separating an idea is a means of emphasis. Unpredictability is almost inherent, which is, in our view, in contrast with the respect for the reader and with the responsibility for full information transfer.

Research into Microstructure

Methodology

We understand microstructure as an interplay of text semantics, syntax, and stylistics. The same set of papers (as in the study into mezzostructure) was interpreted in terms of microstructure.

Findings

The most common signals of the clash between Anglo-American and Slovak writing styles yielded by the analysis are: pluralis auctoris and baroqueness. Our typology of the latter includes: principle of repetition, recurring clustering of three items, padding, artificial elaborateness, and matrioshka effect.

Pluralis Auctoris. A typical feature of the Slovak academic text is so-called pluralis auctoris or pluralis modestiae, i.e., the pronoun "we" is used to refer to a single author. Slovak scholars recognize the use of pluralis auctoris as an indicator of scientific objectivity of a scholarly paper and its author's modesty. Using first person plural pronoun thus implies backgrounding the scholar, depersonalizing, and foregrounding the research and its outcomes. The examples in Table 15.5 evidence practice by a single author.

Table 15.5. The table provides examples of the usage of pluralis auctoris in Slovak and its translation into English.

Slovak usage	Semantic translation	Suggested functional translation
Zámerne používame slovné spojenie . . .	We intentionally use the phrase . . .	I intentionally use the phrase . . .
. . . týmto spôsobom sa budeme odvolávať na dielo . . .	. . . in this way we will refer to the work . . .	. . . in this way, I refer to the work . . .
Spôsoby, akými XY vedie naráciu, sme sa v stručnosti snažili naznačiť v úvode predloženej štúdie.	At the beginning of the present study, we tried to briefly indicate, the ways in which XY leads the narrative.	In the introduction, I outlined XY's ways of pursuing the narrative.

Table 15.6. The table illustrates the usage of unnecessary synonyms, thus unnecessary repeating of the content that in the translation needs to be eliminated.

Types of synonyms	Slovak usage	Semantic translation	Suggested functional translation
different origin	vzdelávacia a edukačná činnosť	educational and educational activity	1/ education 2/ educational activities
paraphrasing	vzdelávacie výsledky a školská úspešnosť	educational results and school success	student's educational/school results/ achievement

Recurring Clustering of Three Items. Slovak authors like to adopt a fairy-tale-like rhetoric in that their expressions come in groups of three. Our view is, when this occurs once in a submission, it is not disturbing. However, if such clustering is repeated with different word classes in one paragraph, the reader may perceive it annoying. The following exemplify semantic translation of the Slovak original:

[1] . . . elements <u>cooperate</u>, <u>complement</u> each other, and <u>regroup</u> within each other

[2] . . . we encounter differences in <u>communication</u>, <u>thinking</u>, and <u>behavior</u>

[3] An integral part of success is, therefore, first and foremost, <u>tolerance</u>, <u>understanding</u>, and <u>acceptance</u> of the culture.

Table 15.7. The table illustrates verbal padding on the phrase level.

Slovak usage	Semantic translation	Suggested functional translation
V kontexte podpory rozvoja . . .	In the context of support of development of . . .	(in order) to support the development of . . .
V kontexte príspevku . . .	In the context of the article . . .	In the paper . . .
S cieľom dosiahnutia . . .	With the aim to achieve . . .	(in order) to achieve . . .
Pružný systém podporných opatrení v podobe jednotlivých profesionálov	A flexible system of support measures in the form of individual professionals	A flexible system of support measures including Ø [. . .] field-specific experts.
Môže zasahovať aj do oblasti športovej edukológie	It may also overlap with the field of sports education	It may also overlap with Ø sports education.

Padding. Padding (Bilá, Kačmárová & Vaňková, forthcoming) is taken to represent microstylistic redundancy from the perspective of English; we identified padding on the level of a phrase, a part of a clause, and a whole clause (Tables 15.7–15.9). The examples demonstrate that redundant segments (printed in italics in source texts and their semantic translations into English) make their English renderings too verbose, less succinct, and less concise. Oftentimes, a redundant segment disrupts the flow of thought thus requiring more processing time on the reader's part. Therefore, we adopted such translation solutions that make syntactic structures more condensed and that reduce the processing effort on the reader's part; they are referred to as resegmentations by Pym (2016).

Table 15.8. The table illustrates padding within a part of a clause.

Slovak usage	Semantic translation	Suggested functional translation
… aby sa zo školy stalo miesto podporujúce aktivitu a kreativitu dieťaťa	… so that a school became a place supporting the child's activity and creativity	So that school may Ø support a child's agency and creativity.
Na skutočnosť, že vzťah medzi rodičmi a školou by sa nemal obmedzovať len na kontakt a spoluprácu v prípade výskytu problémov, poukazujú XY (2018).	XY (2018) point at the fact that the relationship between parents and school should not be limited to contact and cooperation in the case of problem occurrence.	Ø The parent-school relationship should not be limited to dialogue and cooperation merely in problem-solving situations (XY, 2018)
… prostredníctvom svojej základnej jednotky, ktorú tvorí text.	… through its base unit which is text.	… through its essential unit – Ø text.

Table 15.9. The table illustrates padding in terms of whole clause redundancy.

Slovak usage	Semantic translation	Suggested functional translation
Vybrané výsledky prezentované v nasledujúcich častiach príspevku vychádzajú zo zistení autorského výskumu.	Selected results presented in the following sections of the paper are based on the findings of the author's research.	Ø
Obom aspektom sa budeme bližšie venovať v nasledujúcom texte.	We will deal with both aspects in more detail in the following text.	Ø

Artificial Elaborateness. By artificial elaborateness, we mean pretentious language, very popular among long-established Slovak scholars. We understand pretentious language in two areas: syntactic and lexical. Syntactic pretentiousness (see Table 15.10) implies syntactic over-complexity, piling up phrases creating the illusion of embroidery to make the impression of sophistication (Bilá, Kačmárová & Vaňková, forthcoming). Lexical pretentiousness (Table 15.11) is represented by the Slovak authors' preference for foreign-sounding (Latinate, English) expressions although their Slovak counterparts are available. In some cases, even poetic expressions may "trespass" academic prose.

Table 15.10. The table shows unnecessary piling up of phrases in Slovak and their elimination in translation.

	Noun phrase	Verb phrase

Slovak original	Spolupráca *v zmysle*
	 (v zmysle) prejavenia
	   (prejavenia) [. . .] záujmu
	     [pravidelného]
	 a
	 (v zmysle) informovania sa
	   (informovania sa) *o* fungovaní
	     (o fungovaní) dieťaťa
	     (o fungovaní) . . . *v* [. . .] *systéme*
	       [*školskom a rodinnom*]
		ostáva v úzadí.

English semantic translation	Cooperation in terms of
	 (in terms of) showing
	   (showing) [. . .] interest
	     [regular]
	 and
	 (in terms of) becoming informed
	   (becoming informed) about functioning
	     (about functioning) of a child
	     (about functioning) . . . in [. . .] system
	       [school and family]
		remains backgrounded.

Suggested functional translation	Cooperation Ø manifested as Ø [attention to] continuous [. . .] to to a child's Ø school performance and behavior in a family	tends to be backgrounded.

Matrioshka Effect. By the term matrioshka effect, we call attention to the fact that the gist is either hidden in the bulky language (see Example 2 above on ostentatious syntax in a single paragraph) or delayed until the end of the paper. Slovak stylistics is not process-oriented, i.e., authors are not trained in the sense of instructions like state the thesis and your argument in the introduction, provide support for your claim next to it (not two paragraphs later), do not introduce a new claim unless the first one is finished, do not ask questions in the conclusion, etc.

In theory, authors are aware of a three-part structure, of the required vocabulary and syntax, but this is never practiced and thus not mastered. As a result, reader-friendliness is not an issue, as a Slovak author is educated to see the text as a monologue, and it is up to the reader to be able to interpret what the author has in mind. A reader uncovers what is at the core through continuous opening of matrioshka dolls to reveal something of the same sort inside.

Table 15.11. The table exemplifies omnipresence of foreign words or assumed sophistication in texts by Slovak authors and their optimization in translation.

Slovak usage	Semantic translation	Suggested functional translation
... prejavom je požiadavka odklonu od dôrazu na mechanické reprodukovanie a príklonu k aktívnym formám vyučovania	... the manifestation is the requirement of deviating from the emphasis on mechanical reproduction and of inclining to active forms of teaching	... the manifestation of which is shifting the emphasis from mechanical drilling to active learning.
V úzadí ostáva spolupráca v zmysle prejavenia pravidelného záujmu a informovania sa o fungovaní dieťaťa v školskom a rodinnom systéme.	In the background remains co-operation in the sense of manifesting a regular interest in informing about the child's functioning in the school and family systems.	Cooperation manifested as continuous attention to a child's school performance and behaviour in his/her family Ø tends to be backgrounded.
Napriek v podstate minimálnemu explicitnému postulovaniu potreby výskumu uplatnenia jazyka, ...	Despite essentially minimal explicit postulating of the need for research into the language use, ...	Although the Ø need for research into the language use in sports was infrequently explicitly claimed.
s cieľom doplniť mozaiku poznania o možnosti prínosu	in order to complete the mosaic of knowledge of the possibilities of benefit	enhance Ø the knowledge benefits

CONCLUSION AND IMPLICATIONS

The conceptual analysis into the Slovak linguistics tradition made it clear that Slovak stylistics is product-oriented, i.e., it deals with different text types but not with writing as a process. An academic piece is an intersection of text type, genre, and technique. However, the technique represents a mere list of features that a particular genre within a particular text type allegedly has; yet the pure instruction is not a concern. The outcome is thus often idiosyncratic and reflects how an author has adopted and adapted the general principles. The general principles of academic text are as follows: It is intended for the expert public, it is objective, and it is monologic. The rest is to be modified and tailor-made by an author. This is understood as providing space for self-reflection, for an author's right to deciding that the text is not schematic, template-like; rather, it enables an author to express their voice.

Expressing authorial voice can be understood as a clash when two lingua-cultures meet. One culture may see it as taking liberty to use and organize language as convenient to fulfill a set objective, which is generally accepted, tolerated, or viewed as natural and not frowned upon. In another culture, an authorial voice is reflected through the originality of the approach to a research problem statement and dealing with it, which is welcome in that culture. The clash happens when authors educated in one lingua-culture need to express themselves in another lingua-culture; in other words, when a native lingua-culture needs to be translated into a foreign lingua-culture with a differing writing style and eventually accepted by the target audience. Specific discrepancies are instantiated in the present empirical analysis.

The empirical analysis evidences problems on three levels: (1) macrostructure or proper sharing of information (theoretical and empirical); (2) mezzostructure or proper text segmentation into sections; and (3) microstructure or adherence to the stylistic conventions of the Anglo-American writing style (the usage of syntax, vocabulary, etc. in line with economy of expression). Authors educated in other-than-Saxonic writing styles (in this case, Slovak) encounter problems in each of the three aspects. This is substantiated by the conducted analysis. The problems on the macrostructure level include research problem statement and aim statement. The problems on the mezzostructure include haphazard text segmentation, paragraph under- or over-development, improper placement of an argument, and lack of support. The problems on the microstructure level include improper self-reference (pluralis auctoris for a single author) and a set of features falling under the cover term baroqueness or "too much of everything." The features that the analysis yielded include principle of repetition, recurring clustering of three items, padding, artificial elaborateness, and matryoshka effect.

The mentioned features materialize the clash between Slovak and Anglo-American writing styles. In translation, they require some text modification or creation of the voice that is compatible with the receiving lingua-culture. The non-conformity issue may well be due to non-conscious adherence to a certain linguistic tradition and to the ignorance of a different lingua-culture, namely a different writing style. The present study focuses on the Slovak language as a representative of Slavic languages, which, as of now, are not delimited within a specific writing style. We claim that the poor success of Slovak authors aspiring to publish in English journals is caused by the status of English as lingua academica as it implicitly, though pertinently, highlights the dialectal relationship between language and style.

The core of the clash derives from the presence of different writing styles on par with different lingua-cultures. This brings us closer to the need to deal with the conceptualization of academic writing in the Slovak lingua-culture and its impact on Slovak authors' written production. Accounting for this, establishing writing-for-translation stylistics looks like a necessary step towards the internationalization of Slovak academic prose. Understanding English as a lingua academica (not only) by Slovak authors necessarily lies in its being an amalgam of macro-, mezzo- and micro-structure, which needs to be addressed within practice-based writing-for-translation stylistics. We believe that the present study on Slovak writing style may serve as an impetus for other-than-Saxonic lingua-cultures to contribute their observation on the local practice to enhance the awareness of the existence of different writing styles.

REFERENCES

Bilá, M. & Kačmárová, A. (2021). Úvod do akademického/vedeckého písania. *Vedecké písanie (nielen) pre doktorandov*. Prešovská univerzita v Prešove, 22–40. http://www.pulib.sk/web/kniznica/elpub/dokument/Kacmarova9.

Bilá, M. & Kačmárová, A. & Vaňková, I. (2020). The contours of English as a lingua franca in scholarly publishing. *Lingua et Vita, 17*/2020, 21–27. https://lingua etvita.sk/www_write/files/issues/2020/17/d_02_21az27_jkk_bila_kacmarova_vankova_172020.pdf.

Bilá, M. & Kačmárová, A. & Vaňková, I. (Forthcoming). Stylistic redundancy in research papers: Padding as interlingual pleonasm in translation.

Bowe, H. & Martin, K. (2007). *Communication across cultures: Mutual understanding in a global world*. Cambridge University Press.

Chamonikolasová, J. (2005). Comparing the structures of texts written in English and Czech. *Slovak Studies in English I (Conference Proceedings)*. Univerzita Komenského, 77–84.

Clyne, M. (1994). *Inter-cultural communication at work: Cultural values in discourse.* Cambridge University Press.
Čmejrková, S. (1996). Academic writing in Czech and English. In E. Ventola & A. Mauranen (Eds.), *Academic Writing: Intercultural and textual issues* (pp. 137–152). John Benjamins Publishing Company. https://doi.org/10.1075/pbns.41.
Dahl, S. (2004). *Intercultural research: The current state of knowledge.* Middlesex University Discussion Paper No. 26. http://doi.org/10.2139/ssrn.658202.
Galtung, J. (1981). Structure, culture, and intellectual style: An essay comparing Saxonic, Teutonic, Gallic and Nipponic approaches. *Social Science Information, 20*(6), 817–856. https://doi.org/10.1177/053901848102000601.
Hybenová, Ľ. & Saganová, R. (2012). *Slohy pre všetkých*. Školmédia.
Kačmárová, A., Bilá, M. & Vaňková, I. (2018). *The conceptualizing of conceptualization.* Prešovská univerzita v Prešove. http://www.pulib.sk/web/kniznica/elpub/dokument/Kacmarova6.
Mistrík, J. (1997). *Štylistika*. Slovenské pedagogické nakladateľstvo.
Pym, A. (2016). *Translation solutions for many languages: Histories of a flawed dream.* Bloomsbury Academic.
Walková, M. (2014). Rozdiely medzi slovenským a angloamerickým odborným štýlom na príklade jazykovedných textov. *Jazyk a kultúra, 19–20*.

CHAPTER 16.

WAC COMPARED TO OTHER "ACROSS THE CURRICULUMS"

David R. Russell

Iowa State University

WAC is one of many "across-the-curriculum" reform movements in U.S. higher education. There have been efforts to extend specific content or skills across the curriculum in mathematics, the Great Books, philosophy, information literacy (e.g., library skills), oral communication, diversity, multiculturalism, ethics, global studies, and others. In addition, there have been broader reform movements: progressive education, general education, assessment, and professional development ("teaching excellence" centers). This chapter compares WAC to several of these in order to notice ways that WAC has been similar to and different from others, and what those similarities and differences might tell us about options for the future. I will begin with the movements based on specific disciplinary content or skills and move to broader educational reform movements.

WAC has had a much longer and more extensive reach than any of the other specific "across the curriculums." Most remained very small and confined to relatively few intuitions. For example, the critical thinking across the curriculum movement, organized in 1980, splintered early, and generally has an institutional presence more ephemeral than WAC even in its early years. Where critical thinking across the curriculum is organized, it primarily sells teaching materials and training seminars (Paul, n.d.). The notable exception is the Quinnipiac University Writing and Critical Thinking (QUWACT) initiative, which is a central part of their Center for Teaching and Learning. It provides materials for faculty and has held seven biennial national conferences on Critical Thinking and Writing. The Great Books movement began much earlier, with John Erskine's course at Columbia in 1920, but its spread was sporadic (today only about 200 universities of over 4000 offer a Great Books course or program, even as an option) and its organization is left to what are essentially publishers, such as the Great Books Foundation (*College Great Books Programs*, n.d.; *The Great Books Foundation*, n.d.).

The closest comparison with WAC is the movement in mathematics, called numeracy education or quantitative reasoning (QR) across the curriculum. In an excellent article, Cinnamon Hillyard (2012) points out that the numeracy education movement followed a similar pattern to WAC (in part because of WAC's influence) although it was about 15 years later. Like WAC, it was sparked by nationally publicized complaints: for writing, "Why Johnny Can't Write" (Sheils, 1975) and for math, *Innumeracy* (Paulos, 1988). Each produced discussions and reports in the profession. A few institutions began (or developed) programs to address the newly salient need, supported by national grants (NEH WAC grants in 1977 and following; NSF MATC grants in 1994 and following) to fund faculty workshops and other initiatives. A SIG formed in the national professional organization (WAC Network in 1981; SIGMAA-QL in 2004), followed by a regular national conference (Steen & Madison, 2015)—WAC starting in 1993; NNN starting in 2005 in conjunction with various related professional organizations (National Numeracy Network, n.d.). NNN founded the journal *Numeracy* in 2008.

In terms of structure, both have worked to move first-year courses toward a different conceptual orientation: to focus on writing to learn and preparation for writing in the disciplines in FYC, and to focus on quantitative reasoning and applications in introductory math. Both have also worked toward outreach to faculty in other disciplines and departments.

The differences are equally striking. On the one hand, WAC has had a remarkable impact, with more than 50 percent of institutions reporting some program in 2008 (up from 31 percent in 1988), while numeracy education has had far less reach thus far (perhaps not surprising given the 15-year lag), though there have been no national surveys (Thaiss & Porter, 2010). On the other hand, numeracy education founded an incorporated National Numeracy Network in 2005, some 15 years before WAC created a formal organization (apart from an annual 90-minute special interest group at the Conference on College Composition and Communication). Another difference is that WAC is often supported by—and supports—a large network of writing centers, with a long history of service to the wider university community, whereas mathematics tutoring centers typically do not have that campus-wide history or outreach (Palmquist et al., 2020).

Oral communication across the curriculum (styled CXC) is another movement that was inspired by WAC. It began only a few years later and has important similarities. Programs began at a few institutions in the late 1970s. They aim to change the orientation of introductory speech (what they call "the basic course") from public speaking to interpersonal, organizational, group, intercultural, gender, nonverbal, and other types of non-written communication. And they offer their expertise to faculty in other disciplines, to improve not only their students' speaking but also their learning, especially through improved interpersonal and group communication (Vrchota & Russell, 2013). They have followed the lead of WAC by founding communication centers to foster "speaking across the curriculum"—the title of the newsletter of the National Association of Communication Centers, founded in 2001 (with a journal published since 2004). Some 70 communication centers were identified in 2012 (Yook & Atkins-Sayre, 2012), with many more founded since due to the efforts of the national association.

Clearly the number of CXC and QR centers is far fewer than writing centers, but this only points to the recency of the efforts in communication and mathematics and, more importantly, to the potential for combining efforts. There have been many successful across-the-curriculum programs and centers that combine two or more of the three. For example, Carleton's QuIRK program (Quantitative Inquiry, Reasoning, and Knowledge) was in large part successful because it aligned its efforts with the campus writing program (Hillyard, 2012, p. 15). Similarly, the Campus Speaking and Writing Program at North Carolina State is a decades-old collaboration between the departments of English and Communication (Adler-Kassner & Harrington, 2010). All three of these disciplinary and skill areas are foundational to students' success across the curriculum and offer multi-section first-year courses, so it is not surprising they have been the leading movements across the curriculum.

As an option for the future of WAC, combining efforts with CXC and QR is obvious, not only because of the importance of the three but because of their increasing synergy. QR is essential for representing information visually, and this is now central to the digital environment. Similarly, oral and written communication are merging as tools for converting oral, written, and visual information to one another increase in quality, quantity, and reach. This change has of course been central to recent writing studies. (Indeed, the shift from written to multimodal communication in writing studies is behind speech communication using "CXC" instead of "communication across the curriculum," to distinguish the two efforts.) WAC as the leader has much to share, in terms of dealing with skeptics within and beyond the discipline, for example.

Now that WAC, CXC, and QR all have national organizations, it is possible to begin at least informal communication among them. One initial effort might be to identify programs that combine two or three media and put them in communication with one another. They might share successes and challenges, develop best practices, and even collaborate on research and outreach to national higher education (HE) organizations.

Turning now from movements focused on specific disciplines, content, or skills to the broader movements that have worked across the curriculum in U.S. higher education in the last half century or more, one finds two very early predecessors that stand out: the progressive education movement and the general or liberal education movement.

The progressive education movement began in the late 19th century and had a formal structure, though it lasted only 36 years (1919–1955). It was revived in the 1990s and again in 2014 as the Progressive Education Network (PEN) (*History*, n.d.). Its ideas are still profoundly influential and controversial—and a brief listing of them shows their influence on WAC:

- Emphasis on learning by doing—hands-on projects, experiential learning
- Integrated curriculum focused on thematic units
- Strong emphasis on problem solving and critical thinking
- Group work and development of social skills
- Understanding and action as the goals of learning as opposed to rote knowledge
- Collaborative and cooperative learning projects
- Education for social responsibility and democracy
- Integration of community service and service learning projects into the daily curriculum
- Selection of subject content by looking forward to ask what skills will be needed in future society
- De-emphasis on textbooks in favor of varied learning resources
- Emphasis on lifelong learning and social skills
- Assessment by evaluation of projects and productions [over exams] ("Progressive," 2022)

Clearly WAC fits in that tradition (Russell, 2002), but the PEN is not a large or influential organization, and its influence is diffuse. Moreover, it is focused on K-12. Yet WAC can still draw inspiration from its long history, as WAC is at bottom an attempt to reform pedagogy—though a reform that takes disciplinarity more seriously than the progressive education movement has tended to.

The general or liberal education movement was founded after World War II, to counteract authoritarian regimes and defend democracies. That movement had the *Journal of General Education*, founded in 1946 by Earl J. McGrath, who was the driving force in the movement (Russell, 2002). A formal organization did not arise for another 14 years, the Association for General and Liberal Studies, but it now has an annual conference, a working board, and an executive director ("Association," n.d.). As an organization, it is like progressive education in that it has relatively few members and little direct influence. But as a concept and a tradition, it carries a great deal of weight. Indeed, a number of WAC programs were founded as part of a general education reform on campus or took advantage of that effort to get a seat at the reformers' table. Some are even housed in general education administrative units and central to these efforts (Condon & Rutz, 2012).

As Sue H. McLeod and Eric Miraglia (2001, p. 11) pointed out 20 years ago, WAC is part of a third wave of general education reform movement that swept the U.S. in the 1980s and 1990s, which included many of the other "across-the-curriculum" disciplinary, content, and skills movements discussed above. General education was traditionally about curriculum, what students are taught, but as McLeod and Miraglia noted, that third wave was also about pedagogy. And that is even more true today. In that sense, WAC is like general education in that it tries to reform both what students learn in all their courses ("adding" writing) but also how they learn (through writing—and the concomitant writing pedagogies of revision, group work, peer review, assessment beyond machine-scored tests, and so on). The two movements are more than ever ripe for collaboration.

It is worth pointing out here that there is a learning community movement, active since the 1980s, that has been closely associated with WAC. Like other "across the curriculums," learning communities are formed in any discipline with the aim of changing pedagogy to more student-centered forms. A number of WAC programs grew out of or supported learning community initiatives (McLeod & Miraglia, 2001), including one of the very first learning communities, at the University of Washington (Graham, 1992).

WAC also bears a close and complex relation to two more recent national reform efforts: professional development and assessment. Both have a large reach and exert powerful influence from the top down on higher education.

What has been called the faculty development movement in higher education began in the 1960s and was organized officially in 1976 as the Professional and Organizational Development Network in Higher Education (POD), as part of the American Association for Higher Education (with its own journal, the *POD Quarterly*). This makes it roughly the same age as WAC. It has more than 1400 members. POD, like WAC, has a significant institutional presence. In the most recent survey, 2010, some 20 percent of all 2-year and 4-year institutions had an active faculty development program (Kuhlenschmidt, 2011), with 21 percent overall, 72 percent in doctoral institutions versus 14 percent in bachelors. By comparison, the 2008 WAC program survey showed 51 percent overall, 65 percent doctoral, and 60 percent bachelors. WAC is at bottom a form of professional development, and it is not surprising that many WAC programs are housed in POD units and share personnel (how many is unclear). Indeed, one of the most important studies of faculty development was done by a team that included WAC researchers and program developers Carol Rutz and William Condon (2012). Clearly there is room for continuing and expanded collaboration and integration—though there are dangers in an integration that may leave a WAC program without a secure identity and funding, as we shall see.

A final higher education reform movement that has had an effect on WAC is what is called the assessment or accountability movement, which took hold with the neo-liberal turn of the 1980s. With national funding for WAC drying up in the Reagan era, WAC turned to the assessment movement as a way to leverage faculty and department/curriculum reform—an alternative to mass testing that put the power into the hands of the faculty who were teaching the curricula. Pioneering work began in the 1990s at North Carolina State, spurred by new interest in assessment (Anson & Dannels, 2009). The founders of that program consulted widely, advocating for WAC programs based on the faculty in a department or curriculum assessing their students and developing a recursive plan for improving curriculum and teaching. In some places such curriculum/department-based WAC found a very strong and sustainable foothold. Perhaps the most successful of these department/curriculum-based programs is at the University of Minnesota Twin Cities, where a Ford Foundation grant allowed Pamela Flash and her team to create the Writing Enriched Curriculum. Consultants work with the faculty who teach a curriculum over a three-year iterative cycle, through a recursive process of gathering data (e.g., surveys of students, faculty, alumni, employers); analytically mapping current uses of writing in each course; and collaboratively planning further enhancements, implementing them, and assessing them, by gathering more data, and so on through another three-year cycle (Flash, 2016).

A common variation of this—also pioneered at North Carolina State by Chris Anson—is to have a working group of faculty members who teach a particular curriculum carry on a multi-year research project on writing in their field among their students, along with a writing consultant. The University of Central Florida, for example, has a program that has reached most departments. A team of department faculty analyze the uses of writing for learning in their department, identify a problem, institute a solution, and evaluate it—all repeated over the next three-year cycle (Zemliansky & Berry, 2017). And most recently, Elizabeth Wardle at Miami of Ohio has improved upon this through involving departments even more fully (Glotfelter et al., 2022).

In these programs, the faculty teaching a curriculum truly own writing and are responsible for it; thus, their values are central. The faculty members have the expertise in writing in their discipline, and must define and redefine writing for themselves, their curriculum, and thus their students. Full integration is the goal—learning through writing. Although writing consultants may teach mini lessons initially, with faculty present, they work behind the scenes mainly, to consult and support. In this model, faculty members teaching a curriculum are held accountable—and hold each other accountable.

The concern over assessment in WAC, so prevalent in the 1990s, as part of the larger standards and accountability/assessment push in higher education, has not been so prevalent in 21st century discussions. One way assessment has played out in 21st century WAC is through alternative forms of assessment, now often organized around an ePortfolio. But documenting the value of programs through directly assessing the writing of individual students has given way to a variety of options, direct and indirect, for assessing programs, courses, and students' performance. A range of measures often brings in a range of stakeholders, such as alumni, employers, departments (as we have seen), students-as-peers, students-as-tutors, and so on. Perhaps because WAC programs in many places have endured the test of time, the goal is often not assessment per se (for rendering a judgment on whether a program should be funded) but rather providing data—and forums where stakeholder discussions happen—for long-range improvement of programs. Assessment then becomes a tool for creating sustainability (Carter, 2002; Condon & Rutz, 2012; Willett et al., 2014; Yancey, 2018).

All of these depend on developing a consultancy (rather than a missionary) relationship with faculty in the disciplines, which Jeffrey Jablonski (2006) analyzed in his helpful how-to book for WAC practitioners. More recently, an analysis of programs led to the book, *Sustainable WAC: A whole systems approach to launching and developing writing across the curriculum programs*, which lays out a range of options for continuous evaluation and change. As we shall see, these efforts have produced a national organizational structure to facilitate professional development for WAC practitioners (Cox et al., 2018).

~~~

In the first edition of my history of the WAC movement, published in 1992, I noted that WAC was a remarkably long-lived educational reform movement in the history of American higher education, and was all the more remarkable because it did not develop a formal organizational structure. Even more remarkably, that situation continued another 25 years. However, in 2018, WAC finally gained a formal organizational structure, the Association for Writing Across the Curriculum (AWAC). The movement is no longer purely grassroots, and I will give some reasons here why that is a very good thing, in terms of its future longevity.

In many ways, the grassroots served WAC well. Many people may not have noticed, over the last 50 years, that WAC had no national organization because it had other structures. It had a special interest group of the CCCC, the International Network of Writing Across the Curriculum Programs (INWAC), founded by Christopher Thaiss in 1981. INWAC met for an hour and a half once a year for table discussions, led by a group of experienced WAC consultants and Thaiss, who also published an annual directory of programs. A listserv, WAC-L, has existed since the 1990s. And the WAC Clearinghouse, at Colorado State University, operated as a kind of quasi-official website for the movement, with its own board and funding sources (Thaiss, 2004).

The other longstanding national organization, the biennial WAC conference, was passed from one volunteer institution to another without a formal organization. That conference remained quite successful, attracting several hundred participants every two years. It over time changed to reflect trends in writing studies, especially diversity and inclusion, and supported research on student writing with a particular emphasis on disciplinary differences, especially in STEM fields. There was also one regional organization, the Northeast Writing Across the Curriculum Consortium (NEWACC), founded in 2007 by a group of WAC directors ("Northeast," n.d.).

Moves toward a national organization began in 2012 with the development of a national Statement of WAC Principles and Practices by an ad hoc committee of INWAC, spearheaded by Michelle Cox of Cornell. Ratified by INWAC in 2014 and CCCC in 2015, the seven-page introduction to WAC basics served a number of purposes, particularly in making arguments for resources to administrators and other stakeholders ("Statement," 2014).

Led by the same group of mid-career researchers who had spearheaded the Statement, there were efforts to broaden the leadership of WAC and make it more accessible to newcomers by adopting a formal mission statement, goals, structures for rotating elected officers, permanent volunteer committees, and so on, building on the ad hoc grassroots structure the founding generation had successfully pursued.

Formal discussions about creating an umbrella organization for WAC began in 2016, prompted by the impending retirement of the founder of INWAC, Thaiss, and other pioneers of WAC. After getting feedback on bylaws at CCCC 2018, a call for members went out, and the first official meeting of AWAC took place at IWAC in June 2018, followed by incorporation as a non-profit. Elections were held, and a rotating leadership took over, with ten committees, a website, and perhaps most importantly, a three-day summer professional development institute, which quickly sold out. The new umbrella organization included as committees WAC-GO (a graduate student organization), the IWAC conference, and the new WAC Summer Institute ("History of AWAC," n.d.).

AWAC represents an important development. WAC now has a national organization parallel to similar writing organizations that are independent of CCCC and NCTE, such as those for writing centers, writing program administrators, and so on. As Thaiss noted in 2016, WAC has previously been unable to create "an agenda to focus efforts, issue position statements, establish and publish standards, conduct statistical surveys of members, and, maybe most basic, ensure continuity through an orderly process of succeeding leadership" (p. 139). In addition, a dues-paying membership—both individual and institutional—provides support.

The work that a national organization can do is nicely summarized by the committees of AWAC. In addition to committees for the biennial conference, the summer institute, and graduate students, there are committees for advocacy (in such areas as equitable working conditions for those teaching WAC courses), communication, diversity and inclusion (e.g., to make AWAC and WAC practitioners reflect better the student population), international collaborations (responding to the tremendous expansion of work noted above), mentoring (of WAC consultants and other stakeholders), partnerships (with the many other writing-focused organizations, at all levels), and research and publication (which has flourished but has been dispersed and unorganized).

Before the founding of AWAC, I was concerned that, as Rita Malenczyk argued in 2012, WAC might be "disappearing"—absorbed into the broader general education reform, or one of the many other reform efforts with which it is associated, such as faculty development programs. Those involved in WAC are also involved in those efforts, and often wear several professional "hats" (as almost everyone who does WAC work does). They might come to identify mainly with other efforts, or WAC might be so integrated into larger agendas and programs and would lose their identity and specific funding. As Condon and Rutz (2012) argue in their excellent analysis of types of WAC programs:

> WAC becomes seamlessly incorporated into an institution's approach to teaching and learning—seemingly a positive development—WAC can disappear as an entity, throwing the institution back into some of the problems that gave rise to WAC in the first place. As a given WAC program progresses into Type 4 [full integration and beyond], momentum threatens to consume it, so that those who are in charge of WAC must continue to emphasize its location. (p. 379

WAC disappearing is always possible, in that collaboration might become absorption, perceived as a "natural" function that requires no sustaining, no special identity as a movement.

But there is now a national professional organization, which can allow WAC to be an intimate partner with other initiatives while maintaining its organizational and institutional identity. Although such absorption can and has happened at the local level, at the national level WAC has not been absorbed into general education or faculty development. Indeed, it has perhaps a larger presence than either of the other two within higher education institutions. In my view, this is mainly because WAC has taken seriously the profound organizing principle of higher education and of modern knowledge: disciplinarity. In other words, WAC has depended on WID, though that has always been a tension within the overarching WAC movement, a productive tension. The general in general education and the universal in professional development are necessary to take into account—but rarely sufficient, at least to secure their institutional relevance and longevity. It is necessary to work with faculty on their own terms and in their own terms, and the WAC movement has continued to do that, messy as it always is. The assessment movement allowed WAC to capitalize on the value of specialization—and faculty control. Recent developments in the writing enriched curriculum, where WAC professionals take a consulting role in ongoing iterative development by faculty teaching a curriculum (not only a course), bode well for the sustainability of WAC in the long run (Cox et al., 2018). None of the other "across-the-curriculum" efforts have taken disciplinary knowledge and practices as seriously and as thoroughly as WAC, in my view. They have tended to remain at the level of general strategies. And that has limited their reach and, perhaps, longevity.

One might rightly argue that the deeper reason none of the other "across-the-curriculum" movements has had the reach or staying power of WAC is that writing is so very important to the work of higher education and of every profession students enter. But organizationally and institutionally, WAC was and is supported by the overall presence of composition/writing studies, with its writing courses, writing centers, and writing programs, all organized nationally. Chris Anson and Karla Lyles (2011) did a statistical examination of writing-related articles in 14 disciplinary journals that publish on pedagogy. They found that WAC's growth "coincided with—and in many ways helped create and shape—the professionalization of composition as a field" (Anson & Lyles, 2011, p. 8). This is an advantage that none of the other "across the curriculums" has had.

In summary, the WAC movement has taken its place with other educational reform movements of the late 20th century and is now more firmly established than ever in the 21st. In 2002, I wrote that the future of WAC would be about "forging alliances, expanding with new connections" (p. 332). Some 20 years later, the new organizational structures in place for WAC at last allow those alliances to be formalized and the connections developed over time, systematically between organizations and their various committee structures, as well as through personal connections at the grassroots level.

Yet there remain crucial needs in terms of alliances and connections. One is that WAC be more responsive to the other "across-the-curriculum" themes that have occupied general education: diversity, multiculturalism, ethics, global studies, and so on. Making common cause with those organizations in higher education that study and promote these will allow WAC to address as never before issues of nationality, race, gender, class, and more generally the very problems that inspired the formation of general/liberal education after World War II: the battles between democratic and authoritarian government, between liberty and tyranny. Fortunately, AWAC has committees charged with addressing these issues.

Another is the organization of research, at three levels. First, there are some fundamental questions about how writing relates to learning and to development over time, which WAC research might help to answer if there were a concerted effort that involved researchers in K-12, psychology, and other fields, both in the US and internationally. There has been relatively little collaboration of that type (as there often has been in other regions of the world, notably Latin America and Europe). Second, there are programmatic questions that involve large-scale institutional research—a scale that would require cooperation with national organizations. In my view, the model in the US is the collaboration between WAC researchers and the National Survey of Student Engagement (NSSE), which provided the largest-ever study of the effects of writing on students' perception of their engagement with learning. Third, WAC can partner more effectively with research on learning in the disciplines conducted by the disciplines. While there has been research in most every discipline on ways to improve learning through writing (including, for example, mortuary science and forest pest management), relatively few disciplines have taken on board writing as an important project of ongoing research and theorizing over time. The exceptions, though, are important ones. Engineering, science (particularly at the secondary school level), and mathematics have large-scale research efforts stretching back many years into the relationships between writing and learning specifically in those fields. WAC researchers have in some cases partnered with them, but much more is possible. The AWAC committee on research and publications now exists to do these very things.

A final crucial need is that WAC form, at last, those alliances and connections with other organizations involved with educational reform and accreditation, such as The Professional and Organizational Development (POD) Network in Higher Education, American Association for Higher Education (AAHEA), and the Association of American Colleges and Universities (AAC&U), as well as American Association of University Professors (AAUP) potentially. There might be sessions on WAC at every meeting of these organizations, as there have been at times in the past. Indeed, this would be going back to the future. It was the NEH that sponsored the seminars that in many ways gave birth to WAC. And it was Carol Schneider, a long-time president of the AAC&U, who organized a decade of conferences on Writing and Thinking in the late 1980s through the early 1990s at the University of Chicago—featuring Wayne Booth, Joe Williams, and Elaine Maimon. Teams attended from all over the nation to learn WAC principles (Soven, 2006). And yes, there are AWAC committees for advocacy and partnerships.

General education, critical thinking, faculty development, the assessment movement, and a number of other powerful and ongoing reform efforts did not absorb WAC, as Malenczyk in 2012 predicted general education would. And all indications are that WAC will be able to continue to hold to its identity while allying with and connecting with other reforms, perhaps for another half century.

REFERENCES

Adler-Kassner, L. & Harrington, S. (2010). Responsibility and composition's future in the twenty-first century: Reframing "accountability." *College Composition and Communication, 62*(1), 73–99. https://www.jstor.org/stable/27917885.

Anson, C. A. & Dannels, D. (2009). Profiling programs: Formative uses of departmental consultations in the assessment of communication across the curriculum. *Across the Disciplines, 6*, 1–15. https://doi.org/10.37514/atd-j.2009.6.1.05.

Anson, C. M. & Lyles, K. (2011). The intradisciplinary influence of composition and WAC, part two: 1986–2006. *The WAC Journal, 22*, 7–19. https://doi.org/10.37514/wac-j.2011.22.1.02.

Association for General and Liberal Studies. (n.d.). About us. *AGLS*. Retrieved January 13, 2023, from https://www.agls.org/organization/about-us/.

Carter, M. (2002). A process for establishing outcomes-based assessment plans for writing and speaking in the disciplines. *Language and Learning across the Disciplines, 6*(1), 4–29. https://doi.org/10.37514/lld-j.2003.6.1.02.

College Great Books Programs. (n.d.). Retrieved January 12, 2023, from https://www.coretexts.org/programs/college-great-books.

Condon, W. & Rutz, C. (2012). A taxonomy of writing across the curriculum programs: Evolving to serve broader agendas. *College Composition and Communication, 64*(2), 357–382. https://www.jstor.org/stable/43490756.

Cox, M., Galin, J. R. & Melzer, D. (2018). *Sustainable WAC: A whole systems approach to launching and developing writing across the curriculum programs.* National Council of Teachers of English.

Flash, P. (2016). From apprised to revised: Faculty in the disciplines change what they never knew they knew. In K. B. Yancey (Ed.), *A rhetoric of reflection* (pp. 237–249). Utah State University Press. https://doi.org/10.7330/9781607325161.c011.

Glotfelter, A., Martin, C., Olejnik, M., Updike, A. & Wardle, E. (Eds.). (2022). Writing-related faculty development for deep change. *Changing conceptions, changing practices: Innovating teaching across disciplines*. Utah State University Press.

Graham, J. (1992). Writing components, writing adjuncts, writing links. In S. H. McLeod & M. I. Soven (Eds.), *Writing across the curriculum: A guide to developing programs* (pp. 78–93). The WAC Clearinghouse; University Press of Colorado. https://wac.colostate.edu/docs/books/mcleod_soven/2000/chapter8.pdf.

Hillyard, C. (2012). Comparative study of the numeracy education and writing across the curriculum movements: Ideas for future growth. *Numeracy, 5*(2). http://doi.org/10.5038/1936-4660.5.2.2.

History of AWAC—Association for Writing Across the Curriculum. (n.d.). Retrieved January 13, 2023, from https://wacassociation.org/history-of-awac/.

History. (n.d.). PEN—Progressive Education Network. Retrieved January 13, 2023, from https://progressiveeducationnetwork.org/history/.

Jablonski, J. (2006). *Academic writing consulting and WAC: Methods and models for guiding cross-curricular literacy work.* Hampton Press.

Kuhlenschmidt, S. (2011). Distribution and penetration of teaching-learning development units in higher education: Implications for strategic planning and research. *To Improve the Academy, 29*(1), 274–287. https://doi.org/10.1002/j.2334-4822.2011.tb00637.x.

Malenczyk, R. (2012). WAC's disappearing act. In P. K. Matsuda & K. Ritter (Eds.), *Exploring composition studies: Sites, issues, perspectives* (pp. 89–104). Utah State University Press.

McLeod, S. H. & Miraglia, E. (2001). Writing across the curriculum in a time of change. In S. H. McLeod, E. Miraglia, M. Soven & C. Thaiss (Eds.), *WAC for the new millennium: Strategies for continuing writing-across-the-curriculum programs* (pp. 1–27). National Council of Teachers of English.

National Numeracy Network—NNN History. (n.d.). Retrieved January 12, 2023, from https://www.nnn-us.org/NNN-History.

Northeast Writing Across the Curriculum Consortium. (n.d.). Retrieved January 13, 2023, from https://newacc.colostate.edu/.

Palmquist, M., Childers, P., Maimon, E., Mullin, J., Rice, R., Russell, A. & Russell, D. R. (2020). Fifty years of WAC: Where have we been? Where are we going? *Across the Disciplines, 17*(3/4), 5–45. https://doi.org/10.37514/atd-j.2020.17.3.01.

Paul, R. (n.d.). *Critical thinking movement: 3 waves*. The Foundation for Critical Thinking. Retrieved July 22, 2019, from https://www.criticalthinking.org/pages/critical-thinking-movement-3-waves/856.

Paulos, J. A. (1988). *Innumeracy: Mathematical illiteracy and its consequences.* Macmillan.

Progressive education. (2022). In *Wikipedia*. https://en.wikipedia.org/w/index.php?title=Progressive_education&oldid=1129777683.

QuIRK. (n.d.). QuIRK. Retrieved January 12, 2023, from https://serc.carleton.edu/quirk/About_QuIRK.html.

Russell, D. R. (1992). *Writing in the academic disciplines, 1870–1990: A curricular history*. Southern Illinois University.

Russell, D. R. (2002). *Writing in the academic disciplines: A curricular history*. Southern Illinois University.

Rutz, C., Condon, W., Iverson, E. R., Manduca, C. A. & Willett, G. (2012). Faculty professional development and student learning: What is the relationship? *Change: The Magazine of Higher Learning, 44*(3), 40–47. https://doi.org/10.1080/00091383.2012.672915.

Sheils, M. (1975). Why Johnny can't write. *Newsweek, 8*, 58–65.

Soven, M. I. (2006). WAC becomes respectable: The University of Chicago institutes on writing and higher order reasoning. In Mcleod, S. M. & M. I. Soven (Eds.), *Composing a community: A history of writing across the curriculum* (pp. 80–95). Parlor Press.

Statement of WAC Principles and Practices—The WAC Clearinghouse. (2014). Retrieved July 18, 2019, from https://wac.colostate.edu/principles/.

Steen, L. A. & Madison, B. L. (2015). Evolution of numeracy and the National Numeracy Network. *Numeracy, 1*(1), 2. https://evidence.thinkportal.org/handle/123456789/9974.

Thaiss, C. (2006). Still a good place to be: More than 20 years of the national network of WAC programs. In S. M. McLeod & M. I. Soven (Eds.), *Composing a community: A history of writing across the curriculum* (pp. 126–141). Parlor Press.

Thaiss, C. & Porter, T. (2010). The state of WAC/WID in 2010: Methods and results of the US survey of the international WAC/WID mapping project. *College Composition and Communication, 61*(3), 534–570. https://www.jstor.org/stable/40593339.

The Great Books Foundation—Inspiring ideas, dialogue, and lives. (n.d.). The Great Books Foundation. Retrieved January 12, 2023, from https://www.greatbooks.org/.

Vrchota, D. A. & Russell, D. R. (2013). WAC/WID meets CXC/CID: A dialogue between writing studies and communication studies. *The WAC Journal, 24*, 49. https://doi.org/10.37514/wac-j.2013.24.1.03.

Willett, G., Iverson, E. R., Rutz, C. & Manduca, C. A. (2014). Measures matter: Evidence of faculty development effects on faculty and student learning. *Assessing Writing, 20*, 19–36. https://doi.org/10.1016/j.asw.2013.12.001.

Yancey, K. B. (2018). It's tagmemics *and* the Sex Pistols: Current issues in individual and programmatic writing assessment. In S. W. Logan & W. H. Slater (Eds.), *Academic and professional writing in an age of accountability* (pp. 257–275). Southern Illinois University Press.

Yook, E. L. & Atkins-Sayre, W. (2012). *Communication centers and oral communication programs in higher education: Advantages, challenges, and new directions*. Lexington Books.

Zemliansky, P. & Berry, L. (2017). A writing-across-the-curriculum faculty development program: An experience report. *IEEE Transactions on Professional Communication, 60*(3), 306–316. https://doi.org/10.1109/tpc.2017.2702041.

CHAPTER 17.
IMAGINING WAC'S FUTURE: COLONIALITY, DIVERSITY, AND SUSTAINABILITY

Al Harahap
University of Oklahoma

Federico Navarro
Universidad de O'Higgins

Alisa Russell
Wake Forest University

We were tasked with imagining the future of Writing Across the Curriculum (WAC) but quickly realized that we could only do so by honoring our subjectivities and positionalities. Thus, this collective exploration considers three major concepts that we think should drive the future of WAC, each presented with our individual takes: *Coloniality*, *Equity*, and *Sustainability*.

We discuss these concepts not in the predictive but in the aspirational. For this publication, we have decided to preserve a conversational tone to keep the polyphonic nature of our envisioned WAC of the future. The ideas presented here are not a coherent whole, but in staccato, as a chorus. Many of our ideas align, some of them diverge, others perhaps even contradict. With that goal, we'll end with a collective list of action items and questions we might take from here.

COLONIALITY

How international is "international"?—Federico

Decolonial studies have pointed out that coloniality is not necessarily a matter of military and material colonialism by foreign invaders; it is instead a more subtle and pervasive epistemological and symbolic enterprise: a Eurocentric and U.S.-centric, rational-modern, racially-oriented, English-dependent, center-to-periphery, Global North to Global South paradigm of knowledge-making, beliefs, symbols, and ways of communicating. This is illustrated with the North-South divide proposed by Willy Brandt in 1980 (Lees, 2020; see Figure 17.1).

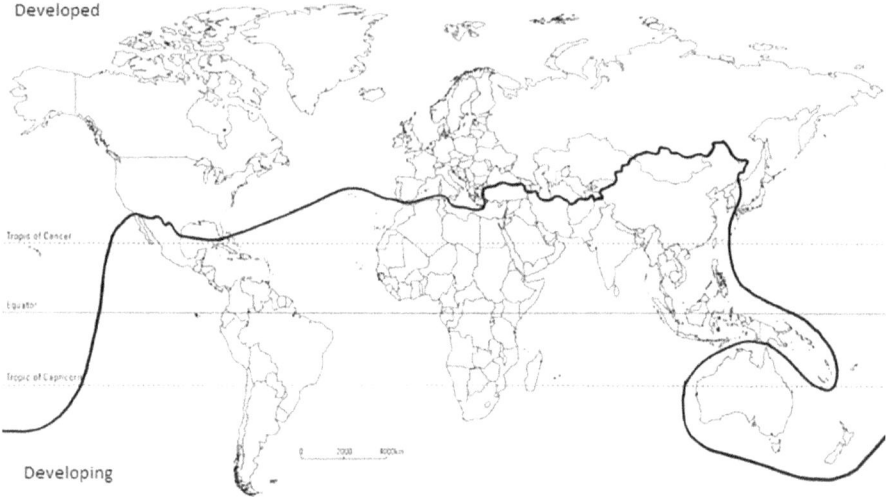

Figure 17.1. Brandt's line (photo by Jovan.gec on Wikimedia Commons).

Consequently, modern-day coloniality is a *coloniality of knowledge* (Maldonado-Torres, 2007). The geopolitical location of scholars, texts, and languages impacts the politics of academic knowledge production. Interestingly, this means that Northern, English-based knowledge production is located in a supposedly *zero point of observation* (Castro-Gómez, 2007) or an *unmarked locality* (Lillis & Curry, 2010) that produces seemingly universal claims (Navarro, 2022).

This is often the case within composition and writing studies. According to Bruce Horner and colleagues (2011), the "field operates with the tacit assumption that scholarship . . . is located—produced, found, and circulated—in English-medium, U.S.-centric publications only" (pp. 271–272). At the same time, the field implicitly circulates a particular narrative, as Christiane Donahue (2009) puts it, of an American "unique knowledge, expertise, and ownership of writing instruction and writing research" with "universal courses, sovereign philosophies and pedagogies, and agreed-on language requirements" (p. 213). Even within writing studies, privileged groups are not required to specify or discuss their locations and viewpoints, which are naturalized as universal, as Jacqueline Joyce Royster and Jean C. Williams (1999) pointed out.

Some of the most prestigious and influential journals in the field help exemplify this point. *Written Communication*, for instance, claims to be "an *international* [emphasis added] multidisciplinary journal that publishes theory and research in writing" (Written Communication, n.d.). However, 73.2 percent of the authors who published there between 2016–2018 were based in central English-speaking countries and regions—namely, the United States, the United Kingdom, Canada, Australia, Hong Kong, New Zealand, and Ireland—while 100 percent of the papers were published in English. Moreover, 90.5 percent of the members of the editorial board are based in the same central English-speaking countries and regions. We find the same situation in *Across the Disciplines*: 100 percent of authors were based in the United States and Canada in articles only published in English between 2016 and 2018, and there is only one member of the editorial review board based outside the United States in a non-English speaking country. Therefore, knowledge produced in these and other similar journals hide their particularly-located gaze to offer a supposed universal take on writing and the teaching of writing.

So the future of WAC could involve considering non-English-speaking literature and traditions to promote North-South research reciprocity and exchange (like this one!). In particular, mainstream journals and publishing companies could effectively democratize international participation and publish in different languages. They could genuinely wonder about the limitations of mainstream knowledge, especially considering their declared or implicit international, universal reach. I believe that the WAC Clearinghouse book collections are pushing the boundaries in the field and fostering more diverse conversations among different traditions. Books have consistently included scholars from many places and more recently have been published in languages other than English. Perhaps more importantly, authors worldwide have increasingly played roles as book editors, chief editors, and peer-reviewers. That is, gatekeeping has been gradually democratized and editorial decision-making has made room for other perspectives to push the boundaries of the field through various ways of knowing that have previously been seen as outside the mainstream.

How does "coloniality" figure into our institutional relations?—Al

I'm speaking from central Oklahoma, the traditional home of the Caddo, Creek, Muscogee, and Seminole Nations and the Wichita Tribes, as well as the traditional migration and trade routes of the Apache, Comanche, Kiowa, and Osage Nations.

I'm also speaking from the figurative lands of rhetoric, composition, and writing studies, which have been and continue to be colonized by the aestheticism of *belles lettres* and the field of literature. In preparing for this address, I've spent some time glossing over patterns in WAC/WID literatures, and just as a very broad, general observation, notice that, corresponding with Sue H.

McLeod et al.'s (2001) *WAC for the New Millennium* and the conception of *Across the Disciplines*, starting in the early aughts, we have increasingly diverged from traditional humanities and letters work, perhaps even more so than our closest sibling fields in writing program administration and writing center work, by warming up to empiricism. And when we don't have numbers, we seem to love using surrogate charts and graphs and tables. I'm unsure, in this moment, if we are creating and preserving our own culture, or if we're just capitulating to the dominant forces of STEM-oriented academia with its culture of big data, impact factors, and other epistemological quantifications. And I wonder if there's some kind of Vygotskian proximal development happening wherein we're so much in service to STEM that we end up assimilating their epistemologies.

So, I'm thinking of "coloniality" in different ways. First, the more literal global, historical events and how one lingering consequence is that English has become the de facto lingua franca of the world, including within the exchanges of global academics, which Federico explored in more depth. And the other, more figuratively, the territoriality of academic disciplines. More specifically, then, I'm thinking of the ways colonial processes work in our institutional WAC/WID initiatives. If we look at various institutional units, whether that's "content" units with academic disciplines/programs or administrative units, these all can be considered "imagined communities." And we can conceptualize them using "imagined geographies." I'm borrowing terms from Benedict Anderson (1983) and Edward Said (1978) respectively, who look at the formation of nation-states, sometimes naturally, other times forcibly, around shared or imposed cultural and political values. If we imagine campus units that WAC/WID has to work with as these imagined communities and imagined geographies, we can start to identify clusters, or "continents," if you will.

We can then ask questions like: What are the dominant cultures in this world? And each institution can be its own world. What have been the sordid sociopolitical and intercultural histories within and between campus communities that affect current inter-unit dynamics? And how can we use these institutional histories and policies? To help explore these questions, we can use a kind of power and relational mapping to inform our WAC outreach, advocacy, and decision-making.

WHAT ABOUT RECIPROCITY?—ALISA

Al's idea of "imagined geographies" has got me thinking about WAC as a connector. We in WAC connect faculty across the disciplines to one another; we connect disciplinary writing to research and principles in writing studies; we connect writing inside the academy to writing beyond the academy. I further see WAC as this generative hub of many cross sections within writing studies: writing assessment, transfer, genre studies, lifespan writing, media studies, problem-based learning. So much WAC work draws on and benefits from these various areas, but then WAC also provides a space to put these areas into conversation. David R. Russell (2020) even recently described technical and professional writing and first-year composition as "two inextricably linked poles of transfer research with WAC/WID in the middle" (p. 478). The middle. The connective tissue. Interstitial.

My question, then, is this: How does WAC act as a conduit—a generative middle space—without subsuming or claiming everything as our own? And on the flip side, how does WAC maintain its visibility and identity amongst all of these connections in order to keep making them?

So, I'm going into my second year as faculty, hired to lead WAC initiatives; I can't call myself a WAC director because there's not a program yet. I'm facing the most classic issues for someone starting up a WAC program: I want buy-in from a variety of stakeholders across campus; I'm trying to learn the various campus initiatives and offices I can partner with and hook our mission into; and I'm working with top-down mandates while trying to cultivate a bottom-up approach to them. Even at this very old-hat, basic WAC-operations level (for which I'm lucky to have so much great scholarship to turn to!), these questions I'm asking about WAC as a connector and what that means in terms of coloniality are palpable.

Take these three short examples that have come up for me: One health and exercise science faculty member recently told me that she's cut out her main writing assignment (even though it cultivates the kind of thinking she would want her students to develop) because it's just too hard to teach. Students come in with writing skills that are too wide-ranging, and she doesn't have the expertise to get them on the same page, so to speak. Meanwhile, in political science, another faculty member insists that his students develop the analytical skills essential to becoming scholars in the field and that he will hand out as many failing grades as needed to push students there. And then over in statistics, a faculty member explained that she only assigns reports aimed at clients since almost none of their students will become academics and will instead be working in industry. I think it would be easy to read these examples and begin sorting or ranking these faculty members based on our own understanding of what writing is and what writing pedagogy should be. But what if we could refrain from immediately drafting responses in our heads? What if we, perhaps, opened space for more questions? What if we saw each of these scenarios as a complex confluence of factors that takes long-term collaboration to understand and find generative ways forward?

Going forward, I think we as WAC scholars and practitioners must wrestle with: What does it really mean to invite ourselves (physically or metaphorically) into others' disciplinary classrooms? Into other fields? What are we inviting in turn? How do we steep our work as connectors in collaboration and reciprocity?

Is it possible to offer all we can *and* receive all we can? To use our position as connector to constantly re-create our identities as a field, as programs, as scholars?

EQUITY

Are we ready to do linguistic justice work across campus?—Al

I want to start by sharing that it has been mentally and emotionally draining to be at conferences like IWAC, in organizations like AWAC, and adjacent ones in writing center and WPA communities, wherein I consistently find myself in spaces and moments where I'm one of only a very few non-white people, sometimes the lone, single one, among 20, 50, or in today's case, upward of 100 people. At a physical conference, I can at least sit toward the front, not see the room behind me, and forget for a moment that's the case. But it has been even more exhausting on Zoom, where everyone is always visible. The concept of equity, for me, is inextricably tied to adequate and proportional representation.

How does this play out in WAC/WID work? Pamela Flash and Teresa Redd's (2021) mid-conference plenary on Wednesday showed, through the illuminating live poll they did, that 78 percent of us who attended and participated feel that the most urgent question or work of WAC scholar-practitioners is "How can we best implement antiracist policies and practices?" So I'm making the assumption that knowing how to advocate for *Students' Right to Their Own Language* (CCCC, 1974) and specifically calls for WAC to be aware of linguistic difference (Matsuda & Jablonski, 2000; Zawacki, 2010; Zawacki & Cox, 2014), antiracist writing assessment (Inoue & Poe, 2012), and linguistic justice (Baker-Bell, 2020) are all administrative and pedagogical concerns that we agree are pressing in our work today.

The big question is: How do we do that? What I think we should do is actually take a step back and ask: Are we ready to do this work? One of the most common grievances I hear from WAC colleagues is that other academic units—often business and STEM, but also generally colleagues who may not have trained in language and writing—are bootstrapping standard-language colonizers who refuse to acknowledge other Englishes in student writing—including, but not limited to, Black and other vernacular Englishes, various international student Englishes, and other U.S.-regional or working class Englishes. Our war stories are replete with these instances. But if you have this grievance, a big question I have for you is: Who is doing this advocacy work? If your WAC/WID programs, writing programs, writing centers, and other stakeholders are homogeneously white, native English speakers and writers, how effective is your message?

Imagining WAC's Future

Over the course of the Breonna Taylor/George Floyd BLM-protests culmination of summer 2020, many antiracism popular books entered our collective consciousness. One of the authors, psychologist Beverly Daniel Tatum, who wrote *Why Are All the Black Kids Sitting Together in the Cafeteria?* (2017) and *Can We Talk about Race?* (2008), claims, through her studies, that children learn exclusionary racism through the example of their parents. Ironically, the white parents she studied tell their children to integrate and play with their non-white friends in their schools, but they themselves only socialize with white friends. So it's a form of the old adage, "Do as I say, not as I do." And to me this highlights the very human disconnect between our ideals and our actions, which, as smart and kind as we are, academics are not immune to.

Figure 17.2 provides a simple, scalar heuristic I've developed to help decide whether or not an academic initiative is ready to do linguistic equity and justice work with colleagues across campus or in other professional spaces:

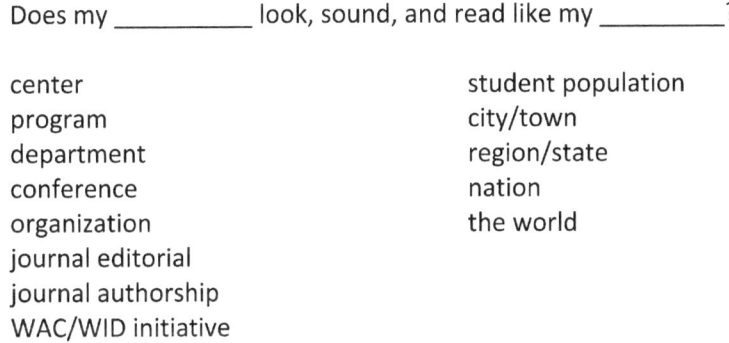

Figure 17.2. Heuristic for linguistic difference and justice work readiness.

Does my [blank] look, sound, and read like [blank]? And you can insert the appropriate variables depending on what the work is. For example: Does my program look, sound, and read like the student population I am advocating so hard for? Does my WAC/WID research project or initiative look, sound, and read like my country or region? And if you claim to be an international-level institution, conference, or journal, does it look, sound, and read like the world?

If the answer is no, I think we need to step back. And I mean that not just for whatever individual programs or initiatives we have going on, but also WAC as a whole subfield itself. Do we really think we are ready to go out there and advocate for antiracism, *Students' Right to Their Own Language*, antiracist assessment, and linguistic justice?

If I am the "linguistically ignorant" content colleague who refuses to acknowledge linguistic difference, and the agents of change you send out to me are always white, native English speakers, looking, sounding, and reading like

259

standard American English, and you tell me to value linguistic difference, but your actions show otherwise, why should I believe a single word you have to say? Perhaps we should work on equity at home first so that we can develop the ethos and integrity to go out there to do that advocacy work—when we're ready.

WHERE ARE THE ACCESS POINTS?—ALISA

When it comes to equity, I keep returning to this question: Where are the access points into WAC? Where are the access points into WAC for upcoming WAC scholars (e.g., graduate students)? For scholars in different disciplines (e.g., those in adjacent or non-adjacent fields who are doing this work)? For faculty at our own institutions? For students at our institutions? And most importantly, are those access points visible and intentional?

WAC is an academic discipline, a programmatic endeavor, a pedagogical approach, a philosophy. When I speak of access points, I am asking what thresholds must be crossed to engage with WAC across these levels and *who* is able to cross them. We know that it's easiest for things to run on autopilot: Social structures, philosophical approaches, and institutions all tend to churn out more of what they already are (e.g., conservatism often leads to more conservatism; whiteness often leads to more whiteness; etc.). If we want diversity, we must intentionally and strategically make visible the access points to engage with WAC. And we must build flexible structures that not only recruit to bring people in but further *value* these expansive views.

As an example, the WAC Graduate Organization runs a Cross-Institutional Mentoring Program, which pairs established scholar-practitioners in WAC with graduate students or early-career faculty at different institutions across an academic year. These cross-institutional mentoring relationships still grow and breathe and take different shapes, but the formal program creates a clear point of access. I had amazing WAC mentors in grad school, but it was because I was lucky and got shoulder-tapped to enter the field (i.e., I was asked to serve as the graduate research assistant for my institution's WAC program before I even knew what W-A-C stood for). That's not intentional. That's not equitable. But even beyond providing clear access points to promote equity, we have to then *value* it through reciprocity. One of the mentors in a recent study of the mentoring program said it like this:

> My mentee also is a person of color, and we have talked regularly about race and racism in academia in general, and in our field. [. . .] This has gotten me thinking about the importance of direct support of graduate students from minoritized groups, not just for those individuals, but for the field. If we

truly want the diversity of our scholarly community to reflect the diversity of our communities and our schools, as I believe most of us really do, I think we need more of the kind of direct, sustained, personal mentoring the Cross-Institutional Mentoring Project is creating. This work does not show up in publication records, or in major named initiatives, but I believe it makes a difference, one scholar at a time, that will change our field as much as the big picture work of big name scholars will. (Russell & Polk, forthcoming)

To this point, I'm starting to hate the term "organic." We often use it when we say we want things to happen or develop organically. I understand the sentiment of that and can even see its usefulness when it's evoked in opposition of strong-arming, or taking over, or moving too fast. But a lot of times, things happening "organically" just means things happening under a cover of occlusion—things happening for those already in the know. Or it means things happening the way they always have. If we wait for our institutions or our programs to organically turn over toward equitable approaches, we're going to be waiting a very long time. We have to make concrete interventions; we have to bake them into our structures, even if that means undoing some existing structures first. I think many are afraid that if we make things more formal, we lose flexibility. But flexibility doesn't have to be the cost of formality; we can stay flexible while still making visible—and expanding—the ways in.

How to teach writing to advance emancipation?—Federico

Until recently, the university system in Chile was relatively small and for a privileged minority. But students in Chile are probably the most active agents of change in society, and their agency has led to structural changes in education in the last decades. For example, the protests in 2011 helped create two new public universities and a national program of higher education with free tuition for low-income families; high school students smile as they hold a banner that reads "no more profit" (Figure 17.3). The demonstrations from 2019, on the other hand, led to the drafting of a new Constitution that aims to expand civil and educational rights; the image in Figure 17.4 shows a female teenager putting herself at risk as she stares at a male, armed member of the military, the very representation of law and order, among the riots and demonstrations. These images illustrate confrontations that emerge when the existing structures of education (and society in general) inevitably face realities that demand change, and consequently open up opportunities for (re)direction.

Figure 17.3. Chilean students' demonstrations in 2011 (photo by Simenon Simenon on Wikimedia Commons, June 30, 2011)

Figure 17.4. Chilean social demonstrations in 2019 which led to a constitutional reform (photo by Migrar Photo).

I currently work for one such new public university, founded in 2015. My first-in-their-family students wouldn't be there, and their university wouldn't be there either, if it weren't for their agency. In fact, the so-called "non-traditional students" are *traditional* students now as they are currently the most frequent university students in Chile and elsewhere; in contrast, universities, faculty, and pedagogies of writing are often the ones that seem at odds with present-day needs and realities in higher education.

However, historically excluded students in Chile embody and express dominant deficit discourses, as in "my abilities were pretty mediocre and not up to the standard required to face university challenges" or "I did not come with a knowledge base from school" (Ávila Reyes et al., 2021). These negative self-perceptions, often related to the type of school students attended and to a supposed lack of preparation, contrast not only with their agency and resilience; we have found that they engage in complex but stigmatized or hidden vernacular practices and often resist received dominant literacy practices (Ávila Reyes et al., 2021). In addition, they deploy self-sponsored strategies that help them build bridges between their authorial identities and higher education tasks and requirements. However, deficit discourses applied to marginalized student communities both hide and devalue students' agency, assets, resilience, and academic achievement, and at the same time, they secure discriminatory gatekeeping systems that function to stifle programmatic changes at our universities.

Based on these findings, we are putting forward an inclusive, equity-based pedagogy of writing designed for teachers across the curriculum (Navarro, 2021), which includes:

- Recognition and active use of vernacular practices students engage in in their communities.
- Writing tasks that make room for students' research, perspectives, and writing decisions, and that refer to meaningful, situated, and controversial topics (related to social struggles or family and community histories, for example).
- Critical reports and parodies of received literacy practices that invite recognition but also resistance, negotiation, and transformation.
- Promotion of mixed genres and code-meshing to train creative and sophisticated writers who play with their semiotic resources and talk and reflect on their choices.

These kinds of tasks and teaching strategies are not entirely new. Nevertheless, the future of WAC could involve systematically exploring what an inclusive, antiracist, socially-just pedagogy of writing should be like. Such equity-based writing pedagogy wouldn't just aim to include or validate students' incomes (Guerra, 2015) and household and community practices but to truly transform our teaching practices and advance emancipation.

SUSTAINABILITY

VISIBILITY OR DISAPPEARANCE?—ALISA

Our last driving concept in looking toward the future of WAC is sustainability. It's a concept I think we all have a felt sense about; it describes something about lasting power, manageable growth, and/or continuing across contextual and generational changes. Of course, how to actually invest in and build toward sustainability can get rather complicated. In Michelle Cox, Jeffrey R. Galin, and Dan Melzer's (2019) book *Sustainable WAC,* they draw on no less than complexity theory, systems theory, social network theory, resilience theory, and sustainable development theory to propose a whole systems approach for launching and developing WAC programs. So while there are a host of factors that feed into sustainability, I want to draw out a healthy tension I think we'll have to wrestle with: visibility vs. disappearance.

Cox, Galin, and Melzer (2019) describe visibility as the "perception of a WAC program across its networks and projects," emphasizing that WAC "tend[s] toward stagnation and institutional entropy if program visibility is not a priority" (p. 49). At the level of an individual institution, this includes initiatives like "sponsored events, university-wide assessment, data sharing, program review, faculty support, student and faculty recognition, curriculum grants, [and] department-by-department planning" (p. 49). At the level of the field, we can see these moves toward visibility in the long-standing WAC Clearinghouse, our WAC journals, the IWAC conference, and the recent formation of AWAC.

But a word on disappearance: In Rita Malenczyk's (2012) piece "WAC's Disappearing Act," she describes WAC as being "gradually subsumed or dispersed into other disciplines or programmatic structures, and therefore being transformed into something other than what it was before, something perhaps less obviously about writing alone" (p. 90). She doesn't see this as a failure of WAC, but a success (or even a fulfillment) of WAC: that "faculty would embrace the movement so that it became simply part of the scene, with writing something they taught in each class (and something they could write and publish about)" (p. 104). She thus sees the disappearance of WAC as an opportunity for transformation.

We can create all the programs and professional organizations in the world—and I'm for that visibility. I'm for the formality, the division of labor, the collaboration, and the equitable pathways. But these organizations have to be REcreated, constantly. Because sometimes the fulfillment of goals inevitably leads to disappearance, or maybe that disappearance is telling us our original goals or structures are no longer responding to current needs. In other words, we need—and need to seize—these moments of transformation that are made possible by disappearance. We need to regularly invite a variety of voices in to re-visit and question even our most fundamental structures across our campus initiatives, our programs, and our profession: Is this still working? How have the stakes changed? What's been done? What can blend in or disappear to make room for what needs to happen now?

When we look toward the future of WAC, maybe we need the ability to do both: to carve out visibility when we need to, and to disappear when we need to. Or at least, to let *pieces* disappear. This is what gives us the ability to transform and shift our efforts of visibility to meet a constantly changing landscape.

How to Make Indexation Our Own?—Federico

Research is an essential dimension to the sustainability of teaching writing. It can be used tactically (Adler-Kassner, 2008) to convince stakeholders, fight for funding, influence educational policies, reach an academic position, or engage in international conversations. However, we face a challenge: Many stakeholders, policymakers, employers, and international colleagues expect that we publish some of our research in indexed journals, especially indexed in mainstream databases such as Web of Science (WoS) or SCOPUS.

So, in a way WAC sustainability depends on the existence of such indexed journals. But the truth is there are not many such journals when compared to other related fields like sociolinguistics, second language teaching, or higher education studies.

There might be good reasons for this configuration. Some WoS and SCOPUS indexed journals respond to a different epistemology, knowledge-making culture, or rhetoric than that of WAC. Moreover, SCOPUS or WoS are for-profit enterprises, neglect languages other than English, and measure scientific relevance in controversial ways (e.g., impact factor). However, indexation does not mean indexation in a particular way. It just means that a particular journal complies with certain quality and integrity standards which account for good research. As the criteria for indexation may vary, we should advocate for *specific criteria for* indexation instead of *against* indexation.

I will illustrate this point with SciELO (https://scielo.org). This acronym stands for *Scientific electronic library online*, a cooperative, not-for-profit, multilingual, open-access, South-based bibliographic database (Packer, 2009). It was created in Brazil in 1997 and now includes 17 countries, most of them from Latin America, together with South Africa, Spain, and Portugal. It lists almost 400 journals and half a million documents, including authors from all over the world (see Figure 17.5). It is free to publish and download any record, and journals need to be open-access to be indexed.

However, SciELO is not just a repository of open-access papers published in the Southern Hemisphere and written in many languages. Journals have to comply with standards that are common to many other databases, such as double-blind peer review, internationalization, or periodicity. The meaningful contribution of SciELO is to offer research that complies with quality standards and at the same time to be open-access and not-for-profit.

This scientific perspective may resonate with WAC scholars-practitioners as it reminds of WAC initiatives such as the Clearinghouse journals. So the future of WAC could involve indexing our own journals to engage in conversations with stakeholders to sustain our educational claims, programs, and policies. But, at the same time, it could involve fighting for alternative criteria for indexation that put forward free access and democratization of knowledge, together with multiple languages, approaches, and epistemologies.

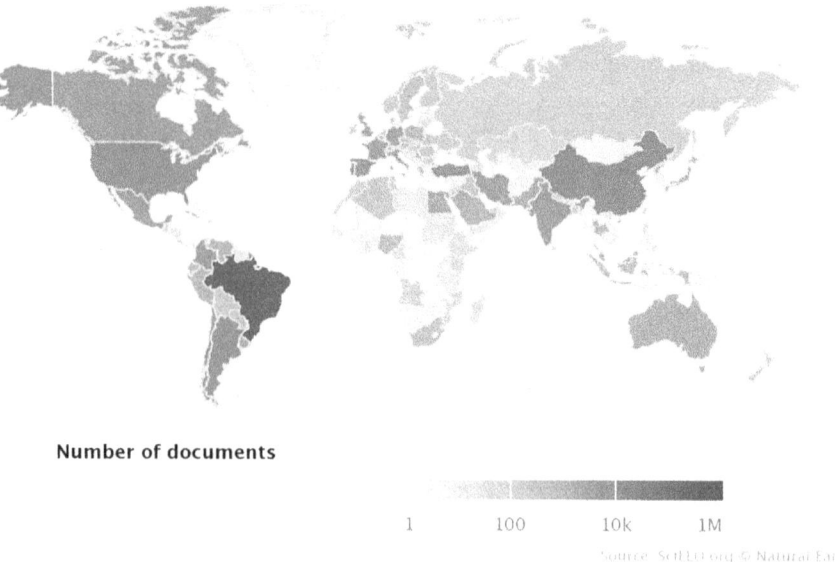

Figure 17.5. SciELO distribution by authors affiliation countries (https://analytics.scielo.org/; May 12, 2023).

Who are we?—Al

I want to dovetail from Alisa's reference to the Cox, Galin, and Melzer (2019) work on sustainable WAC, as well as Federico's deconstruction of the research and publication processes, which are very comprehensive in looking at institutional systems. We're also very good at making the subject of our work the students we teach and the content colleagues we reach out to. But we rarely think and talk about ourselves in reflexive ways. I'm not sure if that's maybe part of the STEM-ification or empiricization of writing studies—the hesitance to acknowledge the subjective. So I'm thinking about the agentic human behind these processes and asking the question: What is our role?

I'm borrowing from writing center discourse, specifically Elizabeth Cowan's (2002) "many hats" metaphor that writing center directors and tutors wear, contextually, depending on with whom they are interacting, and also from Shirley Rose and Irwin Weiser's (1999; 2002) works on "administrators as researcher" and the follow up "administrators as theorist"—all to pose that WAC/WID agents, too, need to be limber in the roles we inhabit.

To build and maintain more sustainable relationships, we need to maintain a high level of self-awareness of ourselves. If, as I mentioned earlier, the many groups and units we interact with on campus all hold different cultures and maintain different values on education and language, one role may be as anthropologist to better understand these differences. Once we do, what then? Are we missionaries? If so, what kind? The kind that go around campus and knock on all colleagues' doors at 8am in the morning to spread the gospels of April Baker-Bell, Asao Inoue, and Carmen Kynard? Are we politicians? If so, what kind? Are we colonizers and invaders? Should we be aggressive in liberating students' writing in other fields? Or do we subtly spread our cultural values like Hollywood does? WAC/WID is at the borders of writing studies. Are we border patrol agents who keep migrants from entering our field? And if they do enter, in what ways are we deporting them, caging them up, or giving them water so that they help rejuvenate our field intellectually?

The point I want to make here is that, to extend the metaphor, to build and maintain sustainable WAC relationships on campus, just like cross-cultural or multilateral international relationships, there isn't one template approach, but that we need to be more mindful, deliberate, and kairotic of the roles we embody and move between.

ACTION ITEMS

Ultimately, there is no "in conclusion" to be made here. At this point, we don't want you to feel a sense of finality for how these ideas factor into our WAC futures; instead, we want all of us—the field, the journals, the organizations, and all the scholar-teacher-practitioners—to forge ahead exploring the questions and ideas we've presented here to see where it takes us.

Each of us must do the individual work of reflecting on how issues of coloniality, equity, and sustainability mark our work. Then we can move toward collective reflection in our programs and across our field. We've presented this cacophonous piece as perhaps a model and starting point for our collective reflection. In this spirit, we are not looking to close things, but to open them.

However, we are also aware that it is easy to get "stuck" in a state of reflection. All three of us have posed many questions throughout this piece, but we don't want to leave you with questions alone. We want to point toward *concrete actions* that might take up or realize the issues of coloniality, equity, and sustainability raised here.

To that end, after we presented this plenary talk, we circulated a Google doc to all IWAC 2020–21 attendees to crowdsource action items that came out of people's individual and collective reflection. We present those items here, almost verbatim as they were written in our crowdsourced document. They are not in any particular order, but instead represent the rhizomatic range of action items we might undertake as we continue to question and reflect on what kind of WAC future we want to build.

- Create plans of reciprocity (with research subjects, with faculty in the disciplines, with colleagues):
    - Create a group to investigate grants or sponsorships available and post these with calls for cross-institutional collaborative proposals.
    - Might we look to people in our field who have done well enough to be able to support or pool support with others to create a one time grant to research teams?
- Consider non-English-speaking literature and traditions to promote North-South research collaborations and exchanges:
    - What about having IWAC and the Institute outside of the US?
    - Listen to and learn from the educational organizations which already use multilingual application and delivery processes for conferences and workshops (like the recent ALES international writing studies symposium).
- Formalize advertisements and application processes for leadership and membership roles (at the institutional and professional levels):
    - How can we better support, and thereby sustain, junior WAC (jWAC) professionals?

- Imagine equity-based WAC pedagogies that draw from diverse students' experiences and incomes:
  - As much of our valuable research like this gets distributed among ourselves mostly, what action items might go beyond imagining to make a wider impact?
  - Revisit my personal teaching philosophy and use it to create a specific statement regarding student assignments (as in: What do we hope to accomplish with those assignments?).
- Regularly invite/conduct reflective check-points (of WAC initiatives, programs, and professional organizations):
  - Alongside but also beyond regular assessment, invite a variety of voices to re-visit even the most fundamental structures and consider possible revisions (what needs to be visible vs. what needs to disappear).
  - Our field's organization statements don't carry much weight—at least institutionally. Might there be cross institutional partners within a state or region, sponsored by funds or which seeks funds to research antiracist writing pedagogy, practices, genres across disciplines?
  - Can we return to collecting local studies that don't get published but, when aggregated, would reveal much about writing across disciplines and contexts? Self-report hasn't worked: Are there grants available to have research teams collect such info? Can we marshall the energy of retirees still invested in the field and those researchers still on payrolls who are interested and invested in collecting local and inter/national research but also have heavy teaching and publication pressures and couldn't do this alone?
- Fight for democratizing open-access indexation criteria to publish research which sustain WAC initiatives:
  - I wonder whether/how IWAC and AWAC might work together to seek/apply for the kind of (substantial) funding that would enable significant longitudinal research to take place. I also wonder if longitudinal research sponsored in any way by IWAC and AWAC might include but also go beyond assessment of WAC programs to look (more) broadly at the writing that students do alongside of, around, aside from, and atop the curriculum as well as after it.

REFERENCES

Adler-Kassner, L. (2008). *The activist WPA: Changing stories about writing and writers*. Utah State University Press.

Anderson, B. (1983). *Imagined communities: Reflections on the origin and spread of nationalism*. Verso.

Ávila Reyes, N., Navarro, F. & Tapia-Ladino, M. (2021). "My abilities were pretty mediocre": Challenging deficit discourses in expanding higher education systems. *Journal of Diversity in Higher Education*. https://doi.org/10.1037/dhe0000366.

Baker-Bell, A. (2020). *Linguistic justice: Black language, literacy, identity, and pedagogy*. Routledge.

Castro-Gómez, S. (2007). Decolonizar la universidad: La hybris del punto cero y el diálogo de saberes [Decolonize the university: The hubris of the zero point and the dialogue of knowledge]. In S. Castro-Gómez & R. Grosfoguel (Eds.), *El giro decolonial: Reflexiones para una diversidad epistémica más allá del capitalismo global [The decolonial turn: Reflections for epistemic diversity beyond global capitalism]* (pp. 79–91). Siglo del Hombre Editores.

Conference on College Composition and Communication. (1974). Students' right to their own language. *College Composition and Communication, XXV*(3), 1–32. https://prod-ncte-cdn.azureedge.net/nctefiles/groups/cccc/newsrtol.pdf.

Cowan, E. (2002). The many hats a tutor wears. *Writing Center*. University of Pittsburgh. https://sites.pitt.edu/~writecen/cowan.html.

Cox, M., Galin, J. R. & Melzer, D. L. (2019). *Sustainable WAC: A whole systems approach to launching and developing WAC programs*. National Council of Teachers of English.

Donahue, C. (2009). "Internationalization" and composition studies: Reorienting the discourse. *College Composition and Communication, 61*(2), 212–243. https://www.jstor.org/stable/40593441.

Flash, P. & Redd, T. (2021, August 2–6). Second plenary: WAC @ 50: Where are we now? [Conference presentation]. Fifteenth International Writing Across the Curriculum Conference, Fort Collins, CO, United States. https://youtu.be/iFOifO6KeGI.

Guerra, J. C. (2015). *Language, culture, identity and citizenship in college classrooms and communities*. Routledge.

Horner, B., NeCamp, S. & Donahue, C. (2011). Toward a multilingual composition scholarship: From English only to a translingual norm. *College Composition and Communication, 63*(2), 269–300. https://www.jstor.org/stable/23131585.

Inoue, A. & Poe, M. (Ed.). (2012). *Race and writing assessment*. Peter Lang.

Lees, N. (2020). The Brandt Line after forty years: The more North-South relations change, the more they stay the same? *Review of International Studies, 47*(1), 85–106. https://doi.org/10.1017/s026021052000039x.

Lillis, T. & Curry, M. J. (2010). *Academic writing in a global context: The politics and practices of publishing in English*. Routledge.

Maldonado-Torres, N. (2007). On the coloniality of being: Contributions to the development of a concept. *Cultural Studies, 21*(2–3), 240–270. https://doi.org/10.1080/09502380601162548.

Malenczyk, R. (2012). WAC's disappearing act. In K. Ritter & P. K. Matsuda (Eds.), *Exploring composition studies: Sites, issues, and perspectives* (pp. 89–104). Utah State University Press. https://doi.org/10.2307/j.ctt4cgjsj.9.

Matsuda, P. K. & Jablonski, J. (2000). Beyond the L2 metaphor: Towards a mutually transformative model of ESL/WAC collaboration. *academic.writing*. https://doi.org/10.37514/AWR-J.2000.1.4.09.

McLeod, S. H., Miraglia, E., Soven, M. & Thaiss, C. (Eds.). (2001). *WAC for the new millennium: Strategies for continuing writing-across-the-curriculum programs*. The WAC Clearinghouse. https://wac.colostate.edu/books/landmarks/millenium/ (Originally published in 2001 by National Council of Teachers of English).

Navarro, F. (2021). (Ed.). *Escritura e inclusión en la universidad: Herramientas para docents* [Writing and inclusion in the university: Tools for teachers]. Editorial Universitaria.

Navarro, F. (2022). The unequal distribution of research roles in transnational composition: Towards illegitimate peripheral participation. In C. Donahue & B. Horner (Eds.), *Teaching and studying transnational composition* (pp. 17–33). Modern Language Association.

Packer, A. L. (2009). The SciELO open access: A gold way from the South. *Canadian Journal of Higher Education, 39*(3), 111–126. https://doi.org/10.47678/cjhe.v39i3.479.

Rose, S. & Weiser, I. (Eds.). (1999). *The writing program administrator as researcher: Inquiry in action and reflection*. Heinemann.

Rose, S. & Weiser, I. (Eds.). (2002). *The writing program administrator as theorist: Making knowledge*. Heinemann.

Royster, J. J. & Williams, J. C. (1999). History in the spaces left: African American presence and narratives of composition studies. *College Composition and Communication, 50*(4), 563–584. https://doi.org/10.2307/358481.

Russell, A. & Polk, T. (forthcoming). Expanding the WAC network: The Cross-Institutional Mentoring Project. In L. Gruwell & C. Lesh (Eds.), *Mentorship and methodology: Reflections, praxis, and futures*.

Russell, D. R. (2020). Retreading, non-ing, and a TPC rationale for sub-disciplining in writing studies. *College English, 82*(5), 472–483. https://library-ncte-org.du.idm.oclc.org/journals/ce/issues/v82-5/30752.

Said, E. (1978). *Orientalism*. Random House.

Tatum, B. D. (2008). *Can we talk about race?: And other conversations in an era of school resegregation*. Beacon Press.

Tatum, B. D. (2017). *Why are all the Black kids sitting together in the cafeteria?: And other conversations about race*. Basic Books.

Written Communication. (n.d.). *Aims and scope*. https://journals.sagepub.com/aims-scope/WCX.

Zawacki, T. M. (2010, May 20–22). Researching the local/writing the international: Developing culturally inclusive WAC programs and practices [Keynote presentation]. IWAC 2010 Conference, Bloomington, IN, United States.

Zawacki, T. M. & Cox, M. (Eds.). (2014). *WAC and second language writers: Research towards linguistically and culturally inclusive programs and practices.* The WAC Clearinghouse; Parlor Press. https://doi.org/10.37514/PER-B.2014.0551.

CONTRIBUTORS

James P. Austin is Assistant Professor of English at Central Connecticut State University, where he teaches writing and administers basic writing courses in the Composition Program. His research has appeared in *Written Communication*, *Civic Engagement in Global Contexts* (Utah State UP), *Emerging Writing Research from the Middle East-North Africa Region* (The WAC Clearinghouse), and elsewhere. He also writes and publishes the occasional short story.

Christopher Basgier is Director of University Writing at Auburn University. In that role, he works with faculty on teaching with writing, and he consults with departments about integrating writing throughout undergraduate and graduate curricula, particularly in support of high impact practices like ePortfolios. His research, which spans writing across the curriculum, genre, threshold concepts, and digital rhetoric, has appeared in venues like *Across the Disciplines, The WAC Journal, Composition Forum,* and *Studies in Higher Education*. He is also active in national organizations like the Association for Writing Across the Curriculum, the Conference on College Composition and Communication, HIPs in the States, and the WAC Clearinghouse.

Elizabeth Baxmeyer has been an English and music instructor at various colleges in Northern California for 14 years. For the last six, she has been a faculty member in the Humanities department at California Northstate University College of Health Sciences in Rancho Cordova, CA, where she runs the podcast studio, co-runs The Calendula Review, CHS's new narrative medicine-focused literary journal, and teaches music appreciation and English composition courses as well as an array of other humanities classes. She received her master's degree in music from Bangor University, Wales, UK with concentrations in Composition and Music for Media and the Arts, and her MFA in Writing and Contemporary Media from Antioch University, Santa Barbara. Her writing has been published in an array of literary journals including *The Examined Life Journal, Querencia Press, Luna Station Quarterly,* and more. Aside from teaching, she is an award-winning sound designer and professional musician.

Brad Benz is Teaching Professor in the Writing Program at the University of Denver, where he has been a faculty member since 2010. His work has been published in *American Speech, Dictionaries, Writing Program Administration,* and *Great Plains Quarterly,* among others. He lives in Denver with his daughter and their dog.

Magdaléna Bilá is a full professor with 32 years of experience in university teaching and scholarly research. She is affiliated at the Institute of Translation and Interpreting, Faculty of Arts, University of Prešov in Prešov, Slovakia. She teaches courses on non-literary translation, stylistics, translation theory, history of translation, and research methods in translation. In her research, she focuses on translational understanding of linguistic landscape, transferring knowledge from translation and translator's points of view, interlingual analysis of metalanguage, and composition of a lexicographic publication. She is currently involved in the research of stylistics of a research paper in translation, negotiating authorial voice in the translation of a research paper. She has authored and co-authored nine monographs, six textbooks, 65 research papers, and edited three books. She is a Fulbright scholarship holder (Notre Dame de Namur University, Belmont, CA, summer semester of 2002).

Julie Birt is Coordinator at the Campus Writing Program at the University of Missouri. Her research follows her interests in helping post-secondary instructors use writing in their college classrooms to reach all students, more specifically, those with a rural background. Outside of her regular research, she enjoys working directly with students to help improve their writing and communication skills in science courses.

Lindy E. Briggette is Assistant Professor of the Practice at Fairfield University, where she teaches in Core Writing and assists with programming and administration of Fairfield's WAC/WID Signature Element. She also teaches courses in Persuasive Writing and Feminist Rhetorics. Her research is focused on feminist rhetorics and archival historiography. Her scholarship has been published in *Peitho* and she has presented at conferences such as Conference on College Composition and Communication, Feminisms and Rhetorics, Rhetoric Society of America, and the UConn Conference on the Teaching of Writing. She holds an MS in Adult Education from the University of Southern Maine, an MA in English/Composition from UMass-Boston, and a Ph.D. in Rhetoric & Composition from the University of Rhode Island. Prior to teaching in rhetoric and composition, she worked as an academic advisor for ten years.

Alejandro Cerón is Associate Professor of Anthropology at the University of Denver, where he co-leads the DU Ethnography Lab. As an anthropologist, he is interested in the social and cultural aspects of health, especially sociocultural epidemiology, public health practice, and the right to health. Prior to earning a doctoral degree in anthropology (University of Washington, 2013), he graduated as physician and Master in Public Health in 2000 and 2006, respectively, from Universidad de San Carlos de Guatemala.

Pamela B. Childers is Caldwell Chair of Composition Emerita from McCallie School, where she directed the Writing Center and the WAC program. Having taught on secondary, postsecondary, and graduate school levels, she is former president of IWCA and an IWAC board member. She is a recipient of the IWCA Scholarship and Outstanding Service awards, and the Distinguished

Fellow Award from the Association for Writing Across the Curriculum. She has published hundreds of essays, articles, and chapters, and presented at regional, national, and international conferences. Her books include *The High School Writing Center: Establishing and Maintaining One*, *Programs and Practices: Writing Across the Secondary School Curriculum* (with Gere and Young), *ARTiculating: Teaching Writing in a Visual World* (with Hobson and Mullin), and *WAC Partnerships Between Secondary and Postsecondary Institutions* (with Blumner). She serves on the Board of Directors of the Colorado West Land Trust and volunteers with multiple nonprofit organizations.

Amy Cicchino is Associate Director for the Center for Teaching and Learning Excellence at Embry-Riddle Aeronautical University in Daytona Beach, Florida. Before joining the CTLE, she worked as an administrator in WAC, writing center, and college composition contexts. She specializes in writing program administration, digital multimodal teaching, and educator development. Her work has appeared in venues such as the *International Journal of ePortfolios*, *WPA: Writing Program Administration*, and the Online Literacy Open Resource (OLOR).

Leslie Cordie is Associate Professor in Adult Education at Auburn University and Affiliate Faculty with the University Writing Center. She holds a bachelor's degree in Nursing from the University of Wisconsin-Milwaukee, an MBA from the University of Texas at Austin, and a Ph.D. in Adult Education and Technical Communication from Colorado State University. Her specialties include instructional and curricula design, professional development, and distance learning. She has over 25 years of experience working and consulting in academic, business, and military environments. She is a Fulbright Scholar with active international collaborations in the West Indies, Ireland, the UK, and Asia.

Rikki Corniola earned her Ph.D. in Biomedical Sciences from the Florida State University College of Medicine. She then relocated across the country to pursue postdoctoral training in cell and molecular neurosciences at the Stanford University School of Medicine. She is Associate Professor of Biomedical Sciences and currently serves as the Assistant Dean of Curriculum and Assessment at the California Northstate University College of Health Sciences, where she has been integral in building the foundational curriculum and fostering cross-disciplinary writing to enhance the learning, engagement, and proficiency of students in the health sciences. Her current interests and work include developing co-curricular programming to enhance student success as students navigate their undergraduate careers focused on entering the health professions. In her spare time, she enjoys cooking with her husband, board gaming with her family, cheering on her children with their athletics, bird watching, and martial arts.

Jill Dahlman is a product of the University of Hawaii system: Hilo for undergraduate and Manoa for graduate. She is Assistant Professor of English for California Northstate University's College of Health Sciences, where she is the co-Director of the writing center and responsible for the faculty professional development series, Mikomiko. She is also responsible for creating the concentration in Writing in the Health Sciences. Prior to this position, she worked at the University of Hawaii system on O'ahu and the University of Nevada Reno. She is the composition and rhetoric editor for the *Rocky Mountain Review*, the peer-reviewed journal for the Rocky Mountain MLA, where she sits on the Executive Board and is in charge of four panels on FYC at its annual conference. She holds various positions on multiple national boards, including The WAC Clearinghouse, the OWCA, and the WS-L.

William Davis received a B.A. in English from Virginia Tech and made his first foray into teaching at the high school level. While earning a master's degree in literature at Northern Arizona University, he taught two levels of college composition courses and served in the university's writing center. He received his Ph.D. in Science and Technology Studies from Virginia Tech and was a founding faculty member at California Northstate University College of Health Sciences. Now an Assistant Professor of Science and Technology Studies at the University of Virginia, he investigates the philosophical and social implications of emerging technologies. Though he no longer delivers English courses, he never stopped teaching composition or engaging critically through writing. Lucid prose, especially when it paves the way for other forms of communication, remains powerful and persuasive.

Dinko Hanaan Dinko is a Ph.D. candidate and a Graduate Teaching Assistant at the Department of Geography and the Environment, University of Denver. His research interest lies in the multiple and differentiated narratives of water insecurity amongst the different segments of society using participatory drone mapping methodologies. His current works examine the socio-political dimensions of water use in local communities and how these interact with broader climatic changes in producing outcomes for different social groups.

Andrea Fabrizio is Associate Dean of Academic Affairs at Hostos Community College/CUNY. She has been a member of the Hostos community since 2003 when she worked at the College as a Writing Fellow. She became a full-time member of the English department in 2008. In her time at Hostos, she has chaired the English department and co-coordinated the Writing-Across-the-Curriculum Initiative with Linda Hirsch. Along with Gregory Marks, she was awarded a $275,000 grant from the Teagle Foundation to lead the implementation of Core Books: A Multi-Campus CUNY Humanities Proposal, which was an initiative inspired by Hostos' application of Columbia University's core curriculum. She is currently a member of the Executive Board of the Association of Departments of English and a member of the Board of Directors for The Great Questions Foundation.

Heather M. Falconer is an Assistant Professor of Professional and Technical Writing and faculty member of the Maine Center for Research in STEM Education at the University of Maine, Orono. She is a Co-Editor for the *Perspectives on Writing* book series, Co-Chair of the Research and Publications Committee of the Association for Writing Across the Curriculum, and serves on multiple editorial and regional boards. Falconer's research has appeared in journals such as *Written Communication*, *The WAC Journal*, and the *Journal of Hispanic Higher Education*, as well as multiple edited collections. Her book, *Masking inequality with good intentions,* is available through the Practices & Possibilities series/The WAC Clearinghouse.

Ming Fang is Associate Teaching Professor in the English Department and Associate Director for the Writing across Curriculum Program at Florida International University, Miami. She teaches both first-year and upper-division writing courses, provides training and support in multilingual writing pedagogy, and also collaborates with faculty across disciplines to integrate writing into content courses. Her research interests include second language writing, multilingual writing pedagogy, transnational writing program administration, and writing across the curriculum. Currently, she serves on the Editorial Board of the WAC Repository.

Christy Goldsmith is Assistant Director of the Campus Writing Program at the University of Missouri. Her research trajectory takes two paths. Through her narrative inquiry into English teachers' identities as writers and as teachers-of-writing, she explores the tensions inherent in teaching writing in secondary schools. Her second strand of research revolves around the teaching and learning of disciplinary literacy, including professional development design at the secondary and post-secondary levels. Prior to her position as CWP Assistant Director, she taught high school English for eight years. She earned her Ph.D. in English education from Mizzou, and she continues to teach courses in English education, disciplinary literacy, and graduate writing.

Caleb González is a Ph.D. candidate specializing in composition studies, writing program administration, and higher education studies. He examines the ways in which writing programs at Hispanic-serving institutions (HSIs), including WAC programs, from a broader lens are shaped by their institutional contexts. Currently, he is a consultant for the Writing Across the Curriculum Program in the Center for the Study and Teaching of Writing at The Ohio State University. He has also served on the Editorial Board for the WAC Clearinghouse since 2019. In 2022, he was a recipient of the K. Patricia Cross Future Leader Award in Higher Education from the American Association of Colleges and Universities (AAC&U). The award recognizes eight doctoral students who show exemplary promise as future leaders of higher education and are committed to academic innovation in the areas of equity, community engagement, and teaching and learning.

Kimberly K. Gunter is Associate Professor at Fairfield University, where they serve as the Director of Core Writing, a program that houses both first-year composition and the WAC/WID Signature Element. In addition to WAC/WID and writing program administration, their research focuses on queer rhetorics and rhetorics of labor. Their publications have appeared in *Enculturation*, *WPA: Writing Program Administration*, the *Journal of Basic Writing*, and elsewhere.

Al Harahap is Lecturer at Queens College, CUNY. He looks at institutionalized writing environments and systems such as writing across the curriculum/in the disciplines, writing centers, and writing programs, both within local institutional and larger national/global contexts.

Kimberly Harrison is Professor of English and Director of the Writing and Rhetoric Program and founding Director of the Writing Across the Curriculum Program at Florida International University in Miami. Her book-length publications include *The Rhetoric of Rebel Women: Civil War Diaries and Confederate Persuasion* (Southern Illinois UP), *A Maryland Bride in the Deep South: The Civil War Diary of Priscilla Bond* (LSU press), *Victorian Sensations: Essays on a Scandalous Genre* (Ohio State UP), and *Contemporary Composition Studies: A Guide to Theorists and Terms* (Greenwood). She has published articles on women's Civil War rhetoric and on writing program administration, and she regularly teaches courses on writing and writing pedagogy.

Linda Hirsch is Professor in the English Department at Hostos Community College/CUNY. She is Director of the Liberal Arts Degree and established and co-coordinates the Hostos Writing and Reading Across-the-Curriculum (WRAC) Program. She holds a Ph.D. in English Education from NYU and is the author of publications on the language and cognitive needs of ELLs across disciplines and WRAC. Her research provided one of the first qualitative and quantitative analyses on the value of WAC with ELL and developmental populations. She also led the creation of a first-year seminar and instituted the first linked ESL/content courses at Hostos. She is the co-founder of the CUNY Writing Centers Association and is also the creator, producer, and host of EdCast, an award-winning TV program examining issues in education airing on CUNY TV and the web (www.youtube.com/cuny). EdCast has received eight Telly awards for excellence in cable broadcasting.

Brandall C. Jones is the Connectivity Director for Kenny Leon's True Colors Theatre Company in Atlanta, Georgia, as well as Partner of MJR Partners, Arts Management Services. An adamant belief that all, no matter what their zip code or background, deserve access to high quality arts has been the driving force of his career. He has previously held positions at The Serenbe Institute and Fulton

County Arts and Culture (FCAC). Currently pursuing an M.A. in Arts Administration at Goucher College, he earned his BFA from the Savannah College of Art and Design (SCAD) with a focus on performing arts and arts administration following performance studies at Stella Adler Conservatory in Los Angeles. He has been named an Emerging Leader of Color by South Arts, Arts Leader of Metro Atlanta by the Atlanta Regional Commission, and awarded the Southern United States fellowship by the International Society of Performing Arts.

Alena Kačmárová is a full professor with 25 years of experience in university teaching and scholarly research. She is affiliated at the Institute of Translation and Interpreting, Faculty of Arts, University of Prešov in Prešov, Slovakia. She teaches courses on English inflectional morphology, English syntax, English academic writing, translation of non-literary text, and writing for publishing. In her research, she focuses on construction and translation of research papers (stylistics and authorial writing style), interlingual analysis of academic styles, intercultural pragmatics, interlingual analysis of linguistics metalanguage, and compilation of a linguistics encyclopedia. She is currently involved in the research into differences between Slovak and English writing styles in academic papers. She has authored and co-authored eight monographs, 13 textbooks, 57 research papers, and edited 11 books. She is a Fulbright scholarship holder (SUNY, Albany, NY, summer semester of 2015).

Megan J. Kelly is Teaching Professor in the Writing Program and Assistant Director of the Writing Center at the University of Denver. Her work focuses on environmental communication, with a particular emphasis on the narrative and rhetorical strategies of student activists in the climate justice movement, and on training peer tutors of writing. She also facilitates writing groups and retreats for faculty.

Kamila Kinyon is Teaching Associate Professor in the University of Denver Writing Program. She has a doctorate in Comparative Literature from the University of Chicago (2000) and an M.A. in TESOL/Linguistics from the University of Utah (1989). Her teaching has focused on the rhetoric of journalism, oral history, and ethnography, which has also been a subject of her recent service and research—including a 2022 article in the *Annals of Anthropological Practice*. Other teaching and research interests include WAC, multilingual writing, visual rhetoric, and Slavic Studies.

Mary Laughlin is is Assistant Professor of the Practice at Fairfield University. As a part of her role in the Core Writing Program, she serves as a WAC/WID consultant and has helped to design professional development initiatives to support the WAC/WID Magis Core signature element. She additionally serves as Core Writing's Library Liaison. Her professional interests include writing pedagogy, writing across the curriculum, and student source usage practices, and she has presented at conferences such as the Conference on College Composition and Communication, the International Writing Across the Curriculum Conference, and the Council of Writing Program Administrators Conference.

Christina M. LaVecchia is Assistant Professor of English (in discipline-based education research) at the University of Cincinnati. Previously she was a Research Fellow at Mayo Clinic and the founding Director of the Writing Across the Curriculum Program and Assistant Professor of English at Neumann University in Aston, PA. Her research spans multiple disciplines: In rhetoric and composition, her work on contemporary composing theories, writing pedagogies, digital literacies, and professional practices appears in *College English*, *Composition Forum*, and *Composition Studies*, among others. Her healthcare collaborations with Mayo Clinic's Knowledge and Evaluation Research (KER) Unit appear in venues like *Patient Education and Counseling*, *Health Expectations*, and *BMJ Open*. Her co-edited collection *Revising Moves: Writing Stories of (Re)Making* is under contract with Utah State University Press.

William J. (Bill) Macauley, Jr. is Professor in the Department of English at the University of Nevada, Reno. He has been teaching since 1987 and directed writing centers and programs for nearly 30 years. Along with these roles, he has done significant work in writing-related assessment across institutions, disciplines, curricula, and courses. His research and scholarship continue to focus on access, empowerment, writing with purpose, and individualized expression while he continues to question academic fairness, access, and cultural openness. These interests have recently resulted in two co-edited collections (with four of his former graduate students) on TAships in Writing Studies. He argues here and at recent conferences that the disciplinarily-diverse and discursively-curious cultures of Writing Across the Curriculum and writing centers are particularly well-suited to forwarding diversity, inclusion, and equity. For the past two years, he has also been offering small-group workshops in writing and meditation/mindfulness across the country.

Heather N. Martin is Teaching Professor in the University Writing Program at the University of Denver, where she leads faculty mentoring initiatives and directs the First-Year Seminar program. Her work has been anthologized in *The Best of Electric Velocipede* and appears in a variety of regional and national publications including *Academic Exchange Quarterly*, *Argot Magazine*, *Cobalt Review*, *Barnstorm*, and *Baltimore Review*. At home, she's mom to two teenagers and several feral chickens.

Christine Martorana is Assistant Teaching Professor in the English Department, Writing and Rhetoric Program at Florida International University. She teaches upper-division undergraduate writing courses in Rhetorical Theory, Writing Studies, and zine writing as well as a graduate-level pedagogy course.

She also serves as a Writing Across the Curriculum consultant and a dual enrollment mentor. Her research interests include multimodal writing, zine writing, and the ways in which both of these approaches can be used to support our multilingual student writers.

Estela Ines Moyano, Dr. of Linguistics (University of Buenos Aires), is Tenured Professor and Coordinator of the Academic and Professional Discourse Competences Program at the Universidad Nacional Guillermo Brown (UNaB); Researcher at the Universidad Nacional de General Sarmiento (UNGS); and Researcher and Coordinator of the Academic Reading and Writing Program (PROLEA) at the Universidad de Flores (UFLO). Her research, based in systemic functional linguistics, explores the description of Spanish, scientific discourse analysis at different specialization levels, and academic literacy programs at different educational levels. She has created and runs academic and professional reading and writing programs across the curriculum in UNGS (former), UFLO (current), and UNaB (current), as well as projects of secondary teacher training in scientific literacy at UNGS. She has many publications in her areas of interest, in Spanish and in English, and directs and participates in the teaching of various postgraduate courses in those areas.

Federico Navarro has a Ph.D. in Linguistics. He is Chair of the School of Education and Professor at the Institute of Education Sciences, Universidad de O'Higgins (Chile). He has served as Chair of the Latin American Association of Writing Studies in Higher Education and Professional Contexts. He has been a principal or co-investigator in 11 research projects on writing and education during the last decade. He has published roughly 150 papers in 12 countries. View his scholarly profile at https://orcid.org/0000–0001-9131–3245.

Mandy Olejnik earned her Ph.D. in Composition and Rhetoric at Miami University (Ohio) and is Assistant Director of Writing Across the Curriculum at the Howe Center for Writing Excellence. She designs and leads faculty workshops, consults with disciplinary faculty on their teaching of writing, researches and assesses WAC programming, and provides special support for graduate-level writing instruction across campus. Her work has appeared in *WPA: Writing Program Administration* and *Transformative Works and Cultures*. She was a learning designer for the online Miami Writing Institute and co-editor of the forthcoming edited collection *Changing Conceptions, Changing Practices: Innovating Teaching Across Disciplines* (Utah State University Press).

Dennis Paoli taught composition, literature, and humanities at Hunter College/CUNY for over four decades. He was Coordinator of the Rockowitz Writing Center from 1987 and Co-coordinator of the Hunter College Writing Across the Curriculum Program from 2001 to his retirement in 2020. He served on the board of the CUNY Writing Centers Association from 1988–2001 and the board of the National, then International, Writing Centers Association from 1996–2001. He has been published and produced in several media and is the Donor-Advisor of The Heidi Paoli Fund for the support of cancer patients and their caregivers.

Juli Parrish is Director of the Writing Center and Teaching Professor in the University Writing Program at the University of Denver. She is a co-editor of the open-access journal *Literacy in Composition Studies* and the edited collection *Literacy and Pedagogy in an Age of Misinformation and Disinformation*. Her work has appeared in *Transformative Works and Cultures*, *Composition Studies*, *Across the Disciplines*, and *South Atlantic Review*, as well as in several edited collections.

Gloria Poveda attended UC Davis as a returning student and received her B.A. in Chicana and Chicano Studies with a minor in Sociology. She then went on to UC Santa Barbara where she completed her M.A. in Chicana and Chicano Studies with an emphasis in Black Studies. Her Ph.D. is from the School of Education at the University of Michigan, Ann Arbor. Her areas of specialization are Foundations, Administration, Research, and Policy, which offered the opportunity to engage a diverse community of doctoral students and faculty members in reimagining education as a central component of the transformation needed to create more inclusive and just societies. Her research is part of a sustainable humanities-social science cluster grounded in leadership and innovation with a central focus in service learning.

Alisa Russell is Assistant Professor in the Writing Program at Wake Forest University, where she also researches and facilitates writing across the curriculum initiatives. Her most recent projects explore genre access in government writing, and her articles have appeared in publications such as *Written Communication*, *Pedagogy*, and *The WAC Journal*.

David R. Russell is Professor Emeritus of English at Iowa State University, where he taught in the Rhetoric and Professional Communication graduate program and served as co-director of the ISUComm Advanced Communication undergraduate program. His research interests are in writing in the disciplines and professions, international writing instruction, and the phenomenology of writing. His book, *Writing in the Academic Disciplines: A Curricular History*, now in its second edition, examines the history of United States writing instruction since 1870. He has published more than 70 refereed articles on writing in the disciplines (WID) and professions, drawing mainly on cultural historical activity theory and rhetorical genre theory. He has recently published articles on the phenomenology of writing, the felt sense of writing under surveillance, embodied cognition in reflection, and genre as social action in relation to recent theories of motivation, all available at https://engl.iastate.edu/directory/david-russell.

Trudy Smoke is Professor Emerita from the Department of English, Hunter College/CUNY where she taught classes in linguistics and rhetoric. She co-coordinated the WAC program from 1999 to 2019 when she retired. She also coordinated the First Year Writing Program at Hunter and has written extensively on composition and ESL issues. Some of her publications include *Thinking Sociolinguistically: How to Plan, Conduct, and Present your Research*; *The World of the Image*; *Language and Linguistics in Context*; *A Writer's Workbook* (4 editions); *Making a Difference*; and *Adult ESL*. She is also a botanical and nature illustrator whose illustrations appear in *The Field Guide to the Street Trees of New York City* and *The Field Guide to the Neighborhood Birds of New York City* (Johns Hopkins University Press). In retirement, she is enjoying tutoring adult learners, drawing, writing, and doing research on lesser-known women botanical artists.

Olivia R. Tracy is Teaching Assistant Professor in the University Writing Program at the University of Denver. Her work has appeared in *Praxis: A Journal of Writing Center Studies* and *The Journal of Haitian Studies*.

Ingrida Vaňková is an associate professor with 16 years of experience in university teaching and scholarly research. She is affiliated at the Institute of Translation and Interpreting, Faculty of Arts, University of Prešov in Prešov, Slovakia. She teaches courses on non-literary translation, lexicology, phraseology, introduction to linguistics, and text analysis. In her research, she focuses on translation, anthropocentrism and subject-centrism in translation studies, linguistic landscape in translation, linguistic anthropology, translation hermeneutics, interlingual analysis of metalanguage (lexicology, word formation, phraseology, lexicography), and composition of a lexicographic publication. She is currently involved in the research of linguistics landscape (tourist text), translator's edge competences, and translator's powers in translation. She has authored and co-authored four monographs, two textbooks, and 25 research papers.

Kathleen Daly Weisse is Assistant Professor and Director of the Writing Center and WAC program at New Mexico State University. Her research interests include antiracist writing instruction, critical data studies, and writing across the curriculum. She has published in *The WAC Journal*, *Rhetoric Review*, and *Across the Disciplines*.

Tiffany Wilgar is Assistant Professor of the Practice at Fairfield University where they teach in Core Writing and served as Assistant Director for the first four years of the program. They also teach Technical Writing and Multimodal Writing at Fairfield. They hold an MA from the University of Nevada, Las Vegas and earned a Ph.D. from the University of South Florida. Their research explores rhetorical presentations of risk in technical documents and artifacts of pop culture associated with the Nevada Test Site, a nuclear testing facility located roughly sixty miles from Las Vegas, Nevada.

Contributors

Christopher Wostenberg is Associate Professor of Chemistry and current Department Chair of Math and Science at California Northstate University–College of Health Sciences (CNU-CHS) in the Sacramento area of California. While his expertise is in biochemistry, he devotes his time volunteering hours in the Media and Communication Center and running professional writing workshops in helping students improve their writing skills. He writes film reviews for CHS Sideline, the student-run publication at CHS. As a supporter and advocate of our military armed forces and veterans, he works with the Veteran Affairs of Northern California Health Care System serving as a board member of their Subcommittee on Research Safety. Additionally, he acts as an eMentor as part of the Sheldon High School's Biotech Academy. In his spare time, he enjoys reading science-fiction, watching all genres of movies, and playing board, card, and video games with his wife and daughter.

Nadia Francine Zamin is Assistant Professor of the Practice at Fairfield University, where she teaches in Core Writing and directs program assessment.

Angela J. Zito is Teaching Faculty with the Writing Center and Writing Across the Curriculum programs at University of Wisconsin-Madison, where she currently serves as Associate Director of WAC and Madison Writing Assistance (a community writing program). She earned her Ph.D. in English Literary Studies, which continues to inform her scholarship of teaching and learning. Her recent research has investigated the teaching and learning of close reading practices in composition courses and the design of writing assignments across disciplines to assess non-writing competencies.

www.ingramcontent.com/pod-product-compliance
Lightning Source LLC
Chambersburg PA
CBHW052133070526
44585CB00017B/1807